Clement Boulton Roylance Kent

The English Radicals

An historical sketch

Clement Boulton Roylance Kent

The English Radicals
An historical sketch

ISBN/EAN: 9783337096960

Printed in Europe, USA, Canada, Australia, Japan

Cover: Foto ©ninafisch / pixelio.de

More available books at **www.hansebooks.com**

THE ENGLISH RADICALS

THE ENGLISH RADICALS

AN HISTORICAL SKETCH

BY

C. B. ROYLANCE KENT

LONGMANS, GREEN, AND CO.
39 PATERNOSTER ROW, LONDON
NEW YORK AND BOMBAY
1899

PREFACE.

It is, I hope, unnecessary for me to say much in order to introduce this book to the reader, but perhaps I may be permitted to say something about its scope and intention. I have made no attempt, it seems almost superfluous to remark, to write a full history of modern English political thought. *Nobis in arto et inglorius labor.* I have surveyed a small portion only of the field of inquiry, but that portion I have examined with some care. My object has been, to state it briefly, this : to trace genealogically the descent of the present-day Radicals, and to show the changes which the party has undergone in this course of evolution; to do—though of course with great differences, and, I fear, very imperfectly—the same kind of thing that M. Brunetière has done with such brilliant results in his *Manual of the History of French Literature;* to exhibit in the successive generations of Radicals the influence of thought upon thought, of doctrine upon doctrine, of books upon books, and of conduct upon conduct. My labour, I trust, will not altogether be in vain. For, first, the history of the Radicals is full of human interest; it presents a gallery of portraits; it is rich in opportunities for studies of psychology and character. Secondly, I venture to believe that to grasp thoroughly the history of the extreme party of movement and progression during the last hundred and thirty years—to see what that party has aimed at, in what it has succeeded, and where and why it has failed—is the best way to obtain a clear understanding of the origins of contemporary politics. It has been said that it is the function of the historian to relate merely, and not to pass judgments upon those whose actions he records; but it would be impossible for him to form no opinions, and perhaps it would be equally impossible, even if it were desirable, for him to conceal them from the reader. I have, however, tried as far as possible to let the story speak for itself; and only in the concluding pages have I ventured to become didactic and to criticise present political affairs.

C. B. ROYLANCE KENT.

CONTENTS.

CHAPTER I.

THE FIRST PERIOD, 1761-1789.

	PAGE
Introductory	1
Different Views of the Movement of Society	2
Radicalism and the Idea of Progress	3-4
Origin of the Word "Radical"	5
The Early Years of the Reign of George III.	6
The Position of the House of Commons	7-8
Whigs and Tories	9-11
Characteristics of this Period	12
The Intercourse with France	13
The Spread of Knowledge	14
Petitions	15
Radicals and Whigs	16
The Birth of English Radicalism	17
Popular Dislike of the House of Commons	18-19
Chatham as a Reformer	20
The Representation of the Land	20-21
Chatham on Short Parliaments	22
Burke as a Reformer	23
Chatham and the Party System	24-25
Unpopularity of Bute and the Scotch	26-27
John Wilkes the First of the Radicals	28
The Germs of Democracy	29
Wilkes; His Life and Personality	30-31
The *North Briton*	32-34
The Trial of Wilkes for Seditious Libel	35
The *Essay on Woman*	36
The Middlesex Election	37-38
The Imprisonment of Wilkes	39
"Wilkemania"	40

The Significance of the Middlesex Elections
The Importance of Wilkes as a Radical
The Relations of Members and Constituencies
Wilkes's Radicalism
Early Political Societies
The Society of the Supporters of the Bill of Rights
John Horne Tooke; His Life and Personality
His Zeal for Wilkes
His Services in the Radical Cause
The Lord Mayor Beckford
Tooke founds the Society of the Supporters of the Bill of Rights
Pledges from Parliamentary Candidates
Quarrel of Tooke and Wilkes
The City of London "Instructs" its Representatives
The Question of Reporting Parliamentary Debates
The Imprisonment of Oliver and Crosby
A Group of Radicals
Mrs. Catherine Macaulay
The Radical Philosophical Thinkers
John Cartwright; His Life and Political Opinions
John Jebb; His Life and Political Opinions
Joseph Priestley; His Life and Political Opinions
Richard Price; His Life and Political Opinions
General Characteristics of the Early Radicals
 1. The Platform.
 2. Political Societies.
 3. Parliamentary Reform.
 4. Relations with the Whigs.
 5. The Delegation Theory of Representation.
 6. Short Parliaments.
 7. The House of Lords.
 8. The Ballot.
 9. Payment of Members.
 10. The Standing Army.

CHAPTER II.
The Second Period, 1789-1831.

The Influence of the French Revolution
Enthusiasm aroused in England
The Jacobinical Radicals

CONTENTS.

	PAGE
Thomas Paine; His Life and Political Opinions	108-117
William Godwin; His Life and Political Opinions	118-126
Changes in the Radicalism of this Period	127-132
1. Attacks on the Crown and House of Lords.	
2. Complaints of Oppressive Taxation.	
3. Anti-Christian Radicalism.	
The Radicals and the French Revolution	132-133
The Unpopularity of the Jacobinical Radicals	135-142
Repressive Legislation and State Trials	143-146, 147
Thomas Hardy	147
The London Corresponding Society	147-149
Thomas Holcroft	149-151
John Thelwall	151-154
The State Trials of Hardy and Others	154-156
The Nadir of Liberalism	157-158
The Society of the Friends of the People	159-161
The Alarmed State of Public Feeling	162-165
Repression of the Radicals	165-167
The Rise of the Philosophical Radicals	168
The Scientific Spirit in Politics	169-172
Jeremy Bentham; His Life and Political Opinions	173-184
The Foundations and Character of His Radicalism	185-191
The School of the Benthamites	192
James Mill; His Life and Political Opinions	193-202
Francis Place	203-207
David Ricardo	207-208
George Grote	209-210
Joseph Hume	211-212
The Younger Philosophical Radicals	213-216
The Foundation of the *Westminster Review*	217-221
The Characteristics of Benthamism	221-229
The Unpopularity of Benthamism	230-231
The Disinterestedness of the Philosophical Radicals	231
The Defects of their Philosophy	232-233
The Superstitious Worship of the Constitution	234-236
Some of the Good Effects of Benthamism	237
The Views of the Philosophical Radicals upon—	
1. Colonies.	
2. Irish Home Rule.	
3. Foreign Policy.	
4. The Sphere of Legislation	238-241

CONTENTS.

The Beginnings of a Radical Party
Radical Hostility towards the Whigs
Sir Samuel Romilly and Brougham
The Tory Rule from 1800 to 1832
Futile Efforts for Reform
The Constituency of Westminster
Place as an Electioneering Organiser
Sir Francis Burdett
Westminster Politics
A Dinner to Cartwright
The Reporting of Debates
The Committal of Sir Francis Burdett
John Cam Hobhouse
Disagreements of the Radicals
Sir Francis Burdett and Bentham
The Burdettites
Sir Francis Burdett attacked by the Radicals
The Delegation Theory of Representation
Sir Charles Wolseley, the "Legislatorial Attorney"
The Hampden and Union Clubs
The Use of the Platform
"Orator" Hunt
The Peterloo Riots
The Apotheosis of Hunt
Repressive Legislation; the Six Acts
The Condition of the Press
Wooler and the *Black Dwarf*
John and Leigh Hunt and the *Examiner*
Black, Albany Fonblanque and the *Morning Chronicle*
William Cobbett; His Life and Political Opinions
Radical Working Men
The Combination Laws
The Beginnings of Socialism
The Rotundists
The Agitation for Reform
Thomas Attwood
The Birmingham Political Union
The Birmingham Radicals
Place and the Reform Agitation
Retrospect of the Second Period

CONTENTS.

CHAPTER III.

THE THIRD AND CONCLUDING PERIOD.

	PAGE
The Method of Treatment	322
The Younger Philosophical Radicals	323
John Stuart Mill; His Life and Political Opinions	324-331
The Reform Act of 1832	332-333
The Radicals in the First Reformed Parliament	334
Charles Buller and Sir William Molesworth	334-335
The Radicals in the Second Reformed Parliament	338
Thomas Wakley	339
Thomas Slingsby Duncombe	340
The Failure of the Parliamentary Radicals	341-342
Radical Mutual Animosities	343-345
The Nadir of Radicalism	346
The Relations of the Radicals and Whigs	347-349
The Earl of Durham	350-351
The Apathy of the Whigs	352
The Conservatives	353
The Causes of Chartism	354-355
The Characteristics of Chartism	356-358
The Drafting of the Charter	359-361
The Demands of the Chartists	362-363
The Methods of the Chartists	364
The Chartist Leaders	365-367
The Causes of their Failure	368-369
The Anti-Corn Law Agitation	370-371
Political Parties and Political Economy	372-374
The Radicals as Political Economists	375
The Radicals and the Anti-Corn Law League	376
The Manchester School	377
John Bright and Richard Cobden	378-389
General Characteristics of the Manchester School	390-393
Its Services to Democracy	394
The Radical Absorption of the Liberals	395-397
The Successes and Failures of the Radicals	398-399
The Causes of their Failures	400-414

    1. Their Passion for Philosophical Systems.
    2. Their Extravagances of Language.
    3. Their Hostility towards the Aristocracy.
    4. Their Contempt for the Natural Conservatism of Mankind.
    5. Their Confusion of the Results of Civilisation and Democracy.

CONTENTS.

	PAGE
The Differences between the Old and New Radicals	414-437

    1. The Delegation Theory of Representation.
    2. The Regard for the House of Commons.
    3. The View of Foreign Politics.
    4. The Sphere of Legislation.
    5. The Optimist Temperament.
    6. The Consistency of Principle.
    7. Individualism.
    8. The Ultimate Principles of Government.
    9. Democracy.

INDEX - - - - - - - - - - - - - 439

CHAPTER I.

THE FIRST PERIOD, 1761-1789.

THE scope of this work will necessarily include some account of the history of political opinion, and of the lives and characters of some of those who have played prominent parts upon the stage of public life. The philosopher and the agitator will alike claim to be considered. For whether we believe that it is the intellectual element in mankind which is the predominant factor in determining their progress, or rather that it is religion and the desire of men to find some supernatural sanction for their conduct which is the strongest evolutionary force, we shall have to take into account the theories of political philosophers. The intellectual state of man, his beliefs, speculations and opinions, must, in any case, constitute one of the most powerful causes which shape and direct the future of the race; they will always more or less determine great political events. Some of the most important changes have had their origin in the closets or lonely walks of disinterested theorists. The minds of these men are seminal; they scatter the seed from which future generations will some day reap the harvest, while other minds are practical and fertile in expedient. These latter belong to the class of men of action, who are, it has been justly said, only the unconscious under-workmen of the thinkers. Bacon said that a knowledge of the speculative principles of young men between the ages of twenty and thirty was one of the great sources of political prophecy; and as thought precedes action, there is no doubt that he was right. Those who weave speculative theories, and those who act upon them, lie in very close relationship; and the history of the one cannot be fully understood without some knowledge of the history of the other. Of both, therefore, something will be said.

At different times and different places men have held very various views about their progress and their future. That there is a movement of some kind in human affairs seems to have been always believed, whenever the matter has been consciously considered. But upon the question whether that movement is one of continuous progress forward, steadily tending to some far-off divine event, or a revolution in a cycle, or an advance towards a golden age, or a backward retrogression, men's thoughts have been very much divided. The ancient philosophers and poets held contradictory views, and were not always consistent with themselves. Hesiod described the progress of mankind as being one of retrogression from a golden to an iron age; Æschylus and Euripides spoke hopefully of progress; while Empedocles and Anaximander believed in cycles. Cicero and Pliny were optimists, while Lucretius imagined that the world and those upon it were hastening to destruction. Virgil—sweetest and saddest of Roman singers — cast regretful glances back to a happier golden age; though he had day-dreams of a time when Saturn's reign should once again return, and Justice plant her feet upon the earth. He was, as Tennyson has said with equal truth and beauty, majestic in his sadness "at the doubtful doom of humankind".

Even Horace seems to have been now and then despondent.

> Damnosa quid non imminuit dies?
> Ætas parentum pejor avis tulit
> Nos nequiores, mox daturos
> Progeniem vitiosiorem.[1]

The notion that mankind was a degenerating race appears to have extensively prevailed during a long extended period; and it may be said that a firm belief in progress is comparatively modern. Descartes tried to prove that the idea of progress was the only rational view; Pascal thought the same; and when Perrault—whose real intention was to flatter Louis XIV. by disparaging the ancients—brought out his epoch-making book on the parallels between the men of antiquity and the moderns, he opened a controversial war in which many disputants took part. In the result the optimistic view prevailed. The contrary belief, that mankind is steadily decaying, or at best only revolving in a kind of vicious circle, has always been readily surrendered for a creed of a more exhilarating kind. In one way or another, in religion or in science, men have discovered the golden anchor of their hope. The doctrine of evolution in these latter days has given them abundant ground for the belief that the human race is working out its way to a better and happier state of things. The progress may be slow and painful; the advance may be, as Goethe said, in spiral lines; or, like the swelling tide, which, though the waves break upon the shore and then retreat, irresistibly moves onwards; there may be meanwhile a martyrdom of man; the struggle for survival may be cruel, and Nature be "red in tooth and claw"; still men

---

[1] Flint's *History of the Philosophy of History*, p. 94; Horace, *Odes*, 3-6.

find consolation in the thought that the end will be found to be very good. Now so long as a community or nation hold hopeful views about the future, those who may be called Radicals, to use the word in its most comprehensive sense, as meaning those who expect much from the reform of human institutions, will certainly be found. These reformers are almost always optimists, taking a sanguine view of things, and seeing visions of a New Jerusalem, or the approach of a millennium; but they expect much, often far too much, of human nature, and they dream dreams which not rarely are as utterly fallacious as any that ever issued from the ivory gate. They believe that improvements are always to be made, which may be true; that almost any change is for the better, and that whatever is, is wrong, which may be false. Hence, as hereafter will appear, when the belief in progress is the strongest, or when in times of distress and discontent the desire for change is keen, then radicalism excites the liveliest enthusiasm. On the other hand, when contentment reigns, and there is satisfaction with the present, then radicalism languishes. The existence of radicalism depends in no small measure, therefore, upon a prevalent belief in the progressive movement of mankind. For reform would be considered vain, if improvement were regarded as impossible; to plough the sands is a task which no man will knowingly undertake.[1]

---

[1] Mazzini divided historians into two classes: those of the circular movement school, and those of the progressive movement school; see his Essay on Carlyle's *French Revolution*. Rénan was in the main right when he said that all Indo-European antiquity had placed Paradise in the beginning, and that whereas all its poets had wept a golden age, Israel placed the age of gold in the future. A remarkable instance of the contemporaneous appearance of optimism and radical fervour is afforded by some incidents in the French Revolution. When, for example, Condorcet's

THE FIRST PERIOD, 1761-1789.   5

The derivation of the word "Radical" is obvious enough; but how and when it first came to be used in its special sense in English politics is not very clear. It was not until about the year 1819[1] that it began to be applied to a separate political party in the country; and it was only then that the Radicals by their activity and zeal succeeded in winning for themselves distinctive recognition as *par excellence* the party of reform. Before this time, indeed, men used to speak of "radical reform"; some seriously, and others, like the writers of the *Anti-Jacobin*, in satire. Radicals there were certainly before, but they were comparatively few, and of too small account to form a political party of their own. Their views and speculations are, however, well worth consideration, as an important element in the history of opinion, and the source from which the radicalism of later days has been derived.

✓Modern English radicalism may be said to have first arisen in the early years of the reign of George III. Yet never did a monarch ascend a throne under more auspicious circumstances. Young and personally popular, he was received with the acclamations of the people; he gloried, he said, in being able to call himself a Briton. The Tories welcomed him with joy, for by this time they

Esquisse d'un Histoire des progrès de l'esprit humain was published, it was ordered by the National Convention to be printed and distributed throughout France at the public expense. The late Mr. Pearson is almost alone amongst modern philosophers in taking a rather pessimistic view. He seems to have thought that the higher races are not likely to progress much farther, but are already entering on a period of restful old age. See his *National Life and Character*.

[1] "It is stated to have been now that the Reformers first assumed the name of Radicals" (Miss Martineau's *History of the Peace*, vol. i., p. 226).

had surrendered their Jacobite ideas, and no longer regarded the Hanoverian House in the light of usurpers; they clung to their idolatry, but changed the idol. They were not, indeed, and never had been, all Jacobites; for the Whigs had purposely confused the two together, in order to cast odium upon all those who were in opposition to the Government. Moreover, the very fact of the existence of the Jacobites had been a check upon the Crown, so that the new King had every reason to rejoice. He found the present full of happiness and the future full of hope. At home the voice of faction was lulled into repose, while abroad the genius of Chatham and the victories of his admirals had raised the fame of England to an almost unexampled height of glory. "Alone this island," it was boasted, "seemed to balance the rest of Europe." Chatham was in the meridian of his fame, and the nation was, as Macaulay said, drunk with joy and pride. The country was happily content, and in no mood to criticise and censure. Even party spirit seemed for a time to have died away.[1] But this happy state of things soon underwent a change, and the new King had scarcely reigned ten years before the party of reform began to raise its head. What then were the causes of this altered state of things?

The balance of the Constitution had since the Settlement of 1688 been gradually upset, and forces were at work which brought about a silent revolution. Formerly the House of Commons had been comparatively weak; it had been compelled to fight its way, and was constantly in conflict with the Crown. In the natural course of

---

[1] The Common Council of the City of London, in a document of the year 1761, refer to "the present happy extinction of parties" (Sharpe's *London and the Kingdom*, vol. iii., p. 70).

things the House stood forward as the champion of the people, and when their rights were threatened, it was always to be found in the forefront of the battle. The Crown had imposed its supremacy by force; it despised the House, and disdained to buy its votes by bribery and corruption. William III., however, held his throne under the strictest obligations to Parliament; obligations which his successors were the more careful to observe, because they were perfectly aware that the rival house of Stuart competed strongly for the affections of the people.[1] The Lower House, therefore, at a bound sprang into a position of importance.[2] But while, on the one hand, its members could no longer be brow-beaten by the Crown, on the other, they ceased to make themselves the natural protectors of the people. In the place of fear the Crown had to substitute corruption; and so it came about that the process began which under Sir Robert Walpole's rule was gradually organised and turned into a system. That every man had his price became a maxim of English political life.[3] Meanwhile, parliamentary representation,

[1] Shelburne justly remarked that the English Constitution owed much to the existence of a Pretender, "with a very just right to the throne upon all Tory or monarchical principles and all old prejudices, but without sufficient capacity to disturb the reigning family"; but who yet kept that family "in perpetual awe" (Fitzmaurice's *Life of Shelburne*, vol. i., pp. 21 and 33). Thomas Paine was of the same opinion; he said that George I. and George II. "were sensible of a rival in the remains of the Stuarts," and were in consequence "on their good behaviour". See his *Rights of Man*.

[2] Hume remarked that "the share of power allotted by our Constitution to the House of Commons is so great that it absolutely commands all the other parts of the government".

[3] Hume remarked that "it is therefore a just political maxim that every man must be supposed a knave". At a later period James Mill (in his *Fragment on Mackintosh*) quotes this passage from Hume's *Essay on*

except in a few constituencies, existed only but in name. The people had very little voice in the selection of their rulers, and were governed sometimes well and sometimes ill by groups of influential Whigs or Tories. Such were the Ministries which were significantly termed the "Cobham Squadron," the "Grenville Connection," and the "Bloomsbury Gang"; and to which Chatham referred when he said that he was not afraid to meet the proudest connections face to face. The system was one which succeeded fairly well, so long as things went smoothly, and the hand of a strong minister was at the helm. While Chatham ruled, the English monarch might have followed the example of the Macedonian Philip, and said that he could sleep so long as he knew that Parmenio was awake. Chatham—who had something of that *facultas dicendi imperatoria* which was ascribed to Julius Cæsar—once said, "I am sure that I can save this country, and that nobody else can"; and the boast was not, perhaps, an idle one. But when Bute stepped in to fill the place from which Chatham had withdrawn, he failed to draw the bow which required the arms and sinews of Ulysses. Disasters followed quickly on the heels of one another; where strength had been, there was only weakness; and the voice of discontent was heard. Then it was that the evils of the prevailing system began to be seen in all their glaring hideousness; hitherto they had remained unnoticed, or, at least, had been complacently endured. To adopt the phrase of Burke, men bore with infirmities until they festered into crimes. It was the perpetration of the crimes that

The Independence of Parliament, in support of his argument that identity of interest between the governors and the governed was the only security for good government.

awakened discontent and caused men to meet together to question and consider; it was the desire to discuss grievances that caused the Radicals to spring into existence.

From the Revolution Settlement of 1688 down to the accession of George III. the soil was being gradually prepared for the development of radicalism. That Settlement, though a compromise and incomplete, paved the way for future enlightenment and freedom. It wrung the sceptre from the hand of superstition, and struck off the fetters which tyranny had imposed. From thenceforth the divine right of kings was in England mentioned only in derision, except by a few belated Jacobites.[1] And though the people at large were little regarded, parliamentary privileges were respected and maintained. Then, as soon as the House of Commons had assumed its proper place, the system of government by party spontaneously arose, and from antecedent causes men naturally fell asunder into two great divisions. These two great parties —which for particular reasons were nicknamed Whigs and Tories—entirely occupied the field between them, and they persistently endured long after they were threatened with extinction. Even as early as 1684 the Marquis of Halifax spoke of them as objects to be ridiculed; he said that English politicians had "played the fool with throwing Whig and Tory one at another as boys do snowballs". Swift, in a letter written to a noble Whig in 1712 speaks of the terms as obsolete; so too Gibbon writes in 1770 of "those foolish, obsolete,

---

[1] "The name of King commands little respect; and to talk of a King as God's Vice-Regent on earth, or to give him any of those magnificent titles which formerly dazzled mankind, would but excite laughter in every one" (Hume, *Essays, Moral and Political*).

odious words, Whig and Tory"; and Shelburne about the same time placed it on record in his papers that in his opinion the old Whig and Tory parties were extinguished. They were, however, founded on perfectly rational distinctions, and were related to one another, not as contraries, but as opposites.¹ Their several principles were these: that whereas the Tories were willing to concede more authority to the Crown, the Whigs made themselves the special guardians of the liberties of the people; that while the Tories dwelt more upon the necessity of maintaining a strong executive and central power, the Whigs hoped more from popular expansion and the development of individual freedom. Or, in other words, the Tories represented the principle of permanence and the Whigs the principle of progression, though these principles were in their particular application not always consistently maintained.² To one or other of these two

¹ This distinction is important. Sir G. C. Lewis insisted on it, saying that things are opposed as contraries when each class or species are so related that the individual members of one are not contained in the other; and as extremes, when there is no fixed line of demarcation, but a gradation from one to the other (*Use and Abuse of Political Terms*, p. 143). So also Coleridge in his *Church and State*: "opposite powers are always of the same kind and tend to union, either by equipoise or a common product". And also De Quincey in his *Essay on the Political Parties of Modern England*: "The kind of opposition between Whig and Tory is not, as the current notions make it, logical; that is, contradictory each of the other".

² That there are two antagonistic forces at work in the state has been insisted upon by two such different writers as Comte and Coleridge. See the former's *System of Positive Polity*, with reference to the statical and dynamical elements in society. See Coleridge's *Church and State*, and J. S. Mill's *System of Logic*, and his "Essay on Coleridge" in the *Dissertations*. In his *Representative Government* Mill seems to have come to the conclusion that the classification of the constituents of social well-being into order and progress is unscientific, because the conditions of both are the same, order being the preservation of existing good, and progress the

THE FIRST PERIOD, 1761-1789.

great parties every one attached himself according to his temperament; for just as it has been said that every man is born an Aristotelian or a Platonist, so it may be as truly affirmed that every man is at heart inclined to the principle of permanence or to the principle of progression. He either dreads anarchy, like Dr. Johnson, who declared that in his time subordination was sadly broken down; that no man, except a jailer, had the same authority as his father had, and that all order was relaxed; or he builds utopian ideals, and like Godwin or Condorcet dreams golden dreams of the perfectibility of man. As of the poet, so of the Whig or Tory, it may be said: *nascitur, non fit.* But though the differences of the Whigs and Tories were acute, and sometimes degenerated into faction and bitter personalities, the two parties were at least agreed in this opinion, that the mass of the people were not to govern for themselves. The Tories claimed to govern as masters; and a Tory prelate summed the matter up by saying that the people had nothing to do with the laws but to obey them.[1] The Whigs on their side claimed to govern as trustees; but as far as the populace was concerned, the distinction seemed to be one without a difference.[2]

increase of that good. "Progress includes order, but order does not include progress. Progress is a greater degree of that of which order is a less." Moreover, progress may be extended to mean the prevention of retrogression.

[1] This saying is attributed to Bishop Horsley (Buckle's *History of Civilisation*, vol. i., p. 500).

[2] The Whig theory of trusteeship is stated explicitly by Burke: " The King is the representative of the people; so are the Lords, so are the judges. They are all *Trustees* for the people as well as the Commons" (*Thoughts on the Cause of Present Discontents*). Again, "all persons possessing any portion of power ought to be strongly and awfully impressed with an idea that they act in trust" (*Reflections on the French Revolution*).

12   THE ENGLISH RADICALS.

With the accession of George III., however, a new spirit insensibly arose among the people ; and though the period from that event until the French Revolution was marked by the return of the Tory party to a share of ministerial place and power, it was one which in many ways was favourable to the spread of Radical ideas. Society, indeed, to use the word in its fashionable sense, though formal and decorous, was with its powder and its patches, its gossips and its *salons*, essentially frivolous within.[1] Yet this *siècle dégoûté*, as Voltaire called it, was one of such intellectual curiosity that it came to be known as the *sæculum rationalisticum*. In matters of religion, scepticism, even among the Tories, with Hume at their head, became the fashionable vogue ; and when Gibbon, "sapping a solemn creed with solemn sneer," declared that all religions were equally true to the people, false to the philosopher, and useful to the statesman, he only summed up into an epigram a sentiment which many thought, but had not openly expressed. But perhaps the most remarkable characteristic of the period was the impetus that was given to the intercourse between the French and English nations.[2] Hitherto that intercourse had not been very great. The French refugees had, indeed, done something towards making English philosophy and English politics familiar to their countrymen,[3] and Voltaire[4] had introduced them to a knowledge of

[1] We might adopt Mr. Austin Dobson's description of a somewhat earlier period :—

"Walpole spoke of a man and his price ;
Nobody's virtue was over nice".
—(Ballad of Beau Brocade.)

[2] See Buckle's *History of Civilisation*, vol. ii., chap. v.

[3] See *Jean-Jacques Rousseau et les Origines du Cosmopolitisme Littéraire*, by Joseph Texte, pp. 21, 22 and 315.

[4] *Idem*, p. 42.

THE FIRST PERIOD, 1761-1789.   13

England's great dramatic poet. Many English books were translated into French, and English customs became extremely popular across the Channel. There arose in France, in fact, a kind of Anglo-mania. The Abbé Morellet told his friend Lord Shelburne that for forty years he had been called an Anglo-maniac and a bad citizen because he had avowed his love for English institutions. Montesquieu professed his admiration for the English Constitution in a manner that led to the most unexpected consequences; and, in fact, even as early as the sixteenth century England was in the possession of reforms which France did not obtain until 1789.[1] The leading English thinkers—Hume is a notable example—were lionised in Paris; " The name of Englishman," says Gibbon, "inspires as great an idea at Paris as that of a Roman could at Carthage after the defeat of Hannibal. Indeed the French are almost excessive." The English on their side repaid this admiration by their unstinted acknowledgments of the lucid elegance of the French literature and language. To make a tour in France was thought to be almost a necessary part of an English education. Nay more; as a literary medium the most likely to reach a numerous class of readers, Gibbon was inclined to prefer the French language to his own. [The period too was one in which the country grew in wealth and population, and commerce advanced by leaps and bounds. Hargreaves, Arkwright, and Crompton revolutionised the spinning trade; Wedgwood laid the foundation of the industry of the potteries, and Watt and Boulton evoked the latent powers of steam. Dean Tucker had, in fact, some warrant for his long-

[1] *Le Développement de la Constitution de la Société politique en Angleterre*, par E. Boutmy, p. 146.

remembered saying that the English people were a shop-keeping nation. Moreover (a love of knowledge for its own sake was becoming widely spread. The great ladies of society formed *blue-stocking* clubs, and met together for debate. Shelburne went so far as to assert that the decline of the authority of Parliament, which was mainly due to its incompetence, was due to the fact that the people were beginning to think and learn for themselves. If this was the case, the result may fairly be ascribed in some degree to the growing power and importance of the press; for notwithstanding the potentiality of much repression in the law, the journalist enjoyed much more freedom than he did in later times. Even Thomas Paine called it "free and open," and the persecuted Priestley allowed that he esteemed it a singular happiness to have lived in an age and country in which he had been at full liberty to investigate, and by preaching and writing to propagate, religious truth.[1]

[1] For the subject of Anglo-mania in France see Carlyle's *French Revolution*, vol. ii., chap. v.; Texte's *J.-J. Rousseau et les Origines du Cosmopolitisme Littéraire*, p. 319; Brunetière's *Manual of the History of French Literature*, pp. 317, 318, 373 and 376; *Lettres de L'Abbé Morellet à Lord Shelburne*, edited by Lord Edmond Fitzmaurice (Letters, 22nd April, 1872; 6th February, 1791); Montesquieu's *Esprit des Lois*, bk. xii., chap. xix., etc. Arthur Young tells us that the Duke de Liancourt sent his two sons to England to be educated "in compliance with the Anglo-mania that then reigned in France" (*Young's Autobiography*, p. 120). For the English admiration of the French language and literature see Gibbon's *Letters* (Letter to his Stepmother, 1763) and *The Early Diary of Frances Burney*, vol. i., p. 286. That there were strong prejudices in England against the French we may infer from the fact that Wilkes, during his mayoralty, would not allow French wines to be used at the banquets at the Mansion House. For the blue-stocking clubs see *The Early Diary of Frances Burney*, vol. ii., pp. 138, 139 and 296. A ladies' club for debate was called La Belle Assemblée (*ibid.*, vol. ii., p. 305). For the spread of education and the freedom of the press, see Fitzmaurice's *Life*

Such, very briefly, were the characteristics of the period
in which English Radicalism had its birth. The first
germs of popular agitation began at this time to develop
and ferment, and the people to show the first signs of
spontaneously moving and acting for themselves. In a
word, they now began to cease from dumb gestures and
to articulate. Public meetings were convened, political
associations and societies were formed, and petitions to
the Crown or Parliament were numerously signed. That
these petitions sometimes merited the scorn that Dr.
Johnson poured upon them is very probable. " This
petitioning," he said, " is a new mode of distressing
Government, and a mighty easy one. I will undertake
to get petitions against quarter-guineas or half-guineas
with the help of a little hot wine." Very humorous is
his account of the way in which a petition was got up :
' The progress of a petition is well known. An ejected
placeman goes down to his county or his borough, tells
his friends of his inability to serve them, and his constituents of the corruptions of Government. . . . The
petition is read and universally approved. Those who
are sober enough to write add their names, and the rest
would sign it if they could. . . . The petition is then
handed from town to town, and from house to house, and
wherever it comes the inhabitants flock together that they
may see that which must be sent to the King. Names
are easily collected : one man signs because he hates the
Papists ; another because he had vowed destruction to the
turnpikes ; one because it will vex the parson ; another
because he owes his landlord nothing ; one because he is
rich ; another because he is poor ; one to show that he is

of Shelburne, vol. ii., p. 363; Conway's *Life of Paine*, vol. i., p. 169;
Rutt's *Life of Priestley*, vol. i., p. 349; Boswell's *Johnson* (1769).

not afraid, and another to show that he can write." Yet the practice of petitioning was one which could not be treated with contempt, and it even had its risks. More than one lord-lieutenant of a county was dismissed from his position for signing petitions which were distasteful to the Crown. The Platform, the Press, and the Right of Petition—the three P's of liberty—were all in turn used, and powerfully and effectively used, by those who were deeply dissatisfied with the existing state of things. From the Tories, who thought that the King should not only reign but govern, there was nothing, so they imagined, to be hoped, and from the Whigs but little more. To the early Radicals the Whig creed seemed a cold and lifeless thing, that gave no promise of expansion nor of any regenerating power. Impetuous and impatient, they thought that the movement of the party of progression was intolerably slow; and they began by degrees to profess distinctive principles and to form a separate group. Philosophically speaking, the Radicals must be regarded as the vanguard of the Whigs; they supply the motive force; they represent the principle of movement in its most lively and energetic shape; and though they have almost always ostensibly pursued the same end as the Whigs, they have differed profoundly in their means, and even more in their principles and theories. It therefore came about that the Radicals and Whigs were divided from one another by some sharp and clearly cut distinctions.[1]

[1] Johnson's *False Alarm*; Fitzmaurice's *Life of Shelburne*, vol. iii., p. 68; Boswell's *Johnson* (1770): "A prince of ability might, and should be, the directing soul and spirit of his own administration; in short, his own minister, and not the mere head of a party". It is not easy to define the terms Whig and Tory. Hume's definition may suffice for his own time: A Tory is "a lover of monarchy, without abandoning liberty, and a partisan

THE FIRST PERIOD, 1761-1789.

It would be impossible to fix the date exactly of a growth whose root is deeply imbedded in the recesses of the past; yet the statement of Mr. Lecky's that "the year 1769 is very remarkable in political history, for it witnessed the birth of English Radicalism," may be taken to be approximately true. It was then, as Mr. Lecky says, that "the first serious attempts to reform and control Parliament by pressure from without, making its members habitually subservient to their constituents," were made.[1] For it is one of the most remarkable facts in English history, that the efforts of the earliest Radicals were directed, not against the House of Lords, nor even primarily against the Crown, but against the House of Commons. The House of Lords did too little to excite any feeling of hostility; they were even accused by Burke of showing a want of spirit. As for the Crown, its power and influence, indeed, had grown far beyond what the authors of the Revolution of 1688 had expected or intended. Influence had gradually usurped the place which once prerogative had held. The House of Hanover, at first *isolée* and unpopular with the majority of the nation, strengthened its arm to resist the machinations of the dynasty it had displaced.[2] Yet it was the popular Chamber that became the object of suspicion to the people;

of the family of Stuart "; a Whig is "a lover of liberty without renouncing monarchy, and a friend of the Settlement in the Protestant line". For other definitions see De Quincey's Essay, *A Tory's Account of Toryism, Whiggism and Radicalism*, and Coleridge's *Church and State*.

[1] Lecky's *History of England in the Eighteenth Century*, vol. iii., p. 174; Buckle's *History of Civilisation*, vol. i., p. 434; Cooke's *History of Party*, vol. iii., p. 187. It is a curious coincidence that the Duke of Wellington, who lived to be such an implacable enemy of the Radicals, should have been born in 1769.

[2] Boswell's *Johnson*, 1779; and Boswell's *Tour in the Hebrides*, 1773; see also Fitzmaurice's *Life of Shelburne*, vol. i., p. 30.

and so far from being regarded as the bulwark of their liberties, it was actually reproached as the enemy of freedom and the usurper of their rights. As Burke said, "the distempers of monarchy were the great subjects of apprehension and redress in the last century; in this, the distempers of Parliament". The Crown was only blamed for resting on a parliamentary system, which was to the last degree vicious and corrupt. George III. did not sin against the light; he was not master of his fate; he did not create the system, but found it already in existence; and as he was not endowed by nature with the wisdom of a statesman, he helped rather to inflame the evil than to cure it. He was, in fact, an excellent country gentleman, who had been called by fate to rule an empire. As for the parliamentary representatives, if they did not fear the Crown, neither cared they for the people; for while public opinion was hardly formed, or only heard in whispers, the subservience of the Commons was secured by the bestowal of places, sinecures and pensions which the Crown had at its disposal. Dr. Johnson hit the mark, as with his massive sagacity he almost always did, when he observed that the House of Commons "being no longer under the power of the Crown" had to be "bribed";[1] nor was it without a touch of humour that Burke compared a member of Parliament to Æsop's weasel that went in very lean, but grew so fat and sleek that it became unable to escape by the hole by which it entered. Parliamentary elections became too often a mere money contest with the Treasury.[2] The

---

[1] Boswell's *Johnson*, 1779.

[2] It is significant that Burke when arguing against triennial Parliaments said that he would not like to commit the country gentlemen every three years to a contest with the Treasury (*Speech on the Present*

system was a bad one, but at that time there was none other open. It defiled almost every one it touched, and must have produced injurious effects, which were unknown to an ignorant and unsuspecting people. Yet even so, a popular agitation was aroused, of which the early Radicals became the natural spokesmen; and it necessarily followed that amongst those who clamoured for the reform of Parliament their voices were the loudest. That they were the popular party was to some extent fortuitous, because it was to the people at large that they were obliged to turn for help. [In a state where democracy is rampant a Radical party might, it is conceivable, be conservative in feeling; but in England the Radicals were, in the main, democratic from the first. Though urgent for reform, they shared that aim with others to whom they were abhorrent; their distinctive mark or note lay rather in their principles and methods.

[Parliamentary reform then was the object upon which the early Radicals concentrated their energies and attention. But there were many Whigs and some Tories who were quite as much in favour of some measure of reform; where they differed from the Radicals was not in the end but in the means.] Sometimes, indeed, even upon the means there was no difference of opinion. Two such Tories as Swift and Bolingbroke expressed themselves in favour of what afterwards became an essentially Radical reform—the shortening of Parliaments. Swift said he admired "that Gothic institution which made Parliaments annual". Chatham was the first statesman of the front rank to declare himself strongly in favour of reform; but he meant reform of a kind very different from that which

Discontents). Chatham writing to Shelburne in 1770 made use of very similar language (*Chatham's Correspondence*, vol. iv., p. 156).

the Radicals demanded. The theory—so dear to English Radicals—that the possession of the suffrage was a *personal* or *natural* right, he strenuously opposed. Property and, above all, landed property—the "soil," as he liked to call it—should, he thought, be represented. "The representation of the counties," he said, "is still preserved pure and uncorrupted"; and holding this opinion he wished that the number of county members should be raised, and thus "a new portion of health" be infused into the Constitution. The small boroughs he contemptuously called "the rotten parts," which he thought should be cut off; but fearing that "amputation might be death," he would have been content with the addition of some "Knights of the Shire," who "approach nearest to the constitutional representation of the country because they represent the soil". The theory of the representation of the land—antagonistic as it is to the Radical theory of the representation of the person—has, indeed, been held by almost every statesman and political thinker of importance, whether Whig or Tory, from early times almost until the present day; if it even now can be said to be extinct. Swift said it was absurd that men "who do not possess a foot of land in the country" should sit in Parliament for boroughs; while Bolingbroke described the landed gentry "as the true owners of our political vessel"; "the moneyed men," he said, "are but passengers in it". Shelburne agreed with Chatham: "I have never heard," he said, "a reflecting man doubt on the county representation being the greatest restorative possible of the Constitution". Burke was of the same opinion: "As property," he said, "is sluggish, inert and timid, it never can be safe from the invasions of ability, unless it be out of all proportion predominant in the representation. It must be represented too in great masses of accumulation or it is not rightly protected." That Dr. Johnson should maintain that influence must be in proportion to property, and that it was right that it should be, is only what might have been expected. Coleridge, *more suo*, took the philosophic view that the representation of the landed interest was the only security for the principle of permanence; and even Benjamin Franklin—who certainly had not a Tory bias—thought that the franchise belonged as of right to freeholders only. Though it is true that the counties were usually the strongholds of the Tories—Gibbon tells us that the Tories used to style themselves the country gentlemen—yet the belief in the representation of the land as the keystone of the Constitution was held also by the Whigs; and it was not until the abolition of the Corn Laws and the rise of the great industrial centres that the belief was in any way shaken or diminished. It was, in fact, a natural product of the time when the landed and agricultural interests formed the very foundation of the state. A curious illustration of this once-prevailing theory is afforded by the long-continued custom that county members only had the privilege of wearing spurs within the House of Commons.[1]

Upon the question of short Parliaments Chatham never, perhaps, passed a final judgment. When in 1770

[1] *Chatham's Correspondence*, vol. iii., p. 406; Swift's *Essay on Public Absurdities*; Bolingbroke's *Patriot King*; Leslie Stephens' *English Thought in the Eighteenth Century*, vol. ii., p. 178; Fitzmaurice's *Life of Shelburne*, vol. ii., p. 223; Burke's *Reflections on the French Revolution*; Boswell's *Journal of a Tour in the Hebrides*; Lecky's *Democracy and Liberty*, vol. i., p. 2; Gibbon's *Memoirs*. Lord Colchester (when he sat in Parliament as Mr. Abbot) says that he was blamed for being disorderly in wearing spurs, the privilege of county members. See his *Diaries and Correspondence*, vol. i., p. 45.

the Common Council thanked him for his promise to try to restore Parliaments to their original purity "by shortening their duration, and introducing a more full and equal representation," he replied that he could not recommend triennial Parliaments, but that he would not oppose them if the country unmistakably demanded them. In a letter to Shelburne he expressed the same opinion, though a year later in writing to Lord Temple he declared that "to shorten the duration of Parliaments" would be just as seasonable as to increase the county members. Speaking in the House of Lords in 1771 he declared himself a convert to triennial Parliaments—the most definite pronouncement on the subject he ever made. But the position of Chatham was almost, if not quite, unique in English history. The Great Commoner was enthroned in the affections of the people; he derived his power from popularity; he was, as Dr. Johnson well remarked, not like Walpole, a minister given by the King to the people, but a minister given by the people to the King; or, to use a phrase of Gibbon, he was "carried on the shoulders of the people".[1] He would in these days have been called a Tory democrat, and he was evidently in sympathy with many of the popular ideas. "For myself," he said, "I am resolved to be in earnest for the public, and shall be a scarecrow of violence to the gentle warblers of the grove, the moderate Whigs and temperate statesmen."[2] But thorough reformer as he believed himself to be, his mind was "bottomed" upon principles which differed profoundly from those which the Radicals professed.

---

[1] *Gibbon's Letters*, vol. ii., p. 236. Chatham described himself as accountable to the people for his conduct (*Annual Register*, 1761).

[2] Letter to Calcraft, 1770, *Chatham's Correspondence*, vol. iii., p. 464, vol. iv., pp. 156, 174; Sharpe's *London and the Kingdom*, vol. iii., p. 104.

The case of Burke may be compared with that of Chatham. He too in his own way was a reformer; and though in many ways he disagreed with Chatham, his difference with the Radicals was ever more profound. He uttered sentiments, indeed, which breathe the purest spirit of democracy. Such phrases as, " I like a clamour where there is an abuse "; the people are " the masters "; Parliament must not defraud " its employers "; the people are " its natural lords "; in all disputes between the people and their rulers, " the presumption is at least on a par in favour of the people "; " to give a specific sanction to the general sense of the community is the true end of the legislature "; " let us identify, let us incorporate ourselves with the people "; show him to have had popular sympathies at heart. His political conduct too was in harmony with the sentiments which he openly expressed. In the case of the Middlesex election, upon questions of privilege, of parliamentary reporting, of financial reform, and of the diminution of corruption, he was found to be upon the side of liberty. But if there ever was a man who from his heart and soul loathed Radical reform, that man was surely Burke; his detestation of it amounted almost to a mania or disease. He called the Radicals " a corps of schemers " and " a rotten subdivision of a faction ". Of the reasons for his hatred something more specific hereafter will be said; and it must be here enough to state that to short Parliaments and a wider extension of the suffrage he was vehemently opposed. His remedy was rather a limited franchise, but one of independency and of weight. Above all, he indignantly rejected those two essential principles of radicalism: first, that the suffrage is a right that is *natural* or *personal* ; and, secondly, that a parliamentary representative is a mere *delegate* or mouthpiece, who should be under the strictest obligations to obey the instructions of those who had elected him. It is no wonder that Burke became to the Radicals a peculiar object of dislike; for to a fanatic moderation is specially abhorrent.[1]

Parliamentary reform was then by no means a Radical monopoly. So far, indeed, was this from being the case that the man who in the eighteenth century brought reform of Parliament nearest to its consummation was, as will be seen, the younger Pitt himself, who was the bitterest foe the Radicals ever had. It remains yet to consider more minutely how they differed from the reforming Whigs and Tories.

It has been said that English Radicalism first became distinctly visible in the year 1769; but for several years before there were clearly signs of an impending change. For what was the position of affairs since the accession of George III.? This short space of time was one which, though not marked by any extraordinary events, was yet pregnant with results. Politically speaking, it was one of great confusion, and was attended by discredit. It was pre-eminently a period of experiments. The elder Pitt resigned, and the Bute, Grenville, Bedford and Rockingham Administrations followed one another in rapid succession. The party system had, for the time

[1] Cartwright evidently despised Burke: "It is left," he said, "to such reformers as Mr. Burke to talk of the people's liberties, and at the same time to deny or explain away their rights" (*Life of Cartwright*, vol. ii., p. 349). Even Bentham seems to have lost command of his temper when, speaking of Burke, he called him a "madman," an "incendiary," "a caster of verbal filth," a possessor of an "unqualified thirst for lucre" (Montague's Introduction to Bentham's *Fragment on Government*, p. 17). It is worth noting that the first use of the word *franchise* to mean the right to vote for a representative has been traced to Burke's *Reflections on the French Revolution*. See the *Oxford Historical Dictionary*.

being, completely broken down, to be replaced by factious combinations, such as the "King's Friends," or the "Patriots". When Dr. Johnson described patriotism as the last refuge of a scoundrel he had abundant warrant for a saying that, apart from special circumstances, would affront our moral sense. For this state of things Chatham, great Minister though he was, must be held largely responsible. He revolted against party, and conceived the notion of forming, with the assistance of the King, a Ministry composed of men from every section. To the King, indeed, his reverence was extreme; when he left the royal presence he bowed so low that his long nose could be seen between his knees; a peep into the royal closet, as Burke said, almost intoxicated him.[1] "Measures, not men," was the rule of conduct he set before himself. When in after years Wilkes, as City Chamberlain, presented the freedom of the city to the younger Pitt he said, "Your noble father, sir, annihilated party".[2] That is an exaggerated statement of the case. He tried to do so, but he failed; and when he formed a Ministry, it resembled a tessellated pavement that was curiously inlaid, rather than a body of men bound together by unity of principle or unanimity of sentiment.[3] The result brought discredit both upon himself and on his King. At first both Sovereign and Minister were equally the favourites

[1] Russell's *Memorials of Fox*, vol. iv., p. 17, note. It is noteworthy that the King repaid Chatham's devotion by speaking of him as "a trumpet of sedition," and "that perfidious man" (Sir G. C. Lewis' *Administrations of Great Britain from 1783 to 1830*).

[2] Almon's *Memoirs of Wilkes*, vol. iv., p. 204.

[3] Burke called the maxim, "measures, not men," an insignificant one (Cavendish's *Parliamentary Debates*, 1769). And again: "This country will never be well governed until we see those who are connected by unanimity of sentiment hold the reins of power" (*ibid.*, 1768).

of the people. When, for example, in 1760 the first stone of Blackfriars Bridge was laid, an inscription in honour of Pitt was engraved upon it, and the bridge was known as Pitt's; and when he went into the City he was overwhelmed with a storm of acclamations.[1] But these halcyon days soon passed away. The popularity of the King, who was suspected of unduly stretching his prerogative under the influence of his mother, became quickly dimmed and faded. "George, be King!"[2] such were the words which—so rumour had it—she daily dinned into his ears. It was commonly believed that a plan was early formed "of carrying the prerogative to very unusual heights". One morning some placards were discovered about the Royal Exchange inscribed with the words, "No Petticoat Government! No Scotch Favourite!" And without doubt they expressed openly what many men were thinking. Sometimes the crowd would burn in effigy a petticoat and jack-boot, just to give a gentle hint of their opinion of the Queen-Dowager and of Bute. The Scotch, who were the mainstay of the Jacobites, were in England unpopular to a degree which it is now difficult to realise; for to see Bute, a Scotsman, Premier, and some old Jacobites basking in the sun of royal favour, was more than many Englishmen were able to endure. They took their revenge, therefore, in a rough and ready manner. Hume bitterly complained of the dislike of the Scotch that was shown during his residence in London, where plays with Scotch names were hissed from the stage. Churchill lent the weapons of his satire to aid the vulgar prejudice, from which even such men as Dr. Johnson and Shelburne were

[1] Sharpe's *London and the Kingdom*, vol. iii., pp. 65 and 69.
[2] Horace Walpole's *Memoirs of the Reign of George III.*, vol. i., p. 16.

not free. The latter, with all his wide sympathies, went so far as to say that he could scarce conceive a Scotchman capable of liberality and impartiality. The populace amused themselves by giving vent to their opinions in a characteristic manner: they paraded a figure dressed up in a plaid and blue ribbon leading an ass royally crowned; and it required no great acumen to interpret the hidden meaning of the symbols. But the displeasure of the country reached its height when Pitt "stumbled upstairs"; or, in other words, accepted a peerage and a pension. It would, perhaps, be too much to assert, as Lord Chesterfield did of Pulteney, that he shrank into insignificancy and an earldom; but he forfeited some of the confidence and affection of the people.[1] Now all these things were, if not the causes, at all events the symptoms of unrest, which reached a culminating point in 1769, in many ways a memorable year. For it witnessed the very beginnings of movements which were destined to revolutionise the political and commercial life of England. By a remarkable coincidence the birth-year of Radicalism was the very year in which Watt and Arkwright took out their earliest patents, from which such wonderful results were afterwards to flow.

[1] Boswell's *Johnson* (1761); Hume's *Essays, Moral and Political;* Rae's *Life of Adam Smith*, p. 195; Walpole's *Letters*, vol. i. (13th Nov., 1761); Walpole's *Memoirs*, vol. i., p. 16; Churchill's *Prophecy of Famine;* Fitzmaurice's *Life of Shelburne*, vol. iii., p. 441; Thorold Rogers' *Historical Gleanings*, p. 156. The antipathy between the Scotch and English was of old standing: in the reign of James I. the Statute of Stabbing was enacted in order to put a stop to the use of the knife by natives of the one country upon those of the other. In connection with Chatham's peerage it is worth noting that the younger Pitt, when quite a boy, perceived how much more influential was the position of a member of the House of Commons; he said he was glad he was not the eldest son. See Lord Ashbourne's *Pitt*.

The period of English history from 1760 to 1769, with its maze of factious intrigues, its insignificant cabals and personal animosities, is one of which it is difficult to give a clear account. In the world of politics there was no commanding figure who stood shoulders high above the crowd. The influence of Chatham was already on the wane; the younger Pitt—though one of those who strangle serpents in their cradles—was still at school; and it was not until 1768 that Fox, then a youth of nineteen, was elected as the representative of Midhurst. It was only in 1766 that Burke entered public life as member for Wendover, and as Lord Rockingham's private secretary; and his reputation was at this time that of an author who was budding into fame. To society in 1761 he was known merely as a young man who had "not worn off his authorism yet".[1] But amid the welter of events there stands out in strong relief the person of John Wilkes, than whom no stranger figure has ever appeared upon the stage of English public life; and if the eye is fixed upon him, the political significance of the events with which he was connected will not be hard to understand. This extraordinary man may justly claim to be the first of English Radicals; and that he was so is a further illustration of the saying that chance plays a great part in the destinies of men. His career has been too often wrongly understood. The earliest form of radicalism was, as has already been remarked, an attempt "to reform and control Parliament by pressure from without"; and it was because the House of Commons flouted Wilkes, and—through him—trampled on the rights of the Middlesex electors, that he became an ardent Radical. To control Parliament from without, to pre-

---

[1] Horace Walpole's *Letters*, vol. iv., 1761.

vent it riding rough-shod over the rights of the electors, became the public mission of his life. Having no settled political convictions of his own, he found the popular forces already put in motion, and turned them to account. The spirit of democracy was already in the air, but, generally speaking, the mass of the people were, from the political point of view, a negligible quantity. Parliamentary elections were but seldom the subject of a contest, and only in London, Westminster, Southwark, and the county of Middlesex did they arouse a large amount of interest.[1] The popular conscience had, indeed, scarcely been awakened. The right of petitioning the Crown or Parliament was almost the only means which the people had of making their voices clearly heard; and that right, indeed, was sedulously cherished. Its exercise involved the right of public meeting, and county gatherings were now and then convened either to frame petitions or to offer addresses to the throne. Here was the germ of what was destined afterwards to become a mighty power. The use of the hustings, moreover, at elections, had a democratic tendency, because it made men more or less acquainted with the conduct of affairs, even when they had not the right to vote. During the first years of the reign of George III. a distinct forward step was taken, for the first attempts were made by constituencies to exact pledges from their parliamentary representatives—an event of great importance from the Radical point of view. In the City of London, indeed, the custom seems to have already been in force; for it is recorded that in 1761 the Common Council issued *instructions* to the City Members, " as was its wont ". But perhaps the case of Gloucester was the first to awaken much

---

[1] Jephson's *Rise and Progress of the Platform*, vol. i., p. 21.

attention. In that city in the year 1763 the people met together and passed a resolution condemning the new duty on cider, and directed a pledge to be taken from the next parliamentary candidate to vote for its repeal.[1]

It was while this spirit was abroad that Wilkes appeared upon the scene, and his career affords a lively picture of the first Radical agitation and of an important political campaign. Born at Clerkenwell in 1727, the son of a distiller, he was educated first at Hertford and afterwards at Leyden, whither he was sent by his father, who was ardently attached to the principles of 1688. He was not, to say the least, endowed by nature with much comeliness of feature, but his squint and sallow skin were made the most of in Hogarth's caricature. Horace Walpole described his countenance as "horrid"; and long afterwards Byron called him—

> A merry cock-eyed curious-looking sprite.

Brougham too spoke of his "inhuman squint and demoniac grin". Yet he had his compensations. He was wittily resourceful and adroit, and so ready in expedients that it was said that if he were stripped naked and thrown over Westminster Bridge on one day, he would on the next be found in Pall Mall, dressed in the height of fashion and with money in his pocket. He was infinitely clever, and one of the greatest masters of repartee who ever lived; and when he chose could be infinitely pleasant. He even contrived to be something of a dandy. Gibbon said that he scarcely ever met with a better companion; that he had inexhaustible spirits and a fund of wit and humour. That he could make himself agree-

---

[1] Sharpe's *London and the Kingdom*, vol. iii., p. 70. Walpole in one of his *Letters* (vol. iv., 1761) speaks of the City as having "given instructions" to its Members.

able it is impossible to doubt ; for even Dr. Johnson was constrained to admit that he had much variety of talk, some scholarship and the manners of a gentleman.[1] The King himself was charmed with his bearing and demeanour, and declared that he had never seen " so wellbred a Lord Mayor".[2] That he had the instincts of a scholar we know from his edition of *Theophrastus*— the elegance of which Lord Mansfield and all bibliophiles were willing to allow.[3] Of his early dissipations, of his boon companions and their orgies we are not concerned to speak, for it is not Wilkes the man but Wilkes the politician who is of interest to us here. Though born in a family of Whig traditions, he does not seem to have been troubled with any deep convictions. Needy, restless and aspiring, he told Gibbon very frankly that during a time of public turmoil he had resolved to make his fortune. The first of the Radicals, in short, was a political adventurer who, thanks to the mistakes of his opponents and his own impudent audacity, contrived to make himself for a brief period the hero of the hour.

Wilkes early aspired to a parliamentary career. In 1754 he unsuccessfully wooed the suffrages of Berwick, but three years later and once again in 1761 he was elected for Aylesbury at a cost which helped to complete

[1] Byron's *Vision of Judgment* (stanza 65) ; Rogers' *Historical Gleanings* (first series), p. 179. Leigh Hunt (*Autobiography*) says that Wilkes sometimes wore scarlet trimmed with gold. He was by almost universal testimony a very plain-looking man. He was described by Dr. Thomas Campbell (speaking of the year 1775) as labouring under "baldness, increpitude, and want of teeth". See *Edinburgh Review* for October, 1859. Mrs. Thrale suggested that he had grown to look prematurely old because the life of wit is so laborious. There is a portrait of Wilkes by Richard Earldom in the National Portrait Gallery.

[2] Sharpe's *London and the Kingdom*, vol. iii., p. 152.

[3] Nichols' *Literary Anecdotes of the Eighteenth Century*, vol. ix.

the ruin of his fortune.¹ Moderation had no charm for a nature that delighted in controversy and loved the joy of battle, and he soon appeared in the lists as the antagonist of Bute. That nobleman made use of the medium of the press to vindicate his policy, and employed Smollett, the historian and novelist, to write for him in a paper called the *Briton*.² Wilkes saw his opportunity, and replied by creating the *North Briton* as a rival publication. Rarely, if ever, has the foundation of a new journal been an event of such historical importance. For the *North Briton* was among the first journals to make politics its leading object, and perhaps the very first of all to give in full the names of public men—a practice which at that time was considered rather daring.³ It was written with a good deal of verve and pungent wit. The poet, Churchill, was the most brilliant *collaborateur* upon the staff. Dr. Johnson, it is true, thought him "a shallow fellow" and a "blockhead," but Horace Walpole described him as an abler man than Wilkes, though his equal in licentiousness. As a satirical poet, indeed, he has been seldom equalled or excelled.⁴ It is no wonder, therefore, that the *North Briton* created a sensation and had an enormous circula-

[1] Almon's *Memoirs and Correspondence of Wilkes*, vol. i., p. 33. It is said that the Delaval family, who held political sway over the borough of Berwick, engaged a vessel to bring their supporters from London, but that Wilkes bribed the captain to steer for Norway, where he landed the electors. See the article in the *Cornhill Magazine*, December, 1897, on "Wilkes" by W. B. Duffield.

[2] Almon's *Memoirs*, vol. i., pp. 91-2. Walpole's *Memoirs*, vol. i., pp. 177-79.

[3] Walpole's *Memoirs*, vol. i., pp. 177-79.

[4] H. Walpole's *Letters*, vol. v., 1765, note. Churchill died during a visit to his friend Wilkes at Boulogne in 1764. Cowper called him the "great" Churchill; Southey praised his poems and his honesty of purpose, and Campbell ranked him as a satirist next to Pope and Dryden.

THE FIRST PERIOD, 1761-1789. 33

tion.[1] It attacked the court and the Scotch favourites with a freedom that was unprecedented then, but which at the present time, when everything is criticised, seems not to be in any way remarkable. Horace Walpole, at least, thought that it was conducted with unheard of acrimony and licence, and, doubtless, this was a novelty that tickled the palates of its readers. The following satire on the Scotch satellites of Bute may be taken as a sample of its wit: " Some time since died Mr. John Bull, a very worthy, plain, honest old gentleman of Saxon descent. He was choked by inadvertently swallowing a thistle which he had placed by way of ornament on the top of his salad! For many years before he had enjoyed a remarkably good state of health."[2] But there were things in the *North Briton* that were written seriously and were intended to have been as seriously received. Here, for instance, is a passage where the voice of democracy speaks aloud and with no uncertain sound: " Government is a just execution of the laws which were instituted for the people for their preservation; but if the people's implements, to whom they have trusted the execution of those laws, or any power for their preservation, should convert such execution to their destruction, have they not a right to intermeddle? Nay, have they not a right to resume the power they have delegated, and to punish their servants who have abused it? If a King can do no wrong, his ministers may, and are accountable to the people for their conduct."[3] Language of this kind must have been, we may be sure, to the King and his ministers exceedingly distasteful; and it is remarkable for its specific affirmation of the doctrine, which is peculiarly Radical,

[1] Stephens' *Memoirs of Tooke*, vol. i., p. 91.
[2] *North Briton*, Number 7. [3] *Ibid.*, Number 19.

3

that parliamentary representatives are simply *delegates*. The passage contains one of the earliest statements of the theory. Yet, notwithstanding, the *North Briton* for a time proceeded gaily on its course; it called forth opposition journals, such as Arthur Murphy's *Auditor*, and that was all. But in 1763 the blow at last descended. In the celebrated *Number 45*, which appeared on the 23rd of April, the King's speech was criticised with what was thought to be a scandalous severity.[1] The writer asserted that the King's speech was the speech of the minister; that it was "the most abandoned instance of ministerial effrontery"; that "all foreigners, especially the King of Prussia," would hold the minister in contempt and abhorrence; that the King is "responsible to his people for the choice of his ministers, but that the favourite has given too just cause for him to escape the general odium". The indictment does not seem so very terrible, yet *Number 45* was declared by the law officers to be "an infamous and seditious libel". The usual consequences followed. Wilkes, who before had been known only to the public as a clever and successful journalist, immediately obtained his desired notoriety. He was indicted for the libel, and thanks to the blunders of the Government and the personal hostility of the King,[2] he was enabled to pose as a hero and a martyr. Three capital blunders were committed: he was arrested on a general warrant in which no individual names were mentioned; his papers were seized; and his privilege from arrest as a Member of

[1] Walpole's *Memoirs*, vol. i., pp. 177-79. Lord Macaulay in his second essay on Chatham says that Number 45 "contained nothing so strong as may in our time be found daily in *The Times* and *Morning Chronicle* ".

[2] The King told Lord North that " the expulsion of Mr. Wilkes appears to be very essential and must be effected " (Sharpe's *London and the Kingdom*, vol. iii., p. 82).

Parliament was disregarded. When he was remanded to the Tower by the Court of Common Pleas, he was received by the mob with cries of " Liberty! liberty! Wilkes for ever and no Excise ".[1] At the Tower his power of wit did not forsake him. He begged not to be placed in a cell where a Scotchman had ever been imprisoned;[2] and he had even the assurance to express a preference for the dungeon which Sir William Windham once had occupied. The satirical dart was shrewdly aimed, for his enemy, Lord Egremont, then a Secretary of State, was Sir William Windham's son.[3] More extraordinary still was the scene that followed the conclusion of the trial. When Wilkes sat down on finishing the speech in his defence, the audience burst out into tumultuous applause, and he was attended home by a multitude of people. Bonfires and illuminations brought to an end a memorable day.[4] The judge, Chief Justice Pratt, afterwards Lord Camden, who ordered Wilkes to be discharged, obtained his full share of popularity; his busts and pictures were hawked about the country; and he was represented on many a tavern sign-post in the act of laying down the law. He was presented with the freedom of the City, and his portrait by Sir Joshua Reynolds, which was fitly placed within the Guildhall, bore an inscription in honour of the zealous assertor of English liberty by law.[5]

[1] Appendix to the *North Briton*.
[2] Wilkes shared the prejudice against the Scotch. On one occasion Boswell when dining in the City complained that he had lost his pocket handkerchief: " It is," said Wilkes, " only the ostentation of a Scotchman who wishes to show that he possesses one ".
[3] Walpole's *Memoirs*, vol. i., pp. 277-79.
[4] Appendix to the *North Briton*.
[5] Sharpe's *London and the Kingdom*, vol. iii., p. 78. The Latin inscription is ascribed to Dr. Johnson. See also Campbell's *Lives of the Chancellors*, vol. v., pp. 248-52.

Wilkes had so far been triumphant, but if the matter had been dropped, he probably would have been soon forgotten. But the Government thought otherwise, and they entered on a course of what looked like persecution. He was first deprived of his command as colonel of the Bucks Militia.[1] Then the Houses of Parliament opened the attack. In the House of Lords Lord Sandwich produced a poem, alleged to have been the work of Wilkes, an obscene parody on Pope's *Essay on Man* called the *Essay on Woman*. Because the name of Bishop Warburton, a spiritual peer, was mentioned in the poem, it was denounced by Sandwich as a grievous breach of privilege. That the poem was licentious there is very little doubt, but in justice to Wilkes it must be said that it was printed privately, while many more profligate works have been given to the world and very little said. From Sandwich the attack came with a very bad grace; and, as Lord de Spencer said, it was the first time he had ever heard the devil preaching against sin.[2] Then the House of Commons took its part in the assault, and entered on a quarrel which it long pertinaciously maintained, but from which it finally retired defeated and discredited. When Wilkes complained of his arrest the House passed a resolution to the effect that *Number 45* was " a scandalous and seditious libel, containing expressions

[1] Almon's *Memoirs*, vol i., p. 130.
[2] *Ibid.*, vol. i., p. 256. Wilkes, in a letter to the electors of Aylesbury speaks of the *Essay on Woman* as "a ludicrous poem" and an "idle poem," and says that he had printed "not quite a fourth part at his private press". He declares that "the most vile blasphemies were forged and published as part of it," and that he had only ridiculed the creed "which the great Tillotson wished the Church of England fairly rid of". Macaulay thought the work not more profligate than some of Pope's published poems (Essay on Hallam's *Constitutional History*).

of the most unexampled insolence and contumely towards his Majesty, the grossest aspersions upon the Houses of Parliament," and ordered the paper to be burned by the common hangman. The attempt to carry out the order in front of the Royal Exchange was turned into a scene of wild disorder; the paper was rescued from the flames, the sheriff was pelted by the mob, and Harley the Lord Mayor, the Tory member for the City, was injured in his carriage.[1]

Thus ended the first act of the drama, and Wilkes withdrew to France, where he became a *persona grata* in society. There we need not now pursue him. The House of Commons, in defiance of all precedent, resolved that in cases of seditious libel no privilege existed, and ordered his expulsion. For refusing to appear, as the author of *Number 45* and of the *Essay on Woman*, to answer a charge of libel in the law courts, he was outlawed. On the other hand, he obtained heavy damages against an Under Secretary of State for the illegal seizure of his papers, and it is probable that Lord Rockingham and others—who were not sorry to keep him out of the way —sent him some pecuniary assistance. In 1767 he returned to England, and wrote submissive letters to the Duke of Grafton and the King. He complained that he was suffering from the vengeance of those persons whose "ignorance, insufficiency, and treachery" he had laboured to expose.[2] But it was all to no purpose. He then re-

[1] Almon's *Memoirs*, vol. ii., p. 88; Walpole's *Memoirs*, vol. i., p. 330; Rockingham *Memoirs*, vol. ii., pp. 96-98.

[2] Rogers' *Historical Gleanings* (second series), p. 167; Texte's *J.-J. Rousseau et les Origines du Cosmopolitisme Littéraire*, p. 314. Wilkes is said to have astonished Paris by his "*éloquence fougueuse*," and to have been called a "*brouillon*" by Rousseau. Walpole's *Memoirs*, vol. i., pp. 322, 350, 388; vol. iii., pp. 5, 6; Rockingham *Memoirs*, vol. ii., p. 236;

solved upon a daring step: he offered himself, though unsuccessfully, as a parliamentary candidate for the City. Nothing daunted by defeat, he immediately came forward to woo the suffrages of Middlesex, and the election proved to be one of the most exciting and dramatic ever known in English history. Bets on his chances were converted into stock and freely dealt in; all persons on the way to the place of the election were compelled to wear a blue cockade, and bits of paper with the inscription "Wilkes and Number 45"; the carriage of Sir William Proctor, the rival candidate, was overturned; the number "45" was scratched on carriage doors as a passport for free passage through the streets; and the Austrian Ambassador was dragged from his coach, and the number chalked upon the soles of his boots. It is said that Cruden (the author of the *Concordance* of the Bible) amused himself by rubbing out the figures "45" wherever he saw them in the streets, but the labour was too great for even his persistency. Every house was illuminated at the dictation of the mob, and the mansions of Bute and several others were attacked and badly damaged. The whole scene was one of the wildest saturnalia; an eye-witness declaring that he had seen in his own presence more than one hundred persons knocked down and several killed.[1] Wilkes was triumphantly returned, and in his address of thanks to his constituents he made use of a remarkable expression; that is to say, he asked them to give him their *instructions*.[2] For a Member of Parliament to admit that he and his electors stood in any

The Appendix to the *North Briton*; Nichols' *Literary Anecdotes*, vol. ix., p. 457.

[1] Cavendish's *Debates*, 1768.
[2] Walpole's *Memoirs*, vol. iii., p. 190.

THE FIRST PERIOD, 1761-1789. 39

such relation was something new, and an event of some importance in the history of political opinion. If the Middlesex election were notable for nothing else, it would be notable for this.

Wilkes' triumph, however, soon suffered an eclipse, for he was committed to prison as an outlaw. On the way to the jail the mob took the horses from his coach and dragged it to Cornhill; a riot in St. George's Fields ensued, and a man was killed by soldiers who were called out to help to keep the peace. Wilkes himself escaped into a tavern, from whence he afterwards surrendered.[1] His outlawry was then removed; but for the libels contained in *Number 45*, and the *Essay on Woman*, he was fined £1000, and sentenced to twenty-two months' imprisonment. But the punishment served only to increase his popularity; he received visitors like Rockingham and Burke; his admirers sent him presents of game, fish and fruit; from the Duchess of Queensberry and Lady Betty Germaine he received £100 apiece; and the large sum of £1200 was subscribed for him in Charleston in America.[2] But more was yet to follow. He published a letter from Lord Weymouth, a Secretary of State, to the magistrates of the Lambeth Quarter Sessions, with a preface, in which he roundly charged the Minister with having deliberately caused what he called the Massacre of St.

---

[1] Almon's *Memoirs*, vol. ii. p. 273; Walpole's *Memoirs*, vol. iii., pp. 205-6. Burke wittily compared Wilkes carried in triumph by the mob to Horace's description of Pindar elevated on the wings of poetical inspiration: "numerisque fertur rege solutis" (*Odes*, iv., 8) (Maxall's *Memoirs of His Own Time*, vol. ii., p. 278). The witticism is said to have greatly delighted Dr. Johnson (Boswell's *Life*, 1778). Wilkes, too, is said to have much appreciated the joke (Boswell's *Journal of a Tour in the Hebrides*).

[2] Nichols' *Literary Anecdotes*, vol. ix., p. 497.

George's Fields.¹ This insult was the piling of Pelion upon Ossa, and could not be endured; and though the matter was one which concerned the House of Lords alone, the House of Commons, by a totally irregular proceeding, resolved once more that Wilkes should be expelled. Then followed an extraordinary series of events. Wilkes underwent a sort of apotheosis, and "Wilkemania," as it was called, reached extraordinary heights. "If," said Franklin, "Wilkes had had a good character, and the King a bad one, the former might have turned the latter out of his kingdom." "Wilkes and Liberty" was the catchword of the hour, and his enemies called "45" the Number of the Beast. "He is," said Horace Walpole, "reverenced as a saint by the mob, and if he dies, I suppose the people will squint themselves into convulsions at his tomb in honour of his memory." His admirers, indeed, would not allow that he was plain; he squinted, they thought, no more than a gentleman should. Diderot sent him congratulations, and even Whitefield offered up prayer on his behalf.² Twice in succession Wilkes was re-elected for Middlesex, and twice was his election declared void by the House. The Government then resolved to run a rival candidate, and one Colonel Luttrell was found willing to undertake the contest. The risk was not a small one, and even the Colonel, who was a man of iron nerves, and did not want in personal courage, insured his life. He was pelted by the mob at Hyde Park

---

¹ Almon's *Memoirs*, vol. ii., p. 273; Walpole's *Memoirs*, vol. iii., pp. 205-6.

² Walpole's *Letters*, vol. v. (1768); Walpole's *Memoirs*, vol. iii., p. 206, and *Letters*, vol. v. (1772); Rockingham *Memoirs*, vol. ii., p. 235; Appendix to the *North Briton*. Boswell, in his *Journal of a Tour in the Hebrides*, notes that in a remote part of the country he saw a print of Hogarth's picture of Wilkes.

Corner, and was only rescued from the violence of the mob by the timely aid of some of his opponents.[1] A malignant press aspersed his reputation: "He has," said Junius, "discovered a new line in human character; he has disgraced the name of Luttrell".[2] Wilkes, of course, was re-elected, but the House declared his election null and void, and that Luttrell was entitled to fill the vacant seat. By this extraordinary act Wilkes was finally excluded. As the Middlesex election was the culminating point in his political life, it remains to estimate its full significance and meaning.

In the history of radicalism the Middlesex election is an event of great importance; for, when divested of all the personal incidents which have encrusted and obscured it, it is plainly seen to have been fundamentally a conflict between the House of Commons and the people. That House claimed not only to be free from the control of the electors, but even to override their wishes when clearly and repeatedly declared. It was no wonder that party passions were inflamed to fever-heat. Dr. Johnson said that the question was whether Middlesex should be represented by a criminal from jail; Dr. Parr, who had given his vote for Wilkes, lost, in consequence, the headmastership of Harrow;[3] the King dismissed from their

[1] Sharpe's *London and the Kingdom*, vol. iii., p. 87; Fitzmaurice's *Shelburne*, vol. i., p. 188; Almon's *Memoir of Wilkes*, vol. iii., p. 4; Stephens' *Memoir of Wilkes*, vol. i., p. 101.

[2] Junius, *Letters*, No. 40.

[3] De Quincey's Essay on *Whiggism in its Relation to Literature*. Dr. Johnson perhaps wished to pay off an old score against Wilkes. The latter, on reading in the grammatical introduction to Dr. Johnson's *Dictionary* that the letter "h" seldom or never begins any but the first syllable, exclaimed: "The author of this observation must be a man of quick apprehension and of a most comprehensive genius" (Fraser Rae's *Wilkes, Sheridan and Fox*, p. 16).

appointments some Members of Parliament who had voted on the Opposition side. That Wilkes was something of a demagogue and agitator is very clear; and not less so is the fact that he suffered persecution, and that his personal and political opponents blundered badly and played into his hands. In his public life he was more sinned against than sinning. Burke was quite right when he declared that Wilkes by "his opposition to the court cabal had become an object of their persecution and the popular favour"; that his punishment was a "pretence"; and that no man believed that he was being made to expiate the fault of his indecent publications. As for the Middlesex election, it seemed to Burke "a tragi-comedy acted by his Majesty's servants, at the desire of several persons of quality, for the benefit of Mr. Wilkes and at the expense of the Constitution"; and he praised the resolute and strenuous resistance which Wilkes showed against oppression.[1] Junius with his usual acumen took in the whole situation at a glance: he said that the Government had made Wilkes a person of importance, and his cause the cause of the people as well as of himself; that "the rays of the royal indignation collected upon him served only to illuminate"; that he had only to be pardoned to become "a silent senator".[2] The King was even more foolish than his Ministers in conceiving a strong sentiment of personal antipathy to Wilkes; and it was a bit of common gossip that the young princes sometimes annoyed their royal father by opening the door of the room where he was sitting and calling out, "Wilkes and Number 45 for ever!" That Wilkes was a persecuted man is a

---

[1] Burke's *Thoughts on the Present Discontents;* Almon's *Memoirs of Wilkes,* vol. iii., p. 6.

[2] Junius, *Letters,* Nos. 35 and 51.

matter of no political importance whatever; it matters not whether he had the virtues of a stoic or was the basest of mankind. But in the *rôle* of politician he played a leading part; and it must in justice be allowed that, for a man who was ugly, who was no orator and who had rather a shady reputation, to have attained the position that he did was something of a feat. But his career was not a mere display of political athletics; it was in its essential facts much more than that. Through the medium of the *North Briton* he greatly stimulated the press as an organ of political importance; he was the first to bring forward into prominence the question of the relations of the parliamentary representatives and the people, and so to open up the way for the discussion of parliamentary reform. When he entered Parliament, an almost unknown man, reform was scarcely so much as thought of; when he left it, a hero and a martyr, it was a subject that was in many minds and on many lips. He was among the first members of Parliament to adopt openly in his address to his constituents a view of the relationship of a representative to his electors, which subsequently was destined to become an essential part of the creed of the English Radical party; the view, namely, that parliamentary representatives are *delegates* and nothing else. That is a doctrine which implicitly admits the unrestricted right of the people at large to control Parliament by pressure from without; and the enunciation of this right is, from the point of view of the history of political opinion, a matter of no little interest and importance. Lastly, Wilkes was among the first to show that the House of Commons might be no less inimical than the Crown to the liberties of the people, and that parliamentary privilege might be turned into an engine of oppression. His political career was, indeed, a concrete example of the fact. Even some of his enemies allowed that he had performed a public service. Horace Walpole, for example, said that " the storm that saved us was raised in taverns and night cellars ". That is a remark that is hardly fair to Wilkes; but having made it, he draws the somewhat rash deduction that nations are commonly saved by the worst men in them. That, again, is a remark that is more cynical than true. The fact is that Wilkes became the first of the Radicals by accident; not out of choice but by the cogency of circumstances. It so happened that a great question of parliamentary privilege was fought out during his career. Formerly—as Junius justly said— it was the interest of the people that the privilege of Parliament should be left unlimited and undefined, but in the time of Wilkes the contrary was the case. The House of Commons, in depriving the Middlesex electors of their right to freedom of election, had "scandalously abused" the trust it had accepted; when it declared that Luttrell was their legal representative it virtually transferred the right of legislation from those whom the people had chosen to those whom they had not.[1]

The expulsion of Wilkes was so gross a perversion of parliamentary law and custom that he did not lack defenders even among those who disliked his personality. Burke, as it has been seen, was one of these. So, too, was Chatham, who called Wilkes the blasphemer of his God and the libeller of his King, and said that he did not deserve "to be ranked among the human species"; he even brought in a bill to reverse the decision of the Commons. He avowed in his place in the Lords that Luttrell was no representative of the people. Lord

[1] Walpole's *Memoirs*, vol. i., p. 182; Junius, *Letters*, Nos. 11, 35, 44.

Camden followed his example; and Sir George Saville in the Commons said he looked upon the House as sitting illegally after their illegal act. Townshend refused to pay his land tax on the ground that Middlesex was not legally represented.[1] The popular side was in fact not exclusively monopolised by Wilkes and his supporters. The agitation was only radical in character, because the question fundamentally at issue was that of the control of Parliament by pressure from without; and it is solely on account of the part that Wilkes played in connection with that question that he has any claim to be considered as a Radical at all. In many ways he differed greatly from the Radicals of later times. He was not an orator who stumped the country; he played no prominent part upon the hustings; during the most important crisis of his life the prison doors were closed upon him, and he was silent by compulsion. Moreover, public speaking had not yet become a common practice in the country. It was rather to his journalistic talents that he owed his power and popularity. Witty and facile with his pen, he drew after him a host of eager readers who enjoyed his pungent sallies; and from this point of view he may be considered as a prototype of Cobbett. In the House of Commons, when he was at last allowed to hold his seat in peace, his speeches were moderate and sensible. He took the Whig side in the American war and on the question of parliamentary reform; and when he retired

[1] Walpole's *Memoirs*, vol. iv., pp. 34, 38; Rockingham *Memoirs*, vol. ii., pp. 74-79, 212; Almon's *Memoirs of Wilkes*, vol. ii., p. 29; Walpole's *Letters*, vol. iv. (1763); Cavendish's *Debates* (1770). It is interesting to note that the minority of seventy-two who voted against Wilkes' expulsion dined together afterwards at the Thatched House Tavern. Amongst them was Wedderburn, the subsequent Tory Lord Loughborough (Campbell's *Lives of the Chancellors*, vol. vi., p. 83).

from the House in 1790 he made a profession of his faith in a limited monarchy, a monarchy, that is to say, "which is not above law, but is founded upon law, and secures freedom to the subject".[1]

But though Wilkes himself was a Radical of only a very moderate type—a Radical, indeed, upon only a single point of great constitutional importance—his expulsion led to results which no one had foreseen, and were exceedingly far-reaching. The Wilkes agitation, indeed, was even less important in itself than its immediate effects. Of these the most momentous was the impetus that was given to the practice of holding public meetings. The populace hitherto had but rarely made its voice heard upon the platform; but the Middlesex electors now set a precedent, which once made has never been forgotten; they called a public meeting at Mile End to express their indignation and to vindicate their rights. It has been said that this was "the first public meeting ever assembled in England, the first in which it was attempted to enlighten Englishmen respecting their political rights"; and even if this proposition were not literally true, the assemblage of the Middlesex electors would yet remain an epoch-making incident. It was a sign that the people were awaking to a consciousness of strength, and was, therefore, an event in the history of radicalism of great significance. A second result was one of hardly less importance; and that was the institution of political societies. The time and soil were favourable to their growth. Some like "Appleby's," the "Standard Tavern," the "Retrospection"—springing from seeds which had been cast in stony places—took

[1] Mr. Gladstone called Wilkes "that unworthy representative of good principles" (Tollemache's *Talks with Mr. Gladstone*, p. 121).

no root and quickly withered. They were merely the ephemeral creatures of a day. But the Society of the Supporters of the Bill of Rights, though its life too was but a brief one, has special claims to be considered.[1]

The inception of this Society in the year 1769, avowedly to assist Wilkes to vindicate his rights, and to promote the cause of parliamentary reform, was mainly due to the indefatigable energy of one who is in the history of radicalism a person of hardly less importance than the famous Wilkes himself. The names of the two men are inseparably associated together as sworn friends and bitter foes. John Horne Tooke was born in 1736, the son of a poulterer in Newport Market, Westminster, who supplied the household of the Prince of Wales. Mr. Horne, the elder—though the Prince of Wales did not pay his bills—made a sufficient fortune to enable him to educate his clever son at Westminster, Eton and St. John's College, Cambridge. Horne Tooke—for he subsequently took the second name—entered the Inner Temple as a student, but changing his mind took orders in the Church. As Vicar of New Brentford he so strongly made his influence felt that the place was called his bishopric. Never, perhaps, did any one so mistake his profession; for he possessed in an eminent degree the talents that make for success at the bar, and there can be very little doubt that, if he had been called, he would have been one of the most brilliant lawyers of his time. A man of good presence and comely in his features, he had fascinating

[1] Rockingham *Memoirs*, vol. ii., p. 94; Buckle's *History of Civilisation*, vol i., p. 434; Stephens' *Memoirs of Tooke*, vol. i., p. 163; Herbert Spencer's *Descriptive Sociology*, table v. Cp. Boutmy's *Le Développement de la Constitution et de la société politique en Angleterre*, p. 157: "Les réunions politiques semblent ignorées de la loi et les mœurs; le premier *meeting* mentionné par l'histoire est de 1769".

manners and was a brilliant conversationalist; while his keen and ready wit, his power of mordant satire, his fluency of speech and indomitable courage made him a dangerous antagonist in any polemical encounter. His caustic tongue, which he could not always curb, must have made him many enemies in private. His knowledge was neither extensive nor profound, but he made the most of what he had, and plied his pen with vivacity and skill. His *Diversions of Purley*—upon which his fame as an author mainly rests—is said to have delighted Fox and Melbourne, and even now is not devoid of interest. Godwin called him "the great philologist," and that the book had some merit may be gathered from the fact that James Mill reviewed it in his *Literary Journal*, and himself borrowed from it some of his philosophical ideas. Even the Tory Dr. Johnson allowed his claim to be a man of letters, and expressed the hope that the Government would not put him in the pillory: "He has," he said "too much literature for that". But if shallow, Tooke was logical and strenuous, "a keen, iron man," as Coleridge aptly styled him.[1] Brought up in Whig traditions,

[1] Stephens' *Memoirs of Tooke;* Hazlitt's *Spirit of the Age;* Foster' *Eclectic Review;* *Memorials of Fox,* vol. iii., p. 143; *Greville Memoirs* (first series), vol. iii., p. 131; Kegan Paul's *Godwin,* vol. i., p. 147; Bain's *James Mill,* p. 55; Coleridge's *Table Talk.* Coleridge writing to Wedgwood in 1800 thus describes Tooke: "He is a clear-headed old man, as every man must needs be who attends to the real import of words, but there is sort of charlatanry in his manner that did not please me. He makes such a mystery of plain and palpable things and never tells you anything without first exciting and detaining your curiosity" (Cottle's *Reminiscences of Coleridge and Southey,* p. 431). The Abbé Morellet writing Lord Shelburne (January, 1803) said that the *Diversions of Purley* is full of new and profound ideas (*Lettres de l'Abbé Morellet à Lord Shelburne* edited by Lord Edmond Fitzmaurice). There is a portrait of Tooke in the National Portrait Gallery by Thomas Hardy.

THE FIRST PERIOD, 1761-1789.

he soon showed a democratic bent and wrote a song to celebrate the liberation of Wilkes from the Tower. In 1765 he published anonymously *The Petition of an Englishman*, a lampoon directed against Bute and Mansfield. In this same year he went abroad, and in Paris was introduced to Wilkes who at this time was his idol. Of the private relations of the two men—which place neither of them in a favourable light—it does not concern us here to speak. Returning home, Vicar of New Brentford though he was, he threw himself with ardour into the Middlesex elections; his enthusiasm was such that he declared that "in a cause so just and holy he would dye his black coat red". His zeal for Wilkes at this time knew no bounds; he made himself his plenipotentiary factor. His energy was inexhaustible; he searched for evidence against a magistrate who had given the order to the soldiers to fire during the riot in St. George's Fields, and against those who had caused the death of a man during the election at New Brentford; he even took the trouble to become qualified to vote as an elector at Bedford in order to oppose the duke who was its patron. As a protagonist in the struggle between the House of Commons and the people he was, therefore, almost as prominent as Wilkes. But it is in connection with several addresses and petitions to the King, and indirectly, therefore, with the public meetings at which those addresses and petitions were adopted, that Tooke has immortalised his name. In the history of the struggle of the people to control Parliament by pressure from without, these meetings and petitions are of such interest and importance that Tooke and Wilkes may well be classed together as the earliest of the Radicals.

Tooke was, indeed, like Wilkes, never an extremist in

his views. He opposed universal suffrage, which was the irreducible minimum demanded by the Radicals of a thorough-going type; he accepted Pitt's proposals for reform; and he was certainly not a republican in theory. But in so far as radicalism means the popular control of Parliament, he was a Radical indeed; for his whole public life was directed to amplify and strengthen that control. At meetings called together for the purpose of moving addresses and petitions, he performed services the value of which it would be hard to overestimate. He moved, for instance, the Address of the Middlesex Electors, in terms which for that time were startlingly outspoken and audacious: "The ministers," so the address proceeded, "have torn away the very heart-strings of the Constitution. . . . That the liberties of the people have been most grossly violated by the corrupt influence of ministers since the days of Sir Rober Walpole is too notorious to require illustration or com ment." Still more remarkable were the addresses pre sented by the City Corporation, and there can be littl doubt that for their composition Horne Tooke was i the main responsible. The Livery first proceeded t elect as sheriffs Townshend and Sawbridge, the propose and seconder of Wilkes, and then "amid applause tha actually shook the hall" adopted a petition praying th King to dissolve Parliament. The petitioners declare that "the majority of the House of Commons hav deprived your people of their dearest rights. They hav done a deed more ruinous in its consequences than tt levying of ship-money by Charles I., or the dispensir power assumed by James II. . . . The present House o Commons does not represent the people." The petitic was carried with unanimous applause. The King, wl was not accustomed to listen to language such as this, was exceedingly incensed, and the servile House of Commons passed a resolution that the right of petitioning had been outrageously abused. But Tooke was not to be suppressed. He sent a copy of the petition to the *Public Advertiser*—a leading journal which was at this time read at Court—together with a description of the manner in which the King had received the petitioners, and how he had burst out laughing when the deputation left the room. It was, he said, a case of Nero fiddling while Rome was burning. Nor was the Livery inclined to allow itself to be put down without a struggle, and Tooke's pen was once again employed to draw up a remonstrance to the King. His Majesty refused to grant a dissolution, and spoke of the remonstrance as "this stuff". Then followed a memorable scene. To the surprise of everybody present, the Lord Mayor Beckford, who led the deputation, took the unprecedented step of making a reply, which Tooke is said to have previously composed. A tremendous sensation was produced throughout the country; and the event delighted even Chatham, stately courtier though he was. "The spirit of old England," he said, " spoke that never-to-be-forgotten day." If Tooke had done nothing else but compose the petition, the remonstrance, and the reply that Beckford delivered to the King, he would have performed an inestimable service to the cause of the people in their contest with a corrupt and servile House of Commons. These were great blows struck in the Radical behalf. Bentham said that he did not like Tooke because he thought that his zeal was not prompted by what he thought the highest of all motives —those of enlightened benevolence; but whatever his motives may have been, his deeds were very memorable.[1] But to have done all this was not enough to satiate the indefatigable energy of Tooke; and he forthwith took up with ardour the formation of what was perhaps the first of English political societies; the Society, that is to say, of the Supporters of the Bill of Rights. Clubs, such as White's and Boodle's, there were, indeed, already; but they were rather social than political, and it occasionally happened that men whom party ties had brought together would frequent a common meeting-place. The Jacobites, for example, were known to patronise the Cocoa Tree Tavern in St. James's.[2] The institution of the Society of the Bill of Rights, therefore, marked a notable advance. The first meeting was held at the London Tavern in February, 1769, and among the original members were almost all the leading Radicals including Wilkes himself, his counsel Serjeant Glynn, and Aldermen Sawbridge, Oliver and Townshend. The object of the Society were twofold: to give Wilkes, who in lavish prodigality, litigation and elections had run through handsome fortune, some pecuniary assistance, and to promote parliamentary reform. At the first meeting no less than £3023 was collected in the room, and not only were many of Wilkes's debts liquidated or compounded but his fines were paid, his election expenses were provided

[1] Stephens' *Memoirs of Tooke*, vol. i., pp. 146-50, 152-56; Rockingham *Memoirs*, vol. ii., pp. 99-101; Sharpe's *London and the Kingdom*, v iii., pp. 91 *seq.*, 98, 102; Rogers' *Table Talk;* Prentice's *Historical Sketch of Manchester*, p. 384. Tooke used to illustrate the moderation of his views by saying that if those who pretended to meliorate the government wished to go as far as Windsor, he would beg to be set down at Hounslow

[2] Stephens' *Memoirs of Tooke*, vol. i., p. 163; Almon's *Memoir Wilkes*, vol. iii., p. 14. Gibbon's *Letters*, vol. i., p. 84 (Mr. Prothero note).

for, and a considerable balance was presented to him as a gift. Not less than £16,000 was in this way raised and expended, so that in its first object the Society was certainly successful. Rarely, if ever, has any politician been as liberally treated as Wilkes was by his friends. The second object, by far the most important from the historical point of view, was advanced but little, if at all; but the Society, by drawing up a list of pledges to be taken from parliamentary candidates, gave its sanction to the theory that parliamentary representatives are merely delegates. A candidate for the future, so it decided, should be asked to pledge himself to vote for a full and equal parliamentary franchise; for annual Parliaments; for the exclusion from the House of Commons of persons holding Crown places and emoluments; for the redress of Irish grievances; for the restoration of the right of self-government to America; to abstain from bribery; to vote for the impeachment of the Ministers who had instigated the so-called massacre in St. George's Fields, and violated the rights of the Middlesex electors.[1] It matters not that no candidate was ever actually submitted to the tests; what is noticeable is that the first English political society was radical in character; that it demanded something like complete control by electors over parliamentary representatives; that it sanctioned annual Parliaments, a favourite hobby of the Radicals, and "a full and equal" franchise. The last phrase is ambiguous, but if it be equivalent to universal suffrage, then the Radical tone of the Society only becomes more apparent than before. But though of great importance in the history of political opinion the Bill of Rights Society was

[1] Almon's *Memoir of Wilkes*, vol. iii., p. 14; Stephens' *Memoirs of Tooke*, vol. i., p. 162.

not destined to live long; for its members, as too often has happened in Radical associations, fell out among themselves. In this instance, at least, the quarrels of lovers were not the renewal of love. Some of the members thought that Wilkes had been assisted quite enough, while others insisted on his being placed on a footing of easy independence. A split ensued; the society was dissolved; and a new society, from which the Wilkite section was excluded, was created. Of this society, the Constitutional, something more will yet be heard. Meanwhile the public was treated to the unedifying spectacle of the two tribunes of the people, Tooke and Wilkes, engaged in abusing one another. In the City the battle raged with extraordinary fury, and two opposing factions contested the municipal elections. We need not peer into the details of the quarrel. It will be enough to note that Tooke played a dangerous game in opposing the favourite of the people, and that he lost some of the popularity that he undoubtedly deserved. When he failed to defeat Wilkes in the election for the Shrievalty of the City, his effigy in full canonicals was burnt before the Mansion House. But the multitude has a short memory for benefits conferred. The sight of the first two English Radicals at death-grips is, at any rate, extremely characteristic.[1]

In other ways, moreover, the career of Wilkes was productive of remarkable results. It, for example, greatly

[1] Fitzmaurice's *Life of Shelburne*, vol. ii., pp. 287-92; Rockingham *Memoirs*, vol. ii., p. 74. The quarrel was of some political importance, and Shelburne took the side of Tooke. Goldsmith went out of his way to write newspaper articles against Wilkes. The career of Wilkes in the City seems to have excited some interest on the continent (*Lettre de l'Abbé Morellet à Lord Shelburne* (5th November, 1772), edited by Lord Edmond Fitzmaurice).

increased the political importance of the metropolis, and helped to make the City of London and the County of Middlesex the rallying-point of Radicals. There are few things in English political life more remarkable than the change which has come over the political condition of the City. Now placidly Conservative, it was formerly the hotbed of democracy.[1] During the first half of the reign of George III. the petitions, addresses and remonstrances from the Livery and Aldermen to the Crown or Parliament followed one another in bewildering and rapid succession. The language employed was sometimes anything but temperate, and the King on one occasion called a petition " a flagrant piece of impertinence ". In one of his letters, dated in the year 1769, Horace Walpole makes the singular remark that London, for the first time in its life, has not dictated to England. The significance of the saying is fully illustrated by the clear evidence of contemporary history.[2] Wilkes himself became the regular City man. He was elected Alderman for Farringdon Without, then Sheriff and Lord Mayor in 1774. In the same year he was re-elected Member for Middlesex, and the House of Commons, drinking the cup of humiliation to the full, expunged from its journals the record of his expulsion. In 1779 he was chosen City Chamberlain, and in that capacity conferred the freedom of the City upon Pitt.[3] Almost all the leading Radicals were at this time connected with the City. There was John Sawbridge, the brother of a lady, Mrs. Macaulay, who was even a greater Radical than himself. Sawbridge, as Sheriff, had

[1] Jephson's *Rise and Progress of the Platform*, vol. i., p. 19.
[2] Sharpe's *London and the Kingdom*, vol. iii., p. 136; Horace Walpole's *Letters* (1769).
[3] Almon's *Memoir of Wilkes*, vol. iii., pp. 1, 6, 172 and 179.

five times returned Wilkes as Member for Middlesex, and he represented the City in three successive Parliaments, where he distinguished himself by his zeal for reform. He had, said Horace Walpole, the republican spirit of Algernon Sidney.[1] There was William Beckford, twice Lord Mayor and Member for the City, a somewhat noisy, vulgar, overbearing man, with a cockney accent and a taste for quoting Latin, who hung his house with decorations when Wilkes came out of prison, and could maintain a self-possession which not even the royal presence was able to abash; there was Serjeant Glynn, the Recorder, who stood by Wilkes in good report and ill; there was Brass Crosby, once Lord Mayor, and Member for Honiton, rough in manners and appearance, but the sturdy and sagacious friend of liberty; and Richard Oliver, who had both served the office of chief magistrate and was Member for the City, a man of polished manners, but who fought courageously and suffered for what he believed to be a righteous cause.[2] Nor was it only as regards their *personnel* that the Radicals were closely connected with the City; for nowhere else was the delegation theory of parliamentary representation—a theory peculiarly in harmony with the principles of radicalism—carried into practice with such logical exactness. William Beckford, for example, in 1769, went so far as to declare that he would obey the *instructions* of the Livery *even if they were contrary to his judgment*. Again, when in 1772 the Lord Mayor Nash refused to convene a Common Hall for

[1] Rockingham *Memoirs*, vol. ii., pp. 96 and 169; Wraxall's *Memoirs of His Own Time*, vol. iii., p. 676; Stephens' *Memoirs of Tooke*, vol. ii., pp. 2, 278 and 283; Walpole's *Memoirs*, vol. iii., p. 285.

[2] Stephens' *Memoirs of Tooke*, vol. ii., pp. 279-84. On one occasion at a *levée* Wilkes told the King that Serjeant Glynn was a Wilkite but that he himself was not.

the purpose of instructing the City Members to support Sawbridge in his efforts in the House of Commons to obtain triennial Parliaments, the Livery themselves drew up instructions, affirming that some of the Members had failed to do their duty, and that, therefore, it was necessary that they should exercise their "*indisputable right of instructing you, our representatives*". In the following year Alderman Bull, when standing as a parliamentary candidate for the City, actually signed a written pledge which the Livery had drafted, and both Wilkes and Serjeant Glynn, when candidates for Middlesex, were prevailed upon to do the like; and they solemnly engaged themselves to promote in Parliament the objects which the Livery had at heart. Alderman Oliver, however, it is pleasant to observe, had too much self-respect to follow their example and was elected, notwithstanding, to represent the City. It is of some interest to note that the constituencies of Bristol, Bath and Southwark, in the matter of taking pledges, are said to have followed the example of the City.[1]

The first Radical agitation arose over an attempt of the House of Commons to escape from the control of the electors; the second, which followed shortly afterwards, though different in character, was due to a cause which, when narrowly examined, was essentially the same. On this occasion the House did not refuse admission to a member who had been properly elected, but it told the electors very plainly that they should not be informed of what their representatives were doing at St. Stephen's. To refuse that information is, it is obvious, to put a grave obstacle in the way of the popular control; and it was

[1] Horace Walpole's *Memoirs*, vol. iii., pp. 332, 339, and 342; Sharpe's *London and the Kingdom*, vol. iii., pp. 131, 141, 144 and 145.

therefore not a thing to which the Radicals, least of all, could be expected to assent.¹ The discussion of politics in newspapers was not at first a common practice, and when discussed at all, it was usually only in journals devoted to the purpose. Of this class the *North Briton* may be taken to represent the type. In consequence there arose a special class of writers who may be called political pamphleteers, such as Wilkes and Churchill, and their opponents Arthur Murphy, Robert Lloyd, Philip Francis and Malloch, the literary executor of Bolingbroke. But when George III. began his reign the ordinary newspapers were beginning to take cognisance of political affairs, and a great impulse was given to journalistic enterprise. That there was room for improvement may be inferred from the existence of journals which could find no better names than the *Whisperer* and the *Parliamentary Spy*. Among the newer and better class, which now bid for popularity, were the *Morning Chronicle*, the *Post*, the *Herald*, the *London Evening Post*, the *Middlesex Journal*, and the *Public Advertiser*.² It is not, therefore, a matter of surprise that a demand spontaneously arose for the dissemination of a better knowledge of parliamentary debates. No people, indeed, that had advanced far along the path of progress would be content to remain in placid ignorance of the conduct of affairs

¹ Jebb, for instance, said: "The usurped power of excluding the subject from the galleries of the Commons' House of Parliament, more especially as exercised of late years, appears to me a direct violation of one of the most important privileges of the people" (Disney's *Life of Jebb*, vol. ii., p. 465. Cp. Boutmy's *Le Développement de la Constitution et de la Société politique en Angleterre*, p. 158, where he calls parliamentary reporting "cette première condition de gouvernement libre").

² Lecky's *History of England*, vol. iii., p. 232; Stephens' *Memoirs of Tooke*, vol. i., pp. 162, 383-88; Campbell's *Lives of the Chancellors*, vol. v., p. 97, note.

THE FIRST PERIOD, 1761-1789.

in their legislative chambers; and it is not the least remarkable of the signs of the awakening of the people that at this time the debates began to be reported in journals which were within the reach of any but the poorest. Hitherto the arrangements for reporting were rather primitive. So indifferent were the public that there were even large gaps in parliamentary history, and it is only thanks to the notes of Sir H. Cavendish that we have any record of the reports for the years from 1768 to 1771. The Parliament of this period has become historically famous as the unreported Parliament. Such reports of the debates as reached the public ears were almost unintelligible. Two magazines there were, namely, the *London* and the *Gentleman's*, which professed to give reports, but they only spoke with bated breath. Dr. Johnson in the pages of the *Gentleman's* wrote the reports of the so-called Senate of Lilliput, and not daring to assign to each speaker the speech that he delivered, he gave merely the names of the debaters in a catalogue. His materials were scanty, and he eked them out by indulging in imaginative flights. He was even charged with fabricating bad arguments which he put into Sir Robert Walpole's mouth. This was a state of things that plainly could no longer be endured, and several journals began to cater for their readers with better reports than any yet attempted. That they were very inaccurate is only natural under the conditions that prevailed. Wedderburn — better known afterwards under the title of Lord Loughborough — once remarked of a speech of his that was reported in the newspapers in this sarcastic vein: "Why, to be sure, there are in that report a few things which I did say, but many things which I am glad I did not say, and some things which I wish I could have said ". His experience, no doubt, was that of many others. Moreover a door was left open to a subtle species of corruption. Woodfall, for example, who was for his feats as a reporter nicknamed " memory Woodfall," is said to have been paid £400 a year for reporting in the *Morning Chronicle* the speeches of Fox and Sheridan better than those of Pitt and Dundas. And Woodfall was one of the most distinguished of his class. The profession of a journalist was still one which was held and long continued to be held in very low repute.[1] But however that may be, parliamentary reporting suddenly became a burning question. It was in 1771 that Colonel Onslow called the attention of the House to the fact that its debates were being reported in the newspapers, and he moved that the resolutions—which in 1728 had been passed upon the subject—be read. By these resolutions the newspaper reporting of debates was declared to be "*an indignity to and breach of privilege of the House,*" and offenders were ordered to be punished. In the course of discussion an ex-Speaker, Mr. Onslow, asserted the Parliamentary law and custom very clearly; reporting in the newspapers was, he said, "*a modern practice completely unprecedented, and in direct violation of the privileges of the House of Commons*". The Colonel's motion was carried, as might have been expected from the temper of the House. The next day he rose again in his place, and complained that the *Gazetteer* and the *New Daily Advertiser* had published a misrepresentation of his speeches. The printers of the papers, Thompson and Wheble, were thereupon directed to attend the House.

---

[1] *The Correspondence and Diaries of J. W. Croker*, vol. iii., p. 291; Stephens' *Memoirs of Tooke*, vol. i., pp. 326, 327; Walpole's *Letters* (vol. vi., 1791); Campbell's *Lives of the Chancellors*, vol. vi., p. 93; Gibbon's *Letters*, vol. ii., p. 91 (note by Mr. Prothero).

THE FIRST PERIOD, 1761-1789. 61

Wilkes and Tooke now saw their opportunity and prevailed upon the printers to disobey the order. Then the House passed a resolution that an address should be presented to the King, praying him to issue a royal proclamation to order the arrest of the offenders. His Majesty—who in a letter to Lord North had called the printers "miscreants," and affirmed that "this strange and lawless method of publishing debates in the papers should be stopped"—was only too glad to comply with the request. Yet, in defiance of both King and Parliament, the reports were merrily continued, and in the following month the Colonel called the attention of the House to the fact that six more papers, the *Morning Chronicle*, the *St. James's Chronicle*, the *London Packet*, the *Whitehall Evening Post*, the *General Evening Post*, and the *London Evening Post*, were publishing reports.[1] A hot discussion followed, and, perhaps, the very first example of the use of obstructive tactics in the House. Twenty-three divisions were taken, and the debate was not closed until the morning sunlight was streaming through the windows. "Posterity," said Burke, in a speech in which he afterwards referred to the debate, "will bless the pertinacity of that day."[2] Then followed a series of events which were hardly less dramatic than those which had occurred in connection with Wilkes and his expulsion. Verily the times seemed out of joint. The printers of the incriminated journals were urged to persevere by the Bill of Rights Society, which provided them with funds.[3]

[1] Cavendish's *Debates*, 1771; Stephens' *Memoirs of Tooke*, vol. i., pp. 329 and 344; Almon's *Memoirs of Wilkes*, vol. v., pp. 51-53; H. Walpole's *Memoirs*, vol. iv., pp. 286-88.

[2] Cavendish's *Debates*, 1771.

[3] Stephens' *Memoirs of Tooke*, vol. i., p. 162; H. Walpole's *Memoirs*, vol iv., pp. 286-88, 290-95, 301-2.

Then the printer, one Miller, of the *London Evening Post*, was summoned to the House; he refused upon the ground that he was a Liveryman of the City, and a messenger who had been sent to fetch him was himself arrested for assault. Brought before the Lord Mayor Crosby and Aldermen Oliver and Wilkes, who were sitting as magistrates at the Mansion House, the messenger was declared to have been legally arrested. Then Crosby and Oliver were ordered to attend in their places in the House, and were accompanied thither by great demonstrations of applause. At Westminster a riotous mob assembled and the approaches to Parliament were blocked; Lord North's carriage was wrecked, and the brothers Charles and Stephen Fox were pelted and rather roughly handled. The signing of the warrant for the arrest of the messenger of the House was declared a breach of privilege, and Crosby and Oliver were committed to prison; an event which Gibbon characteristically described as the sending of "two wild beasts . . . to the menagerie in the Tower".[1] The news of the committal was received by the people with a burst of indignation. On the Tower Hill the figures of the obnoxious persons were carried in carts, beheaded by a chimney-sweep and committed to the flames. Oliver and Crosby were received with every mark of honour in the City, and the Corporation presented them and Wilkes with silver cups in memory of the zeal they had displayed in the protection of the printers. Wilkes seized the opportunity to emphasise his Radical proclivities by choosing the death of Julius Cæsar as a design for his cup, and the following lines from Churchill for an inscription:—

> May every tyrant feel
> The keen deep searchings of a patriot's steel.

[1] Letter to his stepmother, 1771.

The House of Commons never did a worse day's business than in sending Crosby and Oliver to the Tower, unless it was when it resolved that Wilkes should be expelled. Once more, by taking a perverted view of privilege, it came into conflict with the nation, and played into the hands of the Radicals; and just as Wilkes had at last been allowed to take his seat, so parliamentary reporting was tacitly allowed to be continued. The publication of the division lists was, however, not permitted for a long time yet to come. Even Mr. Gladstone, thinking that it should be left to the discretion of each member to tell his constituents how he voted, was opposed to this reform.[1]

The early Radicals obtained the support of many men of other parties for their practical demands, and it is, therefore, not always easy to distinguish between the thorough-going Radicals and such Whigs and Tories who both viewed with disfavour the undue straining of parliamentary privilege and were not disinclined to some measure of moderate reform. Yet there were some unbending Radicals whose strongly marked features may still easily be recognised. Amongst them was a small and interesting group of persons who, though strong Radicals in theory, played no part in the conduct of affairs. Horace Walpole tells us that in 1769 there was a little band who openly avowed themselves republicans. But to be a republican was not necessarily to be a Radical. Republicans there had been, indeed, before; men like Harrington, famous as the author of *Oceana*, or Algernon Sidney, whom Thomson in his *Seasons* has styled the "British Cassius". But though republicans,

[1] Walpole's *Memoirs*, vol. iv., p. 307; Sharpe's *London and the Kingdom*, vol. iii., p. 119; Robbins' *Early Life of W. E. Gladstone*, p. 204.

they were not democrats but oligarchs, men who for the most part held their views as a kind of *arrière-pensée*, and were very far from wishing

> To cast the kingdoms old
> Into another mould.

They belonged to the class of the "high-bred republicans," whom Burke said existed in his time.[1] But from the year 1769 onwards the professed republicans were usually fervent Radicals as well. Of these Mrs. Catherine Macaulay is perhaps the one who was the most widely known, and is still the best remembered. The sister of John Sawbridge, of City fame, she was a woman of strong character and of a masculine and energetic mind. Born in 1731, she married first Dr. Macaulay of Bath, and upon his death the Rev. William Graham, of Misterton in Leicestershire. A considerable traveller, she moved in the society of some of the most distinguished people of her day; she met Turgot in Paris and Washington in America. As an historian and political pamphleteer she enjoyed a fame which, if not lasting, was certainly not small. Her *English History*, though now well-nigh forgotten, was highly praised by Horace Walpole, who commended its manly strength and philosophic gravity, and compared it with the works of Tacitus and Robertson. Mirabeau is said to have desired to have it translated into French. As a controversialist she did not want in courage, and entered into the lists with Burke himself, to whose *Reflections on the French Revolution* and *Thoughts on*

---

[1] Burke's *French Revolution*. The republicans of modern days have been influenced in an extraordinary degree by the heroes of antiquity who were not democrats in the proper sense at all. A French writer has said with some justice that it was Plutarch who made the French Revolution (Bodley's *France*, vol. ii., p. 174).

THE FIRST PERIOD, 1761-1789. 65

the Present Discontents, she had the temerity to reply. With that sublime self-confidence that is often so characteristic of the Radicals, she offered Paoli to frame a Constitution for the Corsicans.[1] As a talker of the type that is eager and aggressive, she was the most notorious woman of her day, but she found her match in Dr. Johnson, who cordially disliked her and said that he on one occasion (metaphorically speaking) "stripped her to the very skin". On hearing that she was not above paying some attention to the adornment of her person, he observed that she was more usefully employed with her toilette than with her pen, and that it was better she should redden her own cheeks than blacken other people's characters. She was, however, a sincere republican and a thorough-going Radical. When Dr. Johnson told her that she ought to recollect that there is a monarchy in heaven, she replied, "If I thought so, sir, I should never wish to go there". A woman who could say that must have been very much in earnest. Her republican sentiments she never attempted to conceal; nay rather, with a courage unusual for the time, she compassed sea and land to make a single proselyte. Of the other members of the group which Horace Walpole had in mind there is not much to be said. *Stat nominis umbra* — and that is almost all. There was Thomas Hollis, who, though not a man of great intellectual force, seems to have been animated by a sincere and disinterested zeal for the welfare of mankind. He used an ample fortune in indulging in the hobby of printing new editions of Milton and Algernon

---

[1] Walpole's *Memoirs*, vol. iii., pp. 176, 331; Walpole's *Letters*, vol. vi. (1791). Her offer to frame a Corsican Constitution may be compared with Bentham's offers to draw up various codes and constitutions. It is a singular fact that Rousseau was asked to legislate for Corsica and Poland.

Sidney, and of presenting democratic literature to European libraries. The bindings of the books that he presented he directed to be stamped with caps of liberty and daggers. The last name to be mentioned is that of Thomas Day, who as the author of *Sandford and Merton* has just escaped oblivion. This eccentric individual, under the influence of Rousseau, resolved to live the life of simplicity and nature; he abhorred the use of hair-powder; he thought a comb and brush were enervating luxuries; and he fell at last a victim to his theories. Thinking the breaking in of horses to be unnatural and cruel, he suffered fatal injuries while driving in his carriage a raw and untrained colt.[1]

There remains to be considered another class of Radicals who are the most interesting and important of them all—the speculative writers who greatly influenced contemporary thought. For it is into their ultimate principles, deep down into the rock-bed of their philosophy and theory, that we must look for the distinguishing marks of the Radicals at this early period of their history. The thinkers of the party, the disinterested theorists, who gave the movement its colour and direction, were distinguished by some well-marked mental and moral characteristics. How far, indeed, the actions of mankind are influenced by speculative theories, and how far, on the other hand, theorists are influenced by the movements of society, it is often difficult to say. Cause and effect in human affairs lie in such very close connection, they so subtly act and react

---

[1] Dr. Johnson, who liked to ridicule the Radicals, when asked to give a toast, used to say, "If you ask for a gentleman I shall always give you Mr. Hollis, if for a lady, Mrs. Macaulay, sir" (Nichols' *Literary Anecdotes*, vol. vi., pp. 157-58; Dowden's *The French Revolution and English Literature*).

on one another, that they are not easy to distinguish. Coleridge thought that "all the epoch-forming revolutions of the Christian world have coincided with the rise and fall of metaphysical systems". In England, however, the practical genius of the people has not been affected in this way to the same extent as other nationalities, and political philosophies have not so much gone before as followed after. Their object has been rather to justify the actual than to guide and anticipate the future. And so it was to some extent with the early speculative theories of the Radicals. The Radical politicians had already, so to speak, the raw material of thought; they had already put some of the theories into practice, though unconsciously and not of set deliberation; while the thinkers followed after, and tried to find a philosophic basis for what had actually been done. Who the thinkers were and what was the nature of the philosophic basis that they found are questions which demand to be earnestly considered.[1]

Among the early Radical thinkers and philosophers there are four who stand pre-eminent—John Cartwright, John Jebb, Richard Price and Joseph Priestley—and they may be taken to represent the type.

John Cartwright, or Major Cartwright as he commonly was called, was born in 1740, of a good family, at Marnham in Nottinghamshire. Entering the navy at an early age, he served for a time on the Newfoundland Station; but perhaps finding his energies too cramped, he soon threw up his commission. This father of reform, as he has been very justly called, on retiring from the service began a course of lifelong effort in devising schemes for the benefit or what—and that is a very different matter—he conceived to be the benefit of his country. Of all the great historical

[1] Coleridge, *The Statesman's Manual.*

Radicals there is no more pleasing figure than that of this genuine and sincere, this single-minded, simple-hearted man. Never was any politician so absolutely clear of any Machiavelian touch. Through a long life—for he died at the age of eighty-four—he laboured indefatigably for what he believed to be the right; with no hope of advancement for himself and with an absolute surrender of his own immediate interests. To know him was to love him. His courage, his zeal, his transparent honesty of purpose, endeared him even to those who differed from him in their political opinions; his only personal enemies were to be found among the Radicals themselves. His tall and spare figure, his benignant but pale and careworn face, his dark wig and long brown coat, must for many years have been familiar sights at every gathering of reformers.[1] But so short-lived is fame that of the multitudes that pass through Burton Crescent there are few who step aside to look at Cartwright's statue—already stained by time and weather—or to consider what manner of man he was. He began to write in 1772, and his published works number more than eighty pamphlets, all fired with patriotic zeal, but now well-nigh forgotten. Few would care to read now through these arid wastes of printed matter with their endless repetitions; if it were a choice between Cartwright and the galleys it is possible that some would choose the latter. An elaborate scheme for providing a perpetual supply of oak for the Royal Navy was the subject to which he devoted his first work; and as the Government

---

[1] *Life and Correspondence of Major Cartwright*, vol. ii., p. 40. *Life and Correspondence of Thomas Slingsby Duncombe*, vol. i., p. 79. He was nicknamed by some the "mother of reform" on account of his womanly ways.

in part adopted his suggestions without, as he averred, making their acknowledgments, we probably should not greatly err if we ascribed in some degree his Radical propensities to a rankling sense of the injustice which he thought that he had suffered. A pamphlet on American Independence was published in 1774, and when his next work, *Take Your Choice*, which is said to be the earliest work on parliamentary reform,[1] was published in 1776 he already was enjoying an established reputation as a writer on political affairs. Of his other works, *Give Us Our Rights*, *The Commonwealth in Danger* and the *Appeal, Civil and Military*, only need be mentioned here, and they may be taken to represent the whole. *Ex uno disce omnes;* where there is so much repetition, the philosophy of Cartwright may be easily summed up; and though he went on writing until almost within sight of the Reform Act, his views underwent so little change that his latest publications and his earliest are perfectly consistent. In Cartwright the dogmas of early Radicalism were quintessentialised; he is the express image of the advanced political thought of the era which the French Revolution closed. His political philosophy—if so primitive a doctrine can be properly styled philosophy at all—was of the simplest. Its ultimate foundation was based upon the theory of personal representation, which he is said to have originated,[2] that is to say, upon the belief in the abstract

[1] Earl Stanhope contests this claim by reason of a work published by him in 1774.
[2] *Life of Dr. Currie*, vol. ii., p. 307 *seq*. Lord John Russell wrongly ascribed the origination of the personal theory to Jebb (Buckle's *History of Civilisation*, vol. i., p. 435). At a later period in English history John Stuart Mill made use of the term personal representation as an equivalent to proportional representation. This difference in the two uses of the term must be carefully borne in mind (Mill's *Autobiography*, p. 302).

right of every man to have a vote. Upon this ground-plan, this abstraction, so characteristic of the revolutionary thinker, he raised his superstructure. His premises are simplicity itself: "there are some things in which every man of common sense may be infallible"; "the principles of politics are the principles of reason, morality and religion"; "the Scripture is the ultimate criterion both in public and private conduct"; there wants "but half a dozen honest men to save a city"; a knowledge of "a few of the plain maxims of the law of nature and the clearest doctrines of Christianity" is all that is wanted for a statesman; "the title to liberty is the immediate gift of God, and is not derived from mouldy parchments"; "*I ought to have a vote because I am a man*"; "good governments, founded on just principles, are always easy to be understood"; "a government not easily comprehended must be a snare"; "a Constitution should be *written* and taught to children with the Lord's Prayer and the Ten Commandments". These and similar sentiments formed, to use Bolingbroke's felicitous expression, his *philosophia prima*; and they led him at once to short Parliaments and universal suffrage. The Septennial Act, he said, suspends "the political liberty of the nation for six parts in seven of human life".[1] From his premises there of course followed the conclusion that parliamentary representatives are *delegates*; and no one has laid down the theory more explicitly than Cartwright.

[1] This reads like an echo of Rousseau: "The English nation thinks that it is free, but it is greatly mistaken; for it is only during the election of Members of Parliament; as soon as they are elected, it is enslaved and counts for nothing. The use which it makes of the brief moments of freedom renders the loss of liberty well deserved" (*Social Contract*, Bk. 3, sec. 15. See also his *Letters from the Mountain*, viii.).

THE FIRST PERIOD, 1761-1789.

He called them the "*proxies*" and "*attorneys*" of the electing body "*to transact its business and receive its wages*". "Shall the instrument," he asks with indignation, "pretend to originality or independence of action?" To put that doctrine into practice would be to degrade a Member of Parliament into the position of a tool; and it was perhaps a consciousness of this fact that caused Cartwright to make the reservation that if Parliament were reformed, the giving of instructions by constituents would then become unnecessary. But that was only a pious aspiration. His conclusions and his premises are equally characteristic of primitive radicalism; his firm belief in abstract rights; his love of simplicity; his desire to return, not, indeed, to a state of nature, but to the uncorrupted constitution of Anglo-Saxon times, which he regarded as a sort of golden age; his dislike of standing armies; his theories on the suffrage, and the relations of members and constituents, are all distinctive of the advanced political thinkers of his time. There was something quite pathetic in his love of Anglo-Saxon times, and his unshakable belief in our ancient institutions as a panacea for every ill. *Juvat integros accedere fontes*. "Our standing army," he said, adopting some words of Hume, is "a mortal distemper in the British Constitution of which it must inevitably perish"; and it should be at once replaced by the *posse comitatus* or Saxon militia, the true military force of our country, the work of the godlike Alfred; an institution which, he declared, a low-minded lawyer could not appreciate and which the impure touch of the politician would profane. If this national militia were revived, all thought of invasion would be abandoned; for "an armed inhabitancy" is the cheap defence of nations; a navy, which "is not a proper arm of defence," might then safely be dispensed with, because "that a completely armed nation is invasion-proof, without the aid of a single ship is a self-evident proposition"; the national debt might under such conditions be eventually extinguished and taxes to a large extent abolished. His creed was essentially that of a revolutionary thinker; he controverted in set terms the opportunist doctrine of expediency in government, calling it an "*ignis fatuus*," which a long experience had convinced him was " a suspicious counsellor," " an excellent servant and the worst of masters ". Still more characteristically he hated moderation, as commonly conceived, and with Mazzini he stigmatised compromise as not only dangerous but immoral. " Moderation," he said, " in conduct is wisdom, but moderation in principle is dishonour, and moderation in justice is injustice." Believing sublimely in himself, as a politician he was terribly in earnest; for a man to say that he had nothing to do with politics was, he thought, as bad as saying that he had nothing to do with morality. But his want of flexibility made him obstinate, and sometimes hopelessly unpractical in the conduct of affairs.[1] " Your husband, madam," said a Member of Parliament to his wife, " is the best-bred obstinate man I ever was acquainted with." The *naïveté* of some of his ideas, to say the truth, made him to be looked on as something of a "crank"; as when he argued that the natural order of the universe, recurring in an annual sequence, clearly showed that a Parliament should not be elected for a longer period than a year; or

---

[1] A practical politician like Francis Place thought him " exceedingly troublesome and sometimes exceedingly absurd ". Place gives an amusing account of how the " old gentleman " would sometimes come to dine with him and regale himself on raisins and weak gin and water (*Life of Francis Place*, by Graham Wallas, p. 63).

THE FIRST PERIOD, 1761-1789. 73

when he ordered caps of liberty to be blazoned on the banners and the buttons of the Nottinghamshire Militia, of which he was the Major ; or when he modelled a special kind of pike for his proposed national "armed inhabitancy". But his integrity, his " purity of principle and consistency of conduct," to use the words applied to him by Fox, were of the highest. Though several times a parliamentary candidate, he was too high principled to make use of the ordinary electioneering methods. " A candidate," he said, " ought to know that the duty of an elector is as sacred as that of a juror, and that a verdict and a vote ought to be given precisely on the same principles." Never did any politician take up such a lofty moral standpoint. " My vote," he said, " I hold in trust; it belongs to my country, and my country alone shall have it" ; his candidature he called the undertaking of " a painful and unprofitable office " ; nor would he regard his position, when elected, as something to be turned to his " own profit and emolument "—a very different point of view from that which was only too commonly adopted. He refused both to accept any "wages" or to spend anything in consideration of a vote. That he never entered Parliament is only what might have been expected, but it is a fact which is hardly to the credit of his country. To sum up the matter very briefly, it might be said, as Lord Tennyson said of Garibaldi, that Cartwright had " the divine stupidity of a hero ".[1]

[1] *Life and Correspondence of Major Cartwright*, vol. i., pp. 82, 91, 60, 65; vol. ii., p. 40 ; *The Appeal, Civil and Military : A Letter to the Electors of Nottingham* (1803). So little did Cartwright like anything resembling the ways of a demagogue that during the excitement of the Middlesex elections he said that Wilkes ought to be hanged, " if he can be legally tucked up". The pike which he specially designed he showed to " Orator " Hunt ; it had a double shaft to protect the hands from sabre cuts (*Memoirs of Hunt*, vol. ii., p. 285).

John Jebb contests with Cartwright the distinction of being the earliest of the expounders of the principles of radicalism; and during his all too brief career he proved himself no less an earnest worker in the cause of parliamentary reform. Upon general lines the two men worked together, though not agreed on every detail. Jebb, indeed, was much the abler man. Born in 1736, the son of an Irish dean, he was educated at Trinity College, Dublin, and at Cambridge, where he greatly distinguished himself as second wrangler. He took orders, became a college lecturer, and actively engaged himself in university affairs. A change in his theological opinions impelled him to give up a living in the Church, and to resign his college lectureship. With rare energy and courage he entered upon an entirely fresh career, took a medical degree, and practised successfully as a doctor. In political affairs he soon made himself conspicuous, taking, as he did, a leading part in the meetings of electors and reform associations in Westminster and London. The foundation of the Society for Constitutional Information was also largely due to his energy and zeal. In his political philosophy he did not differ much from Cartwright; he agreed that every man had an abstract right to have a vote, saying that every restriction of the right was "an infringement of the law of nature"; that a parliamentary representative was a delegate and nothing more; that a proper reform would be a return "to the primæval principles of the constitution of the country"; that the standing army should be replaced by a national militia. Like Cartwright, too, he disliked a middle course: "Don't tell me," he said, "of a moderate man, he is always a rascal". But as a reformer he was prepared to go to even greater lengths.

THE FIRST PERIOD, 1761-1789. 75

Annual Parliaments he thought were not enough; they must be sessional, or they would not be constitutional. Against Pitt's Reform Bill—a large and generous measure —he vigorously protested; because he thought it was "deficient with respect to any probable good effect in stemming the torrent of corruption". He even called the Bill "a solemn farce," and doubted Pitt's sincerity; he was, he said, "politically speaking, the worst man living"; and would—and here Jebb showed something like prophetic insight—be likely "to go greater lengths to destroy liberty than any minister ever did before him". Upon his own views of the relationship of members and constituents Jebb was never weary of insisting; a member of Parliament he deemed a "proxy," an "agent," the "servant of the people," the organ of their will; and he drew up the following declaration to be made by the candidates at Westminster at the election to be held in 1782: "I do declare upon my honour, that upon a fair signification of the wishes of a majority of my constituents, I will either act *in conformity to their instructions* or embrace the first opportunity of resigning my seat". But even such a declaration was not enough for Jebb; for he did not shrink from expressing the opinion that the people have at any time a right to resume their powers; that if the counties in solemn council were to declare that the House of Commons was dissolved, such a declaration would be truly constitutional; and that regulations for the conduct of elections, if made at such a council, would, "if assented to by the nobles and the King," have all the authority of law. That is equivalent to saying that the people might legally supersede the House of Commons; and though the conclusion seems a startling one, it was but a logical deduction from the premises of the new Radical philosophy. If the people are the principals, and members of Parliament only agents, then the principals reserve the right to revoke the authority they have granted.[1]

Though Richard Price and Joseph Priestley must be classed with Jebb and Cartwright amongst the earliest of the writers upon the principles of radicalism, yet they stand upon a somewhat different footing. These eminent men were two of the most distinguished Nonconformist ministers that England has produced; and though not primarily political thinkers, nor very active politicians, their contributions to political philosophy, by a curious irony of fate, produced effects more lasting than any one could have ventured to anticipate.[2]

Joseph Priestley, "patriot, saint and sage," as Coleridge once addressed him, was born in 1733 not far from Leeds. His parents were humble but respectable Dissenters who gave their son as good an education as they were able to afford. After having studied at the Nonconformist Academy at Daventry, he took charge of congregations at Needham Market and at Northwich. He then became a tutor at an academy at Warrington, until in 1772 his remarkable abilities attracted the notice of Lord Shelburne, who made him his librarian at Bowood, where he remained for a period of eight years. It was thought by Shelburne's friends that the advanced views

[1] Disney's *Life of Jebb*, vol. i., pp. 156, 167, 197; vol. ii., pp. 463, 486, 479, 494, 503; vol. iii. (Political Papers), pp. 14, 19; *Life of Cartwright*, vol. i., p. 352.

[2] Price and Priestley's fame had quickly spread to France. The Abbé Morellet greatly admired them. He called them "less dissenters": "j'aime less dissenters et aussi les dissenters politiques" (*Lettres de l'Abbé Morellet à Lord Shelburne*, edited by Lord Edmond Fitzmaurice; *Lettres*, 10th February, 1776; 30th December, 1777).

of his librarian might bring odium on his patron, and so they parted upon terms that were honourable to both, and Priestley went to Birmingham, where he ministered to a Dissenting congregation, and lived happily among his books and scientific instruments until the riots compelled his departure to America. But during all this time his busy brain had been at work. His spare and erect figure, his animated talk, and his lucidity of style, betrayed an intellect that was wonderfully active and alert; while his "mild radiance" and his serenity of countenance—so that "he seemed present with God by recollection, and with man by cheerfulness"—testified to a finely balanced temperament. His talents were as versatile as his activities were multiform, and both to theology and science he made contributions that were numerous and valuable; for while on the one hand he was among the very first of the English Unitarians,[1] on the other he laid the foundation of the industry in aerated waters. His observations on the constituents of the air would alone have been enough to make him long remembered. But it is not of Priestley as theologian or chemist that it concerns us here to speak, but of Priestley as a political philosopher. In this direction his work was small in bulk, and it is probable that he valued it the least, though it is by no means certain that in the long run it did not produce the most results. An *Essay on the First Principles of Government*, written when he was teaching boys at Warrington in 1768, two anonymous pamphlets on the war in America, a volume of *Letters to*

[1] Cottle's *Reminiscences of Coleridge and Southey*, p. 336: "I think Priestley must be considered the author of modern Unitarianism". This saying is attributed to Coleridge (Coleridge's *Table Talk*). There is a portrait of Priestley in the National Portrait Gallery by Mrs. Sharples.

Burke, published in 1791, which went through three editions, and a *Dialogue on the General Principles of Government*, comprise the whole of his writing on political philosophy. These were not indeed profound, nor can it be said that at the time of their publication they had much influence on opinion. The fundamental distinction that he drew between two kinds of liberty, political and civil, has, indeed, nothing to support it. His position is not very easy to define. Dean Tucker called him "the fairest, the most open and ingenuous of all Mr. Locke's disciples, excepting honest, undissembling Rousseau"; and there is no doubt that he owed much to the philosophy of Locke. Priestley's practical conclusions were much the same as those of Jebb and Cartwright, believing, as he did, that "all civil power is ultimately derived from the people," who have a right of "deposing and punishing" their governors; that septennial Parliaments are "a direct usurpation of the rights of the people"; and that "the generality of Governments have hitherto been little else than a combination of the few against the many". But these sentiments were tempered with a saving practical good sense. He held with Pope, for instance, that that Government is best which is the "best administered"; and he agreed with the admirers of the British Constitution, that, as compared with that of any other country, it was "the best actual scheme of civil polity" existing. Yet his philosophy was marked by all the distinctive characteristics of the Radicals of the revolutionary age. He believed in the natural rights of man, and that in small states only can perfect liberty be had;[1] he was moved by all the radiant hope, and the

---

[1] This opinion was held by Rousseau, and it is noteworthy that it was long maintained in the United States by the Democrat or State-

rosy optimism with which the French Revolution filled
many fervid minds; he had faith in the perfectibility
of man; and he prophesied the near approach of a time
when all national prejudice would be extinguished, when
men would beat their swords into plough-shares, and
their spears into pruning-hooks; when the very idea of
distant colonial possessions would be ridiculed; when no
civil war could occur, not even in America; when standing armies, "those instruments of tyranny," would be
unknown, and government would be "unspeakably less
expensive". The end he thought would be "glorious
and paradisaical beyond what our imagination can conceive". If a warning were desired against the danger
of making prophecies in politics, no better example than
that of Priestley could be found. Then he was strongly
individualist, opposing Church establishments, and unelastic systems of education by the State; and affirming
that governments are "burdensome and oppressive," and
"injurious to the *natural rights* and civil liberties of mankind, when they lay a man under unnecessary restrictions". Priestley's views, indeed, were transitional in
character; they belonged partly to the period which the
French Revolution closed, and partly to the period which
it ushered in. He may be said to have linked two systems of philosophy together, for he was in fact the lineal
ancestor of the utilitarian philosophy, which Bentham
worked out with such remarkable results. The tie which
affiliates the famous philosopher to Priestley is one of the
most curious and interesting incidents in the history of
literature. It happened that Bentham was one day reading at a circulating library at Harper's coffee-house in

Rights Party, of which Thomas Jefferson, who had imbibed much of the
French revolutionary thought, was the founder.

Oxford, when he met with Priestley's *Essay on the First Principles of Government*. A single sentence in it caught his alert and penetrating eye: "*The good and happiness of the members of any State, is the great standard by which everything relating to that State must be finally determined*". To the present generation that does not seem a very startling proposition. But it was otherwise with Bentham. "At the sight of it," he says, "I cried out as it were in an inward ecstasy, like Archimedes on the discovery of the fundamental principles of hydrostatics, εὕρηκα." For here was the germ of Bentham's famous principle of government, the greatest happiness of the greatest number. The Essay contained another proposition which is extremely characteristic of the Benthamite philosophy: "*Governors will not consult the interest of the people, except it be their own interest too, because governors are but men*". That is a belief which lay at the very root of Bentham's principles of government, and its statement in the Essay must almost certainly have attracted his attention. It is, therefore, not too much to say that as the lineal ancestor of the School of Philosophical Radicals, even more than as a theologian or man of science, Priestley has exerted a lasting influence on the progress of events. And that is a fact which may be perfectly consistent with Brougham's statement that, though the most voluminous of writers, Priestley had the fewest readers.[1]

Ten years before Priestley saw the light, Richard Price

[1] Rutt's *Life of Priestley*, vol. i., p. 52; Priestley's *Essay on the Principles of Government*; Priestley's *Letters to Burke*; Fitzmaurice's *Life of Shelburne*, vol. ii., p. 244; Huxley's *Essays on Science and Education* (Address on Priestley); Wurtzburg's *History of Chemical Theory*; Montague's *Introduction to Bentham's Fragment on Government*, p. 34; Coleridge's *Religious Musings*; *Autobiography of Mary Anne Schimmelpenninck* (third edition), pp. 31, 32 and 72.

was born at Tynton in Glamorganshire. His family were Dissenters, and he was brought up to be a minister. For thirteen years he was chaplain at Stoke Newington and preached in various meeting-houses. In the Old Jewry he gave a course of sermons which made him so favourably known that he was called to an important charge at Newington Green. As a writer on theology and moral philosophy he quickly achieved a reputation, and his dissertations on *Providence* and *The Junction of Virtuous Men in a Future State* were so highly thought of by Lord Shelburne that he sought out the acquaintance of the writer and remained his friend and patron to the end. In the sphere of economics and finance Price made suggestions which, if not always sustained by later thinkers, were original and valuable, and greatly influenced the financial policy of Pitt. Adam Smith, indeed, called him " a most superficial philosopher, and by no means an able calculator "—surely an ill-considered judgment; for the *Treatise on Reversionary Payments*, the *Appeal to the Public on the National Debt*, urging the creation of a sinking fund, the *Essay on the Population of England*, all attracted much attention and were important contributions to economic science. His fame was wafted to America, and the United States Congress honoured him by asking him to settle there, and to give his assistance in the regulation of the finances of the newly founded State. But it is with Price, not as theologian or political economist, but as political philosopher that we are primarily concerned, and in this capacity his fate resembled that of Priestley ; for he played no prominent part in politics, he wrote but little on the subject, but that little produced a great effect. His fame as a political thinker rests mainly upon a pamphlet and—what is probably unique—upon a sermon. His

Observations on Civil Liberty and the Justice and Policy of the War with America was published in 1776, with such extraordinary success that a cheap edition of 60,000 copies was speedily disposed of. It drew replies from Burke and Johnson, and the City of London admitted him a freeman to testify their admiration for his principles. The sermon on the *Love of Our Country* was preached in the Old Jewry on the anniversary festival of the Revolution Society, in 1789, and was so powerful that the audience almost broke out into applause. Its pathos moved Priestley nigh to tears. But it did not serve merely to awaken the passing emotion of its hearers. Afterwards published by request, it proved to be the red rag that drew Burke into the arena, and was the immediate cause of the production of the most powerful apology for conservatism that has ever been written: the *Reflections on the French Revolution*. It is, therefore, not too much to say that, considered in the light of its effects, whether transient or permanent, no more remarkable sermon was ever delivered from a pulpit. The *Observations on Civil Liberty*, and the sermon, together with some speeches which he afterwards delivered, determine Price's place among the Radicals. Considered as philosophy, his political writings cannot be rightly called profound, but they are enough to justify the title—which Cartwright conferred upon him—of the "Apostle of Liberty". His political principles were based upon the assumption of certain abstract rights of man; with Rousseau he held that perfect liberty "can be only enjoyed in small States where every member is capable of giving his suffrage in person, and of being chosen to the public offices"; he was opposed to standing armies; he was strongly individualist, declaring his belief that "all government, even within a State, becomes tyrannical, as far as it is a needless and wanton exercise of power or is carried farther than is absolutely necessary to preserve the peace and to secure the safety of the State". In the sermon—" a very extraordinary miscellaneous one," as Burke called it—he asserted the fundamental propositions of democracy; he declared that by the Revolution of 1688 the English people acquired the right to choose their own governors and to cashier them for misconduct; that George III. should consider himself as more properly the servant than the sovereign; that he is almost the only lawful sovereign in the world, because the only one who owed his crown to the choice of the people; that representation is the only source of legitimate government; and when representation is defective—as it was in England—it then becomes a "nuisance". In these propositions there was really nothing new beyond their vigorous assertion; for they were the principles — long openly professed—by the Society for commemorating the glorious Revolution of 1688; and the sermon might perhaps have passed unnoticed if the Revolution Society had not expressed a lively sympathy with the French Revolutionary party. From Whiggism that Society—at least it so appeared—was fast drifting to the rapids of revolutionary anarchism. Lastly, Price shared Priestley's firm belief in the joyful future that lay before mankind, and in the blessings that would flow from "the glorious example given in France," and he looked forward to an early consummation of a compact between that country and his own " for promoting peace on earth, good-will among men". The optimistic temperament is almost always characteristic of those who hold strong Radical opinions; and during the early days of the French revolutionary movement—before it lapsed into a course of bloody crime

—that temperament was madly heated and inflamed. The sanguine spirit ran riot in the veins of the reformers. Even the discreet and sober Price was whirled along by the wild gusts of enthusiasm which swept across the world. But in 1791 he died, worn out by suffering and disease: " God's finger touched him and he slept ". *Felix opportunitate mortis :* Happy he who died in the sure and certain hope of a glorious future for mankind ; who did not live to see the time of disillusions.[1]

During the period now before us—from 1761 to 1789—English political life underwent some gradual changes, upon which, in their relation to the progress of Radical opinion, some observations may be made. When the storm which the Middlesex elections and the printers' case had raised began to lull, a heavy ground-swell of democratic sentiment went heaving onwards. Public meetings and political associations, for example, were more and more made use of as a means for bringing pressure upon Parliament and making it subservient to popular control. Where Middlesex led the way Yorkshire quickly followed after, and at a meeting held at York a petition to the Crown asking for a dissolution, and approved by two such sturdy Whigs as Lord Rockingham and Sir George Saville, was signed by no less than 10,000 freeholders. Many other counties followed suit ; so that the platform became more and more a usual channel for the expression of popular opinion. Ex-ministers, like Fox and Shelburne, did not disdain now and then to make a platform speech ; and Burke by his memorable orations to his constituents at Bristol raised the custom of addressing public meetings

[1] See Morgan's *Memoir of Dr. Price ;* Fitzmaurice's *Life of Shelburne* vol. iii., p. 95 ; Rutt's *Life of Priestley*, vol. i., p. 57 ; Rae's *Adam Smith* p. 400 ; Cartwright's *Appeal, Civil and Military.*

THE FIRST PERIOD, 1761-1789. 85

at parliamentary elections to a position of importance greater than it ever occupied before. The next step was the formation of county political associations, and here too Yorkshire was conspicuous for its zeal. Committees were formed which sent deputies to London for the purpose of creating a National Reform Association, amongst whom were Jebb, and the Rev. Christopher Wyvill—an earnest Whig to whom we are indebted for much historical information. The deputies met at St. Alban's Tavern and drew up a memorial recommending the formation of the National Association for reform, which was subsequently created. The constituency of Westminster—a district which was one of great political importance and was destined even to surpass the City as a hotbed of democracy —showed extraordinary zeal in following what Jebb called "the glorious examples" set by Middlesex. A Westminster committee was chosen, public meetings were convened, at which short Parliaments and a more equal representation were demanded, and Fox and Sheridan took active parts. Throughout the country generally numerous petitions to the Crown and Parliament were signed ; no less than forty being presented to the House of Commons in the year 1780 alone. It was then that the House passed a resolution that it was their duty to redress the grievances complained of ; an act which marks a great advance since the time of Wilkes's expulsion in the direction of the democratic theory of the right of the people to control their representatives.[1]

[1] Jephson's *Rise and Progress of the Platform*, vol. i., chaps. iii. and iv. ; Rockingham *Memoirs*, vol. ii., pp. 104-6, 136-38, 412 ; Wraxall's *Memoirs of His Time*, vol. iii., p. 119 ; Disney's *Life of Jebb*, vol. i., p. 119 ; Fitzmaurice's *Life of Shelburne*, vol. iii., p. 75, 79-82 ; *Life of Cartwright*, vol. i., p. 134.

Apart from the associations of the counties were the political societies or clubs. The formation of these "disputing societies," as Sir Samuel Romilly called them, was a marked feature of the time. To the Bill of Rights Society there has already been occasion to refer. Of the rest, the Constitutional-Society—which owed its birth to the seceders from the Bill of Rights Society—was among the most important. Its members were men of pronounced Whig and Radical opinions, and, if we may believe Sir Samuel Romilly, were, a few of them, "men of great talents," but mostly "well-meaning but foolish persons". It purchased and circulated books among its members, and published works of advanced political thought, which probably no ordinary publisher could be persuaded to produce. Such a work was Sir William Jones's *Dialogue on the Principles of Government between a Scholar and a Peasant*, for the publication of which in Wales the Dean of St. Asaph, Dr. Shipley, was subsequently prosecuted. The Society—to its credit be it said—devoted some portion of its income to charitable objects; as when it voted £100 "for the relief of the widows, orphans, and aged parents of our beloved American fellow-subjects murdered by the King's troops at Lexington"; and, therefore, was, as Burke remarked with a sort of condescending sneer, of a "charitable, and so far of a laudable, nature". The Society for Constitutional Information held much the same position as the Constitutional Society, and the members of one were frequently members of the other. It was, however, a little more Radical in character; "to procure short Parliaments, and more equal representation of the people," and to disseminate "sound political knowledge to the people at large" were the avowed objects of its care.[1]

The question of parliamentary reform, both in the House of Commons and the country was during this period advanced a long step forward. In the House the Radical members, like Sawbridge, by motions nearly annual, kept it continually alive; and the serenity of the gilded chamber does not seem to have been very much disturbed when the Duke of Richmond—at that time going through a phase of extreme radicalism—introduced a thorough-going bill to legalise annual Parliaments, manhood suffrage, and electoral districts. But it was not until 1782, when Pitt took the subject up himself, that reform came within measurable distance of achievement. It then ceased to be merely an idle aspiration, and entered the region of the practical. In that year he moved for a select committee to examine the state of the representation in a speech which was remarkable for its vehement attack upon the corrupt influence of the Crown, and the purchase of rotten boroughs by Indian millionaires. The motion was lost by only twenty votes, and the division was the best which the reformers were to get until 1831. In the following week he spoke in support of a bill, which Sawbridge introduced, to institute short Parliaments. Again, in 1783, he moved his famous resolutions on reform. An expectant audience crammed the House and hung upon his lips. This is not the place to give in detail the scheme which he proposed, but it is pertinent to remark that to add one hundred

---

[1] *Memoirs of the Life of Sir S. Romilly*, vol. i., p. 86; *Life of Jebb*, vol. i., p. 161; Nichols' *Literary Anecdotes*, vol. vi., pp. 443, 452. The subscription to the society for Constitutional Information was two and a half guineas annually (*Life of Francis Place*, by Graham Wallas, p. 21).

county members was one of its most important features. The old theory of the representation of the soil had, therefore, lost nothing of its force. The hopes of the reformers were of course raised to an unprecedented height, for victory now seemed to be well within their grasp; and a circular was sent out by Wyvill, the chairman of a reform committee, in which Pitt's name was used more freely than that statesman was disposed to like. But if his private correspondence with Wilberforce and the Duke of Rutland reflect his real opinions, there can be no doubt that Pitt was perfectly sincere at this time on the subject of reform; it would be carried sooner or later, he said, and the sooner the better. In 1785 he introduced a bill to carry out his resolutions. It was variously received. It is not wonderful to find that some of the strongest opponents of the measure were to be found amongst the Radicals; they objected to the clauses which provided for the buying out of the proprietors of rotten boroughs, and they thought that the omission to shorten the duration of Parliaments was a fatal blot upon the bill. They even questioned Pitt's sincerity. A golden opportunity was lost; for when in 1790 the subject was brought again before the House, the French Revolution was beginning to throw its dark shadow on the country, and Pitt was then found to be in opposition to any measure of reform.[1]

[1] That the feeling of the country was in favour of the predominance of the landed interest may be inferred from a resolution passed by a meeting of deputies from county associations in 1781: "That the addition of at least one hundred members of the House of Commons to be chosen in due proportion in the different counties of the kingdom of Great Britain, would be a measure tending strongly to correct that gross inadequacy (in the representation), and the extensive public evils arising from it" (Wyvill's *Political Papers*, vol. i., second series).

THE FIRST PERIOD, 1761-1789. 89

Upon a general view of this first period of Radical activity a few observations may be made. In some ways the Radicals differed greatly from those of later times. As was natural at first, they were not clearly distinguished from the Whigs; the use of the word Radical in a political sense, indeed, was never even heard of. When Dr. Johnson addressed a man as "a vile Whig," and said that the first Whig was the devil and that he hated to see a Whig in a parson's gown, it is evident that he was thinking of the extreme section of the Whigs which afterwards came to be spoken of as Radical. Then the early Radicals acted on general lines in close alliance with the Whigs. Upon two important questions, which during this period were much before the country, economical reform and the war with the American colonies, the Whigs acted *proprio motu* and required no spurring on. In the name of economy one of the earliest of the popular agitations in the country was carried on, and some Radical sentiments were uttered; but the actual accomplishment of this reform was mainly due to Burke. Upon the American War the Whigs from the very first took the liberal point of view, for they instinctively perceived that the defeat of the colonists would not make for liberty at home. As Fox said to Rockingham, the Americans were acting on Whig principles.[1] The pen of the Radicals was, indeed, active in the cause; for in 1774 Cartwright, risking the displeasure of the Government, published his *Letters on American Independence*; in 1776 Price wrote his *Observations*, and in 1780 Horne Tooke and Price, in co-operation, their pamphlet on the policy of the war; but the triumph of liberty should in the main be put down to the credit of the Whigs. And though Cartwright, good soul, hung

[1] Lord J. Russell's *Memorials and Correspondence of Fox*, vol. i., p. 146.

up a copy of the Declaration of American Independence in his dining-room, Fox and his party in the Commons wore a uniform of buff and blue—the colours which Washington had chosen for his troops. Upon the question of religious liberty the Radicals did not display the large-mindedness and zeal which might have been expected of them. They were, many of them, Dissenters, like Price and Priestley, and, as such, opposed the Established Church; but they seem to have wished to confine perfect freedom of religion to themselves, and in this matter the Whigs really played the better part. The same Council of the City of London which embraced the cause of " Wilkes and Liberty," in 1780 passed a resolution against Roman Catholic emancipation, and even *instructed* the representatives of the City to vote for the repeal of those sections of Lord Saville's Act of 1778 which permitted Roman Catholics to buy land and found educational establishments. But this outbreak of narrow bigotry did not suffice, for the Council petitioned Parliament to repeal the Act entirely. Such is the record of a body in which at this time radicalism may be said to have been focussed. Parliamentary reform was a question which the early Radicals, it may freely be admitted, made more particularly their own, though they were not always agreed among themselves. Whether Parliaments should be triennial, annual or sessional, was a matter upon which they never formed any unanimous opinion. Some of them would have been content to have stopped somewhere short of universal suffrage, while others had some dim perception of the fact that an equal right to a vote is not exactly the same thing as a right to an equal vote. But, as there has already been occasion to remark, upon this question of reform the Radicals were never in exclusive

THE FIRST PERIOD, 1761-1789. 91

possession of the field. A few members of all parties agreed that reform of some kind was desirable, if not absolutely necessary. The only question was upon what principles it should be made. The Radical principle of the abstract or personal right to have the suffrage was diametrically opposed to the principle—held alike by Whig and Tory—of the representation of the soil. This difference of fundamental principle caused then a strongly marked-out line of cleavage between the Radicals and the other parties in the State ; and the line has by no means been obliterated yet. But this point, upon which something has been already said, need not be laboured further. With regard to the important questions of parliamentary privilege and reporting, the early Radicals, though they here too had the advantage of being helped by many leading Whigs, performed services of the greatest interest and importance. They bore in the fullest sense the burden and heat of the day, and it should never be forgotten that it was Wilkes, Oliver and Crosby who suffered obloquy and went to prison in defence of principles which it was of the greatest moment to maintain.

There still remain a few points which are worth a passing notice. First, it is of interest to observe that the Radical movement was during its earlier stages essentially middle-class or *bourgeois*. At a later period, as will afterwards be seen, the agitation descended to the lower strata of society. But at first, the persons who were the real fighters in the battle were a limited class of voters, whose rights were being infringed. The mass of the unenfranchised, being affected only indirectly, looked on with some indifference, and if the mob caused disgraceful scenes, it was because the turbulent always love to seize occasions for disturbance. Every agitation is equally welcome to the rowdy. Next, the methods of Radical agitation were quite different from what they afterwards became. There was very little public speaking; the Radicals had not an orator among them. The time for the platform was not yet. Nor, the case of the *North Briton* notwithstanding, was journalism the great controversial medium that it afterwards became. It lived but a poor anæmic life. But the age was one in which the pamphlet reigned supreme, and the master-minds of radicalism were pre-eminently pamphleteers. Cartwright, Jebb, Price and Priestley were the thinkers and writers; the seedsmen of Radical principles and sentiments; but they did not write systematic treatises on political philosophy. That was the work of a later age. But they gave their thoughts to the world in pamphlet form, because that form was the most convenient for reaching the minds of the reading and educated classes. It is also worthy of remark that the questions which were of most concern to the Radicals were not in all respects the same as those of later times. The essential principles of radicalism—the abstract right of man to vote, and the right of the people to control Parliament by pressure from without—indeed, have never varied; but they have many facets, and may be looked at from different points of view. The nature of the relations that existed between Members of Parliament and their constituents, for example, was at this time much debated. The theory of the "agent" or "delegate" was, as has been seen, a cardinal principle in the philosophy of Cartwright and of Jebb; it was a logical deduction from the abstract rights of man. Lord North, on the other hand, rejected it with scorn; Members, he said, were not to act as deputies of the people; but they should use their own discretion and

THE FIRST PERIOD, 1761-1789.

seek no other guidance; while Lord Rockingham declared it would be "a disgraceful bondage" for a Member to submit himself to tests. In the House of Commons in 1769 the matter was made the subject of a vigorous debate. Alderman Beckford, in the course of the discussion, said that he had received instructions which he would not disregard, and that to act upon them was, in his opinion, in accordance with the law and custom of Parliament from very early times; Sir Joseph Mawbey said that to receive instructions he regarded as an "honour"; while the opponents of the theory found a tower of strength in Burke, who said that the theory, unfounded on reason as it was, would, if acted upon, ultimately destroy the Constitution. It is remarkable how constantly the subject was referred to in the speeches and the pamphlets of the period. Dr. Johnson said, for instance, that true patriots do not obey a mandate, and Burke repeatedly recurred to it. He was —he says in his *Appeal from the New to the Old Whigs*— "the first man who on the hustings, at a popular election, *rejected the authority of instructions from constituents*". There was hardly any notion which he so scornfully rejected as that, so beloved of the Radicals, of "*members for districts*". "Cornwall," he said, "elects as many members as all Scotland. But is Cornwall better taken care of than Scotland?" With this subject that of short Parliaments lies in very close connection; and it was one which at this time seems to have aroused almost as much attention. There were two things which formerly made short Parliaments appear a matter of more importance than they have since become: first, the fact that Parliaments actually lasted longer on the average, and general elections did not so frequently occur; and, secondly, the fact that the right of ministers who had not the confidence of Parliament to appeal to the constituencies had not become an established part of parliamentary law and custom. It was only in 1784 that the right was for the first time successfully asserted; and its establishment gave a further guarantee that Parliament faithfully reflected the feelings of the people. There were, indeed, some practical reasons which made short Parliaments very undesirable; for a dissolution opened the flood-gates of corruption, and let loose a torrent of violence and disorder; and as Dr. Johnson well remarked, the populace wished for new Parliaments, not because they expected more from them, but because a "year of election is a year of jollity, and, what is still more delightful, a year of equality". The glutton and the drunkard would feast without cost, and the drone live without work. Yet, these objections notwithstanding, a shortening of Parliaments commended itself to some who were very far from holding Radical opinions. Lord Shelburne, for example, speaking of short Parliaments and equal representation, said that the people "have, and always had, a clear inalienable undefeasible right to the one and the other, in their fullest extent, upon a stronger ground than that of any Act or Acts of Parliament"; and Chatham seems to have arrived at the ultimate conclusion that triennial Parliaments might safely be conceded.[1]

[1] Wraxall's *Memoirs*, vol. iii., p. 408; Cavendish's *Debates;* Dr. Johnson's *Patriot;* Wyvill's *Political Papers*, vol. iv. (first series), Letter from Lord Shelburne to John Audrey; Lewis' *Essays on the Administrations of Great Britain*, pp. 75-77. Swift, in a letter to Pope, expressed an opinion in favour of annual Parliaments, because " in long ones there groweth up a commerce of corruption between the ministry and deputies ".

Three other questions—namely, those of the House of Lords, the ballot, and payment of Members—which were pushed into the forefront by the Radicals of later generations, seem not at first to have been thought of much importance from the democratic point of view. The House of Lords was little criticised either by way of praise or censure ; for until Pitt and his successors added greatly to its numbers, it was usually in harmony with the wishes and the feelings of the nation ; and in this connection it is of interest to remark that in 1831 of the 112 peers created before 1790 no less than 108 voted for the Reform Bill, and only four against it. One of the most Radical of Reform Bills ever drafted was introduced into the Upper House ; and though the Duke of Richmond afterwards recanted, he forfeited the Premiership upon Lord Rockingham's decease. And if the Peers were censured, it was not because they were too active, but because they did too little. Burke said that he wished they had more spirit.[1] Of their place in public estimation an illustration may be cited from the year 1797, though it is to anticipate to some extent. In that year the printers and proprietors of the *Morning Chronicle* were fined £50 and committed to Newgate for three months for a very curious libel upon the House of Lords. The language complained of was as follows : " The House of Lords must now be admitted to be highly important as a political assembly, notwithstanding it has of late appeared to be nothing more than a Chamber where *the ministers' decrees are registered for form's sake.* Some of their lordships are determined to

---

[1] Dr. Johnson, however, said that the House of Lords "made noble stands" when the House of Commons dared not do it, and that the House of Commons only dared to contradict the people during the last two years before the time of dissolution (Boswell's *Journal of a Tour in the Hebrides*).

vindicate their importance. It is there that the dresses of the opera dancers are regulated." The sting of the assertion lay in its proximity to the truth. Indeed it is not too much to say that the abolition of the House of Lords formed at first no part of the practical programme of the Radicals; a fact to which Cartwright himself can testify. "I sincerely hope," he said, "that the peerage of England will at length wisely provide for their own *permanency* in our establishment by heartily promoting such a reform as shall restore to the people one branch at least of the legislature as a genuine representative."[1]

The introduction of the ballot was just as little thought of as the abolition of the House of Lords, and if discussed at all, it was only in an academic way. Harrington proposed the ballot in that portion of his *Oceana* which deals with the model of the Commonwealth; and Hume, Tory though he was, in his essay on the *Idea of a Perfect Commonwealth* expressed his admiration for Harrington's proposal. But the ballot did not commend itself to the majority of English minds, which liked publicity of voting, and thought, as Wyvill says, that secrecy might suit a place like Venice where it covered "intrigues and cabals". But it was generally looked upon as essentially un-English, though now and then a writer would be found to argue for it.[2]

The question of the payment of Members of Parliament was of a less abstract nature, and the proposal to pay them

---

[1] Lecky's *Democracy and Liberty*, vol. i., p. 310; Cartwright's *Appeal, Civil and Military*; Fitzmaurice's *Shelburne*, vol. iii., p. 546.

[2] Benjamin Flower (died 1829) was one of those who advocated the ballot. It was one of the charges against Muir, who was tried in Scotland for high treason and transported, that he had recommended Flower's writings (Rutt's *Life of Priestley*, vol. ii., p. 221).

THE FIRST PERIOD, 1761-1789.

found rather more support. There was, to begin with, a certain amount of ancient custom in its favour. Andrew Marvell, for example, received from his constituents at Hull the sum of six shillings and eightpence per day per session " for knight's pence, being their fees as burgesses of Parliament ". So too Lord Halifax seems to refer to such payment as a well-established custom; for, speaking of the election of military men to Parliament, he remarks: " The wages he hath as a member, and those he receiveth as an officer, are paid for services that are very differing ". It was at any rate to this practice of antiquity that those who advocated payment were accustomed to refer. A sub-committee at Westminster in 1780 recommended in their report " that all members serving in Parliament be entitled to reasonable wages *according to the wholesome practice of ancient times*"; and Benjamin Franklin, who observed that in former times electors sent representatives to Parliament rather "as a duty than a privilege," suggested that the reason why they took this point of view was because the " deputies were to be paid wages by their constituents ". Cartwright, indeed, rejected the proposal for himself out of sheer integrity of mind; nor does he seem to have spoken strongly in its favour. The payment of members, therefore, was at this time rather a pious aspiration than a thing imperiously demanded as of right.[1]

[1] Wyvill's *Political Papers* (first series), vol. ii., vol. iii., vol. v. (*Considerations on the Twofold Mode of Election Adopted by the French*, by C. Wyvill); *Life of Cartwright*, vol. i., p. 236; Disney's *Life of Jebb*, vol. iii. (Report of the Westminster Sub-Committee, 1780); The Marquis of Halifax's *Some Cautions Offered to the Consideration of Those Who are to Choose Members to Serve in the Ensuing Parliament;* and note by Miss Foxcroft to this passage in the second volume of her work on *Lord Halifax*. It appears that wages were secured to members by a statute of

THE ENGLISH RADICALS.

The opposition of the Radicals to a standing army at this time is a subject of not a little interest, because the distrust that lay at the root of it has not entirely disappeared. It has only assumed another form. The modern Radical does not demand the total abolition of the army; he dare not, if he would. But he rails at "bloated armaments," and cavils at the "estimates". The feeling of dislike to a regular standing army, however, was bottomed on some principles of reason, and, in fact, dated from the period of the Commonwealth. The "mailed fist" of Oliver Cromwell struck too hard to be easily forgotten, and *In the Declaration of Rights* of 1688 it was enacted that the maintenance of a standing army in time of peace, without the consent of Parliament, was contrary to law. The distrust was felt almost universally, even by the Tories. "A standing army," said Swift, "whether in time of peace or war, is a direct absurdity; for it is no part of our business to be a warlike nation, otherwise than by our fleets." So too Lord Chesterfield, speaking in the House of Lords, called such an institution a danger to liberty. Barracks were even more dreaded than the soldier; and it was this fear to which Blackstone was referring when he laid it down as a constitutional principle that the soldiers should be "intermixed with the people," and not live in separate camps. Even as late as 1793 we find both Fox and Grey opposing a Bill of Pitt's for building barracks. I is worth notice, too, that lovers of liberty abroad—the Abbé Morellet for example—envied the English because

1322, which fell into desuetude, and in 1676 the right was declared i the law courts. See also Sir William Anson's *Law and Custom of th Constitution*, vol. i., p. 119. The usual payments were four shillings day for knights of the shire and two shillings for citizens and burgesses

THE FIRST PERIOD, 1761-1789. 99

they were not encumbered by the burden of an army. Now in the minds of the Radicals, who saw in a standing army a weapon of oppression in the hands of the Crown or Parliament, this feeling of antipathy was enormously intensified; and Jebb and Cartwright believed that the only way of safety for the people was their being all skilled in bearing arms. Add to the natural feeling of distrust the single fact that the armed national militia was the ancient Saxon practice, and there was yet another reason why the Radicals should have wished to see the old custom disinterred from the dust of centuries and revived.[1] For in the primæval mind of radicalism there was an element of simplicity, just as there was in early man, or as there is in savage life. Hence the simple institutions of antiquity, or of the early Saxon times, were perfectly congenial to the minds of men like Cartwright. The mere fact that an institution, since abandoned, had been known to former ages, was in itself enough to commend it to his favour; and the appeal to ancient practice was one of the commonest of his arguments. The case of annual Parliaments is typical. The fact that both triennial and septennial Parliaments had been later innovations was deemed to be a reason for reverting to what had been the earlier institution. Annual Parliaments, said Jebb, would, in fact, not be a novelty at all; there would not be any new creation, but a simple restoration only. That the old order of condi-

[1] Gardiner's *Cromwell's Place in History*, p. 106; Swift's *Essay on Public Absurdities;* Campbell's *Lives of the Chancellors*, vol. v., p. 34; Disney's *Life of Jebb* (vol. iii., Political Papers); *Lettres de l'Abbé Morellet à Lord Shelburne*, edited by Lord Edmond Fitzmaurice (5th Jan., 1777). If the Abbé had been living in France now he would have had some justification for his fear of a standing army. Cp. Ferrero's *Le Militairisme et la Société Moderne*.

tions had given place to new, and that triennial and septennial Parliaments had been established in order the better to meet an altered state of things, were ideas that either did not occur to him at all, or if they did, were quickly brushed aside. And so it was with the standing army; that too—so it was thought by these Radical philosophers—was a late and cankerous growth upon that fine old Saxon custom, the armed national militia.[1]

[1] As the British Army is reconstituted annually by the Mutiny Act, it is not strictly speaking a "standing army". I employ the term in the sense of a professional as opposed to a volunteer army.

CHAPTER II.

THE SECOND PERIOD, 1789-1831.

THE English Radicals during the first period may be said, figuratively speaking, to have passed through the stages of infancy and youth; and to be now entering on a second period—that of middle life—which is the subject matter of this chapter. And though from age to age in history there runs an unbroken thread of continuity, yet this second period, in its broad outlines, may be sharply distinguished from the first. Nations, said Rénan, are like the Seven Sleepers of Ephesus; spellbound they slumber from century to century, but every now and then they are delivered from the charm, and, thus awakened, they toss uneasily from side to side. Then it is that the great events of human history occur. Thus it was in France during those portentous years from 1789 to 1794; the people arose from their long sleep as with a start, and, as though with a convulsive struggle of the limbs, threw surrounding objects down with a reverberating crash. In England the French Revolution completely changed the course of history. At the moment when that event began, the hopes of the reformers were bright and full of promise, but transient and fallacious. Those, indeed, for the Radicals, were halcyon days; sunlit islets in the stormy sea of life. For even the House of Commons seemed willing to take up reform in earnest; and, during its earlier stages, the Revolution was hailed by many generous natures with a transport of delight. There hung over that event a deadly iridescence which exercised upon some men a kind of fascination. Among the first of these was Price. In November, 1789, the English Revolution Society commemorated the centenary of the great events of 1689; and so natural and proper did the celebration seem, that the House of Commons, with Pitt's approval, passed a Bill—which the Lords afterwards rejected—to invest the festivities with the solemnity derived from the sanction of the nation. Yet here was the beginning and source of many troubles. It was on the occasion of this commemoration that Price preached his famous sermon, and on the evening of the day on which it was delivered, he moved a congratulatory address to the French National Assembly. The next year he acted as a steward at a dinner to celebrate the anniversary of the fall of the Bastille, and ended an eloquent address by proposing an alliance between France and England "for perpetuating peace and making the world happy"; "the passions of kings and their ministers," he said, "have too often and too long involved nations in the calamities of war," but the National Assembly have laid the axe to this source of human misery. There is something quite pathetic about the spontaneous enthusiasm of the noble-hearted Price. "What an eventful period is this!"—to quote from his sermon—"I am thankful that I have lived to see it; and I could almost say, 'Lord, now lettest Thou Thy servant depart in peace, for mine eyes have seen Thy salvation'." It is no wonder that the more cynical observers, like Horace Walpole, thought him something of a visionary with his head a little turned. Priestley was hardly less enthusiastic over what he called "the glorious effulgence of liberty in France"; and the overthrow of the French Church was of course especially welcome to Dissenters, who saw in it an event of good omen for themselves. But the first acts in the drama of the French Revolution delighted all who welcomed freedom in whatever shape it came. Fox, for instance, said that "he for one admired the new Constitution of France, considered altogether, as the most stupendous and glorious edifice of liberty which has been erected on the foundation of human integrity in any time or country". When he heard of the fall of the Bastille, he exclaimed: "How much it is the greatest event that ever happened in the world and how much the best!"[1] Horne Tooke treasured a fragment of stone from the Bastille and kept it in his study, and Erskine, who visited Paris in 1790, is said on his return to have worn the uniform of the Jacobins, with the inscription "*Vivre libre ou mourir*" upon the buttons. Even aristocrats were kindled by the revolutionary flame. Earl Lauderdale— then Lord Maitland—went to Paris and harangued the mob;[2] while Earl Stanhope—Citizen Stanhope, as he loved to call himself—who presided at a dinner to celebrate the fall of the Bastille, and was an eccentric individual not without a touch of genius—was a thoroughgoing Radical. Both Lord Lyndhurst and Canning, as young men, went through the Jacobinical phase of

[1] Yet it afterwards transpired that at its fall the Bastille contained seven prisoners only, of whom four were accused of forgery, one was an idiot, and one was detained at the request of his family (Dowden's *French Revolution and English Literature*, p. 10).

[2] When he returned home Lord Maitland said to the Duchess of Gordon: "I hope, madam, ere long to have the pleasure of introducing Mrs. Maitland to Mrs. Gordon" (Rae's *Life of Adam Smith*, p. 390).

thought; and the latter, when a student at the Temple, was visited by Godwin, who begged him to place himself at the head of a revolutionary group. Even the sober-minded Huskisson acted for a time as secretary to a Paris revolutionary club; a fact which was afterwards remembered, and that too in a manner not to his advantage. But it was the poets with "the vision and the faculty divine" who were the most intoxicated with the delirium of joy. To their rapt fancy France seemed standing on the top of golden hours.

> Bliss was it in that dawn to be alive,
> But to be young was very heaven.

So thought Wordsworth in the first flush of his revolutionary fervour. Nor was the muse of Coleridge silent; his lyre was sounded in praise of Godwin, Priestley, Earl Stanhope and Horne Tooke.[1] Even Burns—" the inspired fawn," as he has been felicitously called—was known in far Dumfries as a "son of sedition"; and he is said to have purchased the guns of a condemned smuggler that had gone ashore in Solway Firth, and to have sent them as a present to the French National Assembly. The academic calm of Oxford was ruffled by the storm. Landor, "the unsubduable," at this time an undergraduate, was known as "the mad Jacobin," and created a sensation by his revolt against the custom of powdering the hair.[2] So too it was with Southey, likewise an Oxford student, who by his own confession was at this time a republican in theory; who found it hard, he said, "to

---

[1] Coleridge said of himself: "No man was more enthusiastic than I was for France and the Revolution; it had all my wishes, none of my expectations" (*Table Talk*, vol. ii., p. 72).

[2] His tutor warned him that he would be stoned for a republican if he persisted (Colvin's *Landor*, p. 16).

pay respect to men remarkable for great wigs and little wisdom," and insisted on wearing his locks *in statu naturali*. His feelings found a vent in *Wat Tyler*, a dramatic poem that breathed the fiercest democratic sentiments, and (being afterwards surreptitiously published) became the source of considerable trouble. Perhaps it was to this poem that Coleridge was referring when he told Southey that he was making " the adamantine gate of democracy turn on its golden hinges to most sweet music ". *Redeunt saturnia regna :* such was the burden of the poets' songs at this revolutionary crisis. But their words were the generous overflow of the opulence of youth ; sparks thrown off, so to speak, from the glowing forge of life. Impatient of delay in the realisation of the visions of their fancy, a small band of them, with Southey and Coleridge at their head, resolved to emigrate to America, there to found a new society of what they called " pantisocrats ".[1] But the scheme collapsed when brought into contact with the hard reality of facts. All this enthusiasm, indeed, was to a large extent an ebullition of animal spirits in the young. For radicalism is pre-eminently the creed of

[1] Walpole's *Letters*, vol. vi. (1790) : " Mr. Burke's pamphlet," he says, " has quite turned Dr. Price's head. He got upon a table at their club, and toasted our Parliament becoming a National Assembly." Walpole called Price Earl Stanhope's " suffragan ". See also Russell's *Memoirs of Fox*, vol. ii., p. 360 ; Stanhope's *Life of Pitt*, vol. i., p. 46 ; Campbell's *Lives of the Chancellors*, vol. vi., p. 451 ; Lord Holland's *Memoirs of the Whig Party*, vol. i., pp. 35-37 ; where the author describes Earl Stanhope as " in some senses of the word the truest Jacobin " he had ever known. Campbell's *Lives of the Chancellors*, vol. viii., p. 17 ; Lockhart's *Life of Scott*, vol. vii., p. 124 ; Sir W. Scott's *Journals*, vol. ii., p. 161 ; Dowden's *French Revolution and English Literature ; Letters of William Wilberforce*, vol. ii. (1817) ; *Life and Correspondence of Southey*, vol. i., pp. 170, 213 ; vol. iv., p. 186 ; Henley's *Introduction to the Centenary Burns ; Diaries and Correspondence of George Rose*, vol. ii., p. 158.

salad days; as Taine has well said: "At twenty years old when a young man enters the world his reason is hurt at the same time as his pride. . . . Thence it comes that the majority of young men are more or less Jacobins on leaving college; it is an infirmity of youth." Aristotle said that a young man is not a fit student of political philosophy, and from Taine's point of view he had reason for his saying. At all events both Bacon and Shakespeare have given the remark the seal of their approval.[1] But these young eleutheromaniacs were in no real sense Radicals at all. They were merely passing through a natural phase of thought, for the development of which the circumstances of the time were peculiarly favourable. "Of my former errors," said Coleridge, "I shall be no more ashamed than of my change of body, natural to increase of age. . . . My feelings and imagination did not remain unkindled in this general conflagration, and I confess I should be more inclined to be ashamed than proud of myself, if they had." The mistakes of these young men arose from an exaggerated optimism, in which the Radical temperament too commonly indulges; for there is a kind of intellectual smoking of opium or of

[1] Max Nordau's *Degeneration*, p. 263; Taine's *Les Origines de la France Contemporaine*, vol. ii., pp. 11-12; Aristotle's *Ethics*, 1-3, where he says: "διὰ τῆς πολιτικῆς οὐκ ἔστιν οἰκεῖος ἀκροατὴς ὁ νέος". Cp. Bacon's *Advancement of Learning*, bk. ii.: "Is not the opinion of Aristotle worthy to be regarded, wherein he saith that young men are not fit auditors of moral philosophy, because they are not settled from the boiling-heat of their affections nor attempered with time and experience?" Cp. Shakespeare's *Troilus and Cressida*, act ii., scene 2:—
"Not much
Unlike young men, whom Aristotle thought
Unfit to hear moral philosophy".
See Mr. Sidney's *Life of Shakespeare*, where he shows that Bacon and Shakespeare meant political philosophy.

hashish which bathes the mind in golden dreams. "There was a time," said Southey, "when I believed in the persuasibility of man and had the mania of *man-making.*" Experience taught him better; or, to adopt a phrase from Hazlitt, he "missed his way in Utopia and found it in old Sarum". But there was another class of men whose radicalism was not merely a fleeting and impressionable sensibility, but was deeply rooted and profound. These were the English Jacobins, who fill a most important place in the history of political opinion.[1]

The Jacobinical Radicals may be distinguished sharply from those of the pre-revolutionary age. Of these, Jebb had already passed away, while Price died in 1791; and though he and Priestley were influenced, indeed, by the new movement in affairs, their work was already in the main accomplished. Cartwright still lived on, but the Revolution found him a doctrinaire reformer, and left him exactly where he was. Wilkes had retired from Parliament to a quiet country seat, where he enjoyed a kind of Indian summer before he felt the wintry grip of death. Horne Tooke, indeed, still preserved much of his old energy and force, and was destined to play a leading part in more capacities than one. He contested the constituency of Westminster with Fox, was tried and acquitted for high treason, and when returned to Parliament, gave rise to a very heated controversy as to the right of a Church of England clergyman to sit there. But even he was less strenuous than of old, and he

[1] Cottle's *Recollections of Coleridge and Southey*, p. 187; Southey's *Life and Correspondence*, vol. i., p. 317. Coleridge thus described this period of transition:—

"Truth I pursued as fancy led the way,
And wiser men than I went worse astray".

became less famous as a politician than as philological inquirer and a social entertainer at his residence at Wimbledon. But other times, other men; the scenes were changed, and new actors were cast for the performance.

In sketching the first period of the history of the Radicals it was possible to present to some extent a separate treatment of the agitators upon the one hand, and the writers and the thinkers on the other. The distinction could not, of course, be made with mathematical exactness; but it was, roughly speaking, of some practical utility. But when an agitation largely takes the form of a vigorous propagandism of political principles—as was actually the case during the earlier part of this revolutionary epoch—a method of treatment such as this cannot be so easily carried out. It will, however, be attempted so far as the limited conditions will allow; and it will, perhaps, be best to say something in the first place about the Radicals who most influenced other minds and left their impress upon contemporary thought. Of these Thomas Paine was certainly the chief.

In the year 1736, in the quiet little town of Thetford, in Norfolk, a child was born whom destiny had fated to stir and agitate the world in a degree far beyond the common lot. This child was Thomas Paine. Born of Quaker parents in a humble class of life, he received only a slender education, and embarked early to make his own career. He was one of those who in his time played many parts. He made stays; he acted as exciseman; he taught in a school, and became exciseman once again. During the first Radical agitation of the Middlesex election he was an exciseman, and the owner of a tobacco mill at Lewes; an obscure individual, but even then noted among his friends for his love of debate and ability in argument. In the noon-day of his life, before he fell on evil days, his personality was pleasing. The lofty brow, the prominent nose, the large and lustrous eyes, which were singularly piercing, bespoke a keen intelligence; while his strong athletic figure seemed to indicate a man who could act as well as think. His neat attire—the snuff-coloured coat, the drab breeches, the olive-velvet vest, the shoe-buckles, the side-curls and powdered hair—must have gone far to make his presence prepossessing. Easy and gracious in his manners, though among strangers rather taciturn, he was a charming companion in the circle of his friends, a brilliant talker, who delighted in paradox and argument.[1] No casual acquaintance would have ventured to predict that this agreeable personage would play an active part in two separate revolutions, or develop in popular tradition into a kind of legendary incarnation of the devil. But so it was. In the year 1774 he emigrated to America, where his natural abilities stood him in good stead, and he quickly made a reputation as a journalist and pamphleteer. In the year 1776, at a single bound, he sprang into notoriety. His pamphlet *Common Sense* was a kind of gospel of American independence, and the name of Thomas Paine was noised abroad upon both sides of the Atlantic.[2] In 1787 he found his way back to England,

---

[1] Thomas Poole thus describes him: "He is an original, amusing fellow. Striking, strong physiognomy. Said a great many quaint things" (*Thomas Poole and His Friends*, by Mrs. Sandford, vol. ii., p. 85). There is a portrait in the National Portrait Gallery after Romney by Millière.

[2] "Rebellious staymaker, unkempt, who feels that he, a single needleman, did by his Common Sense pamphlet, free America; that he can and will free all this world; perhaps even the other" (Carlyle's *French Revolution*).

where for the nonce he threw politics aside, and, having some knowledge of mechanics, he devoted his energy and attention to a design for building bridges. But the dramatic scenes in France kindled afresh in him a spirit which it was always easy to inflame. For just as Price's *Sermon* called Burke into the arena, so did the *Reflections on the French Revolution* goad Paine into a fury. It was, he declared, "a miserable rhapsody in favour of oppression, popery and tyranny". That epoch-making pamphlet —"that most admirable medicine against the French disease," or "Gallic frenzy," as Gibbon called it, was published in 1790, and was more than a success. Many answers were evoked. Some of these were written by several ladies who held advanced opinions; the "Amazonian allies," as Horace Walpole called them, "headed by Kate Macaulay and the virago Barbauld".[1] But of the numerous replies two only are remembered: the *Vindiciæ Gallicæ* of Sir James Mackintosh, and the *Rights of Man* by Thomas Paine. When Paine heard of the approaching publication of Mackintosh's work, he exclaimed that the author had better hasten on, for that after his own book had appeared, there would be no more to be said. And he was right. The *Vindiciæ Gallicæ* had literary merit; it was erudite and polished, but the *Rights of Man* threw it quite into the shade. Now it was that the figure of Thomas Paine, sinister and portentous, flashed meteor-like across the sky. At the Angel Inn at Islington, where he happened to be staying, he rapidly, with his strong incisive pen, threw off the sheets of this memorable pamphlet. The publisher, Johnson, who

---

[1] Another of the "Amazonian allies" was Mary Wollstonecraft, who afterwards married William Godwin, and may fairly claim to be the first to have agitated the cause of women's rights.

took it in hand, became so alarmed that he refused to carry out his contract. So it was entrusted to a small committee of friends—amongst them Godwin and Holcroft—for publication. In the end it was adopted by the Constitutional Society as a kind of democratic Magna Charta, and sent by them to all the corresponding societies in England, France and Scotland. In the following year the second part was written and published. The work had an enormous circulation; and it was alleged that, in order to spread a knowledge of it far and wide, it was used to wrap up sweetmeats sold to children. It was read everywhere, and eagerly listened to by those who could not read it for themselves. In Scotland, where illiterates were less common, it produced a great impression; and at Dundee a tree of liberty was planted. The profits arising from the sale, which were not small, were given by Paine, who, whatever else he may have been, was certainly not a sordid seeker after gain, to the Constitutional Society. Rarely, if ever, has a book attained a success at once so rapid and far-reaching; a success, as Paine himself declared, "beyond anything since the invention of printing". It went through three editions in a fortnight, and made many converts of those who had been of a different way of thinking. In France Paine was elected a French citizen by the National Assembly, and on many a cottage wall his portrait was to be seen in a framework of immortelles; in England there ensued something like a Reign of Terror. If the results be properly considered, the *Rights of Man* might be not unfairly styled one of the most mischievous books that ever has been written. It helped to bring a number of foolish but well-intentioned persons to the dock, to transportation, and the gallows; to cause the suspension of liberty of person and of speech, and to put back all hope of Liberal legislation for almost a generation. But before passing in review the events of this unhappy period, the contributions of Paine to the philosophy of Radicalism have first to be considered.[1]

The reputation of Paine, as a political thinker, rests in the main upon three pamphlets, *Common Sense*, the *Rights of Man*, and the *Address to the Addressers*. The former was written in 1776 and the two others in 1792. A systematic thinker on political philosophy Paine certainly was not; he was even less so than Cartwright, Price or Priestley. It might perhaps be said of him, as has been said of Voltaire, that his writings were a chaos of clear ideas. But as the most prominent representative of a certain type of thought, and as a writer who wielded an extraordinary influence, he takes a pre-eminent position among the Radical leaders of his time. With his keen eye for events which passed before him, with his power of vividly describing his impressions, and his bright incisive style, he would in these days have been a brilliant journalist. As it was, as a political pamphleteer he has rarely been equalled and never been surpassed. Nor did he make an idle boast when he declared that he "had arrived at an eminence in political literature the most difficult of all lines to succeed and excel in". Nothing has ever been written more adequate to the purpose held in view than

---

[1] Rickman's *Life of Paine*, introduction, p. xv., p. 84; Conway's *Life of Paine*, vol. i., *passim;* Kegan Paul's *William Godwin, His Friends and Contemporaries*, vol. i., pp. 69-70. H. Walpole's *Letters*, vol. vi. (1791); *Memoir of Dr. Currie*, vol. i., p. 149; *Memoirs of Romilly*, vol. i., p. 416. Paine assigned to the Society for Constitutional Information the right to publish new editions of his books, and £1000 standing to his credit with his publishers. The portrait which was so popular in France was an engraving by Sharpe after a painting by Romney.

the *Rights of Man* and *Common Sense*; they exactly hit the mark; the language and the sentiments were admirably matched. What the Jacobins were thinking he put into words with brevity and force. Men, he said, have natural rights, which belong to them by virtue of their existence, and civil rights, which arise from their being members of society; government is founded either on power or superstition, or on a contract entered into by each individual person, "each in his own personal and sovereign right"; and a government founded upon such a contract is the only one that ought to arise or to exist. From this it follows that the English government, which has arisen out of conquest, is quite unconstitutional; a fact of which the Septennial Act—a gross piece of usurpation—is an unquestionable proof. The English Constitution must be bad, because it entails upon the nation "the unnecessary expense of supporting three forms and systems of government at once, namely, the monarchical, the aristocratical, and the democratical"; it must also be corrupt, because the part which is based upon the hereditary principle will try to buy up the part which is founded upon reason; the whole is an unnatural compound of monarchy, aristocracy, and some republican materials. The right of reform is inherent in the nation, and the constitutional method of reform would be by means of a convention chosen for the purpose. The King and the House of Lords should be abolished; for the idea of hereditary legislators is as absurd as that of hereditary judges and hereditary juries, and as ridiculous as an hereditary mathematician, wise man, or poet laureate. If there is a king at all, he should be only a *roi fainéant* or gilded figurehead; for "a talented king is worse than a fool," and "a dumb idol better than one animated".

8

"Monarchy," said Lord Halifax, "is liked by people for the bells and tinsel, the outward pomp and gilding; and there must be milk for babes, since the greatest part of mankind are and ever will be included in that list." But Paine would have nothing to say to such a comfortable doctrine, and if the people were ignorant, he was determined to enlighten them. "The palaces of kings," he said, "are built upon the ruins of the powers of paradise." *Quidquid delirant reges, plectuntur Achivi.* A king, in fact, does little but make war and give away places; "a pretty business, indeed, for a man to be allowed £800,000 a year for, and worshipped into the bargain! Of more worth is one honest man to society and in the sight of God than all the crowned ruffians who ever lived." As for the aristocracy, they are "a puppet show"; "mere consumers of rent"; "drones"; a "seraglio of males". It is no wonder, therefore, that the English are ground down by the most tyrannical government in the world. The Revolution of 1688, upon which that government is founded, was nothing but "a job," and William III. as a person was "detestable"; the settlement then established, however, is "already on the wane, eclipsed by the *enlarging orb of reason*, and the luminous revolutions of America and France"; in less than another century it will have gone, like the labours of Burke, "to the family vault of the Capulets"; "the farce of monarchy and aristocracy is in all countries following that of chivalry, and Mr. Burke is dressing for the funeral. Let them pass quietly to the tomb of all other follies, and the mourners be comforted." Moreover, the less of government there is, the better for society; for society is produced by our wants and is a blessing, but government is produced by our wickedness and is a necessary evil. Government is necessary only "to supply the few cases to which society and civilisation are not conveniently competent "; and the more perfect civilisation is, the less occasion has it for government, because the more it regulates its own affairs and governs itself; "laws in fact resemble clothes, in that they are a badge of lost innocence ".

Now in all this there is more vigorous assertion than there is of closely reasoned argument. It used to be said of Dr. Johnson's conversation that if his gun missed fire, he would knock you down with the butt-end, and the same might be said of Paine's literary style. He habitually preferred the butt-end to the trigger; the hammer-blows of his affirmatives descended thick and fast. He had no delicate shades upon his palette, but he worked with glaring colours and a full brush. M. Rénan used to say, "*la verité est dans une nuance*"; but that is a *dictum* which Paine would have been quite unable to appreciate. It was, in fact, not so much what he said, as the way in which he said it, that aroused such passionate indignation, and caused people to speak of him as a "corsair," a 'villain," and the like. He had, indeed, occasional felicities of phrase, as when he said, not quite untruly, that Burke, in speaking of the French Queen, "pitied the plumage, but forgot the dying bird "; felicities which lent a sort of hard metallic brilliancy to what, in the main, was a pitiless and sometimes coarse assault upon established institutions. He had, too, a knack of saying things that bit into the memory, as when he remarked that " it is dangerous in any government to say to a nation, Thou shalt not read "; or that, " thought, by some means or other, is got abroad in the world, and cannot be restrained, though reading may ". But Paine's education and knowledge were not equal to his native vigorous understanding; he was, in truth, to use De Quincey's phrase, "a shallow dogmatist," who, thanks to the aptness of his style, became an unrivalled pamphleteer.

Paine was distinguished in an extraordinary degree by the marks of the eighteenth century radicalism. He was an ardent believer in the power of reason, when allowed to range freely and to penetrate society, to dominate mankind and ultimately to lead it to a happier state of being. He was, therefore, of the optimistic temperament, and was possessed by visionary hopes of the speedy approach of a social and political millennium. He, of course, believed in the abstract and natural rights of man; that deadly upas-tree of elemental thought, from which so much mischief was afterwards to grow. He held the views, which Price and Priestley held, upon the proper sphere of government, and the duties which it ought to undertake; he was indeed, so strongly individualist, that he is in direct descent a lineal ancestor of the anarchist philosophy of later times. He had the same fallacious contempt for history, custom and tradition, which, as will be seen, distinguished Bentham and his school; "the reasonableness and propriety of things," he said, "must be examined abstractedly from custom and usage; principles have no connection with time." Like Jebb and Cartwright he disliked a standing army, and stigmatised barracks as "tyrannical"; like them too he hated compromise. "Those words 'temperate and moderate' are," he said, "words either of political cowardice, or of cunning, or seduction. A thing moderately good, is not so good as it ought to be. Moderation in temper is always a virtue, but moderation in principle a species of vice." That he was a parliamentary reformer it scarcely need be said, though h differed from men like Tooke and Cartwright in the violence of his methods. Parliamentary reform, he said, "is not a subject that is cognisable before Parliament, because no government has a right to alter itself. The right and the exercise of that right appertains to the nation only." Here he is not perfectly consistent, for having described the English Constitution as bad in all essential principles, he goes on to declare that " there is no such thing as an English Constitution. . . . A Constitution is a thing antecedent to government; it is the act of the people creating a government." That is a strong saying; it even exceeded Jebb's contention that the combined assemblies of the counties could legally dissolve the House of Commons, and make rules for the regulation of elections with the assent of the Peerage and the King. All reformers hitherto had spoken, if not with admiration, at least with some measure of respect, for the English Constitution; they would almost have applauded the saying of Lord Halifax, when he called that Constitution "blessed," for in it "dominion and liberty are so happily reconciled". It was, however, reserved for Paine first to vilify it and then to deny its existence altogether.

Of Paine's subsequent career, of the part he played in the French Revolution, of his last years in America, of his *Age of Reason*—a work that finally overwhelmed him in a flood of the *odium theologicum*—it does not concern us here to speak. Dying in poverty and obscurity, he exemplified the saying that "those who make half-revolutions dig their own tombs".[1] It remains to say something of

---

[1] The fate of Paine's mortal remains was singularly in keeping with his tempestuous life. In the year 1819 they were brought by Cobbett from America, and it is said that a town-crier at Bolton was sentenced to nine

the man, who, next to Paine, best represented the prevailing type of radicalism and made the most impression upon contemporary thought. That man was William Godwin. The two were in agreement upon their fundamental principles, but they were the incarnate embodiments of different aspects of the revolutionary movement. For as Paine was the representative of the Jacobins in a hurry, who thought that kings were useless burdens and aristocracies were "gilt pasteboard Caryatides," and demanded their instant abolition; so was Godwin the representative of those who reasoned coldly, and believed in the supreme dominion of the intellect. By the dry light of logical deduction he also became a republican in theory; but he was too imperturbable to wish to hurry on the issue. Of those who worshipped at the altar of the goddess Reason Godwin was the hierophant and priest.

William Godwin was born, the son of a Nonconformist minister, at Wisbeach in Cambridgeshire, in 1756. He was brought up to follow the same profession as his father, and at intervals served several congregations. But thanks to the influence of Fawcet—a man who hoped so much from the French Revolution that he is said to have died of disappointment — his theological views became unsettled, and abandoning the ministry in 1783 he went to live at Somers Town, and entered on a life of literary labour. There for a brief period he contributed to a Whig journal, the *Political Herald*, and though familiar with many of the most distinguished writers of the day, he was to the world at large unknown. But in 1793, as the author of *Political Justice*, he bounded into fame. His

weeks' imprisonment for proclaiming their arrival. In 1836 they passed with Cobbett's effects into the hands of a receiver, since when all trace o them has been lost (Conway's *Life of Paine*, vol. ii.).

appearance was remarkable. The massive head poised on a little body, the placid brow and thoughtful face, the large eyes and elongated nose suggested intellectual power; but his features were impassive and rarely lighted up by the fire of genius within.[1] His lineaments—so Hazlitt tells us—resembled those of Locke's; and Harriet Martineau, who saw him in old age, described his head as striking and his countenance as remarkable. As a talker, indeed, he was trivial and commonplace, not because he wanted thought but because he revelled in abstractions. He was not, therefore, a ready conversationalist; he resembled, as Hazlitt said, a clock that wanted winding up. Never, except perhaps in the case of Oliver Goldsmith, "the inspired idiot," did a man of so much intellectual power show so little of it in the intercourse of life; indeed, in ordinary society he either fell asleep himself or made others do the same. It, therefore, causes no surprise to hear that he fell an easy victim to the ready wit of others more vivacious than himself, and that Tooke—whom Godwin on his side spoke of as "this extraordinary and admirable man"—poured ridicule upon him. Yet Godwin must be ranked, if not among the men of genius, at least among the most notable writers of his time; and in its own way, and amongst a more intellectual class of readers *Political Justice* made a stir that was hardly surpassed by that caused by the *Rights of Man* itself. It was, indeed, caviare to the general; but,

[1] Southey used to remark on Godwin's nose: "As for Godwin himself, he has large noble eyes, and a nose—oh, most abominable nose! language is not vituperative enough to express the effect of its downward elongation" (Cottle's *Recollections of Coleridge and Southey*; Coleridge's *Table Talk*, vol. i., p. 122; Kegan Paul's *William Godwin and His Friends*, vol. i., p. 71). There is a portrait of Godwin in the National Portrait Gallery by Pickersgill.

to quote Hazlitt again, "no work in his time had given such a blow to the philosophical mind of the country. Truth, moral truth, it was supposed, had here taken up its abode; and these were the oracles of thought." Coleridge addressed him in a sonnet as "formed to illumine a sunless world forlorn". Even Wordsworth advised a student at the Temple to throw aside his books on Chemistry and read Godwin on Necessity, while Southey deliberately gave as his opinion that, faulty as the book was in many parts, it was one to make every man think. Not that all critics agreed in their opinions. Sir St Romilly called it the most absurd book he had ever known, and Burke, when asked if he had seen it, replied, "Why, yes, I have seen it, and a mighty stupid looking book it is".[1] But to have been severely criticised by men like these was in itself a proof that it was a work of no ordinary kind. Whether the book was liked or not, it was extremely characteristic of the revolutionary age, and though few would care now to read it for its merits, it will always retain a certain interest as an important factor in the development of political opinion.

Godwin did not come to his opinions without deliberation. For nine years before the publication of *Political Justice*, he tells us that he was a Republican in principle, and that his heart beat high with the great swelling sentiments of liberty when the Revolution in France began. He was a member of the English Revolution Society, and wrote on its behalf an address of sympathy to the French in 1789. He believed that monarchy was a species of government "unavoidably corrupt"; and he agreed with Fénélon's remark that "kings are the most

[1] Mrs. Barbauld said that the book was "borrowed sense and original nonsense".

unfortunate and misled of all human beings"; because they are the dupes of courtiers and never learn the truth. Though he did not agree with Price and Priestley that it is only in small states that perfect liberty can be enjoyed, he entirely disapproved of dependencies and colonies. He thought that a system of government should be simple, because complexity is inimical to the improvement of the mind; that the one true motive for determining conduct was the production of the greatest amount of general good; that the only way to that improvement lay in the cultivation of the understanding; that the attainment of the truth should in all things be the sole consideration; that man should submit to truth and justice only; that submission to a government was to some extent immoral, and that the sphere of government should be, therefore, narrowly restricted. It followed from considerations such as these that the institutions of marriage and property should be abolished. He held that in human nature there was no original tendency to evil, and that "our virtues and our vices may be traced to the incidents which make the history of our lives"; that "all vice is error"; that virtue will be produced by submission to the reason and by the cultivation of the truth; that no play should, therefore, be allowed to the emotions and to the affections; that gratitude, love of country or of persons were absurd, and that a criminal should not be punished, but reasoned with. His ideally virtuous man was a creature dead to passion, who reasoned without flaw.

> He is all fault that hath no fault at all;
> Who loves me must have a touch of earth;
> The low sun makes the colour.

The sentiment embodied in these lines would to Godwin

have seemed a monstrous paradox. He believed that moral and political science might attain to some degree of mathematical exactness. "There is no science which is not capable of additions; there is no art which may not be carried to a still higher perfection. If this be true of all other sciences, why not of morals? If this be true of all other arts, why not of social institutions?" And so too he believed in the perfectibility of man; he even looked forward to a terrestrial immortality; when the whole population will consist of grown men and women only, when generation will not succeed to generation, and truth not have to recommence almost afresh her career at the end of every thirty years. Then "there will be no wars, no administration of justice as it is called, *and no government*. . . . It is not impossible that some of the present race may live to see this in part accomplished . . . but besides this there will be no disease, no anguish, no melancholy and no resentment. Every man will seek with ineffable ardour the good of all."

Such, in brief, were the principles of Godwin, and it is evident that they are thoroughly imbued with the distinctive colouring of the Radical philosophy. Like Paine, whom he described as "a most acute, original and inestimable author," he disliked aristocracies and kings; like Cartwright, he believed in simplicity of government; he was so strongly individualist that he did not "hesitate to conclude universally that *law is an institution of the most pernicious tendency*," and he, therefore, has, with Paine, some share in the distinction of being placed among the founders of the anarchism of modern days.[1] Like Priestley, he dreamed visions of the future; his optimism

[1] See Nettlau's *Bibliographie de l'Anarchie* for further information on this curious and interesting subject.

almost verged on madness. He disapproved of standing armies, thinking that a man who is a soldier merely "must always be uncommonly depraved". It is no wonder that those who talked "rank Godwinism" were generally looked upon with horror. Never did any man live so completely under the domination of the reason to the exclusion of the emotions and the passions as this king of doctrinaire philosophers; and, like Condorcet, who shared his opinions on the perfectibility of man, he might not improperly be likened to a volcano clothed in ice. But he never allowed the fiery elements below to break out into eruption. Thus too, it was in his theory of politics and morals, for he applied the method of pure reason to the study of human hopes, interests, and passions. He looked upon mankind as "a vast collection of incarnate syllogisms"—to use Mr. Leslie Stephens' felicitous expression. And what was the result? Though he thought too well of human nature, though his ends in view were noble, though his famous book made its readers "feel more generously," its conclusions were often obviously absurd. "Its bones were marrowless, its blood was cold"; that is the verdict that has been passed on his philosophy. Upon Godwin himself the results of that philosophy were disastrous in the extreme, though it is simple justice to admit that in later life he so modified it as to mitigate its rigours. In the history of literature there have been writers of renown whose lives have been more dissolute, yet there has been scarcely one whose career, with its long catalogue of sordid meannesses, it is less agreeable to contemplate. Mere nobility of sentiment is the cheapest form of virtue, unless the practice corresponds; and in the case of Godwin—that "Prince of Spongers," as he has been very justly called

—that correspondence was often conspicuously absent. Poor indeed were the rays of emotion which ever warmed that cold and sunless heart, whence all sentiments of affection, gratitude and friendship had been on principle expelled.

> And haply by abstruse research to steal
> From his own nature all the natural man.

Godwin, it would seem, tried to do this, and succeeded.[1]

Godwin did not himself attain to the immortality which he believed that the human race might, if it allowed reason to prevail, in some future time enjoy; but he reached a good old age. He survived the passing of the Reform Act, and saw a new generation of Radicals appear upon the scene. He almost outlived, indeed, his fame as a political philosopher. But it will be convenient to anticipate a little, and to say at once what remains to be said about the place that Godwin holds in the history of radicalism. After the publication of his *chef-d'œuvre*, he took but little part in politics, and subsided more and more into the position of the purely literary man. His answer, in the *Morning Chronicle*, to the charge of Chief Justice Eyre delivered in the great State Trial of Hardy, Tooke and others, turned the scale, it was believed, when their acquittal was hanging in the balance. But he afterwards assumed a position of aloofness from contemporary affairs. When Lady Caroline Lamb, for instance, asked him to give his vote to George Lamb, the Whig candidate

---

[1] Kegan Paul's *William Godwin, His Friends and Contemporaries;* Hazlitt's *Spirit of the Age;* Harriett Martineau's *Autobiography*, vol. i., p. 399; Talfourd's *Memorials of Lamb*, vol. ii., p. 140; Crabb Robinson's *Diary*, vol. i., p. 82; *The Life of Francis Place*, by Graham Wallas, pp. 57-60; Parton's *Life of Aaron Burr*, vol. i., p. 155.

at the Westminster election, he excused himself, and said: "My creed is a short one; I am in principle a Republican, but in practice a Whig. But I am a philosopher. I do not mix in the business of the world." These words, written in 1818, are exactly typical of Godwin, who liked to watch the human drama from a distance. Of his novels, which he made the vehicles of his ideas, of his plays, and of his other literary work, it would be irrelevant to speak. Nor need we dwell upon the details of his life. Of more concern is his place in the history of English political opinion; but that place it is not easy to determine. Godwin, in truth, was something of a paradox; he was at the same time enthusiastic and cold-blooded. His *Political Justice* is paradoxical throughout, and is one of the most extraordinary examples of one-sided reasoning that has ever been composed. Argumentative in form, it leads from one proposition to another, and yet ends in conclusions that are palpably absurd. It is, in fact, a Utopia, like Plato's Republic, that is depicted in the book; a Utopia, after Godwin's ideals, but, no less than the fancied realm of the Laputans, far remote from the actualities of life. This character of idealism, of loftiness of sentiment, of superiority to the commonplace morality, no doubt gave the book its fascinating power, and made Godwin almost the founder of a school, or, at all events, the centre of a literary circle. It is, indeed, in his literary relationships that he interests us most. The husband of Mary Wollstonecraft—the first woman to plead boldly for the rights of her sex—the father-in-law of Shelley, and the friend of Thomas Holcroft, would, if he had written nothing, have had some claim on our attention. But he stood to Shelley as a kind of spiritual father; and his philosophy it was that lay at the root of Shelley's creed. Shelley himself has said that "all the authors of revolution in opinion are necessarily poets," and there can be little doubt but that he must have had Godwin, amongst others, in his mind. The pity is that Shelley did not listen to the practical advice that Godwin, though a philosopher, well knew how to give. "Your views and mine," writes the latter, "as to the improvement of mankind are decisively at issue. . . . One principle that I believe is wanting in you, and in all our too fervent and impetuous reformers, is the thought that almost every institution and form of society is good in its place and the period of time to which it belongs. . . . He that would benefit mankind on a comprehensive scale by changing the principles and elements of society, must learn the hard lesson to put off self, and to contribute by a quiet but incessant activity, like a rill of water, to irrigate and fertilise the intellectual soil." That is an excellent admonition which Shelley, who was in a hurry to be, as he said, "a mender of antiquated abuses," did not follow; and it is extremely characteristic of the writer, who would first kindle the revolutionary flame, and then almost quench it with a stream of calm reflection. When a man's ideals are far removed from the realities of life, his actions will be always inconsistent with the opinions he professes; and so it was with Godwin. But, however this may be, Godwin's position is in the history of radicalism unique. He was neither an agitator, like Wilkes; nor a pamphleteer, like Cartwright; he could not appeal, like Paine, directly to the masses. He was pre-eminently the eighteenth century *philosophe*, the English Diderot or Condorcet; and it would, perhaps, be true to say that he was the last of his race. For the Utilitarian Radicals were essentially a nineteenth century product, and they began another era.[1]

It will be apparent on a brief consideration that the English Radicals during the years 1790 to 1795 underwent a transformation. With the past indeed they did not wholly break; but from being parliamentary reformers, who did not refuse entirely the co-operation of the two great parties in the State, they became violent republicans. The English Constitution, the Crown, the House of Lords had been criticised, indeed, before, but no Radical with any reputation had ever preached their abolition. But Paine had changed all that. Godwin certainly did not to the same extent influence affairs; for though his conclusions, if realised, would have involved the destruction of social institutions, they were too abstract and refined to become ever widely popular. Moreover his style was not alluring, for he could not even grow enthusiastic over the bright visions of his fancy.[2] *Political Justice*—with its contempt for all reform that did not flow from " the clear

---

[1] Torrens' *Life of Melbourne*, vol. i., p. 137; Kegan Paul's *Godwin, His Friends and Contemporaries*, vol. ii., p. 207; Godwin's *Memoir of Mary Wollstonecraft*. It is noteworthy that Godwin said of the *Rights of Women* that "it seems not very improbable that it will be read as long as the English language endures". When, after a too brief married life, Mary Wollstonecraft was dying, she said she was in heaven. The story goes that Godwin replied, "You mean, my dear, that your physical sensations are a little easier". If not true, the story is *ben trovato*. Poe, in a curious essay on *The Philosophy of Composition*, relates that Godwin wrote his novel, *Caleb Williams*, backwards. This is characteristic of Godwin's mechanical intellect.

[2] " It is here that he truly abides with his fellows, in an elysium which his reason has known how to create for itself, and which his love for humanity adorns with all purest delights." So said Condorcet of the philosopher who contemplates the approaching blessedness of society, and perhaps Godwin enjoyed this sort of happiness. See Dowden's *French Revolution* and *English Literature*, and J. Morley's *Miscellanies*, vol. ii.

light of the understanding and the erect and generous feelings of the heart "—was, indeed, just the sort of book to operate as a wholesome douche upon the heated passions of a group of fanatical republicans. But, this reservation notwithstanding, a different class of questions from those which the early Radicals agitated was now pushed into the front. The issue was, in a measure, changed. Parliamentary reform was not, indeed, lost sight of ; it was only thrown into the background, as being the lesser change which the greater would necessarily include. The first step to take, from which, it was argued, all the rest would follow, was to abolish the Crown.

> Others thought kings a useless heavy load,
> Who cost too much and did too little good.
> These were for laying honest David by,
> On principles of pure good husbandry.

The thought contained in Dryden's lines exactly represented that of the English Jacobinical Radicals. "Kings," said Rabelais, "do not live upon a little," and the saying is quoted by Rousseau in his *Social Contract* with approval. That too was Paine's opinion, and he was perhaps the first to make the point of expense a prime argument against the retention of the monarchy. The King's habits were of the simplest, but the royal family was large ; for as Lady Townshend once remarked, they were the cheapest family to see and the dearest to keep that she had ever known. But, however that might be, to indict the Crown for expensiveness was something new. There had already been an agitation for economical reform, but it was a Whig agitation in which Burke had played a leading part. Now, however, expenditure and the weight of taxation were made the very corner-stone of the Radical agitation "We are," said Paine, "oppressed with a heavy national

THE SECOND PERIOD, 1789-1831.

debt, a burden of taxes, an expensive administration of government beyond those of any people in the world. . . . We believe there is no instance to be produced but in England of 7,000,000 of inhabitants which make but little more than 1,000,000 families, paying yearly £17,000,000 of taxes. . . . The enormous expense of government has provoked men to think, by making them feel."[1] And yet there is good evidence to show that at this very time taxation in England was not heavy. Arthur Young, for instance, said of the English : " Compared with the poor of all other countries, their station is that of ease and comfort," and he referred to the " immense wealth and temporal prosperity which are diffused through every class of the community, and of which even the lowest largely partake ". The Abbé Morellet, writing to Lord Shelburne in 1782, said that he considered that the state of England was better than that of any other nation in the world. Wilberforce even accused the middle classes of excessive luxury and dissipated habits. De Tocqueville too remarked that "for centuries the only inequalities of taxation in England were those which had been successively introduced in favour of the necessitous classes. . . . In the eighteenth century it was the poor who enjoyed exemption from taxation in England; in France it was the rich."[2] There was, therefore, in all probability but little substantial ground in fact for Paine's assertions, but it is interesting to note that here was the beginning

[1] *The Address and Declaration of Universal Peace and Liberty; The Address to the Addressers.*

[2] De Tocqueville's *L'Ancien Régime*, quoted by Mr. Lecky in *Democracy and Liberty*, vol. i., p. 279; *An Enquiry into the State of the Public Mind amongst the Lower Classes in a Letter to William Wilberforce*, by Arthur Young; *Lettres de l'Abbé Morellet à Lord Shelburne*, edited by Lord Edmond Fitzmaurice.

of that zeal for penurious economy which became so characteristic of the Radicals, and reached its culminating point some years afterwards in the personality of Joseph Hume. Upon the same ground of expense was based the agitation against the House of Lords, an agitation which was absolutely new; for there has already been occasion to remark that hitherto the House of Commons, and not the House of Lords, had been the object around which the Radical campaign had chiefly centred. Such things as short Parliaments, the payment of members, and the ballot, were merged in larger aims. There is yet another point in which this new class of Radicals differed from the old, which, though in itself not political, produced political effects of very great importance. The point is that of religious opinion and belief. The earlier Radicals were never strong and proselytising infidels. Cartwright was religious; Wilkes, though he had been blasphemous in youth, made annual contributions to the funds for the liberation of the Dissenters from the restraints imposed upon them; Jebb, Price and Priestley all professed some form of Christianity. But Paine and Godwin were strong agnostics and materialists; and though there is no necessary relation between theology and politics, these two writers were the progenitors of that long line of Radicals who united a disbelief in Christianity to their unwavering faith in radicalism as a panacea for human ills. Paine's *Age of Reason*, in particular, was responsible for producing this alliance between two intellectual states which it were best to keep apart. From the Radical point of view it was disastrous, for it brought discredit on the movement. The religiously disposed, and even the professing Christians, who were lax in their principles and conduct, abhorred the very names of those who denied the faith to which the vast majority of the nation, if not by conviction, at least by the tenderness of old associations, was attached. "Genuine Christianity," said Arthur Young, "is inconsistent with revolt or with discontent in the midst of plenty. The true Christian will never be a leveller; will never listen to French politics, or to French philosophy." Wilberforce, who belonged to that class of somewhat narrow Evangelicals, of whom Arthur Young was one, was of the same opinion: "I declare," he said, "my greatest cause of difference with the *Democrats* is their laying and causing people to lay so great a stress on the concerns of this world as to occupy their whole minds and hearts, and to leave a few scanty and lukewarm thoughts for the heavenly treasure". Nor was language such as this a mere effervescence of evangelical fanaticism; for that rather worldly Bishop of Llandaff, Dr. Watson, only expressed the common thought when he declared that those who wished to overthrow the government were not only, generally speaking, "unbelievers themselves, but that they found their hopes of success in the infidelity of the common people". The advocacy of radicalism passed, in short, out of the hands of the Dissenters—who, whatever else they did, never forgot that men in their terrestrial journeys require celestial charts—into the hands of the necessitarians and of the materialists. In consequence, the Radicals never made the progress which they might otherwise have done; they never obtained a firm hold of the allegiance of the people as a whole, even when in times of distress and discontent the circumstances favoured the reception of Radical ideas. As Coleridge said, "it was God's mercy to our age that our

Jacobins were infidels, and a scandal to all sober Christians. Had they been like the old Puritans they would have trodden Church and King to dust—at least for a time." As it was, they alienated more persons by their crude atheism than they did by their political principles.[1]

Such, in brief, were the theoretical principles of radicalism which held the field during the last decade of the eighteenth century. It remains to consider them, as seen in concrete form, and to watch their operation as shaping and modifying forces in the series of causes and effects which make up the history of the period.

The manner in which the uprising of the new school of Jacobinical Radicals first made itself apparent was that of indulging in a good deal of wild rodomontade in congratulatory addresses to the French National Convention. The tone of these addresses was not only very foolish but strongly smacked of treason, as the following specimens will show: "Your wise decrees have enlightened Europe, and, like the rays of the sun, will soon enlighten the four parts of the world.... The impious enmity so long and malignantly kept up in the hearts of a generous people towards the French nation by the manœuvres and intrigues of a perfidious court exists no more but in the hearts of the perverse.... The two nations, united by nature but divided for ages by the intrigues of the courts and the pride of princes.... That destructive *aristocracy* by which our bosom is torn, an aristocracy which has hitherto been the bane of all the countries of the earth,

---

[1] See *An Enquiry into the State of the Public Mind amongst the Lower Classes in a Letter to William Wilberforce*, by Arthur Young (1798); *An Address to the People of Great Britain*, by R. Watson, Bishop of Llandaff; Trevelyan's *Life and Letters of Macaulay*, vol. i., chaps. i. and v.; Coleridge's *Table Talk*, vol. ii., p. 68.

THE SECOND PERIOD, 1789-1831. 133

you have acted wisely in banishing it from France. . . .
Reason is about to make a rapid progress, and it would
not be extraordinary, if in much less space of time than
can be imagined, the French should send addresses of
congratulation to a *National Convention of England*. . . .
But let us hail the speedy approach of general happiness
. . . hail the moment when the ethereal blaze of friendship will spread from pole to pole. . . . Oh, hail!
Britons, hail! The happy period of universal knowledge
advances with slow but steady pace. . . . Frenchmen are
already free, but Britons are preparing to be so."[1] It is
by no means to be wondered at that language such as this
should have produced a widely spread belief that those
who used it hoped to bring about in England a state of
things similar to that which was happening then in
France; a belief which was by no means confined to the
ignorant and vulgar. "The French Revolution was," said
Burke, "an armed doctrine," and both in his deliberate
writings and in his familiar letters he expressed his appre-
hensions plainly. "The spirit of proselytism," he said,
"attends this spirit of fanaticism. They have societies to
cabal and correspond at home and abroad for the propa-
gation of their tenets. . . . England is not left out of the
comprehensive scheme of their malignant charity." And
in a letter to Lord Loughborough he remarked: "There
is a confraternity between the two divisions of the French
faction on the other side of the water and on this"; a

---

[1] Address from the Friends of the People of the Town of Newington to the National Convention; Address from the Revolution Society to the National Convention; Address from several Patriotic Societies to the National Convention; Deputation from the Constitutional Society of London to the National Convention; Resolution passed by the Holborn Society of the Friends of the People.

confraternity which Gibbon—to whose cool temperament and well-ordered life of literary labour the new movement was particularly shocking—described as "new barbarians who labour to confound the order and happiness of society".[1] The result was that a reign of terror and suspicion was engendered, and among all parties a spirit was enkindled which was nothing less than savage. Even Burke called Lafayette "a horrid ruffian," and said that Condorcet—a rare and beautiful nature which Madame Roland compared to "a subtle essence soaked in cotton" — was "capable of the lowest as well as the highest and most determined villainies".[2] Nor was Coleridge, at this time at a white-heat of democratic fervour, less emphatic; and in his lecture-room at Bristol he told his hearers that Pitt had "an actual presence in the sacraments of hell, wherever administered, in all the bread of bitterness, and all the cups of blood". When his audience, sometimes tried beyond their patience, on one occasion hissed, he exclaimed: "I am not at all surprised, when the red-hot prejudices of aristocrats are suddenly plunged into the cold water of reason".[3] If these opinions are typical of the highly educated classes, it is no wonder that those who were not so well informed

[1] Burke's *French Revolution;* Campbell's *Lives of the Chancellors*, vol. vi., pp. 233-34. Arthur Young relates a curious conversation he had with Burke about Gibbon and the French Revolution. "The historian," said Burke, had "heartily repented of the anti-religious part of his work for contributing to free mankind from all restraint on their vices and profligacy, and thereby aiding so much the spirit which produced the horrors which blackened the most detestable of all revolutions" (Arthur Young's *Autobiography*, edited by M. Betham-Edwards, p. 258).

[2] J. Morley's *Miscellanies*, vol. ii., p. 175; Buckle's *History of Civilisation*, vol. i., p. 472.

[3] See Trail's *Coleridge*, p. 19, and Cottle's *Recollections of Coleridge and Southey*, p. 93.

THE SECOND PERIOD, 1789-1831. 135

lapsed into excesses of act as well as of speech, and that there ensued a kind of panic. Upon the Radicals, with Paine at their head, the storm burst with extraordinary fury, and it is of some interest to observe how deeply seated through all ranks of society, from peer to peasant, were the feelings of hostility towards a sect of individuals who, not without sincerity, made promises of a social and political millennium. A few illustrations will suffice. When in 1791 Paine and his friends proposed to celebrate the second anniversary of the fall of the Bastille at the Crown and Anchor Tavern, the landlord, who was afraid of compromising himself, at the last moment closed his doors, and the party adjourned to the Thatched House Tavern, whence they issued an indignant manifesto. Paine was burnt in effigy in different places, and the Fifth of November figures of Guy Fawkes, with pairs of stays beneath their arms, were very much in favour. The so-called "T. P." shoes were in great request among the country gentry, who used to put them on their boot soles by way of illustration of the ease with which they were trampling upon Paine. As for Godwin, he escaped prosecution, because, as Pitt very truly said, a volume that was sold at three guineas could never do much harm among those who had not three shillings to spare. *Political Justice* was in fact too costly to be dangerous. It was not safe, however, to read a newspaper of Radical tendencies, as a gentleman at Bath discovered when the mob pulled down his house about his ears; it was risky to keep a model of a guillotine, as a publican at Chelsea found when he forfeited his licence. It required some courage to associate with a Radical, as the friends of Thelwall found; and men like Thomas Poole of Stowey, the beloved of Coleridge and of Wordsworth, who dared to do so, suffered a kind of social ostracism. Wordsworth, because he had been seen in Thelwall's company, was followed by a spy, and was compelled to quit his house at Alfoxden; and his very silence was construed as a proof that he was hatching a conspiracy. A man, so mysterious and taciturn must be, so people thought, "a desperate French Jacobin". Coleridge, too, who at this time lived at Stowey, was known along the countryside as "a vile Jacobin villain". Even Hannah More—and this surely was the wildest suspicion of them all—did not escape. Many Jacobins, no doubt, were very worthless people, and Coleridge did not speak without warrant when he said that Thelwall was the only honest man among the "acting" democrats, and that "the patriots" were "ragged cattle, a most execrable herd, arrogant because they" were "ignorant, and boastful of the strength of reason because they have never tried it enough to show its weakness".[1] But the populace showed no discrimination. Nor did the upper classes show much judgment about a very trivial matter. The disuse of hairpowder—which the Radicals began with an air of ostentation in order to indicate their sympathies—created quite a scandal, as Poole and Southey discovered to their cost. Thelwall, who was among the very first to adopt the innovation, and to appear at his lectures with his hair *in statu naturali*, produced an extraordinary sensation. Wesley, it is true, had, when at Oxford, given up the use of powder, but then he lived as an ascetic; and the new habit that was introduced upon very different grounds was exceedingly unpopular. The powder question was

---

[1] The Address and Declaration of Universal Peace and Liberty; Kegan Paul's *Godwin, His Friends and Contemporaries*, vol. i., p. 80; Mrs. Sandford's *Thomas Poole and His Friends*, vol. i., p. 234.

THE SECOND PERIOD, 1789-1831. 137

not the unimportant matter that it might now be supposed it was; and the powder tax imposed in 1795 caused some consternation amongst those of both sexes who were vain of their personal appearance. So important was the matter deemed that Coleridge lectured upon it at Bristol, and he even touched upon it in a sermon he preached in a Bath Unitarian chapel. But there can be no doubt that the imposition of the tax did much to hasten on the general disuse of what the Radicals regarded as an aristocratic custom; and it was not long before the queue—an "aristocratical appendage" they called it—followed after. But, however that may be, the English Jacobins must be held in some degree responsible for a change in English habits; and though they did not adopt any Quaker-like simplicity of dress, yet it is from the period of their outbreak of republican enthusiasm that we must date the beginning of the adoption of a plainer style in men's attire.[1]

But these are small matters which pale beside events which were incomparably graver. *Majora canamus.* Through all ranks of society there ran something like an epidemic of "preternatural suspicion," and the worst stories were believed; as, for instance, that a plan had been formed to surprise the Tower and seize the muskets; or that at Manchester a number of people were invited to dinner, and that when the company were assembled an ass bedizened with a blue ribbon and the symbols of royalty was led into the room, where it was killed, with

[1] See Conway's *Life of Paine*, vol. ii., p. 28; Mrs. Sandford's *Thomas Poole and His Friends*, vol. i., pp. 84, 35, 93, 111, 208, 235, 237, 240; *Memoirs of Henry Hart*, vol. i., p. 141; *Wilkes, Sheridan, Fox*, by Fraser Rae, p. 374; *Lives of Boulton and Watt*, by Samuel Smiles, p. 417; *Life of John Thelwall*, by his widow, pp. 203 and 321; Cottle's *Recollections*, p. 181; Southey's *Life of Wesley*, vol. i., p. 63.

ridiculous formalities, and that the pieces of the flesh were afterwards distributed to various political societies. Beneath this symbolic mockery a grim purpose was suspected, and sedition was thought to lurk in the very looks of those who were believed to cherish Jacobin opinions. To refrain from opposition to the French was in itself deemed a proof of treachery, and when Horace Walpole wrote that England was nurturing in her bosom a lot of *philosophising serpents*, he was only echoing the thought that prevailed throughout all circles of respectable society. The Radicals, indeed, at this time very greatly underestimated the strong natural vein of conservatism existing in the nation. A great many people were perfectly contented with the existing state of things. The case of the poet Cowper, hypochondriac though he was, is typical. He would not even read the *Rights of Man;* "No man," he said, "shall convince me that I am improperly governed, when I feel the contrary". A strong sense of opposition to the Radicals was, in fact, aroused throughout the country. This antipathy manifested itself in many different ways. Associations, for example, of influential persons, pledged to support the Government and to counteract sedition, were formed. The mob was less discreet in its loyal exhibitions, and sometimes with its "Church and King" cries created quite a terror. At Manchester a "Church and King" Club was formed, whose members wore a uniform with a representation of the old church upon the buttons; at Liverpool a literary club, consisting of men like Dr. Currie, and Roscoe the historian, became such an object of suspicion that its meetings were suspended. For a publican to admit Jacobins was to run some risk of the deprivation of his licence; and the notice, "No Jacobins admitted here," was no

THE SECOND PERIOD, 1789-1831. 139

uncommon sight. The mass of the people were ignorant and prejudiced to a degree that it is almost impossible to conceive ; they had no respect for liberty; they even welcomed that repressive legislation which all true-hearted Liberals at the end of the eighteenth century so bitterly lamented. As the first Sir Robert Peel said to Fox, the people wanted "no French fraternity. They preferred their religion and their legal freedom with the good roast beef of Old England to the atheism, the liberty and equality, and the broken breeches and soup-meagre of France." That was unquestionably true. It was upon this stubborn mass of Toryism that Jacobinism beat vainly like waves upon a rock. Nay more, the people did not everywhere remain impassive, as the Birmingham Radicals discovered to their cost, when they held a commemoration dinner on the anniversary of the fall of the Bastille. This apparently innocent affair set fire to a quantity of combustible material, which wanted but a spark to light it. The mob scented sedition in the air, and they not unnaturally suspected the Dissenters, who, as a body, were at this time decidedly unpopular. They were generally believed, to use the words of Gibbon, to be waiting "good occasion for some change"; and even Burke, the friend of religious toleration, could not help remarking on what he called "the acid of that sharp and eager description of men". People were stopped and questioned in the streets, and if they declared for "Church and King" were unmolested. "Church and King!" "Down with the Rump!" "No Olivers!" "No false Rights of Man!" were the cries that rent the air. Then an attack was made on the chapels and the houses of the leading Nonconformists, of whom at that time Priestley was the most distinguished member. At a charming residence at Fair Hill he had made himself a home, where — so we are told by a Frenchman who visited him—"everything bespoke industry, peace and happiness". It was upon this bright domestic scene that the irritated mob descended like some barbarian horde. It so happened that at this time there were in Birmingham a number of scientific men—Darwin, Watt, and Wedgwood amongst others, who formed a society, which, from the time fixed for its meetings, was called the Lunar; and it was only natural that Priestley should have joined it.[1] The members, who were nicknamed the "Lunatics," became obnoxious to the people simply because they were philosophers, a term which in the popular mind was associated with Republicans and Jacobins. "No philosophers!" was a common cry in Birmingham. The result was that Priestley, who had prudently declined to be present at the commemoration dinner, had his house burnt about his ears. His library, selected with loving care and admirable judgment, and his scientific instruments, were ruthlessly destroyed. The affair stands eternally disgraceful to all who took a part therein, but it throws a flood of light upon the mad feeling of hostility that the Radicals, by their intemperate conduct, had aroused. Not even learned men, who might have been expected to know better, could maintain the even balance of their minds; for they, too, lapsed into political intolerance. The members of the Royal Society—then, as now, composed of the most distinguished men of science in the country—began to look askance at Priestley, and repeatedly rejected a man whom he had pro-

---

[1] Francis Horner, who visited Birmingham in 1809, found the remnant of the Lunar Society still existing, and found it very interesting (*Memoir of Francis Horner*, vol. ii., p. 2).

posed for election. "Another respectable candidate was," he said, "rejected merely on account of his supposed political principles." Even the King was rather glad that Priestley had been made to suffer. "As the mischief did occur," he said, "it was impossible not to feel pleased at its having fallen on Priestley rather than another, that he might feel the *wickedness* of the doctrines of democracy which he was propagating." And what the King thought the great majority of the people were thinking too. It was, in fact, becoming increasingly apparent that England could no longer afford Priestley a tolerable home. He and Paine were sometimes burnt in effigy together. In a letter to a friend in America he wrote: "I cannot give you an idea of the violence with which every friend of liberty is prosecuted in this country. Little of the liberty of the press on political subjects is now left." And to America, indeed, Priestley finally retired; not, it is true, like Dante to taste the bitterness of exile, to eat another's salt and to mount another's stairs; but, like him, to contemplate the *dolcissime verità*, the sweetest truths of philosophy and science. This, indeed, was his only consolation during the rapid approach to the confines of his life; for of all the Radicals his end was, perhaps, the most pathetic. Torn away from his home and country in old age, he must have felt bitterly the ingratitude of men. When Horace Walpole heard that Priestley's departure was impending, he wrote to Hannah More that he was glad that he was going, and that he hoped he would not learn to scalp his foes and then come back. To such depths did the prejudice of party bring a man of a cultivated mind and of a not unkindly disposition. Priestley, in fact, was, as a politician, much misunderstood; for though a Radical in theory, he was averse from violent methods. But in a time of tumult and excitement, when there was no discrimination, he was confounded with a small number of rash misguided men, who were not content to confine themselves to the use of moral force. And what was harder still, his unpopularity with a section of society pursued him to America.[1]

Unpopularity and social ostracism were penalties which the Radicals had to pay for openly professing their opinions; but there were severer tests of their courage and fidelity to follow. Not only was the whole force of the law put in motion; but new and stringent laws, the so-called "Gagging Bills," were hurriedly passed by a panic-stricken Parliament. Even the *Habeas Corpus* Act was temporarily suspended. The details of the new legislation belong to the general history of the country, and therefore need not be mentioned here. The bills were, of course, bitterly opposed in their passage through the House of Commons by a few liberty-loving Whigs; Fox, for instance, saying that if the bills were passed he would tell the people that obedience to the law "was no longer a question of moral obligation and duty but of prudence". The period that followed was one of the most painful in the history of England. Liberty of speech was all but

---

[1] See Gibbon's *Letters*, vol. ii., pp. 330, 349; *Life of Currie*, vol. i., pp. 38, 467; H. Walpole's *Letters* (1793); Prentice's *Historical Sketches of Manchester*, p. 221; *Memoirs of Romilly*, vol. i., p. 432; Rutt's *Life of Priestley*, vol. i., pp. 116-19; Smiles' *Lives of Boulton and Watt*, pp. 369, 384, 413; Fraser Rae's *Wilkes, Sheridan, Fox*, p. 357; Cobbett's *Political Writings*, vol. v.; *A History of the Last Hundred Days of English Freedom* (Letter iii.). It is curious that while Priestley suffered at the hands of English Tories, Malasherbes and Lavoisier were sent to the guillotine by the Jacobins. "The Republic," they said, "has no need of savants or chemists."

THE SECOND PERIOD, 1789-1831.

stifled ; the press was gagged ; public meetings were prevented ; men were hated and suspected for their political opinions ; letters were opened by the Government ; spies were believed to lurk behind the very walls and beneath the very floors. The terrible position to which the Radicals were brought may best be measured by the series of State trials that now followed thick and fast. One of the first of these was that of Paine himself, who had by this time gone to France to take his place as a member of the National Convention. His astounding letter to the Attorney-General, in which he described the Government of England as perhaps "the greatest perfection of fraud and corruption that ever took place since Governments began," and said that he doubted whether the people of England would any longer tolerate such a man as "Mr. Guelph or any of his profligate sons"; and his defence by Erskine will always make the trial memorable. This act on Erskine's part required not a little courage, and, as it was, he was deprived of his appointment of Attorney-General to the Prince of Wales ; and the chance that Paine had of an acquittal may be inferred from the fact that several proprietors and editors of journals which contained extracts from the *Rights of Man* had already been convicted. Even the pulpit was not safe ; for in the following year the Rev. Mr. Winterbotham was prosecuted for seditious words which he had used in two sermons given at Plymouth. He was fined £200 and sent to prison for a period of four years. Again, one Thomas Walker, of Manchester, and six others were tried on a charge of conspiracy to overthrow the Government and assist a French invasion. It was alleged in the indictment that Walker had exclaimed: "Damn the King ! I would as soon take his head off as tear a bit of paper !" The leading witness for the Crown turned out to be a perjurer, and the prisoners were acquitted. It is no wonder that Sheridan in the House of Commons ridiculed the Government for undertaking such foolish prosecutions: "The Lord Mayor," he said, "had discovered that at the King's Arms in Cornhill was a debating society, where principles of the most dangerous tendency were propagated; where people went to buy treason at sixpence a head; and where it was retailed to them by the glimmering light of an inch of candle; and five minutes, to be measured by the glass, were to be allowed to each traitor to perform his part in overturning the State. . . . There was a camp in a back shop, an arsenal provided with nine muskets, and an exchequer containing nine pounds and one bad shilling; all to be directed against the whole armed force and established Government of Great Britain." Even a private conversation was as dangerous as a sermon, as the fate of John Frost showed. This unhappy person had long been a reformer, and had certainly been imprudent in his conduct. In 1793 he had been sent with Joel Barlow as a deputy to the French Convention, and was present at the trial of the King. On his return home this garrulous busybody was overheard to say to an acquaintance in a coffee-house that he was "for equality and no king". For this utterance he was convicted of sedition, and sentenced to six months' imprisonment, and to stand for an hour in the pillory at Charing Cross. All this was deplorable indeed; but the English prosecutions were humane compared with those in Scotland. The trials of Thomas Muir, of the Rev. Thomas Palmer—once a Church of England clergyman, but now a Unitarian and a Radical politician—of Margarot, and of Gerrald, excited immense indignation by reason

THE SECOND PERIOD, 1789-1831.

of the partiality of the judge, and the severity of the sentences. The summing up of the Lord Justice Clerk throws a flood of light upon the political opinions which at this time were held even by men of ability and culture. It required no proof, he said, to show that "*the British Constitution is the best that ever was since the creation of the world, and it is not possible to make it better.* . . . A Government in every country should be just like a corporation; and, in this country, it is made up of the *landed interest, which alone has a right to be represented;* as for the rabble who have nothing but personal property, what hold has the nation upon them?"[1] The case for the exclusive representation of the landed interest was perhaps never put so strongly. The trial of Gerrald has a distinct pathos of its own. This unfortunate young man—then only twenty-five—was the son of wealthy parents, and had been a pupil of the famous Dr. Parr, who was widely known for his elegant Latinity and his liberal opinions. So angry was he, it is said, with Burke for writing his *Reflections*, and with Paley for writing his *Reasons for Contentment*, that he hung their portraits upside down. Whether Gerrald imbibed his politics from his master it is impossible to say; but he had great talents, an ardent temperament, and a generous disposition; and he soon became a convinced republican in theory. Carried away by youthful fervour, he foolishly took part in a convention modelled after the pattern of the French, and he was put upon his trial for sedition. The courageous

---

[1] It was probably the same judge who at Muir's trial declared that "to say the courts of justice needed reform was seditious, highly criminal, and betrayed a most hostile disposition towards the Constitution". See *A Letter from Sir S. Romilly to Bentham;* Bowring's *Life of Bentham*, Collected Works, vol. x., p. 294.

and eloquent speech he made in his defence, his fine
talents and high character, his sentence to long years of
transportation, his delicate constitution, well known to
be too frail to undergo the cruel sentence, combined to
arouse in his case a large amount of sympathy. But all
efforts to avert or mitigate the sentence were in vain; he
did not long survive the hardships of the hulks. In the
same year, at Edinburgh, Watt and Downie were convicted and sentenced to be hanged, drawn and quartered,
at that time the horrid penalty of treason. So great was
the interest in the trials that Sir Walter Scott, who
wished to hear them, took his place in court at seven
o'clock in the morning, and remained there until the
small hours of the following day.[1]

The trials of Hardy, Horne Tooke, Holcroft, Thelwall
and several others in 1794 for high treason at the Old
Bailey are an event in the history of radicalism of extraordinary interest. The characters of the accused, the
social status of several of the witnesses, the admissions
in their evidence, and the foundations upon which the
charge was laid throw much light upon the position of the
Radicals at this unhappy period. The personalities of
the principal defendants, all men of strong character and
of no ordinary talents, must necessarily have a first claim
to be considered.

Of Horne Tooke something already has been said; we
therefore pass on to Thomas Hardy, who was in several

---

[1] Campbell's *Lives of the Chancellors*, vol. vi., pp. 265, 466; Gurney's *State Trials;* Conway's *Life of Paine*, vol. ii., p. 28; De Quincey's *Whiggism in Relation to Literature;* Fraser Rae's *Wilkes, Sheridan, Fox;* Lockhart's *Life of Scott*, vol. i., p. 218. Fox, writing to Lord Holland, said: "I do not think any of the French *soi-disant* judicial proceedings surpass in injustice and contempt those in Scotland" (Lord J. Russell's *Memorials of C. J. Fox*, vol. iii., p. 61).

ways an interesting person. A shoemaker by trade, he was an excellent example—and one of the very first—of the class of Radical working-men. Next, he was intimately connected with that movement towards political association, which has been a factor of such first-rate importance in the development of radicalism; and of which the Constitutional Society and the Society for Constitutional Information were two of the most notable examples. But hitherto all political societies had drawn their members from the middle and upper classes. It now occurred to Hardy, who must have had some originating power, to form a similar society, whose members should be drawn from the class of artisans. This was clearly a most important step in the direction of the goal of the Radicals' desire—the control of Parliament by pressure from without; for to reach it the intelligent organisation of the people is absolutely necessary. Of this fact this single-minded shoemaker must have had a clear perception, and at a meeting at his house in Westminster he mooted the idea of the formation of the London Corresponding Society. When the Society first met in 1791 it had only eight names upon its books, but so rapid was its growth that some 30,000 members were soon found willing to pay the entrance fee of one shilling and the annual subscription of one penny. Its objects were radical reform; in which universal suffrage, annual Parliaments, and payment of Members of Parliament were specifically included; and "to correspond with other societies that might be formed having the same object in view, as well as with public-spirited individuals". Amongst the latter was Horne Tooke, who was prevailed upon by Hardy, the first secretary, to revise the rules of the society. Its *modus operandi* was to divide itself into sections in different

parts of London, each section sending delegates to a
Central Committee. Books were bought and circulated,
and various topics were debated; the Society, in short,
was eminently successful while it lived. Francis Place,
who was afterwards so famous as a "Benthamite" and
an electioneering organiser in the politics of Westminster,
was one of its most active members, and there is no
reason to doubt his opinion when he says that the Society
was a beneficial and educating influence among the London working-class. It soon, however, fell into suspicion
with the Government, which did not view with favour a
group of men who dubbed one another "citizens". That
was a term that smacked too much of revolution, and
it was only what might have been expected that Burke
should denounce the Society as "the mother of all mischief". Some of its papers fell into the hands of the
Committee of Secrecy of the House of Commons, which
was appointed to inquire into the existence of sedition;
and they doubtless appeared of a compromising nature
at a time when people were half-maddened by suspicion.
It appeared, from the investigations of the Committee,
that the London Corresponding Society had, amongst
other things, condemned the Corn Laws as intended
"to enable the monopolisers of farms to obtain enormous
rents"; and the Game Laws, because through them
"even the farmer . . . is robbed of every constitutional
right of Britons, and subjected to the brutality of a
Bashaw in the form of a County Justice"; that it had
asserted that "it is indispensable to good government
that representatives should be paid for their service to
the public. The want of open and honourable reward
retards the exertion of laudable characters, and subjects
the nation to the fraudulent and delusive practices of

mock patriots." The condemnation of the Corn Laws and the Game Laws was something of a novelty, and might well excite the anger of an Assembly where the landed interest was supreme. In the result it was found by the Parliamentary Committee that the views of the Society were "not intended to be prosecuted by any application to Parliament, but on the contrary, by an open attempt to supersede the House of Commons in its representative capacity, and to assume to itself all the functions and powers of a National Legislature". That was a report which was exceedingly ill-founded in the case of a Society which, as Thelwall said, had only the pen for artillery, and ink for ammunition; but in the long run it was the death-blow of this interesting working-men's association. The state trial of its secretary, Hardy, the Treason and Sedition Acts of 1795, had already caused its ruin before it was finally suppressed in 1798.[1]

Amongst those placed in the dock along with Hardy was Thomas Holcroft, who was nothing if he were not a philosopher, and was even less inclined to play the rôle of traitor. This really admirable person began life under the greatest disadvantages of ignorance and poverty. Born in London in 1745, the son of a journeyman shoe-maker and peddler, who was the poorest of the poor, he spent his childhood in accompanying his father in his travels. He was in turns a horse-trainer's stable-boy at Newmarket, and a servant of Mr. Granville, the well-

[1] Stephens' *Life of Tooke*, vol. ii., p. 82; Crabb Robinson's *Diary*, vol. i., p. 27; Jephson's *Rise and Progress of the Platform*, vol. i., p. 193; Wallas' *Life of Francis Place*, pp. 20-25; Howell's *State Trials*, vol. xxiv.; Reports of the Committee of Secrecy, presented to the House of Commons in 1794 and 1799.

known philanthropist, in London. Yet even under these unauspicious circumstances he contrived to teach himself, and actually sent some contributions to the *Whitehall Evening Post*. He then engaged himself to act under Macklin the comedian, and played with him in Dublin for a time. He was everything by starts, and nothing long. But his natural literary gift could not for ever be repressed; in one so liberally endowed it could not help but find some means for its expression. As a novelist and playwright, Holcroft, indeed, became a considerable literary force. His *Road to Ruin* was a favourite that long held its place upon the boards; and his novels, *Anna St. Ives* and *Hugh Trevor*, published in 1792 and 1797 respectively, were popular successes. They were novels with a purpose, written to give expression to his views on the philosophy of life. Full of the enthusiasm aroused by the French Revolution, and the admiring friend of Godwin, he put into the form of fiction the doctrines that the latter worked out with such elaboration in his *Political Justice*. Like Godwin, he believed that the way to human happiness lay through the submission of the will to the supreme dominion of the reason; that death and disease were due simply to feebleness of mind; and that by the calm exercise of the intelligence truth would in the end triumph over error. He looked forward to a Utopia where the great principles of morality, founded upon reason, would be the constant guide of conduct; where, the spirit of benevolence being universally diffused, international animosities would cease, family attachments be weakened, exclusive friendships end, and gratitude and promises become immoral and absurd. But though an enthusiast, he deprecated violence; he believed only in a gradual improvement through a calm and rational progress. He was, in short, a Radical philosopher of the type of William Godwin; a theorist, a *littérateur* first and a politician afterwards; who rather held himself aloof from practical affairs. But as he never put his views into the formal shape of any serious treatise, his influence on political opinion could never have been great. As a member, however, of the Society for Constitutional Information, he had the bad luck to be suspected of treasonable conduct, and was placed upon his trial. Though honourably acquitted, he was made to appear a much more active Radical than in fact he ever was.[1]

John Thelwall, another of the defendants, was in his own peculiar province a remarkable man, and next to Paine and Godwin the most notable of the group of Jacobinical Radicals. The son of Joseph Thelwall, a well-to-do silk-mercer, he was born in 1764 in Chandos Street, Covent Garden. He was placed by his father in the business, in which it was intended that he should some day become a partner. But, as often happens, the tastes and disposition of the son ran counter to the wishes of the father. To business, in short, the lad discovered an unconquerable aversion, and the time he should have given to the dry details of the ledger he devoted to the more alluring study of literature and painting. Nor could he be persuaded to sacrifice his natural inclinations to the hopes of future riches. He

---

[1] *Memoirs of Thomas Holcroft*, written by himself, three vols. Coleridge, who disliked Holcroft's religious opinions, thought poorly of him, calling him "a man of but small powers, with superficial rather than solid talents, and possessing principles of the most horrible description; a man who at the very moment he denied the existence of the Deity in his heart believed and trembled" (Cottle's *Recollections*, p. 329).

published a volume of poems and a novel, and edited the *Biographical and Imperial Magazine*; and, what is more important in relation to the future development of his mind, he became a member of the Society for Free Debate, which met at the Coachmakers' Hall. The Thelwall of this period, narrow-chested, speaking in harsh tones and with a lisp, and the ardent supporter of the Crown, was as unlike as he could be to the stout-lunged orator and Radical that he afterwards became. Yet he surmounted his physical defects by perseverance, and was converted to the opinions of his opponents in debate. Though he was far from being a learned man, he had a vigorous understanding and could express his ideas in terse and vivid language. His description of Thurlow, as a man "with the Norman conquest in his eyebrow and the feudal system in every feature of his face," is a good example of his power of emphatic phraseology. In a word, if Paine was the Radical pamphleteer, and Godwin and Holcroft the Radical philosophers and literary men, Thelwall was pre-eminently the orator of the party. He was, indeed, the first orator that the Radicals produced; the prototype of Hunt, of Bright and Cobden. It was a boast he used to make that if, when about to suffer execution, he were permitted to address the mob for half an hour he would have no fear of the result, for he would be sure to incite them to his rescue from the gallows. Though he pretended that he had been formed by nature for a poet and that his country had made him an unwilling politician, he was liberally endowed with all the qualities that go to make the platform speaker. No man in his time could play so powerfully upon the emotions of his audience. He gave political lectures, which the Government thwarted whenever it was possible; for they attracted many hearers.[1] Even Burke, in his Olympian manner, contemptuously referred to them: "I shall indulge the hope that no grown gentleman or nobleman of our time will think of finishing at Mr. Thelwall's lectures whatever may have been left incomplete at the old universities of his country". But Thelwall's lectures—which after their delivery he published in weekly numbers under the title of the *Tribune*—could not, in the opinion of the Government, be suffered safely to continue. His objects were, he said, "to confute the sophisms of court jugglers and ministerial hirelings"; to strip off the mask from State hypocrisy and usurpation; and to demonstrate the progress of corruption whereby "the rich are tottering on the verge of bankruptcy and the poor are sinking into the abyss of famine". That was certainly strong language, and it is no wonder that a man who threatened to become a formidable demagogue should have been placed upon his trial; and Thelwall was unquestionably right when he declared that the crime of giving political lectures was his principal offence. After his acquittal he gradually withdrew himself from politics, that turbulent sea of agitation, to a more tranquil course of life. He taught elocution, and professed with some success to cure impediments in speech. Thoroughly honest and sincere, he made and kept the friendships of Thomas Poole, Wordsworth, Lamb and Coleridge; and a man who could do that must have had an engaging personality. A pretty story is told of him when on a visit to Wordsworth at Alfoxden in Somersetshire. "This is a place," said Coleridge, "to

---

[1] Thelwall did not escape the ridicule of the *Anti-Jacobin* poet:—

"Thelwall and ye that lecture as ye go,
And for your pains get pelted,
Praise Lepaux!"

reconcile one to all the jarrings and conflicts of the wide world." "Nay," replied Thelwall, "to make one forget them altogether." There are few Radicals with whom such pleasant memories are associated. That he should have complained bitterly of Godwin, who professed to be his friend, is only further proof of that philosopher's unpleasant disposition.[1]

The trials of Hardy and his fellow-companions in the dock were of great importance to the country; for a victory for the Crown would have struck a deadly blow at liberty, which was already much imperilled. The excitement of the country was raised to fever pitch. The approaches to the court were densely blocked, and the Attorney-General, Sir John Scott, afterwards Lord Eldon, was hissed and hooted by the crowd; while Erskine, who was the leading counsel retained for the defence, had to address the people to induce them to disperse. Those who lived in the provinces went early to the post-offices to obtain the latest news, and the mail-coaches were beset with impatient crowds who were waiting to buy the last editions of the newspapers. But these were merely accidental incidents; the essential interest of the trials lay in the nature of the evidence that was given for the defence. Both Pitt and the Duke of Richmond were examined as to their former intimate relationship with

---

[1] *Life of John Thelwall*, by his widow; *Burke's Letter to a Noble Lord*; Thelwall's *Some Reflections on Burke's Letter*; Thelwall's *The Natural and Constitutional Right of Britons to Annual Parliaments*, etc.; Talfourd's *Memorials of Lamb*, vol. ii., p. 152; Jephson's *Rise and Progress of the Platform*, vol. i., p. 255; Crabb Robinson's *Diary*, vol. i., p. 27; Introduction to Wordsworth's *Anecdote for Fathers*. "A very warm-hearted honest man.... He believes and disbelieves with impassioned confidence," said Coleridge (Mrs. Sandford's *Thomas Poole and His Friends*, vol. i., p. 234).

the party of reform. That they had been zealous reformers they confessed, a fact of which Erskine made the most in his speech for the defence.[1] "The great Earl of Chatham," he said, "began and established the fame and glory of his life upon the very cause in which my unfortunate clients were engaged, and he left it as an inheritance to the present Minister of the Crown, as the foundation of his fame and glory; and his fame and glory were accordingly raised upon it. . . . The Constitutional Society owed its earliest credit with the country, if not its very birth, to the labour of the present Minister, and its professed principles to his grace the Duke of Richmond." That the Earl of Chatham and that Pitt—the first Minister of the Government which had set on foot the prosecution—should once have been reformers, is a fact which throws a flood of light upon a most important point already mentioned, but which Erskine probably never fully realised. In a pamphlet which he published in 1796, he recurs to the essential point of his speech for the defence. "Towards the close of the American War," he writes, "Mr. Pitt (a boy almost) saw the corrupt condition of Parliament, from the defect of the representation of the people, with the eyes of a mature statesman; the eagle eyes of his father had seen it before him, and the thunder of his eloquence had made it tremble. Lord Chatham had detected and exposed the rank corruption of the House of Commons as the sole cause of that fatal quarrel, and left it a legacy to his son to avenge and

[1] Horne Tooke's ready wit was never so wonderfully exhibited as it was at this trial. A single instance must suffice. Wishing to speak for himself in his own defence, he passed a note to Erskine to express his desire. Erskine replied, "If you do, you'll be hanged"; then retorted Tooke, "I'll be hanged if I do".

correct them. The youthful exertions of Mr. Pitt were worthy of the delegation." That is an eloquent passage which proves, however, that Erskine had entirely failed to grasp the essential significance of the facts with which he had to deal; namely, that there were Radical reformers, and Whig and Tory reformers; that Radical reform was, in its primary elements, a different thing from the reform of which Chatham, Pitt, and Burke were, each in their different ways, the earnest advocates. The theory of the personal right to vote, and of Parliamentary representatives being only delegates bound by pledges to instructions, and the demand for annual Parliaments, were of the essence of Radical reform; and reform of that kind was by both Pitt and Chatham as strongly as possible condemned. That is a fact which Erskine either could or would not see. Moreover, the character of the Radical demands had, under the stimulating influence of the French Revolution, changed portentously since Pitt had introduced his measure for reform. A reform, thorough and far-reaching, in Parliamentary representation, would at that time have almost, if not fully, satisfied the claim that the Radicals set up; the claim of the right of the people to control Parliament by pressure from without. But the radicalism that Paine had introduced was something very different; it involved the destruction of the constitutional system; it implied a revolution; and the mere fact that Pitt should have given the evidence he did may be taken as in itself a measure of the change that had occurred. The Government, no doubt, had been needlessly alarmed, and the defendants, in this case at least, were properly acquitted. But Pitt was not altogether wrong when, in moving the suspension of the *Habeas Corpus* Act, he declared that the

THE SECOND PERIOD, 1789-1831. 157

new radicalism "was founded on the modern and monstrous doctrine of the *Rights of Man*".[1]

The close of the eighteenth century marks an epoch in the history of the Radicals. They were then at their nadir of depression, and it will be well to pause for a moment and survey the situation. As a party they had been crushed almost out of existence; Paine had gone to France; Priestley had taken refuge in America; Godwin, whom it was useless to molest, was writing novels; Horne Tooke made a spirited attempt to revive a sinking cause by going into Parliament, but he was disqualified, as a clergyman, from sitting. The English Jacobins, in short, had wrought their own destruction. Nay more, they had struck a blow at liberalism, from which it did not recover until the time of the Reform Act. For, in the first place, the old Whig party was splintered into fragments; it dwindled into the mere shadow of itself; in the House of Commons it could muster scarcely forty members.[2] There was a story told that some one had remarked that the Whig Members might all have driven home together in a single hackney coach: "That," said George Byng, "is a calumny; we

---

[1] Twiss' *Life of Lord Eldon*, vol. i., p. 268; Campbell's *Lives of the Chancellors*, vol. vi., p. 484; Howell's *State Trials*, vol. xxiv.; Erskine's *A View of the Causes and the Consequences of the Present War with France*. Lord Campbell thought that the trials of Hardy and others were unfair; first, because the cases had been prejudged by an Act of Parliament which recited the existence of a dangerous conspiracy; and, secondly, because the judges at the trial had taken part in a preliminary inquiry before the Privy Council (vol. vii., p. 109).

[2] Lord Thurlow said: "There are but forty of them, but there is not one of them who is not ready to be hanged for Fox". Rae's *Wilkes, Sheridan, Fox*, p. 364; Lord John Russell's *Recollections and Suggestions*, p. 268.

should have filled two ". That was a humorous exaggeration of what was an actual fact. Of this forlorn hope, of this devoted band, Fox was by right the natural leader; and he had the good fortune to be supported by Grey, Sheridan and Erskine. But the time was one of retrogression and reaction. Parliamentary reform, religious equality, and the abolition of the slave trade, for which the prospects were once so hopeful, were now practically abandoned causes. When Grey in 1792 moved for an inquiry into the state of the representation—a motion at which Gibbon said he "shuddered"—Pitt opposed it as inopportune; and Burke, in like manner, refused any longer to vote for the repeal of the Test and Corporation Act. Even the slavery abolitionists were suspected of some dark and deep designs. "But in this rage against slavery," wrote Gibbon to Lord Sheffield, " in the numerous petitions against the slave trade, was there no leaven of new democratical principles? no wild ideas of the rights and natural equality of man?" Out of Parliament as well as in it, the cause of liberalism was suffering an eclipse. The two great political educating instruments public meetings and political societies, were except under the most stringent conditions no longer to be handled. Between 1760 and 1790 public speech and public meetings were, indeed, but seldom used as a means to gather and concentrate or to disseminate opinion; but the practice of them was tending to become more and more a common custom. Now, except perhaps at Westminster where Fox and Horne Tooke were not to be intimidated, the public voice was hushed and silenced. Such meetings as there were, for the most part, were convened by the extremists who merely made themselves notorious by the folly and violence of their language. A single instance must suffice

THE SECOND PERIOD, 1789-1831.   159

An address to the King on one occasion was adopted, in which it was asserted that his ministers had "grossly and shamefully deceived him," and that the addressers had actually the right of sending him instructions. The talking of fustian such as this served only to make respectable members of society look upon the hustings with abhorrence.[1] And so it was with political associations. Shunned by almost everybody and suspected by the Government, their glory had departed, and, if not dissolved, they dragged along a hopeless and precarious existence. There was only one society which was an exception to the rule; the Society of the Friends of the People; a Whig body which maintained its ground by reason only of the strict and studied moderation of its tone. Founded in 1792, it had comparatively few members, of whom twenty-eight were parliamentary representatives, amongst them being Fox, Sheridan and Grey.[2] Erskine described them as "persons of rank, talent and character," whose avowed object was "to tranquillise the agitated part of the public, to restore affection for the Legislature . . . to prevent that fermentation of political opinion, which the French Revolution had undoubtedly given rise to, from taking a republican

---

[1] It is worth noting that meetings of the inhabitants at large (as distinguished from meetings of freeholders or householders) were regarded with disfavour; and also that town meetings were considered more Radical in tone than country meetings and therefore likely to injure the cause of moderate reform (Wyvill's *Political Papers*, vol. vi., Letters between Wyvill and Cartwright, 1801).

[2] Lord Holland says that the society originated in an after-dinner conversation at the House of Lord Porchester (afterwards Lord Carnarvon); who, going at that time through a revolutionary phase, refused to join it because it was too moderate (Holland's *Memoirs of the Whig Party*, vol. i., pp. 14-15).

direction in Great Britain ". The Society of the Friends of the People, therefore, is a subject of no little interest and importance, for it enables us clearly to distinguish between radicalism and what was regarded as moderate liberalism at an extremely critical time in English history. In the year 1795 the Society adopted and published a Plan of Reform, which may be regarded as a kind of manifesto of the Whigs. A more trenchant and convincing exposure of the defects in the representation could hardly have been written; but the remedies proposed were moderate and reasonable. They were, to put them briefly, first, that every tax-paying householder (Peers excepted) should vote in the election for one member; secondly, that elections should be all held on the same day; thirdly, that "wages should be paid to members serving in Parliament, and not holding office under the Crown, not by the particular division for which they were elected, but out of the revenue of the public, for the general interest of which the Constitution intends them to serve". Shorter Parliaments are recommended only in the event of these proposals having been actually adopted. It is of great interest to observe here the dividing line between radicalism and whiggism; the personal right to vote, which is equivalent to universal suffrage makes way for household suffrage; the delegate theory of representation is not maintained; the ballot is not asked for; even short Parliaments are not regarded as being of much importance. On the other hand, the payment of members out of public revenues is, somewhat strangely pushed into the forefront. Yet, when Grey presented a petition to Parliament in favour of reform from this eminently respectable society, there were only forty-two members who rose in their places to support him. Even

Pitt said that "the views of the new society were less moderate than their professions to the public"; and that, too, though the greatest care was taken to avoid the slightest occasion for suspicion. The good-natured Major Cartwright, for example, was requested to withdraw his name from the Society, for it was felt that only injury could result from the association of that sturdy and uncompromising Radical. He was at that time the chairman of the Society for Constitutional Information, with which the Whig Society declined all future intercourse; at the same time informing Major Cartwright that they believed his views and objects to be irreconcilable with those real interests on which he professed to inform and enlighten the people.[1]

A few years of revolutionary radicalism had, in fact, reduced English politics to something like a state of chaos. But for the panic that was caused, Pitt and Fox, the great leaders of the two parties arrayed in opposition, might well have worked together; for they had many points in common. Both were by natural temperament reformers; both desired the emancipation of the Catholics, and both pleaded earnestly for the abolition of the slave trade. Yet by the end of the eighteenth century they were divided by a chasm, which it was impossible to pass by any golden bridge of good-will or concession. On both

---

[1] Gibbon's *Letters*, vol. ii. (Mr. Prothero's edition), Letter to Lord Sheffield (1792), and Mr. Prothero's Note, p. 297; Second Report of the Committee of Secrecy of the House of Commons; Stanhope's *Life of Pitt*, vol. ii., pp. 51, 151, 152; Wyvill's *Political Papers*, vol. v., Letter from Wyvill to Burgh (1792); *The Plan of Reform* (published by the Society of the Friends of the People); Erskine's *A View of the Causes and Consequences of the Present War with France*; *Diaries of Lord Colchester*, vol. i., p. 7; Campbell's *Lives of the Chancellors*, vol. v., p. 614; *Letters of William Wilberforce*, vol. i., p. 90; *Life of Cartwright*, vol. ii., p. 346.

sides there were ill-considered judgment and intemperate talk and action. We find Fox, for instance, saying that "the triumph of the French Government over the English does, in fact, afford me a degree of pleasure which it is very difficult to disguise"; while Pitt, on the other hand, denounced Fox and his followers as Jacobins.[1] In like manner, Sheridan, a good Whig, was stigmatised by Mr. Abbott, afterwards Speaker and raised to the peerage under the title of Lord Colchester, as "the most active and mischievous partisan of the republican faction . . . acting himself, heart and soul, with the most desperate Jacobins". A greater misconception could hardly have been formed. There were also foolish acts as well as foolish words; the sense of perspective was almost wholly lost; and things of small importance were magnified in a disproportionate degree. The public mind was in a state of painful tension; the whole atmosphere was charged with electricity. Of the fact a few illustrations—taken out of many—may, without irrelevance, be given; for they will help to put the position of the Radicals in a somewhat clearer light.

In the year 1795, one John Reeves, the president of a society bearing the significant title of the Society against Jacobins and Levellers, published a pamphlet called *Thoughts on English Government*, a foolish work, which illuminated nothing, and might well have been contemned. The purport was to argue that the English Government is purely monarchical, excepting only the Houses of Parliament, which are derivative from the

---

[1] Pitt's state of mind may be inferred from a remark he made in 1795 to Wilberforce: "My head would be off in six months were I to resign" Stanhope's *Life of Pitt*, vol. ii., p. 388; *The Diaries and Correspondence of the Right Hon. George Rose*, vol. i., p. 448.

Crown. "The monarch is the stock from which have sprung those goodly branches of the legislature, the Lords and Commons . . . but they are still only branches which may be lopped off, and the tree is a tree still." The attenuated Whig Opposition were reduced to such extremities that they were glad to seize the opportunity which Reeves's folly now had given them. Sheridan accordingly moved that the pamphlet was a scandalous and seditious libel, and a high breach of privilege of the House; that it should be ordered to be burnt by the common hangman, and the Crown be petitioned to remove the writer from any place of trust. The House directed the Attorney-General to set on foot a prosecution, but Reeves was eventually acquitted. A more signal instance of Whig impotence it would be difficult to conceive. But if the Whigs were destitute of all authority, the Radicals were simply helpless victims. The case of Gilbert Wakefield is in point. This unhappy individual was, if not a profound scholar, a man of refined and cultivated mind; but, withal, he lacked a proper mental balance.[1] His zeal and the generosity of his sentiments awakened the sympathies of many, even when they could not quite agree with him; Fox, for instance, describing him as "thoroughly attached to the principles of liberty and humanity". Yet no Radical ever described a government in more flame-coloured terms than Gilbert Wakefield: "They have occasioned," he said, "a devastation of the human species, infinitely tremendous, beyond the

---

[1] Gilbert Wakefield is now chiefly remembered in connection with his edition of *The Hecuba of Euripides*, upon which Porson made the felicitous quotation:—
"What's Hecuba to him, or he to Hecuba?"
—*Hamlet*, act. ii., sc. ii.

most merciless tyrants of ancient or modern times; the death of a fellow-creature is no more to them than the fall of an autumnal leaf in the pathless desert; land and sea are covered with the carcases of the slain". The force of folly could no farther go. Yet the writer, who was better fitted for an asylum than a gaol, was cruelly sentenced to two years' imprisonment for a seditious libel. Less serious, but not less significant, were the incidents that yet remain to tell. The grave Benchers of Lincoln's Inn, for instance, refused permission to Sir James Mackintosh to give his Lectures on the Law of Nations in their ancient hall; for the author of the *Vindiciæ Gallicæ* had a past which could not be easily forgotten. Fox himself was struck off the Privy Council List for his speech in which he lauded the phrase, "the Sovereignty of the People". The Duke of Norfolk was removed from the Lord Lieutenancy of the West Riding for a similar offence. At a dinner, on Fox's birthday, at the Crown and Anchor Tavern, he had foolishly likened the great Whig orator to Washington, and proposed the toast, "The People our Sovereign"; a democratic sentiment which the Crown, not unnaturally, resented. Yet Fox, for all the King's hostility, was, in all essentials, not a Radical, but a Whig; though the Radicals have sometimes claimed him for themselves. For example, to universal suffrage he always declared himself opposed not so much on abstract grounds as because he believed it was impracticable; "there was," he thought, "no practical mode of collecting such suffrage, and by attempting it . . . fewer individual opinions would be collected than by an appeal to a limited number". In 1793 he acted on this opinion by refusing to present to the House of Commons a petition in favour of this measure of reform,

Again, though he respected Major Cartwright for what he called "his enlightened mind and profound constitutional knowledge, his purity of principle and consistency of conduct," he told him plainly that he differed wholly from him on the question of the extension of the suffrage. But proof, if proof were wanted, of Fox's true position, is forthcoming in the fact that the Radicals themselves repudiated and disclaimed him. Paine denounced him as "a trimmer," because he had called the *Rights of Man* a libel. The principles of the Society of the Friends of the People were the principles of Fox; yet Paine vehemently attacked it as composed of men whose "general motive" was the same as that of every parliamentary Opposition — "power and place". It was, he said, made up "chiefly of those called *Foxites*," who amused the people with a new phrase, that of "temperate and moderate reform," which meant—so he interpreted it—the continuance as long as possible of abuses; "if we cannot hold all, let us hold some". The line of demarcation between the Radicals and Whigs could not have been more distinctly drawn.[1]

The time from the beginning of the nineteenth century up to that epoch-making year, that *annus mirabilis* of 1832, was, for the most part, extremely disheartening for the Radicals, but, when properly regarded, a

---

[1] *Diaries and Correspondence of the Right Hon. George Rose*, vol. i., pp. 153 and 448; *Diaries of Lord Colchester*, vol. i., p. 23; *Life of Cartwright*, vol. i., p. 232; Campbell's *Lives of the Chancellors*, vol. vi., p. 289; Roebuck's *History of the Whig Ministry of 1830*, pp. 183, 188, 198 (notes); Paine's *Address to the Addressers*. Bentham says of Fox: "He was against radical reform of the law. . . . He was both shallow and ignorant, a mere party man." So too Bentham condemned the "moderate reform" programme of the Friends of the People. See *Bowring's Life*, vol. x., p. 364, and Bentham's *Radicalism not Dangerous*.

period from the Radical point of view of extraordinary interest. For it witnessed the rise and the ascent of the most profound and systematic philosophy of radicalism that had ever yet been formulated. But it was a time of national depression and distress, in spite of victories in war, and, for the Radicals, one of drowsy numbness and leaden-eyed despair. Amongst a populace that was either hostile or apathetic, they were impotent and dumb. Even the Whigs at first almost abandoned liberalism as a nearly hopeless cause. "In short," said Fox in a letter to Grey written in 1801, "till I see that the public has some dislike (indignation I do not hope for) to absolute power, I see no use in stating in the House of Commons the principles of liberty and justice."[1] The mass of the population was, in fact, at this time Tory to the core, however much the Radicals were unwilling to confess it. Yet the Radical faith was not extinguished; its dying embers still flickered here and there. The country during this period resembled some volcanic region, honey-combed with subterranean fires, which would sometimes find a vent through rents and fissures in the surface, and burst outwards into flames. There were attempted agitations, which indeed caused some disquiet, but almost always ended in a prosecution and a trial; for the turbulent spirit of radicalism, evoked by distress and discontent, might be kept down, but not extinguished. But the history of the Radicals during the first thirty years of the nineteenth century cannot be rightly apprehended without a recognition of the fact that several classes of Radicals were at work upon parallel and partly independent lines. There were the philosophers, with

[1] *Memorials and Correspondence of Fox* (edited by Lord J. Russell), vol. iii., p. 340.

Bentham at their head; there was the parliamentary group, always small, of which Sir Francis Burdett was for a long time the solitary representative; and, lastly, there were the demagogues and agitators, of whom Hunt and Cobbett, the former on the platform and the latter in the press, were the spokesmen and the leaders. Major Cartwright, now in his decline, still clung with a rare persistency and courage to the promulgation of what he believed to be the true principles of radicalism; but though respected and admired, he was partially eclipsed by the newer and more brilliant lights that had appeared on the horizon. All these Radicals were actively at work in their several different ways, sometimes divergent, sometimes actually opposed to one another, but every now and then moving across each other's paths and coming into contact. But by far the most important were the group of the philosophers, who for years worked quietly in the background, yet in the long run proved themselves to be the most powerful and most formative influence over political opinion that had ever appeared in England. The uprising of the Philosophical Radicals was the greatest force, of a purely speculative kind, that had ever been felt in English politics, and nothing ever did so much to democratise our institutions. The philosophers, therefore, as the most important and influential group of Radicals of the period, have the first claim to be considered.

The law of the three stages in the progress of the human mind, the theological, the metaphysical, and the positive or scientific, is perhaps the most important thesis sustained in the Positive Philosophy of Comte; and it certainly derives some support and illustration from the history of the Radicals. When the divine right of kings was put forward and believed, political opinion was in the primitive or theological condition; when the figment of a contract between the governors and the governed was elaborately argued by the French Eighteenth Century Philosophers, and the theory of the natural rights of man was maintained by the French revolutionists and the early English Radicals, then theology had given way to metaphysics; but when political principles were argued on the ground of experience and expediency, then metaphysics were, in their turn, supplanted by the scientific method. The character of the eighteenth century radicalism was essentially metaphysical, and though no point in time for the change can be accurately fixed, yet it is the peculiar glory of the Philosophical Radicals that they were the first to attempt to put radicalism upon a well-reasoned and scientific basis. Their attempt was imperfect, it is true, and not entirely free from eighteenth century influences; while the earlier Radicals, on the other hand, had occasional glimpses into scientific methods. There was, in fact, no break of continuity, and metaphysical political theories were almost insensibly transmitted into a scientific shape. The transformation, when accomplished, was magnificent, but it was not wrought in a day.

The change from the metaphysical radicalism of the eighteenth century to the more scientific radicalism of the group of thinkers known as "Benthamites," or "Philosophical Radicals," or "Utilitarians," was but a part of a new tendency or movement which, towards the end of the eighteenth century, began to stir in every province of enquiry. A fresh spirit, the spirit of a more accurate and better reasoned method, the spirit of science, in a word, so rich in resources and fruitful in results, was becoming an informing and animating force. The study of the natural sciences was being carried on with an ardour and success which had been hitherto unknown; it had become to some extent even a fashionable pursuit. The mansion of the Earl of Bridgewater, for instance, was a kind of *rendezvous* for men of mechanical ingenuity and talent; and at Bristol the Pneumatic Institution of Dr. Beddoes was a topic of general conversation in the town. It is a curious thing that writers on political philosophy have not uncommonly been men of scientific tastes. Montesquieu, for example, wrote a treatise on the functions of the renal glands, and on the causes of the weight of bodies; Voltaire wrote essays on the nature of fire, the measurement of motive forces, and did much to spread abroad a knowledge of the Newtonian theories. Even Rousseau composed a system of musical notation. Now from this characteristic the prominent Radicals were not exempt; and many of them were of a distinctly scientific turn of mind, and some of them even of scientific eminence.[1] Priestley himself is *par excellence* an example of the fact; for he will always hold an honoured place in the ranks of English chemists. Thomas Paine was a man with a considerable share of mechanical ingenuity, and he devoted much attention to a plan he had invented for making iron bridges. Earl Stanhope, that clever and eccentric nobleman, is another capital instance of the union in one mind of the radical temperament and the scientific bent. This *soi-disant* "citizen" both planned and constructed a steam-ship and a locomotive engine,

---

[1] Cottle's *Recollections of Coleridge and Southey*, pp. 261-262. It is a curious coincidence that this Dr. Beddoes had under his tuition young Lambton, the future radical politician and Earl of Durham. Parton's *Life of Aaron Burr*, vol. ii., p. 173; Brunetière's *Manual of the History of French Literature*, p. 325.

and suggested improvements in the printing press. Some too of the lesser Radicals were more or less distinguished for their love of science or talent for invention. There was Thomas Rickman with whom Paine lodged when he wrote the *Second Part of The Rights of Man*, and who assisted him in the carrying out of his engineering projects; there was Thomas Cooper, who was deputed by the Manchester Constitutional Society to take a congratulatory address to the Jacobin Club in Paris, was denounced by Robespierre as a spy, returned to England, and finally settled in America, where he distinguished himself as a man of science and a judge; there was James Watt, the son of the famous engineer, who accompanied Cooper in his mission, and who had the remarkable experience of preventing a duel between Danton and Robespierre;[1] there was Thomas Christie, a Scotch doctor, an ardent admirer of the French revolutionary party, who went to Paris in 1792, and was employed in the preparation of the polyglot edition of the brand new Constitution. Nor should it be forgotten that Bentham himself was passionately fond of experimental science, and especially of chemistry; and in indulging his taste for the pursuit he found during the troubles of his early life some degree of consolation. On one occasion he bargained with a chemist to have the sweepings of his shop in phials for half-a-crown; on another, he tells us "I spent half-a-guinea on a quantity of phials and hid them in a closet, in which I surreptitiously made a hole to let in the light". To the study of botany he was devoted all his life, and it is characteristic of the man

---

[1] Southey relates this story of Watt: "From him," he says, "I learn this remarkable fact" (*Life and Correspondence of Robert Southey*, vol. vi. p. 209).

THE SECOND PERIOD, 1789-1831. 171

that he preferred it to geology, because he thought it more likely to lead to directly useful and practical results. That the scientific turn of mind, when applied to the sphere of political inquiry, did, at this time, naturally give a mental bias in the radical direction, it is impossible to doubt; and that is why the men of science were regarded with some amount of suspicion and dislike by those whose instincts were conservative. A course of scientific study was believed to have injurious effects on the mental constitution. It was in this spirit that Gibbon condemned the method of mathematical or rigorous demonstration as destructive "of the finer feelings of moral evidence," that Goethe, perhaps, wrote his pamphlet on the abuse of mathematics; that Burke so vehemently assailed the political philosophy of "the geometricians and the chymists," with their ostentatious indifference to "those feelings and habitudes, which are the supports of the moral world". But perhaps no one has expressed more strongly the feeling of aversion from the scientific turn of mind than Southey did. "Chemical and physical studies," he said in a letter to a friend in 1816, "seem, on the contrary, to draw on very prejudicial consequences. Their utility is not to be doubted; but it appears as if man could not devote himself to these pursuits without blunting his finer faculties". That is a hard saying, and one, doubtless, marked by some exaggeration. But the sentiment is worth noting, because it is extremely characteristic of the time when it was uttered; the time, that is to say, when the scientific method was being applied with extraordinary results to the whole field of mental science, and with political consequences which to most minds were exceedingly abhorrent. "The age we live in," said Bentham writing in

1776, " is a busy age ; in which knowledge is rapidly advancing towards perfection. In the natural world, in particular, everything teems with discovery and with improvement ". It was precisely at this time that politics were beginning to enter upon the third or positive stage, the immediate result being the creation of Philosophic Radicalism. Indeed, the general observation may be hazarded that radicalism—the radicalism, that is to say, which claims to be founded upon reason—arises from the habit of looking on politics from the scientific point of view. There is a theological view of politics, as was that of Mr. Gladstone's at least in the earlier part of his career; there is possibly a literary view such as we might conceive Disraeli to have held; but the scientific view belongs mainly to the Radical.[1]

Jeremy Bentham was, in priority of time and by right of his genius and achievements, the first of the Philosophical Radicals; nay, he is, in some respects, the greatest of all the English Radicals whatsoever. In the development of opinion there is never any break of continuity; there is always some thread of thought, however slender, to be traced; one thinker follows close upon another. *Quasi cursores lampada tradunt;* and of this fact the life of Bentham affords an excellent illustration. Born in 1748, he lived until 1832; so that his long span of eighty-four years bridged two periods remote from one another. But his mental development was continuously

---

[1] Lord Holland's *Memoirs of the Whig Party*, vol. i., pp. 35-37; *The Correspondence of William Wilberforce*, vol. i., p. 107; Rickman's *Life of Paine*; Smiles' *Lives of Boulton and Watt*, p. 415; *The Life and Correspondence of Southey*, vol. iv., p. 191; Bowring's *Life of Bentham*, Collected Works, vol. x., pp. 47, 84; Burke's *Letter to a Noble Lord*; Preface to the First Edition of the *Fragment on Government*.

THE SECOND PERIOD, 1789-1831. 173

one of gradual orderly progression ; and his advance from toryism and eighteenth-century metaphysics to radicalism and ratiocinative methods is unfolded before us like some moving diorama. Bentham is in himself the embodiment of a very striking evolution, and to trace that evolution is an essential and necessary part of a historical account of the English Radicals.

Bentham's life, though prolonged to an age far beyond the common lot, was so devoid of interest, so placid and unruffled, that his story can be very briefly told. He was born in Red Lion Street, Houndsditch, the son of an attorney. Very early he gave signs of precocity of talent, and before he was five years old he had learnt the elements of Greek and Latin from his father. A small and weakly boy, he was, when only in his seventh year, sent to Westminster School, where he remained till he was twelve. So well did he progress that at this very early age he matriculated at Queen's College, Oxford. But the boy-. undergraduate derived very little profit from his stay in that ancient seat of learning, and, already an intellectual rebel, he regarded its soporific life with something like disgust. Gibbon said it was a place of "port and prejudice"; an epigram that contained more wit than malice. But Bentham's mind was fired by an honest indignation, and long afterwards he wrote, "mendacity and insincerity—in these I found the effects—the sure and only sure effects of an English university education". The whole atmosphere of Oxford was, in fact, utterly repugnant to a youth of Bentham's turn of mind, in things both great and small, even in the formal dressing of the hair, which at that time was the fashion. Less fortunate than Landor or Southey, who in a later and somewhat laxer age defied the custom, he sullenly

submitted. "Mine," he said, referring to his hair, "was
turned up in the shape of a kidney; a quince or a club
was against the statutes; a kidney was in accordance
with the statutes." The affair was not without its comic
side, but to Bentham the grievance was evidently real.
When he left the University, he entered Lincoln's Inn,
and sat as a student in the Court of the King's Bench
over which Lord Mansfield—at that time the god of his
idolatry—then presided. He was, it is interesting to
note, present at the trial of Wilkes, the great prototype of
radicalism, and he shared in the dislike that was felt for
him in Tory circles. He returned to Oxford to listen to
Blackstone's Lectures, which he heard, he says, with
"rebel ears". Though called to the Bar, he took a
strong dislike to the practice of the law, to the great
disappointment of his father, who saw in his brilliant son
a Lord Chancellor *in posse*.[1] But the days and nights
that he refused to give to the practice of the law he gave
to its reform with unflagging and disinterested zeal. The
outline of the remainder of his life may be very briefly
sketched; for his visits to Lord Shelburne at Bowood,
which were at one time rather frequent, his continental
tour and residence in Russia with his brother, were
merely incidents in a long career of close and unremitting
studentship. Possessed of an independent competence
that was sufficient for his wants, he was enabled to
pursue the even tenour of his way alike removed from
the perilous extremes of opulence and want. In a
residence at Queen's Square Place, Westminster, fitly
called the Hermitage, with a nice garden shaded by old
trees, upon which the poet Milton's house abutted, he

[1] He said that barristers were so called because they barred the
reform of the law.

lived for many years; though during the earlier portion of the time he was accustomed to make a summer change, first at Barrow Green House,[1] Oxted, Surrey, and afterwards at the splendid old mansion, Ford Abbey, near Chard. To Ford Abbey we shall have to accompany Bentham once at least, but it was at Queen's Square Place that his real life was centred. It was there that his great work was in the main accomplished; it was there that he carried on his busy correspondence with would-be reformers in every quarter of the globe; it was there that he received and entertained his numerous friends from every nation, and from every section of society, from working-man to peer, from Place the tailor to Talleyrand the Prince. Every now and then we are privileged to obtain a peep into the interior, and to see Bentham as he lived, either working in his "scribbling-shop," or taking his "ante-jentacular" or post-prandial walks — "circumgyrating" he sometimes called it—round his garden; or sitting *tête-à-tête* at dinner with a specially invited guest, with the table placed upon a platform so arranged as to admit beneath it a current of warm air; or playing on his organ some masterpiece from one of the great composers—for of music he was passionately fond.

Such in very brief outline was the life, and such the manner of it, of one who almost in his own despite, became during his later years the acknowledged leader of the Radicals. Yet no milder-mannered Radical was ever seen; nor one in whose face there beamed more benevolence and kindliness. The dwarfish sickly boy grew up to healthy manhood, and the man's life, notwithstanding

[1] This house was afterwards occupied for a time by another Philosophic Radical, Grote the Historian.

his persistent and long-continued labours, was, thanks to habits of temperance and frugality, lengthened to an old age which was like a lusty winter. Bentham was one of those persons who may be described as having been never really young or never really old ; for in childhood he had some of the wisdom of the man, and in manhood some of the simplicity of the child. Thus he united in himself the characteristics—too often dissociated—of the sage and the philanthropist; and no higher compliment was ever paid him than that of General Foy, who introduced himself in Paris with the words "*vos mœurs et vos écrits sont peints sur votre visage*". His high forehead, his complacent and contemplative face, is said to have so resembled Franklin's, that Ricardo actually bought a bust of the latter by mistake. In his last years Bentham's appearance must have certainly been singular : his long white hair—"the silver livery of age"—floating down his shoulders, his narrow-rimmed straw hat, his brown coat cut with a quaker-like sobriety, his brown trousers, with white worsted stockings drawn up above the knees, his shoes, his quick and shuffling walk, must have combined to make a somewhat striking figure, that would have arrested the attention of the casual passer by, and have told him that here was no ordinary man.[1] Courteous in his manners, cheerful, almost playful in his humours, disinterested in a nearly unparalleled degree, there is no Radical whose whole being it is more agreeable to contemplate. He had all Cartwright's disinterested zeal for human progress, with intellectual powers that were infinitely greater. For Bentham became the acknowledged

[1] There are two portraits of Bentham in the National Portrait Gallery; one painted at the age of eighteen by Thomas Frye; the other at the age of eighty-one by Pickersgill.

THE SECOND PERIOD, 1789-1831.

eader of the Radicals, not by noise or by agitation or by vainglorious self-advertisement, but by sheer force of intellectual effort; and that was certainly for those days, as, indeed, it would be at any time, a remarkable achievement. It remains to describe how he came by his opinions.

Bentham's intellectual life was so full and active, and touched upon so many different points, that to give an adequate account of it would require a volume to itself. There are many aspects of it upon which it would here be irrelevant to speak; because, paradoxical though it may at first appear, Bentham was not, in the political sense of the term, primarily a Radical. For it is of Bentham as a politician that it concerns us here to speak; and he was never what may be called a very active politician; nor were his strictly political writings by any means as voluminous or important as the other works that proceeded from his pen. His *Fragment on Government*, his *Parliamentary Reform Catechism*, his *Radical Reform Bill*, and his *Radicalism not Dangerous*, constitute the bulk of his political writings. From one point of view he was, indeed, a Radical in everything he wrote;[1] for his method, that of thorough and searching analysis, was everywhere the same. He was in every branch of study, to which he gave his mind, the great questioner of things established, and he only carried into his researches on the principles of government exactly the same method which had proved itself so fruitful of results in other fields. His political radicalism was, in fact, a mere incident in his life; and was even, to some extent, an accident, which arose, as will be seen, from personal

[1] It is characteristic of Bentham that one of his favourite quotations was " Veteres avias tibi de pulmone revello " (Persius, *Satires*, v., 92).

12

causes. Still, his political theories lie in very close relationship with the results of his ethical and juridical inquiries, and can hardly be dissociated from them.

Bentham was, as a young man, a Tory of a rather strong type. As he himself said, "the genius of the place I dwelt in, the authority of the State, the voice of the Church in her solemn offices; all these taught me to call Charles a martyr, and his opponents rebels". He idolised Lord Mansfield, while as to Wilkes, he perfectly abhorred him; "I was," to use his own words, "a determined aristocrat". And what is stranger still, he long remained so, even after he had published some of his best and most characteristic work; it is, indeed, not too much to say that during the first two-thirds of his life Bentham was not consciously a Radical at all. Radicalism as a definite political creed only slowly dawned upon him. But from the very first he was one of those youths who cannot rest content unless they satisfy themselves that there are rational grounds existing for the current opinions of society; and even at this time he was, he says, "a quiet reformist". He was dissatisfied, in short, with the practical working of present institutions, which he thought might be easily amended. But of radicalism in Bentham's mind there was as yet no trace. Nevertheless it is plain that the germ was early planted, and it is very interesting to watch its growth until its final bursting into blossom. When quite a child he read with unalloyed delight Fénélon's *Telemachus*, and to this book—which beneath a quaint guise conveyed the writer's notions of political reform—he traced the origin of that great principle of utility which was destined to become the keystone of his intellectual arch. It is, moreover, highly characteristic of the lad that the state of the Laputans, is described in *Gulliver's Travels*, made him "sad," and that he complained of Molière and of Dr. Johnson that their writings did not give him facts. One of his early favourite books was Helvétius' *De l'Esprit*, and he tells us that when he used to go into the country with his stepmother and his father, he would sometimes walk behind them and read as he went along. That Helvétius should have especially attracted him, and have greatly influenced his mind we cannot wonder, because there was much in that philosopher's opinions with which Bentham, by natural inclination, was ready to agree. For Helvétius expressed his belief that ethics should be treated according to the methods of experimental physics, and that all questions of morality were really social questions, because ' the vices of a people lie hid in its legislation ". Again his contempt for precedent and tradition—his averment, for example, that " it is by weakening the foolish veneration of the masses for ancient laws and customs that sovereigns will be enabled to rid the earth of the greater number of the evils that afflict it "—must have appealed to Bentham very strongly.[1] But it was Priestley in his *Essay on Government*, who first taught, he says, his lips to pronounce " the sacred truth," that " the greatest happiness of the greatest number is the foundations of morals and legislation ". For it happened by the merest chance that, when in his twenty-second year, he met with a copy of the *Essay* at Harper's Coffee House in Oxford, and its effect on his mind was instantaneous and immense. The compact and novel phrase was like an illuminating flash amid the darkness; " at the sight of it," he says, " I cried out, as it were, in an inward ecstasy, like Archimedes

[1] Brunetière's *Manual of the History of French Literature*, pp. 327, 330, 333.

on the discovery of the fundamental principle of hydro
statics, εὕρηκα!" From this time forward Bentham'
intellectual course was clear before him; the whole fiel
of thought and action lay mapped out like a chart, an
chaos was transmuted into orderly arrangement. Fo
Priestley his admiration was immense, and he calle
Warrington, where Priestley wrote his treatise, a classi
ground.[1] Yet Priestley was not the first to make use o
this epoch-making phrase; for it was actually employe
by Hutcheson in his *Inquiry Concerning Moral Good an
Evil*, where it seems to have lain neglected and unfruitful
As Bentham continued his researches he came across th
phrase again in an Italian form in Beccaria's illluminat
ing work on Crimes and Punishment, which was pub
lished as early as 1754; and the words *la màssima felicit
nel maggior numero* (a text worked out by the author wit
very great ability) served to confirm his belief in th
correctness of his views. From one other source, he tell
us, he derived fresh argumentative material, upon whic
to build his superstructure; for in David Hume's *Treatis
on Human Nature* he found the thesis that the foundation
of all virtue are laid in utility demonstrated "with th
strongest force of evidence". Such were the hints, th
germs, the prefigurements of the Philosophical or Utili
tarian Radicalism of which Bentham was destined to be
come the founder. The next important step in Bentham'
mental history was his attendance on Blackstone's cours
of lectures on English Law at Oxford. Those lecture
indeed, were a great advance on any yet delivered on th
subject, and, as Bentham justly says, Blackstone was th

[1] Yet Bentham did not like Priestley personally—"Dr. Priestley w
no favourite of mine; I thought him cold and assuming" (Bowring's *Li
of Bentham*, vol. x. of his Collected Works, p. 571).

THE SECOND PERIOD, 1789-1831.

first who taught "jurisprudence to speak the language of the scholar and the gentleman". But its introductory passages were obnoxious to the attacks which Bentham, and he only, knew how to make. He saw his opportunity, and in his *Fragment on Government* he used it to the full. This model of keen and polished criticism was published anonymously in 1776, though his father subsequently let the secret out; and so ably was it written, and so widely recognised were its merits, that it was variously ascribed to Lords Mansfield, Ashburton and Camden. The publication of the book was, indeed, the turning-point in Bentham's life, for it brought him the inestimable friendship of Lord Shelburne, who sought him out in his 'dog-hole in the Temple," and praised the work "outrageously". That very able nobleman, so strangely misunderstood by his contemporaries, and nicknamed " the Jesuit of Berkeley Square," had already provided employment and a competence for one Radical philosopher, Joseph Priestley. He now performed an immense service for another. He made himself Bentham's protector, friend and patron; as Bentham gratefully acknowledged, ' he raised me from the bottomless pit of humiliation, and made me feel that I was something".[1] From this time forward until Shelburne's death their friendship was unclouded, save only for a brief period when Bentham was annoyed because Shelburne failed to keep an alleged promise to bring him into Parliament. For months

[1] Bentham says of Shelburne: "Though desirous of rising, he was desirous of rising by means of the people. He was really *radically* disposed; and he witnessed the French Revolution with sincere delight " Bowring's *Life of Bentham*, vol. x. of his Collected Works, p. 187). The Abbé Morellet told Shelburne that he was occupied with the art of making men happy, "celle que vous aimez" (*Lettres de l'Abbé Morellet à Lord Shelburne*, 26th August, 1774).

together Bentham lived as an honoured guest at Bowood, and yet it was in that hospitable mansion that he went through the experiences that converted him to radicalism. In the preface to the second edition of the *Fragment on Government*—one of the most curious and interesting bits of autobiography in literature—he tells us how this conversion came about. The story he relates is composed of trivial incidents which would be merely ridiculous if they had not led to such important consequences. It is, however, what Carlyle would have called "a genuine human utterance"! When he wrote the *Fragment on Government*, and when he first set foot in Bowood, he never suspected, he says, that the people in power were set against reform; he supposed that they only wanted to know what was good in order to embrace it. But his intercourse with certain great personages entirely disillusioned him. To begin with, Lord Mansfield, who had praised the book, and from whom he expected some kindly hospitality, suffered him to languish in the cold shade of neglect. Then Wedderburn (afterwards Lord Loughborough and Earl of Rosslyn) not only condemned the principle of utility as a "dangerous" one, but he wounded Bentham's *amour propre* by a seeming want of courtesy. Next, Lord Camden stigmatised his book on the *Principles of Morals and Legislation* as difficult of comprehension, and offended Bentham greatly by telling him that he ate too much at Bowood, and that he accompanied his daughter, when she sang, too loudly on the violin. Finally Dunning (afterwards Lord Ashburton) treated him, as he thought, with considerable rudeness. Now all these slights, whether real or imaginary, though, when taken singly, insignificant, produced a great effect upon a temperament which was highly sensitive to impressions from without. Full of suspicions, he came to the conclusion that all these eminent lawyers were angry with him because they saw that his principles, if carried into practice, would be fatal to their interests, and that for that reason they wished to poison Shelburne's mind against him. The intrigue proved, he said, that in England "the particular interest of the rulers is in direct opposition to almost everything that is good". This was not the first time in the history of the world, nor will it be the last, that a man's speculative opinions have been derived from, or strengthened by, his personal experiences; but in the case of Bentham, the fact strikes one as incongruous, for no one ever lived who applied his reasoning faculties with more persistent and unmitigated rigour. Yet he suffered—for he had his human frailties—his mind to be perverted by some trivial incidents, which a man of coarser fibre might have not so much as even noticed.

The effect of the French Revolution upon Bentham was not as great as might have been expected. He was never carried away by the prevailing gusts of enthusiasm; he rather looked upon the movement from the point of view of benevolent neutrality. He was, indeed, consulted by some of the actors in those dramatic scenes, and Mirabeau himself is said to have derived the material for some of his speeches from Bentham through the medium of Dumont; it was, therefore, only what might have been expected that Bentham's name was placed amongst the list of foreigners who were elected French citizens by the National Convention. But Bentham, though he had many of the characteristics of the eighteenth century philosophers, was exempt from the worst of their intellectual vices, which, when given free play in the French

Revolution, converted what might have been a moderate and orderly reform into a scene of bloody chaos. No one has ever more acutely diagnosed the folly of the "pompous" generalities contained in the Declaration of Rights, which in the opinion of many was the especial glory of revolutionary France. "I am sorry," he writes to Brissot, "you have undertaken to publish a Declaration of Rights. It is a metaphysical work—the *ne plus ultra* of metaphysics. It may have been a necessary evil, but it is nevertheless an evil. Political science is not far enough advanced for such a declaration." And again in his *Anarchical Fallacies*: "The things that people stand most in need of being reminded of are, one would think, their duties; for their rights, whatever they may be, they are apt enough to attend to of themselves . . . the great enemies of public peace are the selfish and dissocial passions. . . . What has been the object, the perpetual and palpable object, of this declaration of pretended rights? To add as much force as possible to those passions, already but too strong, to burst the cords that hold them in; to say to the selfish passions, There, everywhere is your prey! to the angry passions, There, everywhere is your enemy!" The abnegation here expressed of metaphysics is no less important than the perception of the danger that lurks in vague and general statements. *Dolus latet in universalibus.* To the neglect of this truth how many fatal errors must be due! Yet Bentham himself sometimes did not avoid the pitfall.[1]

By the beginning of the nineteenth century Bentham

[1] In like manner he condemned the American Declaration of Rights, calling it "a hodge-podge of confusion and absurdity, in which the thing to be proved is all along taken for granted" (Bowring's *Life of Bentham*, vol. x. of Collected Works, p. 63).

THE SECOND PERIOD, 1789-1831.

had probably arrived at the last stage of his political development; he had become a full-blown Radical. Yet, though he was over fifty years of age, he was still in his own country by no means accounted as a prophet. His fame, however, was beginning; for we find him writing to Dumont in 1802 : "Benthamite! What sort of animal is that? I can't find any such word in Boyer's *Dictionary.*" This naïve repudiation of the notion that he was founding a kind of sect or school is at all events conclusive proof that even then he was attracting some followers or disciples. How he arrived at his radicalism has already been described; but it remains yet to consider more in detail those principles of government upon which his creed was based.

Bentham was before everything a law reformer; it was in the field of jurisprudence that he reigned unrivalled and supreme. He found the study of the law a chaos, a tangled "wilderness of single instances," and he left it a science—a science of which he has been not inaptly called the Newton. In some departments, that of the penal law, for instance, he did his work so thoroughly that nothing remained but to put his theories into practice.[1] His writings, their ends being now accomplished, seem many of them so entirely out of date that he has been compared to Samson who perished in the ruins of the temple he destroyed. Compared with his work on law reform, his writings on political science are of very little value; but, strongly prejudiced and inconclusive though they are, they are of very great importance as containing the germ of the philosophical radicalism

[1] As Brissot well said : "Howard had devoted himself to the reform of prisons; Bentham to that of the laws that peopled the prisons" (Bowring's *Life of Bentham,* vol. x., p. 192).

which was destined to be so ably thought out and developed by the small group of friends who gathered round him. The foundation of his creed was based on his belief, so unalterable that it might be described as an *idée fixe* or an obsession, that self-preference was the clue to human nature. He even denied the possibility of disinterested conduct upon the part of any governors whatever; no system of government ever had or could have had, he thought, for its actual and principal end in view the good of any other persons than the very individuals by whom on each occasion the powers of it were exercised. That all governments then existing were cruelly and ineradicably selfish was his deliberate conviction; and, as to the English one, he could not even damn it with faint praise; it was "a cover for rascality"; at the best it was of all bad governments "the least bad". He noticed that the great personages whom he was wont to meet at Bowood were always engaged in a discussion about what *was* and seldom or never about *what ought to be*; and as they had none of them Bentham's master passion for improvement, his observation was undoubtedly correct. But he inferred that they were not merely not anxious for improvement but—a rather rash deduction—that they were actively opposed to it. Now this was undoubtedly a very simple principle and one easy to apply; as he himself said, everything that had served to make the field of politics a labyrinth had vanished; a clue to the interior had been found. It was a principle that made Bentham in theory a determined republican and democrat. Though in answer to the French National Convention, when they elected him a citizen, he declared himself "a Royalist in London," to the principle of monarchy he was bitterly opposed. The King he called the "Corrupter-General";

THE SECOND PERIOD, 1789-1831.

upon the vices of kingship he never wearied of insisting : " In the ethics of a monarch there is," he said, " but one virtue, obsequiousness to his will ; there is but one vice, resistance to it ". Nor did the aristocracy fare any better at his hands ; it is "a many-headed incubus " ; " a member of the aristocracy looks upon himself as the richer by every pleasure he deprives the democracy of " ; " if the lower orders have been called the dregs of the population, the higher may by a much clearer title be termed the scum of it ". As to the ordinary party politics of the country, they merely excited his contempt. " All parties," he said, " are, in fact, at all times resolvable into two ; that which is in possession, and that which is in expectancy of the sweets of government. . . . This state of things is of the essence of mixed monarchy." And again : " The world of politics is by acknowledgment of both parties divided into two opposite regions, the world of major and the world of minor purity ; where the one party places the major, the other places the minor excellence. At the summit of both, high in the region of the clouds, in the portrait drawn by both, sits royal excellence." The English Constitution—the " matchless Constitution " he used ironically to call it—he stigmatised as " aristocracy-ridden " and " lawyer-ridden," and as aiming at " the maximisation of depredation and oppression ".

Such then were the judgments on the English government deliberately formulated and passed by Bentham in all sincerity of conviction. What then were the remedies he proposed for a state of things which, if true, was in the highest degree distressing and alarming ? Radical reform or " the abolition of corruptive influence " was, he thought, the object to be steadily kept in view. But how was this much-wished-for consummation to be reached? In Bentham's opinion radical reform was resolvable into the four elements of secrecy, universality, equality and annuality. What he meant exactly by these terms must be carefully considered.

By secrecy he meant, of course, the vote by ballot. It will be remembered that the earlier class of Radicals were, in the main, opposed to secret voting, which seemed to them to savour of insincerity and cowardice. Cartwright, however, convinced himself at last that without the ballot there could be no real freedom of election, and as Bentham allowed, he was the first to take up strongly this measure of reform. He planned a model ballot-box, and in his *Bill of Rights and Liberties*, which he published in 1817, he gave a description and picture of a so-called polling table. But if Cartwright was the first to advocate the ballot, Bentham was no less zealous in its cause; he thought, indeed, that without this security all other reforms were nothing worth. By universality he meant universal suffrage, but on this subject his opinions were halting and uncertain. He explained that by universality he meant "virtual" universality, in order to make way for the exclusion of idiots, lunatics and criminals. But with the question of female suffrage (which logically follows upon universal suffrage) he never fairly grappled; he, in fact, shirked it in a manner which was hardly worthy of him. To say that "no man appears to mean that females should vote," or that "as to anything approaching a decided opinion, anything of that sort, any attempt towards it, would in this place be altogether premature," is hardly an effective contribution to the discussion of the question. Upon the whole subject of the franchise Bentham was strangely inconsistent and uncertain. While he thought that ability to read should be made an educational qualification for a voter, or, to use his own words, that "non-reading" ought to be a "defalcation," he seems to have been perfectly willing to allow universal suffrage to precede a properly organised system of popular education. He imagined that such a "defalcation" would in practice hardly operate at all, because he fondly believed that all illiterates would learn to read without delay—a sanguine view which actual facts have hardly justified. Moreover, he says he would have been content with household suffrage: "I, for my part," he says, "would gladly compound for household suffrage"; and yet he was perfectly aware that such a limitation it was impossible to maintain upon any rational grounds consistent with his principles. As to equality, he has not expressed his meaning very clearly; but it may be presumed that he was thinking of equal electoral districts. By annuality he meant a general election every year, though here too he expressed himself with hesitation; for he was personally willing to compound for triennial Parliaments, just as he was for household suffrage.

These, then, were the means by which Bentham hoped to overcome the self-preference, the "interest-begotten prejudice," which, he believed, naturally belonged to those placed in authority and power. That an identity of interest in the governors and the governed was the only security for good government, that from such an identity the security would infallibly and necessarily follow, that the majority of the people know their own interest, and, so knowing it, invariably pursue it, were the essential and distinctive propositions of his creed.[1] To attain that security, therefore, all his speculations were directed. It is here that Bentham differed from the Radicals who had gone before him, though he resembled them in many ways. Like them he had a passion for improvement, like them he glowed with an inextinguishable optimism. Speaking of himself in the third person, he said: "Bentham is the most ambitious of the ambitious. His empire—the empire he aspires to —extending to, and comprehending, the whole human race, in all places, in all habitable places of the earth, *at all future time*." Compared with such an aspiration Bacon's claim to have taken all knowledge for his province is modesty itself. "Twenty years after I am dead," he said, "I shall be a despot." He wished that centuries after his death he could come again on earth to watch his principles producing their beneficent results. Here, indeed, was faith that could remove mountains. He seems to have believed that the lot of man could be indefinitely ameliorated by some ingenious reformation of the prisons, as worked out in the plan he called "Panopticon". Like the early Radicals he was a great believer in simplicity in government. "Prejudice and imposture always seek obscurity," "State secrets are State iniquities," "Complication is the nursery of fraud," and similar remarks, were among his favourite sentiments. Like the early Radicals he was a strong parliamentary reformer, in the general sense of demanding an extension of the suffrage, a redistribution of seats, and shorter Parliaments. Like Paine and his followers he denounced

---

[1] Bentham classified the elements of happiness as follows: 1. Subsistence; 2. Abundance; 3. Equality; 4. Security. He thought that the last was much the most important, and from it the rest would follow. See Bowring's edition of *Bentham's Works*, vol. i., p. 33.

the Monarchy, and the House of Lords. So, too, he disliked—though he rather hinted his opinion than openly declared it—the standing army. But in some respects he broke away from the earlier Radical beliefs. As there has already been occasion to remark, he repudiated metaphysical abstractions, and such things as abstract rights. Essentially a practical-reformer,-a born organiser of the business arrangements of society, he looked forward to progress in this direction, rather than built his hopes upon high-sounding declarations of "glittering generalities". Yet he was, like the Radicals before him, a sturdy individualist; he sought to strike off the fetters which had been unnaturally imposed upon society by law and ancient custom; he dreamed of a millennium of an equality of opportunity, and he, therefore, hated privilege. On the other hand, he did not express himself in favour of the theory that parliamentary representatives are merely delegates who ought to obey instructions, and might properly be called upon to bind themselves by pledges; nor did he advocate the payment of members of Parliament by constituencies or by the State. He looked rather to other means to secure what he called the "due dependence" of parliamentary representatives;—annuality of election in the first place, and in the next, some regulations to ensure constant attendance in the House. So suspicious was he of the corrupting influence of Parliament upon its members, that he approved, though with a good deal of hesitation, of a provision inserted in the Spanish Constitution of 1812, that no deputy should be re-eligible. In order to avert the patent disadvantages of this extraordinary arrangement, he recommended the formation of a Continuation Committee to carry on the work of one session into the next. On this question of re-eligibility of representatives Bentham stands alone among the Radicals.

Before entering on a criticism of philosophical radicalism as a whole, it will be convenient to say something of that brilliant and interesting group of men who were more or less Bentham's intimate friends, and moved within the circle of his influence. It is not a little strange that the sage was better known for many years in foreign countries than at home; as Hazlitt well put it, his reputation lay at the circumference, and the lights of his understanding were reflected with increasing lustre at the other side of the globe. His voice had gone forth into all lands. This result was, no doubt, largely due to the self-sacrificing labours of Dumont, a native of Geneva, who deemed Bentham's speculations of such importance to mankind that he devoted his life to putting the philosopher's scattered writings into systematic shape—a by no means easy task. And what is more, he translated them into French, the language that was then the great literary medium. In the United States, indeed, his writings were caviare to the general; for serious works were in that country little read, and to study Bentham was deemed a mark of holding very advanced opinions. In Spain, upon the other hand, contrary to what might have been expected, the Benthamite philosophy was better known and more appreciated than in almost any other country;[1] a fact which may partly be accounted for

[1] Bowring's *Life of Bentham*, vol. x., p. 433; Parton's *Life of Aaron Burr*, vol. i., p. 155; Borrow's *Bible in Spain*, vol. ii., chap. xii., where the Galician Alcade says to Borrow: "The grand Baintham. He who has invented laws for all the world. I hope shortly to see them adopted in this unhappy country of ours." See an article in the *Law Quarterly Review* for January 1895, "A Spanish View of Bentham's Spanish in-

by the efforts of Blaquière, an enthusiastic Benthamite, who moved about the Iberian Peninsula like an itinerant apostle. But it was long before Bentham was widely known in England, and he was actually sixty years of age and only in the beginning of his fame when he was introduced in 1808 to the man who became his greatest disciple, and the most powerful and original expounder of philosophic radicalism. This man was James Mill.

James Mill was born at Northwater Bridge, Forfarshire, in 1773, the son of a shoemaker. He received his education at the Montrose Academy, where among his friends and school-fellows was one who was also destined to become a famous Radical, the notorious Joseph Hume. A studious youth, and showing an early promise of ability, Mill went to complete his education at the University of Edinburgh. After a brief period of a tutorship of the daughter of Sir James Stuart, and having been licensed to preach in the Presbyterian Church, he, like many an able Scotsman before his time and since, found his way to London. There he began his career by writing for John Gifford in the *Anti-Jacobin Review*. He also planned and edited the *Literary Journal*, and for a few years managed the *St. James's Chronicle;* he wrote articles for various periodicals, and his well-known *History of British India*. In a word he lived the life of the laborious man of letters. It was in 1808 that he reached his mental turning-point, and was introduced to Bentham. Mill was at that time living at Stoke Newington, and he used to dine at Queen's Square Place once a week. The two men soon became very intimate, and in 1810 Bentham allowed his friend to live in the house next his

fluence". And yet by a curious irony of fate Spain is now one of the worst governed countries in Europe.

own, once occupied by Milton. After a brief stay Mill moved to Newington Green, but in 1814 he was offered another house by Bentham in Queen's Square Place, where he lived for sixteen years. Nor was this the limit of Bentham's generosity; for he invited the whole Mill family to stay with him at Barrow Green House and Ford Abbey. Their friendship was, therefore, very close, and though they had occasional differences, yet it was only put an end to by Bentham's death in 1832. A man of middle height, of good figure, with a massive head and forehead, and light grey eyes which sparkled with intelligence—he is said to have strongly resembled Charles XII. of Sweden—it is no wonder that Mill made a great impression on the philosopher, who was not slow to recognise his powers. Nor is it to be wondered at that Mill ardently adopted Bentham's views on the principles of government, and became an uncompromising Radical. "I was the spiritual father of Mill," was one of Bentham's sayings, and to the end of his life he always spoke of him with pride. Writing to Chamberlain Clark in 1828 he said: "He was one of the earliest and most influential of my disciples"; and in the same year he wrote to Rammohun Roy: "For these three or four and twenty years he has numbered himself among my disciples; for upwards of twenty years he has been receiving my instructions". This, no doubt, was a claim which was perfectly well-founded, but Mill was an original and independent thinker, who was a slave to no authority. In some branches of inquiry, psychology and political economy for example, he accomplished much, where Bentham did practically nothing. But it is his political writings that we are concerned with here, because they form an elaborate exposition of his own radicalism in particular, and of philosophic radicalism in general. There was nothing, however, in Mill's experiences of life, as there was in those of Bentham, to give him a strongly personal bias in the Radical direction. He was, indeed, a man of humble origin, but he never suffered from the contumely which is too often the reward of patient merit. He merely adopted Bentham's theory of self-preference in governors, and worked it out in detail with extraordinary skill. As a reasoner upon the ultimate principles of government he was much superior to Bentham, who, as has already been remarked, excelled in quite another field, and it is to Mill that the first definite exposition of philosophic radicalism must properly be ascribed.

It has been commonly supposed that Bentham was the founder of a philosophic school, and taught a number of disciples whom he intended to become the propagandists of his creed. His influence was certainly immense; he was like a sun around which many constellations clustered. But the conception of Bentham as the master is not altogether accurate. The use of the word "Benthamite," as has already been seen, struck him with amazement, and his surprise was natural enough; for as far as he personally was concerned, there was never any oral teaching, nor was there any esoteric school that hung upon his lips. His influence was almost entirely derived from the publication of his writings, and he thus obtained an audience fit though few. If he invited guests to dine with him, it was his usual custom to entertain them singly, and he conversed for relaxation merely. Sometimes, indeed, a person who wanted to consult him would not await an invitation, as was once the case with Brougham who wrote him the following extraordinary note : " Grandpapa, I want some pap; I will come for it at your dinner-hour".[1] That Bentham never formed a school, in the proper sense of the term, is expressly stated by James Mill. "It is also," he said, "a matter of fact that until within a very few years of the death of Mr. Bentham the men of any pretension to letters who shared his intimacy and saw enough of him to have the opportunity of learning much from his lips were, in number, two." These were Dumont and Mill himself. The latter became a kind of living bridge between the recluse philosopher and the world, and in no other sense than that of accepting the philosophy of Bentham was there any such thing as a school of Benthamites at all. It would indeed be much more true to say that a school was formed by Mill, who by his earnestness and dialectical skill obtained an extraordinary ascendency over the minds of the young men who came to hear him. "The notion," says J. S. Mill, "that Bentham was surrounded by a band of disciples who received their opinions from his lips is a fable. . . . But my father exercised a far greater personal ascendency. He was sought for the vigour and instructiveness of his conversation, and did use it largely as an instrument for the diffusion of his opinions." Of this fact there is ample testimony. "He was, indeed," says Mrs. Grote, "a propagandist of a high order, equally master of pen and speech. Moreover he possessed the faculty of kindling in his auditors the generous impulses towards the popular side, both in politics and social theories; leading them at the same time to regard the cultivation of individual

---

[1] Sir John Bowring's *Autobiographical Recollections*. Perhaps it was in answer to this note that Bentham wrote to Brougham a letter beginning: "To Master Henry Brougham. Naughty, naughty boy! Pap for you? Oh no! No more of that!"

affections and sympathies as destructive of lofty aims, and indubitably hurtful to the mental character." Of Mill in the capacity of teacher, the Historian of Greece has drawn for us an admirable picture: "His unpremeditated oral exposition was hardly less effective than his prepared work with his pen. . . . Conversation with him was not merely instructive but provocative to the dormant intelligence. Of all persons whom we have known, Mr. Mill was the one who stood least remote from the lofty Platonic ideal of dialectic: τοῦ διδόναι καὶ δέχεσθαι λόγον (the giving and receiving of reasons); competent alike to examine others or to be examined by them upon philosophy." It is therefore to Mill that the gradual formation of the group of thinkers known as Benthamites must be ascribed.

What then were the principles of Government adopted by James Mill, which he so elaborately developed and upon which he raised his superstructure of philosophic radicalism? His philosophy of politics he never expounded in any formal treatise; it is to be gathered rather from sundry scattered articles and from a controversial work upon Sir James Mackintosh's *Dissertation* upon the Principles of Morals. The articles, however, were collected and published in a single volume in 1828. Two of them contained the kernel of his teaching; one the famous article on *Government* written in 1820 for the *Supplement to the Encyclopædia Britannica*, and afterwards reprinted by his friends; and the other, the still more famous article which appeared in the first number of the *Westminster Review* in 1824—an article which John Stuart Mill considered the greatest blow ever struck for radicalism. Like Bentham, he started from the premise that self-love is paramount in politics, and argued that the only security for good government was an identity of interest between the governors and the governed. But he was not content with simple affirmation; he brought together a mass of authority in support of his contention. He went even back to Plato and his description in the *Republic* of the guardians of the State: "Without identity of interest with those they rule, the rulers, instead of being the guardians of the flock, become wolves and its devourers".[1] He relied on the authority of Berkeley: " Self-love being a principle of all others the most universal and the most deeply engraven on our hearts, it is natural to regard things as they are fitted to augment or impair our own happiness ".[2] And so too he relied on David Hume: " Political writers have established it as a maxim, that in contriving any system of government, and fixing the several checks and controls of the Constitution, every man ought to be supposed a knave, and to have no other end in all his actions than private interest. . . . If we find that by the skilful division of power this interest must necessarily in its operation concur with the public, we may pronounce that government to be wise and happy."[3] He even drew some weapons from the armoury of his opponents, as where he quoted Blackstone's saying that self-love is "the universal principle of action "; or Burke's, that "nothing is security to any individual but the common interest of all ".[4] Having satisfied himself

---

[1] See Plato's *Republic*, bks. iii. and v. " There is no author to whom my father thought himself more indebted for his own mental culture than Plato, or whom he more frequently recommended to young students. I can bear similar testimony in regard to myself" (J. S. Mill's *Autobiography*, p. 21).
[2] Berkeley, *Works*, vol. ii., p. 7.
[3] Hume's *Essay on the Independence of Parliament.*
[4] Blackstone's *Commentaries*, Introduction, sec. ii.; and Burke's Letter to the Sheriffs of Bristol.

that he was fortified by adequate authority, he argued that "the end of government" is "to increase to the utmost the pleasures and diminish to the utmost the pains which men derive from each other"; that "the greatest possible happiness of society is attained by issuing to every man the greatest possible quantity of the produce of his labour"; and that the foundation of all government is based upon the fact that "one human being will desire to render the person and property of another subservient to his pleasures". From these premises he deduced that democracy is the only possible form of good government. Aristocracy is bad, because "one man if stronger than another will take from him whatever that other possesses and he desires"; and an aristocracy is a group of persons who are stronger than the rest of the community. For the same reason a monarchy is bad. Both aristocracies and monarchies induce their subjects to conform to their will either by inflicting pain or by bestowing favours, which it can only do by plundering some persons. "Terror is the grand instrument," and to the subjects will finally be left "the bare means of subsistence," and the endurance of "that degree of cruelty which is necessary to keep in existence the most intense terrors". And so too there can be no mixed form of government composed of democracy, aristocracy and monarchy, though Blackstone vainly argued that a balance of the three was the peculiar glory of the English Constitution; because any two of them might combine to swallow up the third, and they would invariably do so. It follows that the solution of all difficulties will probably be found in "the grand discovery of modern times, the system of representation"; for otherwise the conclusion would inevitably follow that good government is impossible. There must be, therefore, a body to act as a check upon the governors, with ability to check; and such a body must have an identity of interest with the mass of the community. The checking body must consist of those who choose the representatives; and those who choose must be the community at large, for otherwise there might not be an identity of interest between them and the community. A democracy, in short, is the only form of government in which a security for good government can possibly exist.

Such, very briefly, were Mill's principles of government in general. In their application to the English Constitution in particular, though he objected to a monarchy in theory, he did not share Bentham's enthusiastic admiration for republics, and was content with constitutional kingship as at least a temporary makeshift. Upon the aristocracy, however, he fell with all his fury; and by the aristocracy he meant much more than the House of Lords. He included in the term the great families who were the owners of the parliamentary seats, the plutocrats who bought their nominations, the English Church and the lawyers—the two "props" he called them— whose support was bribed by patronage, and the standing army, which supplied the force upon which the whole superstructure rested. He divided society into *Ceux qui pillent*—the Ruling Few, and *Ceux qui sont pillés* —the Subject Many; and to prevent the perpetuation of this inequitable system was the *raison d'être* of radicalism. The community at large must, therefore, appoint their parliamentary representatives to act as "watchmen" on the government; but it is necessary also that some plan should be devised in order that the "watchmen" may be watched and compelled to do their duty. This end can only be secured by giving the voters perfect liberty of choice, or, in other words, by the introduction of the ballot; by enabling them to know what their representatives are doing; or, in other words, by freedom of the press and parliamentary reporting; and, lastly, by enabling them to replace their representatives when they wished, or in other words, by short Parliaments. Whether he would have been content with anything less than universal suffrage and annual Parliaments, there is no certain means of knowing, but it is probable that, like Bentham, he would have been willing to accept as an instalment household suffrage and triennial Parliaments. Upon female suffrage, however, he declared himself in no uncertain terms; and this was perhaps the only question upon which he and Bentham greatly differed. The latter, we are told by John Stuart Mill, was wholly on the side of those younger Radicals who favoured female suffrage, and he is said to have declared that James Mill's view about the inaptitude of women was "abominable". But however that may be, Mill disposed of the question in a summary manner with the argument that the interest of women "is involved either in that of their fathers or in that of their husbands". The conclusion is, at all events, explicit, but the reasoning in the opinion of many will not be considered satisfactory.[1]

John Stuart Mill has well remarked that, just as Brutus was called the last of the Romans, so his father might not improperly be styled "the last of the eighteenth century," continuing its tone of thought, though not unmodified nor unimproved, into the nineteenth. That is indisputably true; for in the mind of the elder Mill the tendencies of the two centuries were ever striving for

[1] J. S. Mill's *Autobiography;* Bowring's *Life of Bentham*, Collected Works, vol. x., p. 450.

the mastery. When, for instance, he affirmed that the cultivation of a man's affections and sympathies were inimical to lofty aims and hurtful to the mental character, he adopted a sentiment of Godwin, who was preeminently an eighteenth-century philosopher.[1] But when he adopted Bentham's methods, he was animated with a large measure of the nineteenth century spirit; and it was one of his great merits that he was, as his own son said, the earliest Englishman of any mark to understand thoroughly and adopt Bentham's general views of ethics, government and laws. Those views he assimilated and made his own so completely that he gave "the distinguishing character," to quote John Stuart Mill again, to what was known as Benthamism. James Mill and Bentham might be called the twin hierophants of philosophical radicalism, which was the outcome of the mental characteristics of them both. In the main, James Mill, like Bentham, did not differ very greatly from the Radicals before him. He was, of course, a parliamentary reformer; he was a sturdy individualist; he demanded shorter Parliaments; he disliked the standing army. On the other hand, he was strongly in favour of the ballot. He did not ask for payment of parliamentary representatives, nor did he hold the theory that they were merely delegates who ought to be strictly bound by pledges. He looked rather to short Parliaments, to a free press and the reporting of debates, in order to secure to the community the control over their representatives which he thought they ought to have.[2] Nor did he make a fetish,

[1] It is curious that James Mill seems never to have known Godwin personally (Bain's *James Mill*, p. 80).

[2] Bentham says that Mill held the opinion that a man should not hold office under forty years of age. There does not appear to be any confirmation of this statement (Bowring's *Life of Bentham*, Works, vol. x., p. 450).

THE SECOND PERIOD, 1789-1831. 203

as Cartwright did, and Bentham was inclined to do, of simplicity in government. There was one trait in Mill's character, however, which distinguishes him from other Radicals; that is to say, he was not optimistic; he dreamed no dreams of the dawning of a social or political millennium; at the most he was but soberly hopeful of the future. His outlook on life, indeed, was rather dreary; "he thought," says John Stuart Mill, "human life a poor thing at best, after the freshness of youth and unsatisfied curiosity had gone by". That was a most unusual attitude for one who belonged to the class of sanguine thinkers.[1]

The next, in order of importance, of the Benthamites, and, though not so well remembered as some others, not by any means the least, was Francis Place. To many persons in these days, to most perhaps, his very name will be unknown; so fleeting are human reputations. But he was one of those men who loved quiet power, and kept himself as much as possible in the background; he was, in short, to use an expression which Mr. Gladstone applied to the Earl of Aberdeen, one of the most suppressed characters in history. Born in 1771, when the storm aroused by the Wilkes agitation was subsiding, he entered life under the most inauspicious circumstances. The son of a brutal father, who was turnkey of a debtors' prison in the vicinity of Drury Lane, and to amuse himself used to knock his children down, he received a wretched education, and, when quite a youth, was apprenticed to a leather-breeches maker. In this trade, from strikes and other causes, he suffered great privations, and though a strong constitution enabled him to

[1] John Stuart Mill's *Autobiography*, p. 48; Bain's *James Mill;* Lord Lytton's *England and the English*, Appendix C.

survive them, the iron entered into his soul in a way that he was never able to forget. But from the first he had an ardent love of learning, and by dint of great industry and a naturally vigorous understanding, he contrived to teach himself an amount of knowledge, which, all things considered, was amazing. In 1794 he joined the London Corresponding Society, one of the first of working men's political associations, and began to show his natural bent for political organisation by taking an active part in its meetings and discussions. Of this Society something already has been said, and it need not be repeated here. It must be enough to note that the political programme, which the Society adopted, contained among its items, besides the usual radical demands for universal suffrage and annual Parliaments, a proposal for the payment of parliamentary representatives. This proposal had also commended itself to the moderate Whig Society of the Friends of the People, so that at this time it could not have been considered a revolutionary notion. The Treason and Sedition Acts of 1795, and the coquetting of some of the members of the committee with the United Irishmen in 1798, caused the death of the Society in which Place had played such a very influential part. But he had already become a confirmed agnostic and a Radical of an uncompromising type. For the part he took in publishing a cheap edition of Paine's *Age of Reason* he narrowly escaped imprisonment. Yet all this time he did not neglect his trade: he made leather-breeches well, as he did everything well to which he turned his hand; and in 1799 he had enterprise enough to open a shop for himself at Charing Cross. So well did it succeed that in twenty years he was able to leave it with a fortune. Rarely has a man so completely

THE SECOND PERIOD, 1789-1831. 205

surmounted the bar of circumstances, or so happily grasped the golden fruit that nods upon the bough of opportunity.

It was in 1808, the same year in which James Mill became acquainted with Bentham, that James Mill and Place were introduced to one another. This was the intellectual climacteric of Place's life. He was at this time the prosperous tailor, though a most unprepossessing-looking person and to all outward appearance, with his short thick-set figure, sallow skin, black hair and bushy beard and whiskers, one of the least likely individuals to become the associate and friend of two such philosophers as Mill and Bentham.[1] Yet with both thinkers his friendship became intimate and lasting ; they taught him their philosophy, and he, an excellent man of business, in return performed for them many a useful service and brought them into closer contact with the world, with which, living, as they did, the contemplative life, they might have failed to keep in touch. The picture is a curious one: the tailor on his way to leave a parcel at a customer's house calling at Queen's Square Place where the philosopher resided ; or, again, at Ford Abbey, the philosopher with his long white hair hanging down his shoulders, either writing in his library or " circumgyrating " round his garden, while James Mill. was putting his children through a course of rigorous instruction, and Place was walking round the park with a Latin grammar or some work on economics in his hand. Never surely did any country house shelter such a devoted band of students. The affectionate terms on which Place and Bentham lived

[1] Place was acquainted with Godwin, and though he does not appear to have been influenced by Godwin's philosophy, he lent him a considerable sum of money that was never repaid.

together may be gathered from their letters : " My dear old father" and "Dear good boy" were the terms in which they addressed one another.[1]

It is as a man of action and not as a man of thought that Place claims a foremost position in a history of the Radicals ; as hereafter will be seen. As a thinker he was not so much original as a disseminator of other men's ideas. He was, indeed, a great collector of social and economic facts, and in his house at Charing Cross he brought together a large number of interesting books and pamphlets ; the Civic Library, as it was called, became a kind of *rendezvous* for members of Parliament and others who wished to prosecute inquiries or to consult the owner, whose practical acquaintance with the facts of life among the working class was certainly unrivalled. For it was not for nothing that he had sat upon the tailor's board. His historical importance may be said to lie in the fact that he carried the spirit of philosophical radicalism into the conduct of affairs. Of that spirit he was the living and active incarnation and embodiment. He himself possessed no natural literary gift, though some of his pamphlets and journalistic articles were written in a terse and vigorous style ; but no one did so much to introduce the thoughts of the Benthamite philosophers to the masses of the English reading public ; he reprinted, for example, cheap editions of some of James Mill's most striking articles, and, in particular his famous article on government, which originally appeared in the *Supplement to the Encyclopædia Britannica*. He also brought out with the assistance of Wooler (a now forgotten personage, but notorious in his day) Bentham's *Plan of Parliamentary*

[1] *Life of Francis Place*, by Graham Wallas ; *Memoirs of Sir S. Romilly*, vol. iii.

THE SECOND PERIOD, 1789-1831.   207

Reform in the shape of a catechism. It is, perhaps, not too much to say that if it had not been for Place the propagandism of the Benthamite principles of government would have failed to some extent for want of a proper publication. For the *Westminster Review*, though an admirable organ of philosophic radicalism, appealed only to a very limited class of educated persons. Place's position as a speculative thinker need not further be considered, because he contributed nothing original to the discussion on the principles of government. His *Illustrations and Proofs of the Principle of Population*, a work in which he followed Malthus, and his *Not Paul but Jesus*, a work based on one of Bentham's manuscripts, and edited by Place under the pseudonym of Gamaliel Smith, it would be irrelevant to discuss. But to Place as a practical organiser and political wirepuller, a part which he played supremely well, there will hereafter be occasion to refer.

A less important member of the Benthamites, but one of considerable interest, was David Ricardo. Though of Jewish descent, and partially educated abroad, though a successful stockbroker, who, thanks to his natural business instincts, amassed a considerable fortune, he represented philosophic radicalism in some of its best and most elevated aspects. James Mill became his friend, and exercised great influence upon him; so much so that Bentham said, "I am the spiritual father of Mill, and Mill the spiritual father of Ricardo". It was at Mill's instigation that he sought a seat in Parliament, where he represented Portarlington in Ireland; not the last time that a Radical has won the confidence of the electors of the Sister Isle. It was, no doubt, at Mill's suggestion too, that he wrote and published his most important work on the *Principles of Political Economy and Taxation*. But on the ultimate principles of government he was not, like Mill or Bentham, a profound or original thinker; and though he adopted the tenets of philosophic radicalism, he had no desire to see them pushed to their logical extremes. He saw clearly that the House of Commons was not appointed by the people, but by the Peers and the county aristocracy, and that the only check upon the governors was "the good sense and information of the people themselves, operating through the means of a free press". Yet he saw too that "all great questions are decided in the House of Commons, and that the House of Lords seldom gives any opposition to important measures to which the other House has given its sanction"; and he candidly admitted his belief "that an extension of the suffrage, far short of making it universal, will substantially secure to the people the good government they wish for". On the question of the ballot, however, his opinions were decided: "Without it," he said, "no substantial reform can be obtained.... Mr. Bentham's sagacity did not fail to discover that terror was the great instrument of influence and corruption." Ricardo was, in fact, a Radical of only a very moderate type who looked rather to obtaining what under the circumstances was practical, than to logical and theoretical perfection. It is, perhaps, as the friend of James Mill, and as the man who was the means of bringing him and George Grote into contact, that as a factor in the history of philosophical radicalism he best deserves to be remembered.[1]

It was in 1819 that George Grote, through the medium of Ricardo, became acquainted with James Mill; an in-

[1] *The Works of David Ricardo*, with an Introduction by McCulloch; Mrs. Grote's *Personal Life of George Grote*, p. 21.

roduction from which important results were to follow. Grote was then a young man of twenty-five. Educated at the Charterhouse he did not enjoy the advantage—or disadvantage, as he might have thought it—of a university education; but at an early age was placed by his father in his banking-house in Threadneedle Street. Grote was the first, unless we except Ricardo, of the Radicals taken from the rich mercantile or *bourgeois* class. Hitherto it had been generally the professional men, the journalists and authors, with a small number of eccentric peers, who had produced the persons of the stuff of which the Radical protagonists were made. They had none of them been opulent, and some were entirely dependent on their own labours for a living. Bentham, indeed, inherited a competence, but he was a barrister by profession. The adherence to the party of a man like Grote, a wealthy banker, was an event of some importance, because it gave to the Radicals a prestige in society which they would not otherwise have had. But though Grote was from an early age immersed in the business of the bank, he had from the first an ardent love of learning, and was just the sort of man to profit most by James Mill's didactic conversation. It is evident, indeed, that Mill was the strongest formative influence on the development of his mind; for the great dialectician was a frequent guest at the banker's house in Threadneedle Street, where many questions, especially those of political economy, were strenuously discussed. How strong was the zeal for knowledge displayed by Grote and his associates may be gathered from the fact that for a period they used to meet twice a week at half-past eight o'clock in the morning at Grote's house for the purpose of discussing metaphysics. Such men must have been terribly in earnest. But though from the Radical point of view Grote was an invaluable recruit, it cannot be truly said that he contributed anything original to the principles of government upon which the philosophy of radicalism was based; as John Stuart Mill says, he was by the side of James Mill "a tyro in the great subjects of opinion," but he "rapidly seized" on his ideas. As a philosophical Radical Grote was only the echo, and James Mill was the voice. But for the Radical cause in the House of Commons, in pressing the question of the ballot to the front, he performed inestimable service. Yet Grote was constitutionally timid, and was glad to relinquish the turmoil of Parliament for the more peaceful avocations of the library; an exchange that redounded greatly to the advantage of the literary world. Perhaps no one has summed up his character more truly and succinctly than Cobden, who was introduced to Grote and his wife in 1837: "She is the greater politician of the two. He is a mild and philosophical man, possessing the highest order of moral and intellectual endowments, but wanting something which for need of a better phrase I shall call devil".[1]

Of all the philosophical Radicals the one who in Parliament made the greatest figure was Joseph Hume; yet he was perhaps the one who had the least intellectual grasp of the principles of the Benthamites. His history is a curious one. Born in Forfarshire, he came into contact with James Mill as a schoolfellow at Montrose Academy; but whether he derived any mental stimulus

[1] *Life of Cobden*, by John Morley, vol. i., p. 137; Harriet Martineau's *Autobiography*, vol. i., p. 345; *Personal Life of George Grote*, by Mrs. Grote; John Stuart Mill's *Autobiography*. There is a portrait of Grote in the National Portrait Gallery by Thomas Stewardson.

in the Radical direction at that early age it is impossible to say. He was brought up to the medical profession and practised in India for a time. On his return he was introduced in 1813 to Place. This apparently was the turning-point of his career, for thanks to Place's training, he speedily became a thorough-going Radical. His conversion, of which Place in a letter to Mrs. Grote has left a very singular account, is another example of the extraordinary influence which the philosophical Radicals wielded; of what might be called their proselytising power. This is what Place says of Hume, whom he evidently regarded as a tutor does a pupil: "Mill fixed him upon me some twenty-five years since. I found him devoid of information, dull and selfish. . . . Our intimacy brought obloquy upon both of us, to which he was nearly as callous as I was. He was taunted with 'the tailor his master,' without whom he could do nothing. I was scoffed at as a fool for spending time uselessly upon 'Old Joe,' upon 'the apothecary'. . . . Hume showed his capabilities and his imperturbable perseverance which have beaten down all opposition."[1] To the philosophy of Radicalism Hume contributed practically nothing, but of one aspect of it—the denunciation of the extravagance of the aristocratic rulers—he was the greatest parliamentary exponent that ever lived. Endowed with an iron constitution,[2] and an indomitable will, he made himself the self-appointed auditor of the national accounts. Though a man of only mediocre talents, and ungraceful as a speaker, though somewhat eccentric and perverse,

[1] *Life of Francis Place*, by Graham Wallas, pp. 183-84.
[2] Grote once remarked to Bain: "Do you see what depth of chest Hume has got?" (Bain's *James Mill*, p. 77). There is a portrait of Hume in the National Portrait Gallery by Walton.

he succeeded by dint of his indefatigable persistency
Year after year, and session after session, he preached
the gospel of economy, and scrutinised every item o
expenditure with a microscopic eye; he was the arch
tormentor of the ministers responsible for the proper
application of the money of the nation. His zeal fo
retrenchment, which often infringed on vested interests
made him exceedingly unpopular; Sir Walter Scott, fo
instance, said that he was "the night-workman of th
House of Commons, who lives upon petty abuses".
Yet his rigid scrutiny must have been very beneficial
and there is no more startling change in the history o
radicalism than that the demand for economy—a deman
which in the hands of Joseph Hume was raised almos
into an elemental dogma—should in these latter day
have been all but abandoned. Democracy, indeed, i
somewhat of a spendthrift.

The year 1824 was marked by a change, at first un
noticed, but gradually increasing, in the persons and th
characters of the philosophical Radicals. It was the
that John Stuart Mill, the eldest son of James Mill
entered the circle of the Benthamites. In one sense i
may be said that he had been a Benthamite from in
fancy; for, as is well known, he was most carefull
instructed by his father, and was nourished solely o
his principles and methods. James Mill—whose re
markable household must have been a veritable *erga*
tulum—following the example of the elder Mirabeau an
the father of Frederick the Great, was determined t
cast his son's mind in the mould that he had fashioned
Writing to Bentham in 1812 he said: "However, if

[1] Sir Walter Scott's *Journal*, vol. i., p. 160.

were to die any time before this poor boy is a man, one of the things that would pinch me most sorely would be he being obliged to leave his mind unmade to the degree of excellence of which I hope to make it".[1] In the result, the "poor boy," at an age when other lads have few interests beyond their games, was already a full-fledged and sober-minded Radical. He was, no doubt, as Roebuck tells us, at this early period of his life entirely ignorant of the world, and merely repeated the ideas which he learnt from his father's oral teaching, and from his own study of Bentham's most characteristic treatises. But even so, he was one of those who blossom early;—a marvel of precocity. In 1823 he entered the East India Company's office, where his father held the important position of examiner; and he was thereby enabled to introduce among the Benthamites some fresh and invigorating elements. Bentham was already not far short of eighty years of age, while the lengthening shadows were closing upon Mill, who had long passed the meridian of his life. When, therefore, the younger Mill brought with him a select band of his contemporaries, he infused some new blood, which was rather badly needed. One of the first things that he did was to found the Utilitarian Society, which used to meet in Bentham's house. The members of the Society at first were only three in number, and they were never more than ten, and as it was dissolved after an existence of three years its influence could have been never very great. Yet it is probable that its name was one cause of the fact that ' Utilitarian " became a synonym for " Philosophical " or ' Benthamite," to denote a class of Radicals. Mill tells

[1] Bain's *James Mill*, p. 119.

us that he did not invent the word, but found it in Galt's novel, *The Annals of the Parish*, and that he thought it was appropriate. It is, however, of some interest to note that Bentham seems to have had some prevision of the term; for in a letter to Dumont with reference to the Benthamites he said: "To be sure, a new religion would be an odd sort of thing without a name, accordingly there ought to be one for it, at least for the professors of it Utilitarian (Angl.), *utilitairien* (Gall.), would be more *propre*."[1] The new Society, at any rate, served as a focus for reunion for a number of young men of what Peacock described as "a disquisition set". Sometimes they would meet at James Mill's house and sometimes at Grote's for reading and discussion; and a few years later they took part in the debates of a society, a which all shades of thought were represented, and where Sterling and Maurice and John Stuart Mill himself were among the most conspicuous figures. In the result the philosophical Radicals underwent a kind of transformation. Among the new recruits were Charles and John Austin, John Arthur Roebuck, Hyde and Charles Villiers Strutt (afterwards Lord Belper), and Romilly, the son of Sir Samuel Romilly, who became Master of the Rolls In his early days the brilliant Charles Austin must be accounted by far the most important, for he did the most to render fashionable the Benthamite mode of thought amongst the intellectual young men of the higher classes of society. At the same time he was to a large extent responsible for much of the prejudice and misconception which clouded the popular idea of the philosophical Radicals. For, as John Stuart Mill said, he "presented

---

[1] Bowring's *Life of Bentham*, Works, vol. x., p. 214.

the Benthamic doctrines in the most startling form of which they were susceptible, exaggerating everything in them which tended to consequences offensive to any one's preconceived feelings". But Charles Austin relapsed into the parliamentary barrister, and immersed in a large and lucrative practice, he failed to do for the cause what might have been expected from the brilliant promise of his youth. John Austin was nearly as able as his brother, but he did not possess the arts of practical success from the worldly point of view. And for the Radical cause he did no more than his brother, but from a very different reason. An extreme consciousness of temperament prevented him from taking up the position of a man of strong convictions, while his fastidiousness and nicety of taste seemed to paralyse his pen. In consequence the man who of the younger set of Benthamites made the greatest figure, was one who was not the equal in ability of either of the Austins. This was John Arthur Roebuck. Though born in England in 1802, he was taken to Canada as a child; but in 1824 he returned with nothing in his pocket, but with a highhearted resolve to make his own way in the world. Coming to London he was introduced to John Stuart Mill by Peacock, a mutual friend of both, and he soon began to take an active part in the debates of the Utilitarian Society. In this way he became acquainted with Bentham himself, and with other members of his circle, among them, Francis Place. Impulsive and impressionable, it is no wonder that Roebuck, among surroundings such as these, became an active Radical. But from the first he showed that irritability of temperament and instability of character that went far to ruin his career, and made him the most wayward politician of his time; and

Bentham prophesied truly when he said that Roebuck's temper would do him more harm than his intellect would do him good. In some ways he was superior to the Benthamites, for he was a genuine lover of poetry and the arts, though he denied their value in the formation of the character, and thought that the artistic and poetic tastes were by no means an unmixed good to their possessors. It may, indeed, be questioned, having regard to his subsequent career, whether Roebuck was ever thoroughly "bottomed," to use a phrase of Dr. Johnson's, in the principles of Benthamism; and whether he did not become a Radical from the mere accident of circumstances. But however this may be, he was for many years the most combatant Radical of his time; and in this capacity he will often force himself upon our notice. It must be enough here to remark that as a philosophical Radical he adopted *en bloc* the teachings of Bentham and James Mill, and that he really added nothing new. Upon one question he deviated from the strongly held opinion of John Stuart Mill, and adhered to the older point of view—that is to say, upon the question of female suffrage. But his reasons were peculiar. He thought that the possession of the suffrage would tend to harden and impair the refined and delicate susceptibilities of women. "I would," he said, "as much as is consistent with perfect education, keep women out of contact with actual political strife. This is the only argument which I could ever find worth a rush against giving to women all political rights." That is an opinion which, whatever may be thought of it, is at least worth consideration, and it is a matter of some interest that a Radical should have held it.

With the advent of John Stuart Mill and his con-

THE SECOND PERIOD, 1789-1831.   217

temporaries, philosophic radicalism began to undergo a silent change, and its rigid tenets to be partially modified and softened. But the process was a slow one. Meanwhile in 1824 an event occurred of very great importance in the history of the movement; the foundation, that is to say, of the *Westminster Review*. The large quarterly reviews were at that time in their palmy days, and carried an influence and weight which they have subsequently lost. The first to appear was the *Edinburgh Review*, which owed its inception to the orginality and vigour of Sydney Smith, Brougham and Jeffrey, the great "literary anthropophagus" of his age.[1] The great Whig Review was supported by a very brilliant staff, and so widely was it read that it proved a serious obstacle to the other great party in the State, and one which could not be passed over in neglect. It excited, indeed, an amount of bitter animosity, which it is now difficult to realise. Sir Walter Scott, for instance, said that "politically speaking" it was doing "incalculable harm"; that it degraded the sovereign, exalted the power of the French armies, and the wisdom of their counsels; and disgraced its pages by "disgusting and deleterious doctrine".[2] Though at first a contributor he afterwards refused to receive it in his house. In the result the *Quarterly Review* was launched in 1808 with Gifford for its editor, and John Wilson Croker as one of its main founders and principal contributors. The exertion of great energy, as John Murray the publisher said, was needed "to counteract the baneful effects of the widely circulating and dangerous principles of the *Edinburgh Review* which

[1] *Memoir of Sydney Smith*, vol. i.; Lord Brougham's *Memoirs of His Life and Times*, vol. i., p. 246.
[2] Lockhart's *Life of Scott*, vol. ii., p. 209.

becomes, if possible, more immoral and certainly more openly Jacobinical ".[1] The two Reviews, in fact, were the main organs for the expression and the diffusion of Whig and Tory opinions, before the daily and weekly press attained that position of importance which has finally eclipsed those learned compilations altogether. That the Radicals should wish for a periodical as a propagandist organ was, therefore, what might have been expected. But to produce and maintain an expensive review, which could only enjoy a limited circulation, was a project which could not be carried out except by the display of a good deal of disinterested zeal. Bentham's generosity was equalled by his means, and in 1824 the world of letters and politics was startled by the first appearance of a purely Radical review. The main object of its founders was not so much to attack the Government, which was then in Tory hands, as the Whigs, and the Whig organ, the *Edinburgh Review*. For Whiggism was deemed a more subtle, and therefore a far more dangerous foe, than the most reactionary Toryism; the latter at least was frankly hostile, while the former, under a specious show of friendship, masked a policy of treachery and fraud. This attitude of the Benthamites towards the Whigs, which originated in the truculent assaults of Thomas Paine upon both parties in the State, was at this time a marked characteristic of all Radicals; and it endured even beyond the date of the Reform Act, though that great piece of legislation was almost entirely due to Whig endeavours. The hatred of the Whigs found its most vehement expression in the *Westminster Review*. In the very first number James Mill contributed

---

[1] Smiles' *Memoir of John Murray*, vol. i., p. 154.

an article, which, in his son's opinion, was the most formidable attack on the Whig policy ever made, and the greatest blow ever struck on the Radical behalf. It was a direct assault upon the great Edinburgh organ, poised on its "light wings of saffron and blue," and the "political coquetry" of its writers. It was argued that periodical literature depends for its existence upon immediate success; that such success can only be secured by the patronage of opinions most in vogue, or in other words, the opinions of those in power; that those in power are the aristocracy; that the periodicals must, therefore, favour the aristocracy. It was, moreover, next contended, that whereas the *Quarterly Review* supported the ministerial party, the *Edinburgh* only wished to turn that party out from interested motives; that while it tried to win the favour of the people, it dared not offend the aristocracy; and it therefore engaged in a perpetual system of compromise, and trimming between two interests; that of themselves and of the country. From this it followed that books which received in the *Edinburgh* the most favourable criticism, were those that gave support to aristocratic pretensions to a monopoly of government. As a piece of polemical writing the article could hardly be excelled, and John Stuart Mill expressed the simple truth when he declared that no one but his father was capable of doing it. Certainly no more vigorous attack was ever made by one review upon another; and it could not fail to give the *Westminster* from the very first a position of importance in the world of politics and letters. Its start was assuredly auspicious. The funds were found by Bentham, who, on the refusal of James Mill, appointed Bowring, afterwards Sir John Bowring, then a merchant in the City, but who for some years had been a frequent visitor at Queen's Square Place, to edit the political department; while to Henry Sothern was entrusted the literary side. Messrs. Longman undertook to publish the *Review*, but for reasons connected with their business they relinquished the proposal, and Mr. Baldwin took their place. The *Westminster* was undoubtedly the most powerful and influential organ that the Radicals had ever yet possessed. Many of its articles were written with very great ability; and among the contributors were James and John Stuart Mill, Albany Fonblanque, the brilliant journalist, who afterwards edited the *Examiner*; William J. Fox, formerly a Unitarian minister, and afterwards member for Oldham, and an Anti-Corn Law orator;[1] Dr. Southwood Smith, to whom Bentham's body was handed for dissection, and Colonel Perronet Thompson, who after serving both in the navy and the army, and as Governor of Sierra Leone, was returned to Parliament for Hull, and finally distinguished himself in the campaign against the Corn Laws. But notwithstanding the self-sacrificing zeal and the capacity of the editors and writers, it was not a great success; for from the first it resulted in a pecuniary loss, and, owing to some friction and dissonance of opinion, it created a great deal of dissatisfaction in the minds of those connected with it. James Mill predicted failure under Bowring's management from the outset; and so to some extent it happened; for, says John Stuart Mill, "it is worth noting as a fact in the history of Benthamism, that the periodical organ by which it was best known was from the first extremely unsatisfactory to those

[1] J. S. Mill afterwards thought of making Fox the editor of a review he was projecting (see the "Unpublished Letters from J. S. Mill to Professor Nichol" in the *Fortnightly Review* for May, 1897).

whose opinions on all subjects it was supposed specially to represent". Its subsequent fortunes may be here conveniently related. In 1828 it was bought by Perronet Thompson, and so unpleasant was the feeling caused by the way in which the sale was carried out, that John Stuart Mill declined to contribute any longer. Afterwards in 1834 it passed into the hands of Sir William Molesworth, who merged it with the *London Review*, and appointed John Stuart Mill as editor. That its career should have been embarrassed by reasons of finance was, indeed, to be expected; but the bickerings and jealousies to which it gave occasion might well have been avoided. They were, however, incidental symptoms of that querulousness with which, as will be seen, the Radicals seem to have regarded one another.[1]

Such, very briefly, were some of the chief personal characteristics of the philosophical Radicals; but upon their peculiar type of radicalism some comments must be made. It was different from any that preceded it, and in like manner, though it has not even yet entirely spent its force, it differs in some respects, and those by no means the least important, from the radicalism which is in vogue to-day. The range of the Benthamite philosophy, including as it did, politics and morals, political economy, metaphysics, logic, theology, and analytic psychology, was very wide; there was nothing germane to the study of man in his individual or social aspects that was excluded from the sphere of investigation of this group of diligent inquirers. They were quite unable

---

[1] *Autobiographical Recollections of Sir John Bowring*, pp. 66-7; Bain's *James Mill*, p. 261; *Autobiography of John Stuart Mill*. In the year 1840 the *London and Westminster Review* was transferred to Mr. Hickson, and the old name of the *Westminster* was reverted to.

to endure what Socrates called the βίος ἀνεξέταστος, or life without research. Almost every one of them took up some peculiar province of his own; Bentham, for instance, taking law and legislation, James Mill psychology, and Ricardo political economy; but there was a common spirit that pervaded all their work, and a co-operating zeal that was founded upon a community of feeling. Of this fact the manner of the publication of Bentham's works is in itself an illustration; for it is not too much to say that but for the efforts of his friends, who acted, so to speak, as conduit pipes between him and the outside world, a considerable portion of his writings would to this day have remained obscurely hidden in a mass of dusty manuscripts. "But neither gods, nor men, nor booksellers," said Sydney Smith, "can doubt the necessity of a middleman between Mr. Bentham and the public"; and he said no more than the truth. So singular was his mode of composition, and so careless—the sheets of paper on which he jotted down his thoughts lying scattered like the leaves of the Cumæan Sibyl in her cavern—that it was a work of no small labour to present his work in any intelligible shape.[1] This is not the place to enter into a discussion of Benthamism generally; its ethical basis of self-interest; its dry and dusty method of rigorous analysis; its pitiless exposure of many fondly cherished fallacies;

---

[1] Apart from Dumont's French versions, the following works of Bentham were edited by friends and, in some cases, were constructed from his manuscript notes: J. S. Mill's edition of the *Rationale of Judicial Evidence; The Book of Fallacies*, by Bingham; *Natural Religion*, by Grote (under the pseudonym of Philip Beachamp); James Mill's *Table of the Springs of Action;* Place's *Plan of Parliamentary Reform;* Place's *Not Paul but Jesus* (under the pseudonym of Gamaliel Smith). See *Edinburgh Review*, 1825.

its war upon the feelings and emotions; its purging language, as it was said, of the affections of the soul; its stoical indifference to all pleasures but that derived from the approbation of the conscience; and the curious mixture in the minds of its professors of narrow class-prejudice with a limitless philanthropy. But as philosophical Radicalism was only a subdivision, a particular instance or species of that mental condition or way of looking at things which is spoken of as Benthamism, it will be of some interest to inquire how far the former was permeated and infused with the characteristics of the latter.

Philosophical Radicalism might be described as the result of the application of the Benthamite method of inquiry to the ultimate principles of government. The fundamental basis upon which Benthamism rested was the doctrine of utility. In the utilitarian theory, indeed, there was nothing very new, for the doctrine of enlightened selfishness was at least as old as Epicurus. Nor even as a theory of morals can it be accepted as true without some qualifications, which either Bentham failed to see, or the importance of which he did not comprehend. His moral philosophy was certainly imperfect, because he underestimated motives, and made consequences the sole standard of the morality of conduct; it was enough for him that he considered that such phrases as "law of nature," "right reason," "natural rights," were merely covers for dogmatism, and obstacles to rational inquiry.[1] His method, when applied to the

---

[1] See Lord Lytton's *England and the English*, Appendix B on Bentham's *Philosophy*. It appears from some letters written by J. S. Mill to Professor Nichol, which were published in the *Fortnightly Review* in May, 1897, that J. S. Mill admitted having written this appendix. See also J. S. Mill's *Autobiography*, p. 198.

field of legislation, for which it was admirably fitted, was extraordinarily fertile in results; but in the sphere of political science it was exceedingly defective. In making expediency the test of politics there was really nothing new, for Locke, whom he apostrophised as "the first master of intellectual truth," had anticipated him here; expediency, indeed, was almost a commonplace of statesmen, as well as of opportunist politicians. It is of more interest to note how widely he diverged from the older school of Radicals who assailed the doctrine of expediency as fallacious and immoral. But Bentham, who was a great master of administrative details,[1] made no profound investigations into the ultimate principles of government; it was James Mill who shunned details, and liked to work up to general propositions, who carried on the work which Bentham had only just begun. The nature of those general propositions has been described, and need not be repeated here. In their ultimate form there was nothing revolutionary about them; and the bare statement that "the greatest happiness of the greatest number" ought to be the end of government, could hardly be denied. Locke had already said that "the end of government was the good of mankind," and that was but another version of the fundamental premise of the Benthamite political philosophy. Such, too, was Fox's saying that "the end of all government is the happiness of the governed". It was not so much the matter as the manner; not so much the dogma as its application, that offended and raised such a storm of opposition. For Benthamism was to many, if not to most minds, as a system peculiarly irritating.

[1] Good government, Bentham used to say, only requires aptitude maximised and expense minimised.

THE SECOND PERIOD, 1789-1831.

John Stuart Mill described it as "a combination of Bentham's point of view with that of the modern political economy and with the Hartleian metaphysics"; but if it had been that and nothing more it would not have excited much attention. Nor were the Benthamites disliked because they considered utility to be a sounder principle than a simple declaration of abstract natural rights. It was rather their general view of things, their attitude of mind, which was, as Francis Horner said, "repulsive".[1] Consider Bentham in the first place. His very style of writing—resembling, in his later works, a collection of algebraic symbols—his exhaustive method of analysis, warned readers from his pages.[2] The narrowness of his intellectual vision, which made him blind to many sides of human nature, was, in combination with his dogmatism, exceedingly exasperating. He was an excellent example of what Carlyle calls "the completeness of limited men"; for seeing only a section of the field to be surveyed, he saw that single section with a penetrating glance. But of everything beyond the contracted circle of his vision he was absolutely ignorant. The result was that he looked upon the mind as though it were some mechanical arrangement, and he imagined that morals might be made a simple matter of arithmetic. For it was his deliberate conviction that mathematical

---

[1] *Memoir of Francis Horner*, vol. i., p. 229.

[2] In his use of words Bentham aimed at mathematical exactness: his rule for composition he expressed in the following couplet:—

"For thoughts the same, the same the words should be;
Where differ thoughts, words different let us see".

Bowring's *Life of Bentham*, vol. x., p. 68. It is amusing to find that Bentham not only found fault with James Mill's style, but plumed himself upon his own (see Wallas' *Life of Francis Place*, p. 85).

calculation might be introduced into the field of ethics with "a propriety no less incontestable" than in the field of physics; and he incidentally remarked that the chief use of mathematics was to habituate the mind to pay attention to the subject of proportions in ethical inquiry for in morals, he declared, "utility depends altogether on proportions". So too James Mill, when he told Place that, if he had time to write a book, he would make the human mind as plain as the road from Charing Cross to St Paul's, was, it is evident, labouring under much the same idea. Of the literature of the fancy and of the imagination Bentham did not see the slightest use; of "the fairy way of writing," or of "the natural magic of style," he had not the least appreciation. Nay, rather, such things only excited his contempt, for upon "the pathetic fallacy" —the use of words, that is to say, with emotional associations—he waged unceasing war. Napoleon used to call poetry "a hollow science," and Newton held it in disdain, but their attitude towards it was one of considerate respectfulness compared with that of Bentham "I never," he very frankly said, "read poetry with enjoyment. I read Milton as a duty, Hudibras for the story and the fun." He denounced in round terms all poetry as "misrepresentation," and with Goldsmith he was extremely angry for writing *The Deserted Village*, which he described as both gloomy and untrue. Probably no one ever permitted political prejudice to warp so outrageously his literary judgments. He classed together Sir Walter Scott, Lord Eldon, and Lord Stowell as "a Tory Trinity of Scots"; he assailed Dr. Johnson as "the pompous vamper of common-place morality—of phrases trite without being true," and as a "miserable and misery-propagating ascetic and instrument of despotism".

Scott, he said, was "a servile poet and novelist," and Southey—at that time Poet Laureate—an "ultra-servile sack-guzzler".[1] Upon Blackstone he made a furious assault, quite as much on account of the elegance of his style, as on account of the fallacies which lurked beneath his specious phrasing. "His hand," he said, "was formed to embellish and to corrupt everything it touches. He makes men think they see, in order to prevent them seeing. His is the treasury of vulgar errors. He is the dupe of every prejudice, and the abettor of every abuse." It is no wonder that a man who wrote and talked as Bentham did, and gave vent to such opinions, should have brought some odium on himself. In other ways, moreover, he offended men's susceptibilities. He placed little or no value, for example, upon history, custom, or tradition; he had no reverence for antiquity; "let experience be fertile and custom be barren" was one of his fondly cherished maxims. An appeal to precedent he called an avowed substitute for argument; while he ignored the possibility that the continuance of a custom might be a proof of its utility, and a good reason why it should not be hastily destroyed. Again, he had all that passion for logical arrangement and impatience of anomaly which is so characteristic of the French, and has given rise in France to so much political disturbance—for, as Guizot very truly said, revolutions are relentlessly logical. Then he seems to have imagined that the governments of all nations might be fashioned almost upon a single pattern,

---

[1] Bowring's *Life of Bentham*, Collected Works, vol. x., pp. 57, 124, 518, 83; Montague's Introduction to the *Fragment on Government;* Preface to the Second Edition of the *Fragment on Government; The Life of Place*, by Graham Wallas, p. 91; De Quincey's *Essay on Whiggism in Its Rela-*

though now and then he dropped some *obiter dicta* to th[e] contrary. At all events to the Czar, to Mehemet Ali, t[o] the President of the United States, to Spain and Portug[al] he offered either codes or constitutions; he had wha[t] he himself called the "*cacoëthes codificandi*". But thes[e] mental traits, though singular, might perhaps have bee[n] passed over had Bentham pressed his views withou[t] making a display of his personal antipathies. In his zea[l] for obtaining securities for good government, he vehe[-] mently assailed what in general terms he called th[e] aristocracy; he liked, he said, to drag "the nobilit[y] through the dirt". He was, in fact, what his old enem[y] Dr. Johnson would have described as a good hater. Bu[t] in his capacity of aristocracy-reviler he was far outdon[e] by James Mill, that most acidulated of all censoriou[s] critics. Even Bentham, whose temper at bottom wa[s] benign, remarked upon Mill's acerbity of manner an[d] of speech. He said that his "willingness to do good t[o] others depended too much on his power of making th[e] good done to them subservient to good done to himself'[;] that his "creed of politics" resulted "less from love f[or] the many than from hatred of the few"; that he was to[o] much under the influence of selfish and dissocial affectio[n;] that he tried to subdue his hearers by his "domineerin[g] tone," and to convince them by his "positiveness"; tha[t] his way of speaking was "overbearing" and "oppressive["]. These are hard sayings, and their truth was denied b[y] John Stuart Mill with becoming indignation. But the[re] is too much ground for the belief that they were not wit[h]out foundation. We find Grote, for instance, saying tha[t] the mind of James Mill was marked by "asperity" a[nd]

[1] Bowring's *Life of Bentham*, vol. x., p. 450.

'cynicism"; that he had "a seeming preference" to
dwell upon "the faults and defects of others, even of
the greatest men"; while Mrs. Grote remarked that with
his strong conviction on the superiority of the democratic
form of government "he mingled a scorn and hatred of the
ruling classes which amounted to positive fanaticism".[1]
Roebuck said even worse than that; describing him as a
severe democrat in words who "bowed down to wealth
and position," and was so disdainful of the young men
who came to see him that they ceased visiting his house.[2]
But whatever James Mill's personal failings may have
been, his attitude towards the ruling classes, the lawyers
and the Church, was shared by all the Benthamites.
They looked upon the aristocracy much in the same way
as the Romans did on Carthage, or as Voltaire with his
'Ecrasez l'infame," or Gambetta with his "le cléricalisme, c'est
'ennemi," looked upon priestly influence in France. It is
not surprising that the men who were such bitter critics
aroused a very hostile feeling which found expression in
many different ways. Sir James Mackintosh, for instance,
said that they desired "the credit of having vulgar prejudices"; that they sought distinction by singularity, and
clung to opinions because they were obnoxious; that
they wantonly wounded the most respectable feelings of
mankind; that they regarded an immense display of
method and nomenclature as a sure proof of a corresponding increase of knowledge, and plumed themselves
as being the chosen few to whose care the mysteries of
philosophy were confidentially entrusted. Sydney Smith
was wittily sarcastic. Speaking of a utilitarian, he said:
"That man is so hard you might drive a broad-wheeled

[1] *Personal Life of George Grote*, by Mrs. Grote, pp. 21 and 22.
[2] *Life and Letters of J. A. Roebuck*, by R. E. Leader, pp. 25-29.

waggon over him, and it would produce no impression
if you were to bore holes in him with a gimlet, I am
convinced sawdust would come out of him. That school
treats mankind as if they were mere machines; the
feelings or affections never enter into their calculations
If everything is to be sacrificed to utility why do you bury
your grandmother at all? Why don't you cut her into
small pieces at once and make portable soup of her?"
Carlyle expressed his views in that downright fashion
that might have been expected of him: "It is," he
said of Benthamism, "a determinate *being* what all the
world in a cowardly half and half manner was tending
to be. . . . I call this gross steam-engine utilitarianism an approach towards new faith. It is a laying
down of cant; a saying to oneself: ' Well, then, this
world is a dead iron machine, the god of it gravita
tion and selfish hunger' . . . you may call it heroic
though a heroism with its eyes put out."[2] But in al
their polemical encounters the philosophical Radicals
crossed swords with no one who was the equal of
Macaulay. That redoubtable antagonist, in one of his
articles in the *Edinburgh Review*—an article that was
marked by all his usual brilliancy and wit—submitted
the Benthamite philosophy to a pitiless analysis. Of his
general line of argument it would take too much space
to give a full account, but his final judgment may be
quoted: "They may as well be utilitarians as jockeys

[1] *Memoir of Sydney Smith*, vol. i., pp. 62 and 63.

[2] Carlyle's *Heroes and Hero Worship*. In a letter to Emerson (5th
November, 1836) he thus expressed himself about the *London Review*
"I do not recommend it to you. Hide-bound Radicalism: to me well
nigh insupportable thing! open it not; a breath of Sahara and the
infinite sterile comes from every page of it" (*Correspondence of Carlyle
and Emerson*, vol. i.).

or dandies. And though quibbling about self-interest, and motives and objects of desire, and the greatest happiness of the greatest number, is but a poor employment for a grown man, it certainly hurts the health less than hard drinking, and the fortune less than high play; it is not much more laughable than phrenology, and is immeasurably more humane than cock-fighting." To have used language such as this about Bentham and James Mill, whose eminent abilities were at least entitled to respect, may well be deemed unworthy of Macaulay, and he is said to have regretted it. And it is but simple justice to remark of Bentham and his circle, that their lives were irreproachable, and that they interpreted the principle of utility in their own conduct by much unselfishness of temper. Bentham put the philosophy of happiness into a syllogistic form; the way, he said, to be comfortable is to make others comfortable; the way to make others comfortable is to appear to love them; the way to appear to love them is to love them in reality. Nor were he and his followers by any means arm-chair philosophers, men of the character of Joubert, who, attired in silk, would spend days in bed in order to ward off the emotions; so far from that, they carried the doctrine of utility into the every-day practice of their lives. When, for instance, the use of the gymnasium was introduced into the country, Bentham thought so highly of its possible advantages, that he converted his stables into a place where he and his friends might enjoy the pursuit of physical development. The sight of the philosophers at work on the horizontal bar or the trapeze must have at least added something to the gaiety of nations. And Bentham's end was in keeping with his life, for he did his best to spare his servants pain, and left his body for dissection. But of all this the great English public had no appreciative knowledge, and Macaulay only happily expressed what many men were thinking. There were some who looked upon philosophical radicalism and its authors with abhorrence, but there were probably many more, the less thoughtful and reflective, who never tried to understand it, and to whom Macaulay's closing words must have been an unalloyed delight.[1]

Why Benthamism was an unpopular philosophy it is not hard to understand. It was thought to be irreligious, owing to its attacks upon the Church; to be materialist and selfish, and utterly destructive of the æsthetic perception and the nobler aspirations. Nor were these judgments without warrant. Benthamism was, to say the least, unorthodox; its doctrine of utility was carried to excess; its conception of humanity was narrow, and its idea of government as a system for ingeniously manipulating the selfish affections of the people was degrading.[2] Moreover, in its attacks upon the ruling classes, who, with all their faults, had made England's greatness, was decidedly unjust; though this bitterness may be in part accounted for by the fact—to which we shall have occasion to refer—that the Radicals were disliked, and, to some extent, a persecuted sect. Yet notwithstanding their deficiencies, the Benthamites had many shining merits. In an age not conspicuous for a high standard of morality, their private lives were pure;

[1] Macaulay's *Miscellaneous Writings*, vol. i.; Article on Mill's *Essay on Government, Edinburgh Review* for January, 1874.
[2] Professor Huxley thought that Bentham, by speaking of the "happiness" and not the "good" of the greatest number, had converted a noble into an ignoble principle (see his "Address on Priestley" in his *Essays on Science and Education*).

and if they preached a philosophy of selfishness, they were themselves distinguished by the austerity of their virtues, and their stoical abstinence from pleasure. Their political philosophy, indeed, was vicious in its methods and wrong in its conclusions, as was shown by Macaulay, and has since been amply proved. It was, as John Stuart Mill has said, "the most remarkable example afforded by our own times of the geometrical method in politics". It was founded on the premise that men's actions are always determined by what they conceive to be their worldly interests. From this the conclusion was deduced that the only rulers who will govern in the interests of the governed are those whose selfish interests are in accordance with the desires of the people whom they are called upon to rule; and that the only way to make the interests of the governors and governed identical is to render the former accountable to the latter. But the premise is by no means always true; nor can the concluding propositions be truthfully laid down in reference to all nations at all times. At the most they correctly represent the facts at some times in some places only. They might, perhaps, have been truly said of the state of things in England in the days of Mill and Bentham; but that was not a reason why propositions that were relatively true should be elevated to the rank of universal predicates. But this unwarranted generalisation was precisely the mistake into which those thinkers fell; this was the prime error that lay at the root of their political philosophy. In other words, they reasoned solely on the geometrical or *a priori* method, while they ignored the *a posteriori* or historical method altogether. Macaulay showed in his usual brilliant style that they were wrong; but he himself relied too much on the latter mode of reasoning, to the entire exclusion of the former; whereas the two should be used in combination, and the conclusions of the one be verified by the other. Hence it was that philosophical radicalism was raised upon a structure that was fundamentally defective; and that it aroused such indignation. To affirm that rulers can never be moved by any motive than self-preference seemed a monstrous proposition. But even after making these deductions, philosophical radicalism was not merely, as Macaulay thought, a philosophy that Bacon described as *controversiarum ferax, operum effæta, ad garriendum prompta, ad generandum invalida*. It was much more than that. It was the greatest force of a purely speculative kind ever known in English politics; it introduced a view of things that permeated through and coloured the whole of English life; it produced a silent revolution in English modes of thought; it, more than any other movement, democratised our Constitution. Moreover, its effects were sometimes healthy; it crushed out some superstitions, and exposed some fondly cherished fallacies. Consider the subject of the British Constitution for example. It was worshipped by almost every one with a blind unreasoning reverence as a fetish; and its amendment was regarded as a kind of sacrilegious violation. Lord Halifax said that he admired "our blessed Constitution";[1] even Wilkes described it as "divine"; Horne Tooke said he loved everything that was established; and Cartwright desired not to destroy the Constitution, but to restore it to what he conceived to be its pristine state of purity. Its many good qualities even he was unable to deny; and these he ascribed to

[1] *Character of a Trimmer.*

the fact that it was erected on the common law, and based upon the law of nature and morality. In fact the older class of Radicals were, no less than the Tories, the supporters of the Constitution. It was a commonplace in the speeches from the Throne, and in the election addresses of parliamentary candidates to speak of it as "happy" or as "glorious," and to describe reformers as insidious enemies who laboured to subvert it. When in 1817 the Prince Regent opened Parliament, he declared that it had been felt by his subjects, and acknowledged by other nations, that the Constitution was "the most perfect that has ever fallen to the lot of any people". The reverence for the Constitution was in some minds almost a religion; as it was with Lord Eldon, for example, who told the House of Lords that it was their duty to transmit it to posterity as pure as they received it from their ancestors, and expressed his firm conviction that from the moment of the admission of the Roman Catholics to political power, "the sun of Great Britain would be set". Rarely, indeed, did any one raise his voice against this fulsome panegyric; though Fox once indulged in a little genial raillery when he said that the admirers of the Constitution reminded him of Goneril and Regan when asked by King Lear to say how much they loved him. It was against this ill-considered idolatry that Bentham set his face when he subjected the Constitution to a pitiless dissection, and assaulted Blackstone's placid theory of the balance of King, Lords and Commons. Bentham was the first, it has been said, to speak disrespectfully of the Constitution; he even in one place denied, like Paine, its existence altogether. But if Bentham was wanting in respect, Place was scornfully contemptuous; for he said it was a "nose of wax which every one twists to his purpose". Yet this very form of government was the admiration of the world; and in one of his sportive moods Bentham suggested *The Homage of Foreigners to the British Constitution* as a title for a book.[1] Nor was the jest devoid of meaning. Even in the United States the British Constitution was reverenced by a considerable party. "As it stands at present," said Alexander Hamilton, "with all its supposed defects, it is the most perfect form of Government which ever existed"; and again, said John Adams, who succeeded Washington as President, "Purge that Constitution, and give to its popular branch equality of representation, and it would be the most perfect Constitution ever devised by the wit of man". That seems exaggerated praise; yet in France there were many who believed that it was no more than due. De Maistre, indeed, described the Constitution as "an insular peculiarity utterly unworthy of imitation"; but amongst French thinkers he was singular; and Madame de Staël was right when she remarked that all French Publicists from Montesquieu to Necker had regarded the British Constitution as "the highest point of perfection to which human society could attain," and as "the finest monument of justice and moral grandeur in Europe". England, in short, was the envy of the French, who thought it the happiest country in the world; and it is not too much that Montesquieu's enthusiastic praise was quite as much a cause of the revolution as Rousseau's passionate vagaries. Nor did the

---

[1] *Life of Cartwright*, vol. i., p. 91; Harris' *History of the Radical Party in Parliament*, p. 121; Twiss' *Life of Lord Eldon*, vol. i., p. 492; vol. iii., p. 63; Fraser Rae's *Sheridan, Wilkes, Fox*, p. 428; *Life of Francis Place*, by Graham Wallas, p. 289; Bowring's *Life of Bentham*, Works, vol. x., p. 76.

French exhaust their admiration in merely turning pretty phrases; for when Napoleon fell, and the monarchy was restored, they adopted a parliamentary system which was avowedly copied from the British.[1] Yet Bentham's solvent criticism had its salutary uses; because reverence for the Constitution caused many people to suppose that it could in no wise be improved by any reform however moderate. Upon that state of imperturbable contentment it was well that Bentham should have poured the vials of his wrath. In other ways, too, his teaching was fruitful of desirable results; it spread abroad a spirit of inquiry; it caused men to think, to discriminate, and to exercise their judgment. That "whatever is, is best" was no longer blindly accepted as a maxim. Lastly, philosophical radicalism was aglow with a bright and luminous hope; for it was thought by its founders to be a genuine revelation. "Throughout the whole horizon," said one of their apologists, "of morals and of politics, the consequences were glorious and vast. It might be said without exaggeration that they who sat in darkness had seen a great light. . . . The bones of sages and of patriots stirred within their tombs, that what they dimly saw and followed had become the world's common heritage."[2] With the advent of the new philosophy it is true that men were awakened, so to speak, from their slumbers, and that they chased away some of the superstitious phantoms that had beleaguered and bewitched them. But though utilitarianism was not quite the wonder-working principle that its discoverers supposed it was, yet it was

---

[1] *Memoir of Thomas Jefferson;* Goldwin Smith's *Political History of the United States*, p. 50; Madame de Staël's *Considérations sur la Revolution Française;* *France*, by J. E. C. Bodley, vol. ii., pp. 248, 255,.

[2] *Edinburgh Review*, June, 1829.

no small thing that at a period of our history which was leaden in its dulness—a period when Europe was suffering from what the Germans called a *weltsschmerz*—there should have arisen a band of men who looked beyond the present and had glorious previsions of the future.[1]

Before leaving the subject of philosophical radicalism altogether, there are some features it presented which, though at the first but little noticed, have derived especial interest from their relation to later political developments, and, therefore, demand a brief consideration. There were some ideas thrown out, rather incidentally as *obiter dicta*, than as fundamental propositions, which have since become of great importance. A few of these were the germs or prefigurements of what afterwards became material parts of the adopted policy of the Radicals. The question of the treatment of the colonies is an instance. That question was not one which the Benthamites considered very fully, but their expressed opinions are of interest, because they anticipate what afterwards became the accepted dogmas of those Radicals who were known generally as the Manchester School. The Benthamites, so far as they thought about the colonies at all, seemed to have desired their independence; or at all events not to have regarded them with favour. Bentham wrote a pamphlet styled *Emancipate Your Colonies*, and James Mill said he thought that they were the grand cause of war, and of corruption, because of the patronage which was placed in the hands of the hated aristocracy. Hence he condemned them as a source of the oppression of the people.[2] Roebuck again

[1] The period that lasted, roughly speaking, from 1815 to 1832.

[2] *Life of Francis Place*, by Graham Wallas, p. 329; Bain's *James Mill*.

declared that the cost of the colonies exceeded many times the profits to be derived from trading with them, and that the exercise of colonial patronage by the Government shed "a malign influence" upon the liberties of the mother country, while Joseph Hume affirmed in Parliament that they, "instead of being an addition to the strength of the country, increased its weakness". Nor was this in the beginning a peculiarly Radical point of view, for it was held by some Whig and Tory thinkers. Dean Tucker, for example, had the temerity to say that "the total separation from America" would be "one of the happiest events that has ever happened in Great Britain".[1] But with the growth of our colonies, the anti-colonial policy became more and more distinctive of the Radicals. And so, too, with the case of Ireland. The Home Rule Question, to be sure, did not directly come within the sphere of philosophical radicalism; but Bentham and Place both expressed themselves in favour of some measure of Irish independence.[2] But their opinions were only a foreshadowing of the modern Home Rule doctrine. It is also worthy of remark that James Mill gave utterance to a proposition for which John Bright afterwards contended with all his eloquence and power. "The desire," said Mill, "so often expressed, that we should interfere to establish good government all over the world, is most alarming, and if assented to in any degree would lead to the worst of consequences. The business of a nation is with its own affairs."[3] That is perhaps the first declaration by the

---

[1] Egerton's *Short History of British Colonial Policy*, p. 368.
[2] *Life of Place*, by Graham Wallas, p. 329.
[3] Letter from James Mill to Brougham (1832), Bain's *James Mill*, p. 366

Radicals upon British foreign policy, a subject that for a long time they treated as one beyond their province, but which afterwards became almost as much to them a matter of concern as any question of domestic legislation.[1] One more aspect of Benthamism deserves especial notice, because it stands in striking contrast to the most characteristic feature of the newest form of radicalism. For, perhaps, when all things are considered, the Philosophical Radicals were distinguished by hardly anything so much as their courageous and sturdy individualism. Bentham, with all his nostrums for the better government of the people, desired only to help them to help themselves the more. Like Condorcet, he looked forward rather to equality of right than to equality of fact. It is true that the designer of Panopticon was interested in Robert Owen's philanthropic schemes for the regeneration of humanity, but he had none the less a shrewd perception that the father of English Socialism was something of a dreamer; Owen, he said, begins in vapour and ends in smoke.[2] In the second number of the *Westminster Review*, in an article which was inspired, if not written, by James Mill, the individualist note was very clearly struck: "Liberty," it was remarked, "in its original sense, means freedom from restraint. In this sense every law and every rule of morals is contrary to

---

[1] In a letter written by J. Symonds to Arthur Young in 1795 there is a quotation (from a pamphlet by Israel Mauduit called *Considerations on the German War*) which is a curious anticipation of the later Radical doctrine of non-interference: "Is Britain to make itself the general knight-errant of Europe, to rescue oppressed states, and exhaust itself in order to save men in spite of themselves, who will not do anything towards their own deliverance?" See *Autobiography of Arthur Young*, edited by M. Betham Edwards, p. 25.

[2] Bowring's *Life of Bentham*, vol. x., p. 570.

liberty." James Mill, in fact, regarded Socialist teaching with abhorrence. "Nothing," he said, with reference to a Socialist movement which was beginning to find favour with the people, "can be conceived more mischievous than the doctrines which have been preached to the common people at Birmingham and elsewhere." Such notions to a man of Mill's stern and austere temperament seemed "mad nonsense" and nothing else.[1] But Place is the most notable example of the Benthamite individualism; a fact which is all the more remarkable because the contrary might well have been expected. He had been a working-man himself; he had suffered the extremes of poverty and of hunger; he knew, better than any other Benthamite could know, the kind of lives the poorer classes lead, their wants, their aspirations, their virtues and their faults. Yet he never falsely flattered, nor weakly implored the protection of the State. He was a stern critic, but a just one. Though he had a keen perception of the hardships to which the working-class were exposed in their relations with capitalists, he opposed protective legislation as a thing likely to weaken the power of self-reliance. "All legislative interference," he said, "must be pernicious. Men must be left to themselves to make their own bargains; the law must compel the observance of compacts, the fulfilment of contracts. There it should end. . . . No restrictive laws should exist. Every one should be at liberty to make his own bargain in the best way he can."[2] So strong was his conviction that even in the liquor traffic he thought that there should be absolute free-trade. Philosophical radicalism, in short, was in its general

[1] Bain's *James Mill*, p. 366.
[2] *Life of Francis Place*, by Graham Wallas, pp. 173-75.

view of the organisation of society antagonistic to the type of thought which is now vaguely called collectivism. That antagonism has since greatly waned and dwindled. The full significance of the change that has occurred will in its proper place receive consideration.

During the years that the Philosophical Radicals were rising up and becoming an important and influential force, during the period, that is to say, which, roughly speaking, lasted from the beginning of the century to the year of the Reform Act, the Radical creed had its practical exponents. There were men of action as well as men of thought; and though the two classes came sometimes into contact, though the functions of the one were occasionally performed by individual members of the other, yet, in the main, the course of both was separate and distinct. The division is just sufficiently accurate to be practically useful. It, therefore, now remains to say something of the demagogues, the Members of Parliament, the journalists and others who carried on the Radical campaign in the country; to consider not what was theorised, but what was actually performed.

It is, in the first place, a noticeable fact that it was now that the Radicals began to take, as a party, a definite form or shape, and to be generally recognised as a distinct entity, living a separate and well-marked existence of its own. Hitherto they had been known vaguely as reformers; but that was a term which was too uncertain in its meaning to serve the purpose of a badge. The exact moment when the term "Radical" was first used to designate a separate political party it is impossible to say; but the words "radical reform" were employed comparatively early by Jebb, and in the satires of the *Anti-*

Jacobin.[1] But it was not until about the year 1819 that the Radicals began to be called by the name by which they have ever since been known. Whether in the first place they assumed it themselves, or whether it was given them by others, it is difficult to say; but the latter is more probably the case. In James Mill's famous article, for instance, in the first number of the *Westminster Review*, it is said that the term was meant to be "opprobrious," and that the Whigs used to stigmatise the professors of popular opinions "by some nickname in the slang of the day," such as "Jacobinical" or "Radical". Again, in an article in the *London Review*, written in 1835, we are told that the Radicals were so called in order to class them "with all that is most despicable in the community, till the name began to acquire respect," and that then they were called instead "Destructives". We read that "to be called a Benthamite" was a mark of reproach; that Sir Francis Burdett was "cut" by aristocratic society, and that "only men of the firmest nerves dared to appear as reformers". There can be no doubt, indeed, that the word "Radical" for a long time carried odium with it. It formerly required no small amount of moral courage for a man in good society to openly declare himself a Radical; for such rank apostasy —for so it was considered—estranged him from his friends. Grote, for instance, was constrained to relinquish that enjoyment of intercourse with people of rank and culture for which his birth and eminent talents had so naturally fitted him.[2] The term "Radical," not

[1] Disney's *Memoir of Jebb*, vol. i., p. 194; *The Poetry of the Anti-Jacobin*; Martineau's *History of the Thirty Years' Peace*, vol. i., p. 226.
[2] Mrs. Grote's *Personal Life of George Grote*, p. 43; *London Review*, vol. i. (an Article on the State of the Nation, attributed to James Mill).

without reason, called up in the minds of those who
heard it some ill associations, which not a few members
of the party would have liked to have seen dispelled
by the use of a new and less offensive name. Daniel
O'Connell, for example, who at one period of his life went
through a fit of Benthamism, wished to substitute the
title "Constitutional," but the philosopher of Queen's
Square Place, of course, dismissed the notion as absurd.[1]
The distinction between the Whigs and Radicals was
now so sharply drawn that the latter might justly claim to
form a separate party. Sometimes overtures were made
between the two, but they rarely ended in any practical
results; for the Whigs, as Cartwright said, when asked
to co-operate in a movement for reform, "seemed as shy
as if asked to handle a serpent".[2] The relationship of
the two was touched upon by Bentham in an interesting
letter, where he applied his favourite method of analysis
to his view of English parties. These he divided into
Tories (or Serviles and Absolutes) on the one hand,
and Liberals upon the other; and the latter he sub-
divided into Radicals and Whigs; so that the two Liberal
groups he regarded as the species of a genus.[3] Yet the
Radicals were just as hostile to the Whigs as to the
Tories. The half measures of moderate reform which
the Whigs were willing grudgingly to concede, were
obnoxious to the Radicals, because they savoured of
dishonesty. This bitterness of feeling between the two
sections of the Liberals was a remarkable feature of the
political history of the time, and it lingered on with
hardly less intensity beyond the passing of the Reform

[1] Bowring's *Life of Bentham*, Works, vol. x., p. 596; vol. xi., p. 6.
[2] *Life of Cartwright*, vol. ii., pp. 5, 137.
[3] Bowring's *Life*, vol. x., p. 95.

Act. Between the earlier Radicals and the Whigs the line was less distinctly drawn, and at the present day it tends to become more and more obliterated; but for a long period the antagonism was acute. Place spoke of the "dirty sneaking Whigs, a corrupt and profligate faction"; and said that Erskine, Fox and Sheridan were Tories out of office; Hunt, the demagogue, called them "shoy-hoys," who joined the Tories in keeping the populace in ignorance, in order that they might plunder it; he declared that the English public might be properly styled John Gull and not John Bull; and that the Whigs were like soldiers on half-pay, who expect to be called back to active service; Cobbett denounced them with all the violence of words he could command; they were an "old battered worn-out faction," "a greedy and perfidious" gang, with whom the Radicals could no more co-operate than they could with "the inhabitants of the infernal regions".[1] It can excite no surprise that the Whigs should sometimes have retaliated, as they did at the Newcastle Fox Club, when even so extreme a Whig as Lambton, afterwards the famous Earl of Durham, denounced them as "brawling, ignorant, but mischievous quacks".[2] Mr. Tierney, in moving an amendment to the address in 1819, said of the Radical leaders that he wished to mark in the strongest terms "his contempt of their understanding, his disgust at their proceedings, and his jealousy of their objects". Sir Fowell Buxton in the

[1] *Life of Francis Place*, by Graham Wallas, p. 134; *Memoirs of Henry Hunt*, written by himself, vol. i., pp. 508, 509; vol. ii., pp. 145, 147; *Selections from Cobbett's Political Works*, edited by M. Cobbett and James P. Cobbett, vol. iv., Letter to the Chancellor of the Exchequer, No. 9; vol. v.; *A History of the Last Hundred Days of English Freedom*, Letter 8.

[2] *Life of Francis Place*, by Graham Wallas, p. 201.

same year reprobated the Radicals, and said that he was persuaded that their object was "the subversion of religion and the Constitution"; while Earl Grey asked in the House of Lords in tones of indignation, whether he was suspected of any attachment to those persons "called Radical reformers," who were decided enemies to himself and to the Whig party as a whole.[1] It is evident that between the Radicals and Whigs the antagonism was so profound that the chance of any workable alliance was almost hopeless. For though the two might sometimes agree in details, yet their differences were not differences of accident but of principle; and the gulf was one which it was impossible to bridge, so long as both sides refused to admit of any compromise. Yet both were anxious to obtain the assistance of each other, and between individual members there was sometimes friendly intercourse; though the negotiations for alliance were almost always fruitless. There were Whigs, too, who dallied with the principles of radicalism, who never crossed the Rubicon, but retreated before it was too late. Of these the most distinguished were the liberty-loving and sober-minded Romilly, and the brilliant but wayward and erratic Brougham. Sir Samuel Romilly was on friendly terms with Cartwright, and intimate with Bentham, whom he visited at Ford Abbey; but he remained from first to last the steady advocate of moderate as opposed to Radical Reform. He persistently refused to be allured by any blandishments; in vain the net was set before him. When Cartwright asked him to be a steward at a dinner of the friends of reform, at the Crown and

---

[1] Harris' *History of the Radical Party in Parliament*, pp. 130, 137, 139.

Anchor Tavern, he declined the invitation; when pressed to attend a dinner of the Westminster electors to celebrate the release of Sir Francis Burdett from the Tower, he did the same; and he could not be persuaded to stand as a parliamentary candidate for Middlesex, because he was unwilling to pledge himself to principles which were abhorrent to his nature.[1] Yet he raised his voice on every opportunity in favour of moderate reform; and he even on one occasion supported a proposal to restore triennial Parliaments. But he was none the less a thorough Whig; and when he was a candidate for Westminster, Bentham, who rarely took any part in an election, ventured forth from the recesses of his study, and denounced him as "a lawyer, a Whig, and a friend only to moderate reform".[2] The case of Brougham was similar. That versatile genius, so unstable and illusive, was the despair of the Radicals, who hoped to win him to their cause, but never quite succeeded. The relations that existed between the "queer old hermit," as Bentham called himself, and the young barrister just on the threshold of his fame, present both in a very pleasing light. The patriarch would address Brougham as "my dearest sweet boy," and "dear sweet little Poppett"; while the latter would reply to his "dear grandpapa". In his correspondence with Brougham the supposed dry-as-dust philosopher used to reveal himself in a very playful mood, for he seems to have had a genuine liking for his brilliant but erratic friend. "Insincere as he is," he said, "it is always worth my while to bestow a day on him." Yet he could never capture Brougham, who, on his part, never scrupled to consult him for arguments,

[1] *Memoirs of Sir S. Romilly*, vol. ii., pp. 92, 340, 413-17.
[2] *Ibid.*, vol. iii., p. 365.

which he jocosely called his "pap". There is, said Bentham, a man "who comes here and tells me that he has come to sit at the feet of Gamaliel and imbibe wisdom from my lips, but when I begin to show him that his projected legal reforms have no simplicity or breadth of principle, he suddenly discovers that it is time to go away, and dine with my lord this or my lady that". This would-be disciple was unquestionably Brougham. He was the friend also of James Mill, who, like Bentham, had great expectations of him; and Mill, indeed, on one occasion urged him to come forward as a candidate for Westminster, and even guaranteed that he would pledge himself to a strong measure of reform. But Brougham afterwards retracted.[1] Place also tried to detach him from the Whigs, but he was too astute to be allured from the highway that led to power and riches. He remained a vacillating Whig, who sometimes urged moderate reform, and sometimes doubted its expediency. But of the Radicals he spoke in no uncertain tones. He said that they and their "vile press" should at all hazards be suppressed, that the Whigs should firmly decline any offers of alliance; he condemned Hobhouse for using "the very language of the Cartwright school," and spoke, as well he might, in terms of abhorrence of the "Huntites".[2]

---

[1] Bowring's *Life of Bentham*, vol. x., p. 575; Prentice's *Historical Sketches*, p. 379; Bain's *James Mill*, p. 123. Bentham was fond of writing doggerel verses on Brougham, *e.g.*:—

"Oh, Brougham! a strange mystery you are!
Nil fuit unquam tibi tam dispar.
So foolish and so wise—so great, so small,
Everything now, to-morrow nought at all."

"Frailty! thy name is Woman!
Insincerity! thy name is Brougham."

[2] Brougham's *Memoirs of His Life and Times*, vol. ii., pp. 341, 351.

Sir Samuel Romilly and Brougham are typical examples of those Whigs who, as we have seen, were by no means ill-disposed in their relations to the Radicals; but, their good-will notwithstanding, any durable alliance was utterly impracticable. The unpassable gulf of deep-rooted principle was only rendered more apparent by any attempt in that direction. This isolation was, however, from the point of view of the Radicals, by no means disadvantageous, for it served to make them a more important body than they would otherwise have been; it raised them to something like the status of a party, not strong, indeed, in numbers or influence, but still a party, and that in itself was a considerable achievement.

Such, very briefly, were the political relations of the Radicals during the years that passed from the time when at the end of the eighteenth century they were crushed beneath a mass of repressive legislation, until the Reform Act ushered in a new and brighter age. The period, at first one of war, and latterly one of great depression, was uncongenial to the Radicals. The Tory rule was safe, but in the main was dull and leaden; our rulers were men like Addington, upon whom Canning penned the squib:—

> Ne'er shall thy virtuous thoughts conspire
> To wrap majestic Thames in fire;

or Percival, whom Sydney Smith so unmercifully satirised; or Lord Liverpool, the "arch-mediocrity," whom Madame de Staël described as "having a genius for silence". His long rule had not even the merits of a vivifying despotism. Yet throughout this period the Radicals still remained true to their ideal; to secure for the people the control of Parliament by pressure from without was still the goal of their desire. In Parliament and outside of it, by motions, petitions, public meetings and the like, they laboured to attain that control with invincible persistency. The nature of their efforts, what they won, and where they failed, have now to be considered.

The most direct and obvious way of pressing the claim of the people to parliamentary control was to move for reform within the walls of Parliament itself. That way was not neglected, but it was a well-nigh hopeless task. The Radicals of the school of Thomas Paine had utterly discredited the once progressive party of reform. That party, indeed, was scarcely represented in the House. "I think," said Tooke to Cartwright, "that the cause of reform is dead and buried"; and it required a rare display of faith for Cartwright to declare that he believed in its resurrection.[1] For in truth the outlook for reformers was at the beginning of the century one of blank despair. Futile motions in the House of Commons for the consideration of the question were occasionally made, but they were always overwhelmed in failure. When Sir Francis Burdett, for instance, proposed a scheme of reform in 1808, he could find sixteen members of Parliament only to support him. Meanwhile, the character of parliamentary representation seemed to be receding more and more from the Radical ideal. The case of Sir Samuel Romilly, a man of high integrity, whose veracity it is impossible to doubt, is typical. At the general election in 1807 we find him complaining that parliamentary seats were very dear,

---

[1] *Life of Cartwright*, vol. i., p. 236. The words occur in a letter written by Horne Tooke to Cartwright in 1797, and in the margin of it Cartwright wrote: "But J. C. is a believer in the resurrection".

because the "new ministers" had "bought up all the seats to be disposed of, and at any prices. . . . To come in by a popular election, in the present state of the representation, is quite impossible . . . many men who buy seats, do it as a matter of pecuniary speculation, as a profitable way of employing their money".[1] A bill, indeed, was introduced by Mr. Curwen, to render the trafficking in seats illegal, but it was passed in such a form as to leave a monopoly to the Crown. There were, in fact, with very few exceptions, two avenues only to the House of Commons; and the aspirant had either to accept the nomination of a patron, as Sir Samuel Romilly accepted that of the Duke of Norfolk, or to purchase. Whether the House of Commons thus elected was a corrupt or an inefficient House, or whether it is likely to have been in any way inferior to one that should be elected on the basis of universal suffrage, it is not to our purpose to inquire. It must be enough to note the fact that the control of Parliament by the people was by reason of this pseudo-representative system practically non-existent. If there was any control at all, it was exercised by the Crown or by the patron. The obstacles in the way of popular control seemed almost insurmountable. Yet there was one constituency in the country where the Radical campaign was, thanks to the efforts of a few energetic men, carried on with conspicuous success. The City of London and the City Corporation were in the days of the Wilkite agitation distinguished for their zeal in the democratic cause, but their fervour seems slowly to have died away. It is remarkable, indeed,

---

[1] *Memoirs of the Life of Sir S. Romilly,* vol. ii., p. 200. He gave £3000 for the seat of Wareham, and refused to accept £1000 from a fund formed by the Whig party for political purposes (vol. ii., p. 237).

how even early in the century the City Corporation was attacked for its effeteness by the Radicals. It was, said Place, "corrupt, rotting, infamous"; "a burlesque on the human understanding more contemptible than the most paltry farce played in a booth at Bartholomew's Fair".[1] The democratic centre of gravity, so to speak, had already shifted west to the constituency of Westminster, just as it afterwards shifted to Birmingham and Manchester. Westminster was at this time one of the few places in the country where the electorate was of a fairly democratic character; it was a "scot and lot" borough, where every rate-paying householder possessed the right to vote.[2] The electors had been in the main distinguished for their devotion to the Whigs, and had done themselves no little honour by returning Fox— though he was opposed by the veteran Tooke himself —to Parliament. His election in 1796 was a cause of much enthusiasm. "He was carried," we are told, "in a gilt chair mounted on a small platform, and backed by an alcove of laurels. Immediately before him went a dozen butchers, with marrow bones and cleavers, and three banners inscribed 'Fox and Peace,' 'Fox and Liberty,' 'The Man of the People'." This picturesque account of the electoral manners of the age prefigured what was soon about to happen. When Francis Place opened his tailor's shop at Charing Cross in 1799, he became a householder in Westminster and entitled to a vote. The setting up in business of the leather-breeches maker was probably little noticed at the time, but it was really an

---

[1] *Life of Francis Place*, by Graham Wallas, p. 347.

[2] In 1801 the population of Westminster was about 153,272; and the number of ratepayers about 10,000 (*Life of Place*, by Graham Wallas, p. 39).

THE SECOND PERIOD, 1789-1831.   253

event of some historical importance, because it was Place who was mainly instrumental in causing Westminster to send some of the earliest Radical representatives to Parliament. It was now that he found scope for the employment of his electioneering talent, which he possessed in a very high degree, and in the Westminster electors he had material ready to his hand. This energetic organiser set to work to democratise the constituency and he succeeded. It was in 1807 that he first found his opportunity. Then it was that he began to teach the electors to form committees, and to canvass upon systematic lines. He himself was the life and soul of the election, and he laboured without stint, and not without success. For many a year, indeed, his influence in the politics of Westminster was very great; "such influence," to use Sir Samuel Romilly's words, "as almost to determine the elections for members of Parliament".[1] Though he refused to enter Parliament himself, he had much to do with getting other persons there, and still more with their conduct when they got there. He played, so to speak, the part of parliamentary "coach," as was the case with Joseph Hume, whom he evidently regarded as a tutor does his pupil.[2] For the House itself he had all that contempt which characterised every Radical before the time of the Reform Act; he called it "rascally," and an "atrocious assembly"; while as for individual members, he thought them proud and overbearing, and the servile followers of their patrons.[3] Yet this master-tailor, and friend of Mill and Bentham, was the greatest political wire-puller and election-manager of

[1] *Memoirs of the Life of Sir S. Romilly*, vol. iii.
[2] *Life of Francis Place*, by Graham Wallas, pp. 183-84.
[3] *Ibid.*, 127, 190.

his time. He set the fashion of that systematic organisation of the voters which has since by both parties been considered indispensable; and he is, in the main, responsible for what may be called in general terms the introduction of caucus methods into English politics. It would, perhaps, be no exaggeration to describe him as the lineal ancestor of the National Liberal Federation.

It was in 1807 that Place won his first success in the politics of Westminster by securing the election of Sir Francis Burdett, who had already been known for his steady and consistent radicalism, as a disciple of Horne Tooke and as member for Middlesex. A patrician and a baronet, and a very wealthy man, who, besides being a landowner, had married the daughter of a banker, his adherence to their cause was to the Radicals a thing of inestimable value. Handsome, tall and thin, dignified in port and bearing, civilly familiar in his manner, he was every inch an aristocrat. His must have been a most attractive personality. "A manly understanding," says Hobhouse, a personal friend, "and a tender heart gave a charm to his society such as I have never derived in any other instance from a man whose principal pursuit was politics. He was the delight of both old and young. There was no base alloy in his noble nature." He had, too, in an eminent degree the qualities of the orator. His lofty stature, his mellifluous voice, his sweet and silvery tones, his command of language and easy flow of words, his sincerity of manner, combined to make him one of the most pleasing and impressive speakers of his time. Byron, Hobhouse and Canning all admired his style; even Sir Fowell Buxton, a somewhat bitter critic of the Radicals, confessed that his speech in the House of Commons on the question of the Peterloo riots was a masterpiece. "His speech," he said, "was absolutely the finest, and the clearest, and the fairest display of masterly understanding that I ever heard. . . . Canning was second; if there be any difference between eloquence and sense, this was the difference between him and Burdett."[1] Such was the man whom the Westminster electors made the object of their choice. Burdett had refused to stand again for Middlesex, where, it is said, he had spent £100,000 in contesting petitions made to invalidate his seat; but while declining to offer himself as a candidate for Westminster, he expressed his willingness to sit if the voters carried his election. They did so by a great majority; and from that time till a period beyond the Reform Act, his connection with Westminster was continuous and close. "Westminster's Pride" and "England's Glory" were the terms of endearment by which he was popularly known. Thus it happened that by a curious irony of fate a West-End constituency became the centre and the focus of democratic agitation, as well, indeed, it might, since it contained within its area Bentham and James Mill to represent its political philosophy, Place to organise its voters, and Sir Francis Burdett, afterwards in company with John Cam Hobhouse, to give voice in Parliament to its political convictions. It was rightly named the cradle of parliamentary reform.

The constituency of Westminster during the period

---

[1] Bamford's *Passages in the Life of a Radical*, vol. i., p. 21; *Life and Correspondence of Thomas Slingsby Duncombe*, vol. i., p. 79; Harris' *History of the Radical Party in Parliament*, p. 137; *Edinburgh Review*, vol. cxxxiii., No. 272; *Life of Francis Place*, by Graham Wallas, p. 47. There is a portrait of Sir Francis Burdett in the National Portrait Gallery by Shee.

now before us presents some lively pictures of life and work among the Radicals, which are not only full of interest from the standpoint of the constitutional historian, but throw a flood of light upon the manners of the time. We obtain a glimpse of a meeting in the old Palace Yard, where Cartwright was acclaimed as the patriarch of reform; of dinners of reformers; and of a dinner to Sir Francis Burdett on his release from the Tower. We watch with interest a series of elections full of incident; of contests between Tories, Whigs and Radicals, and sometimes between rival Radicals themselves. We see Romilly elected, soon, by his too untimely death, to make way for a successor; and a lady of a Whig patrician family, not thinking it beneath her to do some electioneering work; we see that brilliant naval officer, Lord Cochrane, expelled from the House, on his conviction upon a charge of fraud (whether justly or not it is impossible to say), but triumphantly sent back by the Westminster electors.[1] We note, with interest, a dinner given in 1818 in honour of Cartwright, whose services to the cause of Radical reform had scarcely received the recognition they deserved. There was a touch of pathos in the closing years of that venerable patriarch who had laboured so long and so faithfully for the people. Yet he never sat in Parliament. When he offered to stand as a candidate for Westminster, he was rudely brushed aside, with a contemptuous disregard that savoured of ingratitude. It may have been, indeed, the fact that, as Place said, he was "utterly incompetent" and a man for whom the electors would not

---

[1] *Life of Cartwright*, vol. ii., p. 138; *Life of Sir S. Romilly*, vol. iii., pp. 145, 365; Torrens' *Life of Melbourne*, vol. i., p. 137. The Whig Lady was Lady Caroline Lamb.

vote. Still Cartwright very naturally viewed his rejection with some bitterness of spirit. "The cause," he said, "of Radical reform was in the conduct pursued towards me personally undermined and betrayed;" and there was perhaps some truth in his assertion, so evidently moved by disappointment, that he had been "unceremoniously dropped and cast off as a worn-out garment, to clear the way for younger and untried reformists". The dinner given to Cartwright must, therefore, have brought some consolation to the old man's wounded feelings. He was too ill to be present, but he sent a written speech. The following toasts, so thoroughly characteristic of the occasion, were proposed: "The people, the only source of political power"; "The King and Constitution, and a speedy recovery to both"; "Take your choice: a civil government or a military despotism; in other words, Burdett's bill or Castlereagh's bayonet". Cartwright's speech, in reply to the toast of his health, partook of the nature of a valedictory address; it was, so to speak, a final and public profession of his faith; his political will and testament. That faith was as unshaken as a rock, for never did he speak with such intensity of immovable conviction. He condemned the majority of the House of Commons in terms which even for Cartwright were severe; it was, he said, "a small and odious faction," an "Algerine faction," who "assemble in divan, and arrange themselves on their usurped benches"; he jeered at the "late farce of mock-elections performed on their incorporated dung-hills by a few slaves"; he declared his unshakable belief that annual Parliaments and universal suffrage had been "demonstrated" to be right by irrefragable proof; and that they were matters of "moral obligation" and "tests of integrity ". Thus faithful to the last in the cause he had made his own lived Major Cartwright, respected and beloved by all who knew his brave unselfish nature. He lingered on until 1825, when the weary wheels of life, worn out by eating time, at last stood still. His eccentricities and obstinate perverseness were forgotten by those who were acquainted with his love for mankind and his self-sacrificing zeal.[1]

The most interesting event in the annals of Westminster, and the one of most importance from the constitutional point of view, was the committal to the Tower of Sir Francis Burdett for a breach of parliamentary privilege. It will be remembered that Wilkes and other early Radicals were the protagonists in combating the pretensions of the House of Commons to privileges inconsistent with the liberties of the people, and in fighting the claim set up in Parliament to prohibit the publication of debates. In those days the attempts to stretch parliamentary privilege unduly, and the refusal to allow the reporting of debates, were judged to be the chief obstacles to that popular control of Parliament which the Radicals demanded. After a brief but angry contest they succeeded, and what may be called the first epoch of radicalism closed. Then attention was directed to a different class of questions, such as the various proposals for reform, and for the amendment of the Constitution, and radicalism in consequence took other shapes. The old conflicts over privilege and parliamentary reporting had well-nigh been forgotten, when suddenly in 1810 they

---

[1] *Life of Cartwright*, vol. iii., pp. 149-51; Wooler's *Black Dwarf*, vol. ii. Though Cartwright was not a utilitarian philosopher, he resembled Bentham in that he bequeathed his body to be dissected at the Royal College of Surgeons in a regular lecture (see his *Life*, vol. iii., p. 262).

blazed up once again in a way entirely unexpected. The standing order of the House for the exclusion of strangers was enforced by Mr. Charles Yorke in a fit of whimsical perversity, with the result that the press gallery was prevented from reporting the debate. The enforcement of the order caused a commotion in the country, and was vigorously condemned. It so happened that the British Forum, a debating society in the city—"a club of chicken orators," as Horace Walpole would have called it—took up the question as a subject for discussion. If the members of the society had stopped there, the matter would have excited no attention; but they went out of their way to advertise and to disseminate a circular, in which they claimed that the enforcement of the order "ought to be censured as an insidious and ill-considered attack upon the liberty of the press, tending to aggravate the discontents of the people, and render the representatives objects of jealousy and suspicion". The author of the paper, John Gale Jones, "a poor emaciated crazy-looking creature, possessed of considerable talents, but as devoid of judgment as any man could well be," was for his escapade committed to the Tower. Sir Francis Burdett, inflamed with righteous indignation, published in Cobbett's *Weekly Register*, a journal which at that time enjoyed an enormous popularity, an article in which he questioned the legality of the committal, and spoke of the House in very disrespectful terms. The House, which was by this time in an irritable mood, judged the article to be a breach of privilege, and sent Sir Francis also to the Tower. Then followed some very extraordinary scenes. The worthy Baronet shut himself in his house in Piccadilly, and having sent a letter to the Speaker to announce his intention to resist, he prepared to undergo a siege. The people rose to protect the man whom they regarded as a hero, and the streets could only be kept clear by the use of a strong military force. An organised attempt was made to bring about his rescue, but though Place was one of those who helped, it proved abortive. A company of soldiers broke into the mansion, where Sir Francis, who seems to have had an eye for good effect, was discovered reading the Magna Charta in Latin to his son. But this display of zeal for constitutional liberty availed him nothing, and he was carried to the Tower, where he had ample time for calm reflection, until Parliament was prorogued. A triumphal procession was arranged to escort him to his home by Place and other friends, but Sir Francis, who had taken fright, and imagined that Place was a Government spy, escaped quietly by a boat upon the river, to the great disgust of the crowd who had assembled to give a hearty welcome to the martyr. The fiasco cost Burdett some of his favour with the people; he was nicknamed "Sir Francis Sly-go"; and even Place called him "a coward and poltroon". It is entirely characteristic of the Radicals that the two men who were the most prominent individuals in the politics of Westminster should for a space of nine years have been not even on speaking terms.[1]

In this incident of the committal of Burdett two questions of great importance, from the Radical point of view, were raised; one involved the right of Parliament to take cognisance of words spoken outside its walls

[1] *Memoirs of the Life of Sir S. Romilly*, vol. ii., pp. 306-13; *Life of Francis Place*, by Graham Wallas, pp. 48-60; Jephson's *Rise and Progress of the Platform*, vol. i., p. 337; Cobbett's *Political Writings*, vol. v.; *A History of the Last Hundred Days of English Freedom*, letter iv.; *Memoirs of Henry Hunt*, vol. ii., pp. 421-23.

THE SECOND PERIOD, 1789-1831.

whether by its own members or by strangers; and the other the right to exclude the public from the galleries, and so to prevent the reporting of the debates. If the control of Parliament by pressure from without be the goal of the Radicals' desire, then they were clearly justified in their refusal to admit the contentions now put forward. To keep the people in ignorance of what Parliament is doing, and to put it beyond the reach of censure, would prove the greatest obstacles to popular control; and the claim of Parliament to do either has tacitly dropped into abeyance. Yet once again another Radical came into violent conflict with the House of Commons upon this very question of parliamentary privilege. This Radical was Hobhouse.

John Cam Hobhouse, better known to later generations under the title of Lord Broughton, was in his early days one of the most brilliant of those who represented the principles of radicalism in Parliament. When quite a boy he was taken by his father to visit Lord Shelburne at Bowood, and there perhaps he derived some inspiration from the genius of the place where Priestley and Bentham found a refuge. He went to Cambridge, where he showed his Liberal propensities in the founding of a Whig Club, and became the intimate of Byron.[1] In

---

[1] Byron afterwards wrote the following squib on Hobhouse when he was a candidate for Westminster:—

"Who are now the people's men?
  My boy Hobby O!
Yourself and Burdett, gentlemen,
  And blackguard Hunt and Cobby O!

"When to the mob you make a speech,
  My boy Hobby O!
How do you keep without their reach
  The watch within your fobby O?"

(Smiles' *Memoir of John Murray*, vol. i.)

1819 he contested the seat of Westminster and was supported by Burdett, who contributed £1000 to defray the expense of the election. The Whig candidate, George Lamb, however, was returned, and Hobhouse indulged himself in a whimsical revenge. He published a pamphlet entitled *A Trifling Mistake in Thomas Lord Erskine's Defence,* in which he had the temerity to ask, "What prevents the people from walking down to the House, and pulling out the members by the ears, locking up their doors, and flinging the key into the Thames?" He answered that "their true practical protectors are to be found at the Horse Guards and the Knightsbridge Barracks". For this astounding piece of insolence he was committed to Newgate by the much offended House. In the following year, however, he was successful in his candidature for Westminster, a seat which he and Burdett continued to represent in Parliament without a break until 1831. Perhaps of all the Radicals who have entered Parliament there has been no one more distinguished for fine scholarship and culture. He will, at least, go down to posterity as the inventor of the phrase, "His Majesty's Opposition".[1]

All this time the demands, which the Radicals have made peculiarly their own, were not allowed to slumber. Take, for instance, the question of the extension of the suffrage. The views of the philosophers of the party, upon this and other kindred questions, have already been considered. What then were the views of the active politicians, who looked rather to achieve the practically possible than the theoretically perfect? In the first place, it would appear that over the extension of the

---

[1] *Edinburgh Review,* vol. cxxxiii., No. 272; *Life of Francis Place,* by Graham Wallas, p. 149.

suffrage opinions were very much divided. The more extreme democrats would be satisfied with nothing less than universal suffrage, while others would have been contented with the admission of householders only to the register of voters. Of the former, Henry Hunt the "Orator," was the spokesman, and he claimed to be the first to "publicly propose" at a meeting of reformers (held at Spa Fields in 1815) that a petition be presented to Parliament for universal suffrage. A meeting of delegates from the various petitioning bodies was actually held at the Crown and Anchor Tavern, where the question was discussed, and a great divergence of opinion was disclosed. Hunt and Bamford carried the meeting with them in favour of the widest extension of the franchise against Cartwright, Cobbett and Burdett, who thought that household suffrage was more easily attainable, and at least a practicable measure.[1] Cobbett and Cartwright both wished for universal suffrage, but they abated their opinions in deference to Burdett, who, as almost the solitary representative of radicalism in the House of Commons, was beyond dispute the leader of his party. He had promised to introduce a Reform Bill into Parliament, so that nothing which had not Burdett's approval was within the sphere of practicable politics. The position which he held at this time in the country was unique. He was the connecting link between the philosophical Radicals on the one hand, and the active politicians on the other. Though not one of the former, he was on friendly terms with Bentham, and drew some of his inspiration from him. He would address him as "my very worthy and approved good master," and

[1] *Memoirs of Henry Hunt*, written by himself, vol. i., Introduction.

Bentham would reply to him as his "much esteemed disciple". Sir Francis, indeed, valued Bentham very highly, and in this respect set an excellent example, which men like Hunt and Cobbett would have done very well in following. He asked Bentham to draw up a Reform Bill, but the philosopher, who knew his limitations, declined upon the ground that he was too busy and insufficiently prepared. Much, indeed, was hoped from the united action of two such men as Bentham and Burdett. But while the former thought that any bill that did not provide for the introduction of the ballot would be absolutely futile, the latter wished to leave it out, because he believed that the prejudice against it could not be overcome, and that its presence would wreck any measure of reform. Eventually, however, in 1818 Burdett proposed some resolutions in favour of reform, in which the inspiration of Bentham is apparent. The preamble contained the proposition that no adequate security for good government can have place but by means of, and in proportion to, a community of interest between the governors and the governed. Here, certainly, were the voices of Bentham and James Mill. The resolutions embodied the demands that the suffrage should be equal, free, and comprehensive; a phrase evidently intended to be vague; that the electors should have power to remove their representatives "at least once in every year"; that the counties should be divided into electoral districts, as far as possible equal in population, and returning a single representative; and that all elections should be held on the same day.[1] The proposed reforms, thus very briefly stated, would have gone far in the direction

---

[1] Bowring's *Life of Bentham*, Works, vol. x., pp. 491-97.

of satisfying the aspirations of the majority, but a small dissentient group of irreconcilable extremists rejected them with scorn. These fanatics would have nothing short of universal suffrage. In the result there was a split between the two wings of the party; between the lower class Radicals on the one hand, and the middle class Radicals, of whom Burdett was the leader, on the other. The position of Burdett is instructive and is worth a brief consideration. For a time, indeed, he seems to have had a distinct following of his own. Cartwright, for example, spoke of "Whigs, Tories, and Burdettites," and Sir Walter Scott described the latter as "men who, rather than want combustibles, will fetch brimstone from hell". That was an opinion which fell naturally from the lips of a high unbending Tory, but, though "Burdett and Liberty!" was sometimes the watchword of the people, and though Bentham once called him the hero of the mob, yet Sir Francis was never in any sense a demagogue. With Hunt, for instance, he was far from being on friendly terms; as is apparent from the tone of contumely and scorn in which the favourite of the mob used to speak of the Burdettites. "They are," he said, "a faction composed principally of petty shopkeepers and little tradesmen, who, under the denomination of tax-paying householders, enlisted themselves under the banners of Sir Francis Burdett," and "a privileged class above the artisans". He complained, too, that he was calumniated by the Burdettites as well as by the Whigs".[1] This remark of Hunt's on the

[1] *Memoirs of Henry Hunt*, written by himself, vol. ii., pp. 75, 82; *Life of Thomas Attwood*, by C. M. Wakefield; *An Appeal to the Nation*, by the Union for Parliamentary Reform (drafted by Cartwright); Lockhart's *Life of Scott*, vol. ii., p. 260. Hunt said that Sir F. Burdett had falsely accused him of having a Government protection in his pocket at Peterloo.

privileged class above the artisans is exceedingly suggestive; for it indicates that radicalism was percolating down to a lower social stratum than it had ever done before. Hitherto, so far from having commended itself to the great mass of the wage-earning population, it had rather been abhorred, and there was no class of people who were so immutably Tory as the mobs who burned down Priestley's house, carried Thomas Paine in effigy, and raised cheers for "Church and King". Radicalism had been rather the faith of the middle class and of fairly educated people, who had read and reflected for themselves; and of this class, still by far the most important, Sir Francis Burdett, who loved liberty more than he did the *profanum vulgus*, was the spokesman and the leader. Notwithstanding his great services, his moderation exasperated those who were impatient at what they conceived to be the slow progress of the cause. Even Place thought him "too rich, too high and too lazy".[1] Suspicion even fell on his sincerity—a suspicion which, perhaps, his subsequent defection justified. But however that may be, Burdett remains an eminent illustration of the fact already mentioned, and to which again there will be occasion to refer, that the Radicals suffered more from the aspersions of their own professed adherents than they did from their political opponents. How he was spoken of by Hunt and Place we have already seen. It remained for Cobbett to accuse him of feeble inconsistency, of jealousy, of envy and ambition that could not brook a rival; of postponing his duties in Parliament to his pursuit of hunting in the country. He charged him with wishing to defer the passing of a reform bill

[1] *Life of Francis Place*, by Graham Wallas, p. 152.

through fear of losing his position as the "one great man" among the Radicals; he threw it in his teeth that he allowed his son to take a commission in a crack regiment in the army; he even suspected that his good intentions had been corrupted by contact with the Court. "The courtly air of Brighton had some effect upon Sir Francis; the very purlieus of a court-barrack are pestilential as to political principle." That Cobbett should have thought so, shows how deeply and unworthily the political life of his time was tainted with suspicion.[1]

The question of the ballot was not one which excited much attention; nor over annual or triennial Parliaments was there occasion found for quarrel; though, generally speaking, those who were for universal suffrage were also for the shorter term. The question of the relation of members of Parliament to their constituencies —a question mooted by the early Radicals, and upon which they expressed their opinions very strongly—is one of more interest, and demands a brief consideration. That parliamentary representatives were simply delegates or attorneys, who might be bound by pledges, was originally an essential dogma of the Radical profession. How far this belief still continued to be held during the period which we are now considering, is a question of some importance in tracing the development of Radical opinion. The general feeling of men of all parties was adverse to

[1] Cobbett's *Political Writings*, vol. v.; *A History of the Last Hundred Days of English Freedom*, letter iv. "I believe," said Cobbett, "that Sir Francis Burdett, for instance, has not the smallest idea of an act of Parliament ever being made without his assistance, if he chooses to assist, which is not very frequently the case" (*Rural Rides*, p. 103). Cobbett's criticisms of Sir Francis Burdett must be taken *cum grano*, because a dispute arose between the two men as to whether a sum of £3000 advanced by the latter to the former was a loan or a gift.

what we have called for the sake of convenience the delegation theory, though there was some divergence of opinion. We find Wilberforce remarking that constituencies cannot be expected to approve every particular of their members' conduct; that on "the great principles" there should be a general agreement, and that a representative should be sent to Parliament as a free agent and not a "slave fettered and shackled". Canning, in a speech delivered at Liverpool in 1812, gave expression to the reasonable view that he claimed to retain an independent judgment, but that if a serious difference of opinion between him and his electors should arise, he would not abuse his trust, but give them the earliest opportunity of recalling or reconsidering their "delegation of it".[1] In the House of Commons the matter gave occasion to a regular debate, and to take two examples of the views on either side, we find Lord Milton protesting with all his might against the notion that members were "merely delegates," and Sir J. Newport as vigorously asserting that the wishes of constituents ought to be obeyed, or the trust should be surrendered. Perhaps no one condemned the delegation theory in stronger language than Lord Eldon. He declared that he would not have sat one moment in the House of Commons, if he had not been at liberty to act upon his own opinions, and that no man would have dared to ask him to sit there "otherwise than upon that understanding". During the debate on the second Reform Bill in the House of Lords, he expressed his "deep sense

---

[1] Canning held that the House of Commons was not "an assembly of delegates," but "a body of men chosen from among the whole community" (see a *Review of Canning's Speeches at the Liverpool Election*, 1812, by William Roscoe).

THE SECOND PERIOD, 1789-1831. 269

of humiliation" that members of the Lower House had bound themselves by pledges. "To convert," he said, "a member of the other House of Parliament into the mere representative of the particular place for which he was returned, instead of the representative of the whole of the Commons of England, was a perversion of one of the best principles of the Constitution." Submission to pledges was, he thought, a "degradation," and that measures ought to be taken to prevent it. In practice there was no uniformity; and at the general election in 1818 we find that some candidates promised to obey instructions, while the majority claimed to be unshackled, unfettered, and unbiassed. But what concerns us most is the view adopted by the Radicals, because the subject has a most important bearing upon that popular control of Parliament which was the ultimate aim of their desires, and the essence of their principles. It has already been observed that the philosophical Radicals made no explicit statement on the matter, and it may fairly be assumed that they believed that, if an identity of interest between the governors and the governed were secured, all the rest would follow. Even Cartwright seems to have thought that, if his suggested reforms were carried out, a perfect harmony would subsist between the electors and the elected, which would render "instructions" quite unnecessary. Yet during the twenty years that preceded the Reform Act, a greater difference of opinion among the Radicals themselves was disclosed than at any time before. Place, for instance, insisted on the view that a representative should submit to pledges and instructions, and he founded the Parliamentary Candidates Society with a view to the more diligent observation of the way in which members gave their votes in Parliament. The

Society, notwithstanding that Bentham actively supported it, enjoyed but a very brief existence, but while it lasted, it recorded the votes of Tory members for electioneering purposes. But Place was not content with this endeavour; he even wrote a pamphlet on the subject—*Pledges to be Given by Candidates.* Here, however, he found himself at issue with several leading Radicals. John Stuart Mill, for instance, in the *Examiner* criticised the pamphlet, and when at a Westminster election Burdett and Hobhouse were asked to pledge themselves to the ballot, the abolition of the house and window taxes, of the newspaper stamp duty, and the repeal of the Septennial Act, they both declared that "none but fools demanded pledges, and none but knaves gave them". Joseph Hume too was scarcely less emphatic; though anxious, he said, to attend to the representations of his constituents, he would in no instance regard himself as bound to vote as they desired, "unless his own convictions went with them". And yet there were some Radicals who took the view of Place. Alderman Waithman, for example, a Radical candidate in the City, declared that on all great questions "it was the duty of the representative to listen to the voice of his constituents," and that their opinions when "fully, fairly, and distinctly expressed . . . ought *implicitly to be obeyed*". Two crucial examples of the practical application of the theory are recorded, and are of considerable interest. The first occurred in 1811 when the Freeholders of Middlesex (then a Radical constituency), met in their club at the Crown and Anchor Tavern, and passed the following resolutions: first, that it be earnestly recommended to the electors of Middlesex and throughout the country to follow the example of Westminster in sending a representative to Parliament free of personal expense, and never to vote for any candidate who had not *subscribed* the following *declaration* :—

"I declare it to be my opinion that representation ought to have at least as wide an extent as taxation in support of the poor, the Church and State; that such representation as a common right ought to be fairly distributed throughout the community; and that Parliaments ought to be brought back to a constitutional duration, that is, not exceeding one year".

The second resolution asked Sir Samuel Romilly to subscribe the declaration and to come forward as a candidate —an invitation which he naturally declined. Here is an extreme instance of demanding written pledges. The second crucial example happened in 1819, and is unique. It was, in fact, an actual attempt to over-ride the law, and to place the election of a parliamentary delegate in the hands, not of the narrow class of voters on the register, but in those of the people themselves. The plan was ingenious, but like many plans of Cartwright's, who probably devised it, it was intrinsically absurd. At a mass meeting held at Birmingham Sir Charles Wolseley, a Staffordshire Baronet of democratic sympathies, was actually elected, amid the thundering acclamations of one undivided multitude, to be "*legislatorial attorney*" for one year, "if so long he executed his trust faithfully"; or to use Cartwright's quaint expression, he was to be "a petition in the form of a living man, instead of one on parchment or paper". The whole scene, which was more ridiculous than dramatic, was in itself a kind of living illustration of the delegation theory implicitly contained in the words "legislatorial attorney". But for the chief actors in the farce the results were somewhat serious. Indicted for unlawful conspiracy, three of them, Edmunds, Maddocks, and Wooler, were sent to prison, and the venerable Cartwright, whom it was wished to spare the indignity of a gaol, was fined a hundred pounds.[1]

The popular control of Parliament was to be obtained by such constitutional changes as short Parliaments and a wide extension of the suffrage. So, at least, thought the Radicals, and to achieve these ends, they used, as far as possible, such instruments or means as they found ready to their hands. The means that most naturally presented themselves were the use of political societies, of the right of petition, of public meetings, and of free discussion in the press. No account of the Radicals would, therefore, be complete, if this important part of the subject were ignored.

The formation of societies, such as the London Corresponding Society, for example, was a very powerful instrument in the hands of the eighteenth century Radicals. As a means whereby to concentrate their energies, to give definite expression to their views, and to disseminate their doctrines, the value of such associations could hardly be exaggerated. But by the end of the century they had all vanished beneath the crushing weight of a severely repressive legislation. Gradually, however, and timidly, they began to rear their heads, and in 1811 two new Radical societies were founded, the Hampden and the Union. The first of these had Mr.

---

[1] Jephson's *Rise and Progress of the Platform*, vol. i., pp. 304, 455-59, 472; Twiss' *Life of Lord Eldon*, vol. iii., pp. 150, etc; Wallas' *Life of Francis Place*, pp. 262, 327; Bowring's *Life of Bentham*, Works, vol. xi., p. 66; *Memoirs of the Life of Sir S. Romilly*, vol. ii., pp. 413-17; *Life of Cartwright*, vol. ii., pp. 165, 169, 221.

Northmore, a gentleman of strong Liberal opinions, as one of the chief of its creators, though it is clear that the indefatigable Cartwright was its animating soul. The scheme of the Society was that of a head or central body with its rooms and offices in London, and a co-ordination of branches in the provinces, and for a time it was carried out with some success. We find Bamford, for example, one of those Radicals of whom the working-class might be proud, helping to establish a branch at Middleton in Lancashire. That it met with many difficulties may be gathered from the fact that it could find no better place than an old Methodist chapel for its meetings. In the metropolis, indeed, things were not as bad as this, and Sir Francis Burdett sometimes occupied the chair. Annual Parliaments, universal suffrage, and equal electoral districts were the main objects upon which the Society concentrated its attention; but when in 1817 a meeting of delegates from the various branches met in London to consider a Reform Bill, the differences of opinion gave rise, as they often did among the Radicals, to a good deal of heated argument. The Hampden, however, soon began to wane and dwindle, and in 1819 it was dissolved. Cartwright accused it of inertness, while others attributed its failure to his own intemperate zeal, that cut off the support of the more moderate reformers. In any case it was self-destroyed by the dissensions of its members.[1]

---

[1] *Life of Cartwright*, vol ii., pp. 24-26, 107, 165; Wallas' *Life of Francis Place*, p. 115; Bamford's *Passages in the Life of a Radical*, vol. i., pp. 9, 11, 16. Cobbett (writing in 1817) said that the Hampden Clubs were hardly worthy of notice, except the one in London, "which consists in reality of Sir Francis Burdett and Major Cartwright" (Cobbett's *Political Writings*, vol. v., "An Address to the Men of Norwich").

The Union Club was founded about the same time as the Hampden, and though perhaps not so important, shares with it the distinction of being the subject of inquiry by a House of Lords Committee. Sir Francis Burdett and Cartwright were the best-known names among its founders, and its principles were annual Parliaments and representation—the basis of political liberty —coextensive with direct taxation. Though its career was very brief, and all it did was to publish an address to the nation on the subject of reform, it was nevertheless suspected by the Government of acting with the Spenceans, an insignificant group, who preached a kind of communism. A petition denying the allegation was presented to Parliament on its behalf. As the Hampden and the Union Clubs were during this period the only examples of Radical societies, and as even they were failures, it is evident that political association was, as an instrument of radicalism, almost entirely ineffective.[1]

The right of petition to the Crown, and especially to the House of Commons, was still constantly employed, and if not fruitful in results, it yet served to keep the Radical cause alive, and well before the public eye. The extremists, however, thought that for the people to petition their servants was absurd. The City of London, though it had given place to Westminster as the focus of democracy, still continued to petition Parliament in favour of reform; and on one occasion the Corporation had the boldness to ask Parliament to expunge from its journals all references to the committal of Sir Francis Burdett and John Gale Jones. That event gave occa-

---

[1] *Life of Cartwright*, vol. ii., pp. 10, 129, 377; Cobbett's *Political Writings*, vol. v.; The Petition of Thomas Cleary, Secretary to the London Union Society.

sion to a large number of petitions from many different sources, but they were sometimes couched in terms so disrespectful that the House refused to entertain them. On the whole it must be said that the use of the petition was not nearly so effective as it was in the days of Beckford and Horne Tooke. Public meetings were more useful, because they aroused more animation, and were therefore more frequently attempted.[1] But they were accompanied so often by scenes of riot and disorder, that they were carried on with difficulty, and were actually injurious to the cause. Those present at the meetings and the officers of the law were continually in conflict. Even Cartwright, who in 1813 stumped the country on a tour, notwithstanding that his maxim was "hold fast by the law," was rudely arrested at Huddersfield on suspicion. Upon the conclusion of the war in 1815 so much distress was caused by the high prices and scarcity of food, that there was no lack for the demagogue of inflammable material; and, in fact, there arose a class of agitators who were paid for their services, and traded on the feelings of the masses. "It was," says Bamford, "a bad practice, however, and gave rise to a set of orators who made a trade of speechifying. . . . He who produced the greatest excitement, the loudest cheering, and the most violent clappings, was the best orator, and was sure to be engaged and well paid; and in order to produce those manifestations the wildest and most extravagant rhodomontade would too often suffice." Of this class of speaker the greatest was the notorious Henry Hunt,

---

[1] It is curious, but worth noting, that the Evangelicals, or Clapham Sect, who generally acted with the Tories, by their anti-slavery campaign gave a good deal of impetus to political agitation (Trevelyan's *Life and Letters of Macaulay*, vol. i., p. 67).

who was commonly called the "Orator," and as the chief representative of the demagogue, or agitator Radical, he claims from us a brief consideration.[1]

Henry Hunt was born at Upavon, in Wiltshire, in 1773. His father was a farmer, and Hunt, who received a fair education, followed his profession. The amusements of the country, hunting and shooting and the like, seem to have occupied a larger share of his attention than they ought, and his farms did not greatly prosper. He would perhaps have remained an unknown countryman for the remainder of his life, if he had not joined the Wiltshire Yeomanry. It was about this time that an incident occurred which proved to be the turning-point of his career. It so happened that Lord Bruce, who was the colonel in command, accused Hunt of shooting pheasants on his preserves, and dismissed him from the corps. Hunt forthwith challenged the colonel to a duel, an offence for which he was committed to the King's Bench Prison for a period of six weeks. During the enforced leisure which he was thus compelled to take, he listened to a good deal of inflammatory talk from a number of discontented persons, who had grievances, real or imaginary, against the existing order of society; and in consequence, though he had entered prison a Tory, he emerged a furious Radical. It was at this time that he became a frequent guest at Horne Tooke's Sunday parties at his house at Wimbledon—an incident in his history that was not without importance. We need not follow Hunt in his varied private fortunes any further, but as the greatest demagogue of his time,

[1] Sharpe's *London and the Kingdom*, vol. iii., pp. 278-80, etc.; *Life of Cartwright*, vol ii., p. 46; Bamford's *Passages in the Life of a Radical*, vol. i., p. 35; Jephson's *Rise and Progress of the Platform*, vol. i., p. 413.

THE SECOND PERIOD, 1789-1831. 277

and one of the greatest of all times, he presents a very interesting figure. Over six feet in height, well-knitted and robust, he looked much more like a jovial farmer than a Radical politician. His light grey eyes, fair complexion, thin lips, regular features and agreeable expression, must have given him a very comely look; and gifted as he was with a fine melodious voice, a great power of passionate delivery, and a wonderful fluency of speech, it is no wonder that he kept the listening people spellbound.[1] His white hat, blue coat, light waistcoat, kersey smalls and top-boots soon became the cynosure of every eye at public meetings. He was, indeed, as Place called him, "the best mob orator of the day," impudent, active, vulgar, and "a pretty sample of an ignorant, turbulent, mischief-making fellow, a highly dangerous one in turbulent times". In the opinion of all the better class of Radicals he was regarded as no better than a nuisance, who did more harm than good to the cause which he pretended to advance. He was, indeed, full of envy and detraction, and jealous of a rival in the affections of the people. That he and Cobbett should have been at times on disagreeable terms cannot be a matter of surprise, for while Hunt thought Cobbett a poltroon, the latter denounced the "Orator" as a despot. What Place's opinion of Hunt was, we have already seen; and that there was no love lost between them is evident from the fact that Hunt repaid him in his own coin by calling him "the leading cock of the rump". Such were the amenities of intercourse among the Radicals. The judgment that Bentham passed on Hunt, though severe, perhaps did not greatly err; for the philosopher clearly

[1] There is a portrait of Hunt in the National Portrait Gallery by Adam Buck.

wished to do him justice. When people laughed at Hunt for selling blacking, Bentham courageously protested; "the feeling thus betrayed," he said, "belongs not to us democrats, but to aristocrats". Yet he declared that in Hunt's pericranium the organ of abusiveness was a good yard long, and that his radicalism did not arise from a love of liberty, but from a hatred of tyranny, mixed with a hatred of anything superior whatsoever. There can be little doubt that Hunt's master-passion was a love of popularity unrestrained by any higher motives or finer feelings.

> So fond of loud report that, not to miss
> Of being known (his last and utmost bliss)
> He rather would be known for what he is.

For to gain notoriety there were no limits to the arts to which he would not descend. He made and sold blacking and herb tea, and he manufactured a concoction as a substitute for coffee, in order to prevent any revenue being collected from the customs duties upon the real article. This histrionic agitator was a past-master of the arts of *réclame* and self-advertisement, and—like his prototype Cleon who of all Athenians had the most persuasive tongue—he soon contrived to make himself the idol of the mob.[1] Tricolour flags and caps of liberty were waved before him as he moved along amidst thunders of applause. So alarmed did the Government become, that in 1817 the Habeas Corpus Act was suspended, and the right of public meeting was suppressed. There were rumours of treasonable plots; private revenge sought gratification in false information to the

---

[1] Bowring's *Life of Bentham*, Collected Works, vol. x., pp. 602, 603. See Thucydides, bk. iii., c. 36, for a description of Cleon ; τῇ τε πόλει τῶν πάντων ἐν τῷ τότε πιθανώτατος,

THE SECOND PERIOD, 1789-1831. 279

police; secret gatherings were held under pretexts, thinly veiled, of benefit and botanical societies, and for the relief of the families of those who for the cause of liberty were languishing in prison. There were processions with banners bearing inscriptions such as "Unity and Strength," "Liberty and Fraternity," "Parliaments Annual," "Suffrage Universal," and crimson caps of liberty with tufts of laurel raised aloft on poles. There were arrests, and even convictions, for treasonable practices; the whole country was in a state of ferment, which in 1819 reached a point where an explosion had at last become inevitable. Then it was that Hunt appeared in all that tinsel magnificence in which he gloried. It so happened that in August of that year a great meeting was organised and brought together in the neighbourhood of Manchester at Peterloo Fields. A black flag was waved aloft with the inscription, "Equal Representation or Death," while a number of women bore a red one with the words, "Let us die like men, and not be sold like slaves". Hunt, the chief speaker, was borne in triumph on a car. How the cavalry charged the mob with such disastrous results, it would be beyond our province to describe; it must be enough to say that the so-called Peterloo massacre inflamed the feelings of the people to a fever pitch.[1] Monster meetings were convened to express the general indignation, and Hunt, the "Champion of Liberty," was received in London in triumph as the hero of the hour. About 300,000 people thronged the streets through which

[1] The feeling thus expressed by Shelley illustrates the indignation of many people over the Peterloo affair: "I await anxiously to hear how the country will express its sense of this bloody murderous oppression of its destroyers" (Letter to C. Ollier, 6th September, 1819).

he passed. The white hat which he wore at Peterloo, and was damaged by a sabre cut, became a kind of symbol for the Radicals, and for a time the trade of dyeing black hats white was very brisk. To put on the white hat was a badge of conversion to the democratic cause. Hunt and others were tried at York for the part they had played in the affair. He was convicted, and sentenced to two and a half years' imprisonment, and to find security for his future good behaviour. His durance vile at Ilchester afforded him the leisure for acts of extraordinary folly, which his admirers abetted and encouraged. He proposed a solemn fast day to commemorate the "massacre"; he went through a mock ceremony of knighting with the "Order of the Cross of Ilchester" his friends who came to visit him, and proposed that any two such knights should have the power to confer a diploma upon any deserving Radical. His head was almost turned by his apotheosis as a deeply suffering martyr. He was "St. Henry," and the "Captive of Ilchester" immured at the "Bastille"; even children were christened "Henry Hunt" in batches. The force of folly could no farther go than this.[1]

In the same year a public meeting was convened at Stockport, which, though not of the same magnitude as that at Peterloo, is not less illustrative of the history of the time. The chief speakers were Sir Charles Wolseley, already famous as the "legislatorial attorney," and the Rev. Joseph Harrison, a local preacher. Their language

[1] *Memoirs of Henry Hunt*, written by himself, 2 vols.; Bamford's *Passages in the Life of a Radical*, vol. i., pp. 16, 45, 156, 198, 208, 249; vol. ii., p. 207; Wallas' *Life of Place*, 120; Cobbett's *Political Writings*, vol. vi., Letter on the Corn Bill (April, 1825); *Diaries and Correspondence of Lord Colchester*, vol. iii., p. 87; Jephson's *Rise and Progress of the Platform*, vol. i., p. 487; *Memoirs of the Court of England during the Regency*, by the Duke of Buckingham, vol. ii., pp. 339-41.

was imbued with the sort of epithets which Coleridge once described as flame-coloured. "The people," said Harrison, "should rise en masse to suppress such a tyrannical Government as the one of this country, and it will not be long, but very soon, that it shall be overturned, and many a bloody battle may be fought, and many a one incarcerated in prison, before it shall be accomplished. . . . The House of Commons are the people's servants. It would be as absurd to petition them as it would be for a master to petition his groom for his horse." Sir Charles Wolseley on his part declared that he was proud to say that he had been at the taking of the Bastille in France, and would be happy to be at the taking of the Bastille in England. It was not a matter for surprise that they were both sentenced to eighteen months' imprisonment for conspiracy to cause a riot. These events were but typical of a most distressing state of things. The condition of terror of 1795, indeed, seemed to be once again revived. Beyond the Tweed things were no better than in England, and we find Sir Walter Scott and other lairds raising a corps of volunteers to put down a revolutionary movement, and dreading a plot to seize the arms stored at Edinburgh Castle. This "præternatural suspicion" culminated in the repressive legislation of the "Six Acts" passed by the so-called "Savage Parliament" in a state of panic in a few weeks towards the close of the year 1819. But a description of the "Six Acts" belongs to the general history of England; and it concerns us here to mention them only by way of illustration of the difficulties by which the Radicals at this time were beset.[1]

[1] *Memoirs of the Court of England during the Regency*, by the Duke of Buckingham, vol. ii., p. 336; *Memoirs of the Court of George the Fourth*, by the same, vol. i., p. 15; Jephson's *Rise and Progress of the Platform*, vol. i., p. 476; Lockhart's *Life of Scott*, vol. iv., pp. 318, 324.

If there was little liberty of public speech, the press was not in much better plight. The publication of parliamentary debates, except on the occasion which led to the imprisonment of Burdett and John Gale Jones, was allowed to continue unimpeded. But the reporting was very poorly done, and journalism was almost at its lowest ebb. When Lord Loughborough late in life was suspected as the author of the *Letters of Junius*, he met the allegation by declaring that he had never contaminated his hands with any connection with a newspaper, and that he would disdain to taint his character with any such employment. In like manner Sir Walter Scott averred that no one "but a thoroughgoing blackguard ought to attempt the daily press". That was a hard saying, but it was not far distant from the truth. The Benchers of Lincoln's Inn reflected the general feeling of educated persons when in 1808 they passed a by-law disqualifying from call to the bar any one who had written for hire in the columns of a daily paper.[1] The agitation for the repeal of the newspaper stamp duties — the so-called "Taxes on Knowledge"—belongs mainly to the period that followed the Reform Act, and it is, therefore, mentioned only here. But it may in general terms be said that the conditions under which the press was carried on were those of struggle and contest with the law. True it is that many of the prosecuted journals or pamphlets were atheistical or blasphemous, and as such had no political character whatever. Richard Carlisle, for example, that well-meaning but obstinate republican and atheist, who spent many years in prison in the cause of

---

[1] Campbell's *Lives of the Chancellors*, vol. vi., p. 348; Sir Walter Scott's *Journal*, p. 262; *Diaries and Correspondence of Lord Colchester*, vol. ii., p. 240.

freedom of the press, is not a personality of much significance in the history of the Radicals. Yet, notwithstanding many disadvantages, their voices were occasionally heard in the columns of the papers, sometimes speaking in bold accents and sometimes in bated breath. We read, for instance, of Place and Bentham helping to support the *Gorgon*, a working-class journal ; and of Place writing in *Hone's Register* against what he called the Gagging Act. The latter paper, however, had a very brief existence.[1] But perhaps the most characteristic example of the purely Radical press was the *Black Dwarf*. This was a London weekly publication which was established in 1817 by T. J. Wooler. Its spirit may be inferred from the words of its prospectus. It was intended to " expose every species of vice and folly, with which this virtuous and enlightened metropolis abounds ". To political delinquency no quarter, it was asserted, would be given; and no mercy would be shown to spiritual imposition. Neither the throne nor the altar would be a sanctuary against the intrusion of the editor. It was no idle boast, for to do him justice, he carried out his promise. As Cartwright said, "in the *Black Dwarf* we have got a giant in talent on our side ". Bentham gave Wooler his support, and allowed him to publish in cheap numbers his *Catechism of Parliamentary Reform*. Wooler, indeed, struck the true Radical note when he declared that to " respect honest prejudices " is like "respecting honest swindling or honest robbery ". Yet this uncompromising zeal did not help him to prolong the life of the *Black Dwarf* beyond 1824. Its circulation dwindled, and Wooler closed his thankless task of instructing what he conceived to be a most

[1] *The History of Trade Unionism*, by Sidney and Beatrice Webb, p. 88 ; Wallas' *Life of Francis Place*, p. 125.

ungrateful public by sorrowfully declaring his belief that they had ceased to take any interest in reform.[1]

There were other journals of a more distinguished and literary style, which, though not avowedly Radical in character, yet gave important services in furtherance of the cause. The chief of these was the *Examiner*, which the brothers John and Leigh Hunt set up in 1808 as a weekly publication. The names of its founders would be in themselves a guarantee of its great superiority to the ordinary stuff that in those days passed for journalism. The *Examiner's raison d'être* was the promotion of Church and parliamentary reform, and though Leigh Hunt admitted that Burdett was his hero, yet the paper was, at most, only ultra-Whig in character. The Hunts were what they themselves called "Whig-Radicals and Liberals". The *Examiner* soon found itself engaged in a contest with the law. In 1809 it suffered from a prosecution (which was subsequently dropped) for some remarks upon Major Hogan's pamphlet accusing the Duke of York as Commander-in-Chief of favouritism and corruption. Again in the following year a second prosecution was begun and discontinued; and on this occasion the offending journal incurred the displeasure of the law for having the temerity to remark that of all monarchs since the Revolution the successor of George III. would have the finest opportunity to make himself nobly popular. A third prosecution followed for an article (reprinted from another journal) upon flogging in the army, but the defendants, who had Brougham for

---

[1] The *Black Dwarf* (to be seen in the British Museum); *The English Historical Review*, an article on the Unstamped Press, 1815-36, October, 1897; *Life of Cartwright*, vol. ii., p. 127; Bain's *James Mill*, p. 434; Bowring's *Life of Bentham*, vol. x., p. 490.

their counsel, were acquitted. At last the Government succeeded. It so happened that the Prince of Wales had promised, or was believed to have promised, the emancipation of the Catholics, but that as Regent he opposed it.[1] The *Examiner* criticised his conduct with a severity that exceeded all ordinary licence; it condemned him as "a violator of his word, a libertine over head and ears in disgrace, a despiser of domestic ties, the companion of gamblers and demireps, a man who has just closed half a century without one single claim on the gratitude of his country or the respect of posterity". For this audacious language the brothers Hunt were sentenced to two years' imprisonment and fined £1000.

This disaster to the Hunts gave Bentham an occasion to show his benevolent good-will. He had reason to be grateful, for they had been useful to the cause that he had so much at heart; they had, as he said, taken him under their protection, and "trumpeted" him every now and then in the pages of the *Examiner*. John Hunt, moreover, he justly called "the tried, undaunted, persevering, intelligent, and upright defender of the people's liberties". But Bentham did not content himself with words, for he went to visit the sufferers in prison, and helped them to while away the tedium of the slowly dragging hours. The picture of the sage playing battledore and shuttlecock with Leigh Hunt is a pleasing one to contemplate; and it is entirely characteristic of his

---

[1] The Prince Regent, in a letter to the Whig leaders, declared that he had no "predilections"; upon which Moore wrote the following satire:—

"I am proud to declare I have no predilections,
My heart is a sieve where some scattered affections
Are just danced about for a moment or two,
And the finer they are, the more sure to go through".

ever-restless mind that he should have seized the opportunity to suggest improvements in the game.¹

The *Examiner* was not the only high-class journal which served as a medium for the Radicals to disseminate their views. The *Morning Chronicle*, formerly a Whig organ, became, under the management of Mr. Black, to a large extent a vehicle of utilitarian radicalism. Black, indeed, was a disciple of James Mill, and was one of the most influential channels through which his master's conversation and personal influence moved the world. But of all journalists the one who did the most for the philosophic Radicals was Albany Fonblanque. Born in 1793, he studied first for the Royal Engineers and secondly for the bar, but want of health prevented him from going any farther. Very early he worshipped at the shrine of Bentham and James Mill; and by the time that he joined the staff of Black, then the editor of the *Morning Chronicle*, he had already become a convinced and thoroughgoing Radical. He brought conspicuous talents to the discharge of his profession; or as a writer in the *Edinburgh Review* remarked with an air of condescension, "no man need be ashamed of a profession of which Albany Fonblanque is a member". He possessed in an equal degree perspicuity and acuteness, vivacity and wit; so that when in 1831 he succeeded Leigh Hunt as manager and proprietor of the *Examiner* the prosperous future of that journal was assured. In his hands it became, to use the words of John Stuart Mill, the principal representative in the newspaper press of Radical opinions; and so it continued until 1847, when Fonblanque retired to become Statistical Secretary to the

---

[1] *Autobiography of Leigh Hunt*, pp. 181-85, 205-7; Bowring's *Life of Bentham*, vol. x., p. 531; Bain's *James Mill*, p. 123.

THE SECOND PERIOD, 1789-1831. 287

Board of Trade. Thus was lost to journalism one of its most brilliant representatives. He died in 1872.[1]

The most celebrated figure at this time in the ranks of journalism, or at all events of Radical journalism, was a very different kind of person. This was William Cobbett, one of the most striking individualities of his time. His native place, where he was born in 1762, was Farnham, Surrey; a locality which calls up some historic memories, for it was afterwards the home of Richard Cobden, and was in the immediate vicinity of Moor Park, with which the names of Swift and Sir William Temple will ever be associated. The son of a small farmer, Cobbett received but a scanty education. If not a peasant of genius like Burns or Carlyle, he was at least one of extraordinary talent; but he did not all at once discover where it lay. After serving some apprenticeship to agriculture and the law, he went into the army, where he seized the opportunity to cultivate his love of learning. In eight years he bought his discharge. He then accused three of his commanding officers of fraud, and was court-martialled for his pains. Failing to appear, he fled to France, and thence to Philadelphia, where he contrived to make a living by teaching English to French emigrants. He soon, however, found his true vocation; for the journalist, like the poet, is rather born than made. He set up a daily paper, which he happily styled the *Porcupine's Gazette*, and subscribed himself as Peter Porcupine. The tone of the paper was worthy of its name, for it bristled with pungent personalities. He bitterly attacked the American Republic, comparing its society to the vessels in a crockery shop, which have

[1] *The Life and Labours of Albany Fonblanque*, by E. B. de Fonblanque J. S. Mill's *Autobiography*, pp. 89, 173.

all been rendered equally worthless by being shattered into fragments of uniform value. The democratic party, the most hostile to England, was peculiarly obnoxious to his feelings; for at this period of his life he was an unmitigated Tory. He nicknamed Franklin "Old Lightning Rod"; he called Washington "a notorious rebel and traitor," and Lafayette "a citizen miscreant". As to the English Radicals, he exhausted upon them his vituperative vocabulary; a thing which in Cobbett's case was something of a feat. Paine he called "the greatest disgrace of mankind," an "infamous and atrocious miscreant," and "Mad Tom";[1] Wilkes was "a miserable adventurer without ancestry, without fortune, without anything but impudence, obscurity and blasphemy to recommend him"; the saintly Price was "the pious old apostle of discord". The unhappy Priestley, who had gone into exile to escape persecution at home, fared even worse; for Cobbett wrote a malicious pamphlet styled *Observations on Priestley's Emigration.* But this campaign of abuse was destined to come to an abrupt and disgraceful termination, for he was fined heavily for a libel upon a well-known Dr. Rush, and fled to England to escape the payment of the penalty. In the old country, where his fame had gone before him, he was welcomed by the Tories as a valuable recruit. Windham, who said in Parliament that Cobbett deserved a golden statue for his writings in America, invited him to dinner, and intro-

---

[1] Yet Cobbett in 1819 brought Paine's bones back to England, so great his veneration for him had become. Byron wrote the following squib on this act of Cobbett's:—
"In digging up your bones, Tom Paine,
Will Cobbett has done well;
You visit him on earth again,
He'll visit you in Hell".

duced him to Pitt, at that time the all-powerful Minister of State. Whether Cobbett received some slight from Pitt it is impossible to say, but it has been asserted that he did. He started a bookseller's business in Pall Mall, under the sign of the Crown, Bible and Mitre, to indicate his principles; but those principles soon underwent a rapid change. The *Political Register*, which he began in 1802, and which with hardly any interruption was continued until his death, and was the main occupation of his life, was at first Tory in its character, but soon became a Radical journal of an advanced and revolutionary type. Whether the transformation was due to the slight which it was alleged that he had received from Pitt, or to the prosecutions that he suffered for some libellous attacks upon the Government, is not a question of any great importance; for the result was in any case the same. What is certain is that in 1810 he was fined £1000, and sentenced to be imprisoned for two years, and that from that time onwards he became the bitter and determined enemy of existing institutions. On his release he became a sort of hero, and was entertained at a dinner by Sir Francis Burdett. A second time he sought refuge in America, where he lived in Long Island for two years, but even at that distance he contrived to issue the *Register* with very little interruption. Whether he left England to escape the crushing legislation which then enthralled the press, or to defy his creditors, whom he seems to have treated very badly, is not very clear; but the latter reason was probably as cogent as the former. At least he was severely criticised by another Radical, Wooler, in an article in the *Black Dwarf* on the "Trial and Desertion of Corporal Cobbett". From the other side of the Atlantic Cobbett replied by charging

Wooler with being dissolute, drunken and vindictive; in short, the two Radicals had a very pretty quarrel. On his return to England he wooed the suffrages first of Coventry and then of Preston, but it was not until 1830, when he was already verging towards his seventieth year, that he was elected for Oldham, which he represented to his death in 1835.

Such, very briefly, were the salient incidents of the life of William Cobbett. It was a stormy controversial life, and quite different from what the casual observer would have guessed from his personal appearance. Tall and strongly built, with sharp grey twinkling eyes, a round and ruddy countenance, he might very well have passed for an English yeoman in comfortable circumstances. When he entered Parliament he was described by one who saw him as "an elderly, respectable-looking, red-faced gentleman, in a dust-coloured coat and drab breeches with gaiters".[1] In general appearance Hunt and Cobbett were very much alike, but though the latter had not the fluency of Hunt, he was much the more intelligent. Hunt was nothing but a blatant rhetorician, but Cobbett, notwithstanding his defects, had some distinguished merits. As a journalist, if not the greatest ever known, he was, for power and far-extending influence, beyond dispute the greatest of his time. He was, says Southey, "an evangelist of the populace". The *Political Register* had a circulation which was immense and constantly increasing. He contrived to evade the stamp duty by publishing it as an open and unfolded sheet, and in 1815 he was able to reduce its price to twopence, from which its nickname of the *Twopenny Trash* originated.

[1] Bamford's passages in the *Life of a Radical*, vol. i., p. 20; *Life and Correspondence of Thomas Slingsby Duncombe*, vol. i., p. 72.

Some idea of the influence exerted by the *Register* may be gathered from the language used by Bentham when he sent to Cobbett his *Parliamentary Reform Catechism* and requested him to publish it: " The celebrity of your name," he said, " compared with the *obscurity of my own*, has suggested to me the idea . . . ," and in this way he hoped to obtain " a degree of circulation so much beyond what *any such name as mine* could give to it ".[1] That is an extraordinary testimony, coming, as it did, from one of the greatest of philosophers. In fact the *Political Register* seems to have been generally recognised as the most powerful organ for the dissemination of opinion. Twice Sir Francis Burdett made use of it, and twice he suffered prosecution by the Government. The first occasion was that of the imprisonment of John Gale Jones, to which we have referred; the second was that of the letter to the Westminster electors on the Peterloo Massacre, when he was fined £2000 and sent to prison for three months. The success of Cobbett's journalism was due less to his opinions, which were often curiously perverse, than to his wonderful lucidity of style. It was clear, direct and incisive in an almost unparalleled degree. Never was pure Anglo-Saxon diction used with such telling and immediate effect. Some popularity was due, no doubt, to the nicknames which he was singularly happy in inventing. They were always suggestive and appropriate, and stuck like bird-lime to those to whom they were applied. " Old Glory Burdett," " Prosperity Robinson," Bentham " the antediluvian lawyer," " Æolus Canning," " pink-nosed Liverpool," and similar phrases, caught the popular taste, and long lingered in the memory. Cobbett's invective,

---

[1] Bowring's *Life of Bentham*, vol. x., p. 458.

though wanting in good taste, was often droll and exceedingly amusing. But quite apart from this, and putting politics aside, he has made for himself a distinct place in English literature, and that place he has won by his vigour, his simplicity and purity of diction. Yet besides his journalistic writings, which number about a hundred volumes, he has not left very much work of literary value. He wrote an excellent English grammar, which had a wide circulation, and of which he said, and perhaps truly, that he knew it was the best. His *Rural Rides* may yet be read with considerable pleasure; but his other books are mainly works of practical utility, or, like his *History of the Protestant Reformation*, are marred by his unconquerable prejudices. How Cobbett, who, from one point of view, possessed so little literary taste and judgment, came by so good a literary style is somewhat of a mystery; but he owed something to Swift, whom he studied as a boy, "the first author after Moses," he said, "I ever read". It is evident too that he made biblical English his model. Yet he spoke of the "soft balderdash of Southey or Sir Walter Scott," and blamed farmers' daughters for spending time in reading it; and declared that "Addison had made it the fashion to admire Milton and Garrick Shakespeare, those writers of bombast and far-fetched conceits and miserable puns". Such wildcat criticism it would be difficult to parallel. Nor does his taste for music or the drama seem to have been in any better case; for he could find no better description of the opera than by talking of "the squalling and squeaking and piping of the Italian singers".

But it is Cobbett's place not in literature but in politics that is to us a matter of concern; and that place is certainly unique. After he had shuffled off his Toryism,

THE SECOND PERIOD, 1789-1831. 293

in his last and longest stage of settled political conviction, he was, indeed, a Radical, but his radicalism was of a type peculiarly his own. For while the Radicals, as a body, made parliamentary reform the final cause of all their agitation, Cobbett viewed it more as a means than as an end. That end was a complete change in the financial system of the country. The public debt, the funding system, paper money, the Bank of England, the absorption of capital in foreign expenditure and subsidies, the profits of loan mongers and stock jobbers, he firmly believed to be the sole causes of the troubles of his country and of the misfortunes of the poor. These things, therefore, he was never weary of denouncing. As it was said of Addison by Dr. Johnson, that he thought justly but thought faintly, so conversely we may say of Cobbett that he thought wrongly but strongly. *Quod vult, valde vult.* He believed "the powerful and widely extended influence of the moneyed interest" to be a standing danger to the country; and by the "moneyed interest" he meant the "loan jobbers, directors, brokers, contractors and farmers-general," who had been engendered "by the excessive amount of the public debt and the almost boundless extension of the issues of paper money". This class of persons he summed up as the *Paper Aristocracy*, while holders of sinecures and pensions he stigmatised as the *Dead Weight*. The paper money he described as "destructive and murderous," and together with the funding system as "of Dutch descent, begotten by Bishop Burnet and born in hell". Bank-notes he classed with gunpowder, as "two of the most damnable inventions that ever sprang from the minds of man under the influence of the devil". Speaking of the mill where the paper for bank-notes was manufactured, he said that he hoped the time would come when a monument would be erected where the mill stood, and that on that spot the words "The Curse of England" would be inscribed. "This spot," he declared, "ought to be accursed in all times henceforth for evermore." The Bank of England he vigorously denounced; it was an "audacious and rapacious body," which from being a company of merchants had "in conjunction with the seat-dealers become the real sovereigns of England". Hence he abhorred the Stock Exchange, and the system that enabled "a hook-nosed round-eyed Jew to bag half a million of money, and to exchange his orange-basket for two or three parks and mansions by watching the turn of the market". He, therefore, disliked the Jews for their connection with finance and opposed their admission into Parliament; he would in these days have been called an anti-Semite. His prejudice against the Quakers was hardly less intense; for if they did not haunt "'Change Alley," they were the leading brokers and dealers in Mark Lane. They were, said Cobbett, "as to the products of the earth what the Jews are as to gold and silver"; "a perfect monster in society," and "a great deal worse than the Jews"; famous for "cool impudent falsehood" and "a monstrous quality of hypocrisy". He even opposed the anti-slavery agitation because it was largely a movement of the Quakers.

Such, in brief, were Cobbett's root principles, which he made subservient to all his actions and everything he wrote, and to which he held with invincible tenacity. To abolish the financial system which he found in operation he made the final aim and object of his life; but with the Parliaments as then constituted he soon perceived that any efforts on his part would be absolutely futile.

In his own despite he became a parliamentary reformer. In an article written in 1806 he gave a very clear expression of his views upon the matter : " Of what has been denominated Parliamentary Reform, I have always disapproved. . . . Of universal suffrage I have witnessed the effects too attentively and with too much disgust even to think of it with approbation. . . . When the funding system, from whatever cause, shall cease to operate upon civil and political liberty, there will be no need of projects for parliamentary reform. The Parliament will, as far as shall be necessary, then reform itself." Gradually, however, he worked his way to the conclusion that parliamentary reform must precede any change in the system of finance. Yet he was never quite the vehement reformer that Cartwright, for example, was. He would certainly at one time have been satisfied with household suffrage ; and for the ballot he did not greatly care. " I am for the ballot," he said, " but it is not a matter of very great importance." Yet he thought it would protect tenants against the undue influence of their landlords, and on the whole he rather favoured it. For annual Parliaments, however, he seems to have been more wishful, and he warned his readers against what he called the " Triennial Trick," which, he said, was intended to divide the friends of parliamentary reform.

To the extent of desiring annual Parliaments, the ballot, and a more liberal diffusion of suffrage, Cobbett was in hearty accord with the main body of the Radicals. Yet on some points he differed from them very widely. In the first place his crotchets on finance awakened very little sympathy; if they did not seem absurd, they were deemed to be beside the mark and trivial when compared with the grand question of parliamentary reform. As

Cobbett himself has acknowledged, Cartwright good-naturedly reproved him for wasting his great talents "on questions of political economy, in exposing the state of the finances, and in discussions about the funding system". Even Joseph Hume, the great investigator of financial abuses, and the terror of the Treasury, Cobbett seems to have regarded with suspicion and contempt. He called him "a parliamentary packer," who was "dazzled with the prospect" of becoming Chancellor of the Exchequer, and loved to make displays of his "talent of deducting by thimblefuls from the stream of public expenditure". As to the philosophical Radicals, their general view of things and mental attitude were as alien to Cobbett's as anything could be. Few men, for instance, have done so much for the science of political economy as James and John Stuart Mill, Ricardo and other members of the utilitarian school. Yet for that science Cobbett had nothing but contempt. "The gabbling," he said, "about exchanges and bullion and market prices of gold and silver is as ridiculous as the disputes of Milton's devils about grace, free will, free knowledge and predestination;" a remark that appears strangely inconsistent when his own writings are considered. Of Adam Smith he said that his darkness had given him the reputation of being deep; and that his bulky volumes contained less sound and useful matter than a single poem by Swift. Ricardo was not only a stockbroker but a Jew, and it is therefore no matter of surprise that Cobbett should have stigmatised his famous work on political economy as "a heap of senseless 'Change Alley jargon, put upon paper and bound up in a book". In fact Thomas Paine, compared with whom Locke, he said, was "a mere babbler," seems to have been Cobbett's main authority in matters of finance; and the crudeness of his views may, therefore, be imagined. On educational questions his differences with the philosophical Radicals were hardly less profound. For the universities and public schools, indeed, he shared Bentham's scornful hatred; he styled them "dens of dunces" which turned out a set of "frivolous idiots". But while Bentham, James Mill and Francis Place were working hard for the better education of the people, Cobbett persistently poured cold water on their efforts. He called the demand for popular education "despicable cant and nonsense"; and he tried to justify his statement by asserting that the children would probably read not truth but falsehood. He affirmed that misery and education were increasing side by side, and he jeered at royal dukes for acting "cheek by jowl" with Methodist parsons in "hatching" methods of instruction. "I do not repudiate popular education," he once said in one of his less polemic moods; "I am for letting people do as they like about it, but I am against taxing the people, in order to enable the Government to appoint a schoolmaster and schoolmistress in every parish." That sentence contains, perhaps, the best word he ever uttered for letting light into the solid cloud of ignorance that in his days rested on the masses of the people.

In some smaller matters also Cobbett's radicalism differed somewhat from that which was in vogue. The early Radicals were usually Dissenters, while those of the philosophical school professed no definite belief. But Cobbett was not only a believer, but a strong Churchman in addition. Of the clergy he was sometimes, as in his *Legacy to Parsons*, a caustic critic; but their chastisement was mild compared with that he meted out to the Dissenters. They were the peculiar objects of his wrath; their preachers were fitted for anything, he said, rather than teaching the people morality; the politics of the whole sect were very bad; their kingdom was not of this world, yet they did not neglect its goods, and some amongst them were among the rankest jobbers in the country. The "saints," as they were ironically called, were, he said, as keen for places, contracts and jobs, as the inhabitants of any perjured borough in the kingdom, and produced "the most consummate knaves" that could be found. Cobbett was certainly in his judgment of the Dissenters not only harsh but exceedingly unjust. And so to with regard to those engaged respectively in commercial and agricultural pursuits. The early parliamentary reformers, it is important to remember, made the increase of the representation of the counties the very foundation of their schemes; the landed interest they regarded as the source from which new health might be infused into the corporate body of the state. That the landed interest was the main interest of the country, that it constituted, so to speak, the life-blood of the country, still continued to be a cardinal belief in the minds of many people, but it was the belief no longer of the reformers but of those who were generally Tories. We find Lord Eldon, for example, declaring *suo more* that "every other interest which entered into the constitution of the country, the manufacturing, the commercial, the professional interests, rested so strongly on the agricultural interest that Parliament would do infinite mischief to every rank and class in the community if they did not carefully foster the interests of agriculture".[1] That was a sentiment which must have found an echo in every Tory mind. But no better statement of the case is to be found than in

[1] Twiss' *Life of Lord Eldon*, vol. ii., p. 538.

THE SECOND PERIOD, 1789-1831.

the report of a parliamentary committee on agricultural distress which was issued in 1821. "Your committee," says the report, "are still more anxious to preserve to the landed interest the weight, station and *ascendency* which it has enjoyed so long and used so beneficially." Now Cobbett's attitude towards the agricultural interest was peculiar; nay rather, inconsistent. He was torn in two opposite directions by a conflict of struggling sympathies; for while he was the stout and constant friend of the peasant and the yeoman farmer, he was hostile to the landed aristocracy. In his animosity to the latter he fully shared the sentiments of every class of Radicals. He called the country gentry "the most base of all the creatures that God ever suffered to disgrace the human shape"; he said he did not see why the farmers as a class should be spoken of as "valuable"; that they were "the great pillars of Pitt and his system," and "the loudest, the most hardened, and the most brutal of all the enemies of freedom in England". The "farming aristocracy," he said, were the object of his abhorrence; they had "all the meanness of the crouching tenant coupled with the arrogance of birth; all the insolence of wealth unchecked by any of those sentiments of honour, which are seldom wholly wanting in men of birth and education". In his invectives on the landlords—the "body-guard of the borough-mongers," as Major Cartwright called them—Cobbett showed himself a thorough Radical; yet in his attitude towards the commercial and manufacturing interests he took up an entirely independent line. For if there has been one thing more than another distinctive of the Radicals from the days of Cobbett downwards, it has been their constant tendency to exalt the trading and manufacturing classes at the expense of those subsisting on the land. The fact, whether we ascribe it to the existence of the corn laws, or to a deeply rooted hatred of the landed aristocracy, or to a genuine conviction of economic principles, is not to be disputed. The idea was given shape by Joseph Hume. Speaking in the House of Commons in 1836 he expressed the opinion that "too much stress was laid upon the supposed importance of the landed interest. Landed proprietors imagined that the country could not do without them; the fact was that they could not do without the country . . . for his own part, he believed that if in this country we did not grow a single grain of wheat, of oats, of barley, or rye, England would still be as great and flourishing as it was at present." It was precisely the notion here contained that formed so marked a feature of the language used by Bright and Cobden in the anti-Corn Law agitation. Now to this theory Cobbett was so violently opposed that he held the most extreme and irrational views upon the other side. "Perish Commerce!" was his watchword. "My satisfaction," he said, "at the prospect of a great diminution in our commerce arises from a conviction, long entertained, that such a diminution would be a great benefit to the country. . . . It is well known that England has been upon the decline of power ever since she became decidedly commercial. . . . The land always calls for hands, and always yields a grateful return. . . . Diminish commerce and manufactures, and we have more labour for the land; and that will, I warrant, bring us more corn. . . . Commerce adds nothing, does in no wise contribute to the real wealth or power of the nation. . . . It has in fact caused only the accursed system of funding, and the national character to be degraded." As to large manufacturing centres, he said he had long been satisfied of "their mischievous consequences," and that they were "a very great evil," and that so far from being, as Ricardo called them, a source of national wealth, they were "monstrous heaps of human bodies"; and London was the "wen". Despite his radicalism Cobbett was, in fact, sometimes carried by his prejudices into the very rankest Toryism.

In some minor points, however, Cobbett adhered to the common Radical opinion. He fought boldly and persistently for the freedom of the press, though with regard to the reporting of parliamentary debates he seems to have imagined that the practice was of advantage more to the governing majority than to the people as a whole; "it was," he said, "a great instrument in favour of the 'Collective,'" as he called Parliament, "by giving them an importance they would not otherwise have had. . . . It has long been a most powerful mode of using the press, and in many cases to a most pernicious purpose." That view was at least original and singular. But when he described the *Times* as "this bell-wether of the well-dressed rabble," and "the oracle of all the fools in the kingdom," it is probable that few Radicals would have disagreed with him. Upon the question of the standing army his opinions were as strong as those of Major Cartwright. "There is no need of a standing army," said Cobbett, "in a country where the very lowest classes are so well off as to have no desire and no interest to disturb the public tranquillity. This was formerly the situation of this miserable country. . . . This system, this order of things, an *immense standing army*, with corps of yeomanry established all over the country, with the press under the superintendence of the magistrates, and with the personal safety of every man taken from him; this system I call the borough-monger system, it having been notoriously adopted in order to resist and to crush the petitioners for parliamentary reform." Here, indeed, is the spirit of radicalism in its most undiluted form. Upon questions of legislative interference Cobbett was upon the side of individual freedom. He condemned the "well-meaning men" who would make laws "for the regulating and restraining of every feeling of the human breast"; and in the same spirit he ridiculed the law that made it criminal to adulterate bread with alum and potatoes, just as though the customers, poor creatures, "had no taste of their own, no palate, no discriminating faculty either in their jaws or in their bowels". In like manner, he did not value the protection of the Corn Laws. He maintained that the price of corn depended not upon any law but upon the crop, and that foreign importations were too small to be of any consequence; that the Corn Laws would do no good to the grower or the landlord but would bring unfounded calumny upon them; that they would cause heartburning among the population and withdraw their attention from what he conceived to be the real cause of the distress. "Speaking as a grower of wheat," he courageously exclaimed, "I wish for none of this sort of protection." Upon free trade as a universal principle it may be doubted whether he had any fixed conviction; for while he once made the sensible remark that "free intercourse between nations is a right of human nature," at another time he said free trade was "humbug," and the product of a set of "garret-bred, smoke-dried, free-trade doctrinaires". Upon the question of colonial possessions he was in accord with Bentham and James Mill. "The whole of the colonies," he said, "of every description, as now managed, are a burden to the country.

The colonies are merely a channel through which to convey English, Scotch and Irish taxes into the pockets of the aristocracy and their dependants. . . . On a limited scale and when necessary to national defence, colonies may sometimes be useful, but stretched about over the world, as ours are, they are the cause of feebleness and not of strength ; they are the cause of poverty and not of wealth." As to the question of foreign interference, his views were by no means in accord with those of the philosophical Radicals or of the Manchester school of later days ; he was rather one of those who would have liked to see his country playing the part of the knight-errant of the world. " To set all Europe free," he said, "there requires only the regaining of their rights by the people of England . . . if once the Chapel of St. Stephen were to contain a set of men really elected by the people of the kingdom, away would go Bourbons, Pope, Monks and Legates, as I now see dead sticks and leaves flying before a stiff breeze from the north." These words are conceived in the spirit of that new radicalism which clamours for the rescue of Armenia.[1]

From this brief sketch of Cobbett's political opinions, it will at once be seen that his position was unique. With all his revolutionary and inflammatory talk, he was by natural temperament something of a Tory, and so continued to the end. In one particular he was, as Lord John Russell said of Sir Francis Burdett, " a high prerogative Tory of the days of Queen Anne"; that is to say, he

[1] Selections from Cobbett's *Political Writings*, edited by John M. Cobbett and James P. Cobbett, 6 vols. ; Cobbett's *Rural Rides ; Historical Gleanings*, by J. E. T. Rogers (second series) ; *Westminster Review*, July, 1835 ; Bamford's *Passages in the Life of a Radical ;* Sir Henry Bulwer's *Historical Characters ;* Forsyth's *Essays, Critical and Narrative.*

held that the right of the Crown to choose its servants should be unfettered, and that ministers should not sit in the House of Commons. "It would," he said, "be very difficult to show how the business of the state would suffer from the banishment of that thing called the Treasury Bench out of the House of Commons;" and he said that he wished to see no member of Parliament ever a servant of the King.[1] But, putting constitutional theories aside, he was, indeed, a thorough Englishman; inconsistent and illogical, and standing in sharp contrast with the Radical philosophers who had the Frenchman's passion for precise order and arrangement. Carlyle has with a few graphic strokes depicted this side of his character; "he is," he said, "the pattern John Bull of his century, strong as the rhinoceros, and with singular humanities and genialities shining through his thick skin, a most brave phenomenon".[2] His sympathies were deeply rooted in English rural life. To the peasants—for he never forgot the class from which he sprung—he remained the constant friend; and perhaps of all interests in life, their interests lay the nearest to his heart. His fellow feeling for the agricultural labourer was greatly to his credit, though it sometimes led him far astray. He said, for instance, that a felon was better treated than a peasant, and with singular perversity he regarded the growth of the potato in the garden of the cottager as at once a cause and sign of degradation. That humble root he accordingly abhorred; it was "base"; its introduction was one of "the greatest evils that England ever knew"; Sir

[1] Cobbett's *Political Writings*, vol. ii. (Letter to Windham, 1806); vol. iii. (Members of Parliament, 1809). Earl Russell's *Recollections and Suggestions*, p. 37.
[2] Carlyle's *Essay on Sir Walter Scott*.

Walter Raleigh, who introduced it, was "one of the greatest villains upon earth"; it had become a favourite form of food "because it is the suitable companion of misery and filth"; he himself could very well remember when "even the poorest of the people" would not eat it, and thought it only fit for hogs. Yet the whole of this terrible indictment arose from his belief that the potato was inferior to bread, and that its use was only forced upon the peasant by his poverty. It was in the same spirit that he loved the old Poor Law that was so indulgent to the labourer, and that he hated Malthus with an inextinguishable rage. A "monster," a "shallow and savage fellow," a "hard-hearted misanthropic economist"; such were the kind of terms he applied to the blameless author of the famous work on population. Yet Cobbett's injustice may in a measure be forgiven, for it was but philanthropy perverted. His faults were, however, great and many. Egotistical and vain, he loved to make himself notorious; as Dr. Johnson said of Richardson, he could not be contented to sail quietly down the stream of reputation without longing to taste the froth from every stroke of the oar. He was jealous and suspicious; he indulged in invective to excess; he sadly wanted tact, as he showed by his contempt for the courtesies of parliamentary life. That many of the leading Radicals disliked and suspected one another was only too often unhappily the case, but Cobbett was perhaps the best hated of them all. Bentham said that he was "almost universally known for a vile rascal," that he was "a man filled with *odium humani generis*," that his "malevolence and lying" were extreme, and that he and Hunt resembled "the rabid animals devouring one another" which are revealed in a drop of water by a microscope. Place called him an "impudent mountebank" and an " unprincipled cowardly bully " ; while Shelley lamented that "so powerful a genius" should have been blended with "the most odious moral qualities ".[1] True it is that by his gross misrepresentations he went far to sap all confidence in public men; but his influence was by no means always evil. His writings, which were very cheaply printed and were very widely read, were in a manner educational; as Bamford said, " the labourers read them, and thenceforward became deliberate and systematic in their proceedings," and less inclined to riot. He had moreover great industry and strength of will ; he sincerely wished the reform of all abuses; he was not a pecuniary self-seeker; he helped to clear the popular mind of such illusions as that the introduction of machinery caused distress, and to familiarise the people with free criticism of affairs and public men. His invective too was often more humorous than malicious. He was, in fact, a man who was not so bad as he liked to make himself appear. He had great faults and great merits; and in his own peculiar style of radicalism he stood alone, having no forerunner and leaving no successor.

It has already been remarked that the Radicals were in the main drawn from the middle class of society. Some of the leaders, it is true, like Thomas Paine and Francis Place, were men of humble origin, who came to the front by dint of their industry and talents; but the mass of the people were inert and indisposed to change. In times o

---

[1] Trevelyan's *Life and Letters of Lord Macaulay*, vol. ii., p. 281 Bowring's *Life of Bentham*, Collected Works, vol. x., pp. 471, 570, 601 *Life of Place*, by Graham Wallas, p. 117; Shelley's *Letter to Peacock* 26th January, 1819.

[2] Bamford's *Passages in the Life of a Radical*, vol. i., p. 7; Prentice' *Historical Sketches and Personal Recollections of Manchester*, p. 88.

distress, however, such as that which in 1815 followed the conclusion of the war, men blame existing institutions and clamour for reform. Hence it was that "Orator" Hunt's persuasive tongue drew many followers from the labouring population. But their radicalism was a transient phase which passed away as prosperity returned. Yet the democratic creed slowly percolated downwards, and there gradually arose a small but very interesting class of Radical working men. Of these, of course, Francis Place was pre-eminently the leading representative. But there were others who deserve at least a passing notice, if it were only for the part they played in the conduct of affairs which led up to the Reform Act of 1832. One of these was Samuel Bamford, a tall gaunt Lancashire weaver; a man of genuine literary taste, who has left us in his *Passages in the Life of a Radical* a very graphic picture of the trials and the troubles that beset those who embarked on the perilous seas of agitation. He did honour to the class from whence he sprung.[1] Not less so did William Lovett. The son of a sea captain at Penzance, he was apprenticed to a rope-maker, but soon made his way to London, where he became a cabinet-maker and store-keeper to the first London Co-operative Trading Association. Joining a small working men's debating club he quickly drifted into politics, in which, as will be seen, he played an active part. This "gentlest of agitators" must have had a fascinating personality. He was, says Place, "a tall, thin, rather melancholy man"; "soured with the perplexities of the world," but "honest-hearted, possessed of great

---

[1] Bamford was a great admirer of Tennyson's poems. The fact was brought to the notice of the Laureate who sent him a copy of his poems with his autograph, and said, "I reckon his admiration as the highest honour I have yet received" (*Life of Lord Tennyson*).

courage and persevering in his conduct ". Clear-sighted, industrious and of business-like capacity, he was invaluable to his fellow-artisans who banded themselves together to agitate for reform.[1] That the first Reform Act of 1832 was carried when and as it was, thanks in no slight measure to the efforts of a small but intelligent class of working men can hardly be disputed; and as that Act marks a decisive epoch in the annals of the Radicals, some account of the events which led up to its passing cannot properly be omitted.

At the beginning of the century the English working class were not, as a rule, inclined to concern themselves with politics. Their interests lay rather in their industrial conditions. An Act of 1799, which in 1800 had been re-enacted with additions, had made it equally illegal for masters and workmen to combine; a piece of legislation which was certainly a legacy of the French Revolution. That event had caused people to view all associations with suspicion and alarm. But while the masters were able to evade the provisions of the law, it was not so with the men. The repeal of the Combination Laws had therefore the first claim on their attention, and was for a time the main object to which their agitation was directed. Of this agitation Francis Place was the life and soul and hero. Now it was that he won his greatest triumph as a parliamentary wire-puller, and turned to good account his influence over the indefatigable Hume. A parliamentary committee was appointed in 1824, and it was mainly due to Place that an overwhelming mass of evidence was marshalled and arrayed, and that the committee

---

[1] *The Life and Struggles of William Lovett*, written by himself; Wallas' *Life of Place*, p. 269; Holyoake's *Sixty Years of an Agitator's Life*; Gammage's *History of the Chartist Movement*.

THE SECOND PERIOD, 1789-1831.

recommended the removal of the restraints on combination. Their recommendation was forthwith embodied in an Act, but the results have differed widely from what some people then anticipated. "Combinations," said Place in a letter to Sir Francis Burdett, "will soon cease to exist. Men have been kept together for long periods only by the oppression of the laws." The dangers of prophecy were never better illustrated.[1]

When after many years of effort the restraints on combination were abolished, the way in the direction of parliamentary reform was cleared of an impediment. A new outlet was sought for energies which had hitherto been otherwise employed, and it was found, partially at least, in the demand for an enlarged and better representation of the people. That demand was now fast rising to the flood. Yet the working class, as a whole, had not pinned their faith upon reform. There were not a few, and those not the least important, who looked rather to a reorganisation of society. The first hint of modern socialism in England was given by Thomas Spence, an eccentric individual, who, after spending some time as a schoolmaster at Newcastle, came to London and began business as a publisher and bookseller. He was imprisoned in 1792 for selling the *Rights of Man*, and on his release he brought out a periodical called *Pigs' Meat, or Lessons for the Swinish Multitude*. In 1801 he was imprisoned once again for publishing *The Restorer of Society to its Natural State*. In his last years he kept a bookstall at the corner of Holborn and Chancery Lane, and in 1814 he died in poverty, leaving a disciple, Thomas Evans, who founded the Society of the Spencean Philanthropists. The nationalisation of the land

[1] *The History of Trade Unionism*, by Sidney and Beatrice Webb, pp. 58, 63-65, 91-97.

was Spence's root-idea, but it was not one that proved attractive, nor brought him many followers. It was rather Robert Owen who by his publication in 1813 of his *New View of Society* unveiled the glamour of socialist ideals.[1] His fanciful pictures of Utopia, then coming with all the freshness of surprise, made many converts among the English working men, and especially among the superior class of intelligent artisans. The demand for Radical reform was, therefore, blended with something very different; for whereas the reformer sought the bettering of institutions as he found them, the socialist yearned to recast them altogether. The first working men's association for pressing forward the question of reform grew out of the Metropolitan Trades Union of 1831, which under the influence of Lovett became less industrial than political, and gradually expanded into the National Union of the Working Classes. This was founded in 1831 by Lovett, who believed that private property was the cause of almost every social ill; and it was extremely socialist in character. Its members used to meet at the Rotunda in Blackfriars-Bridge Road, and were therefore known as the Rotundists. Between the Rotundists and the main-body of the Radicals there now ensued a vigorous struggle over the question of reform. The former, as socialists, denounced the latter as "political economists," and a set of hard-headed, cruel-hearted thinkers. Never was the strongly individualist character of the Radicals brought out with such distinctness as it was on this occasion. "Nothing," said James Mill, in reference to the socialists, "can be conceived more mischievous than the doctrines which have been preached to the common people at Bir-

---

[1] Wallas' *Life of Place*, pp. 61-63.

mingham and elsewhere;" while he described the works of Hodgkin—the ablest socialist writer of his time—as "mad nonsense". Place was not content with words, and he established the Political Union as a counterblast to the Rotundists. He believed that the cause of reform would almost certainly be lost if it fell into their hands, and by dint of great exertion he succeeded in controlling the current of events.[1]

The history of the agitation that culminated in the passing of the Reform Act of 1832 belongs so entirely to English history as a whole that it would be both irrelevant and superfluous to describe it in these pages. It was, too, rather a movement of the Whigs than of the Radicals. But the Radicals lent it their support, and some account, therefore, of their conduct in relation to it in the years 1831 and 1832 cannot entirely be omitted.

Between the beginning of the century and the year 1832 the question of parliamentary reform was on several occasions brought before the House of Commons and debated; and the point at issue between the Whigs and Radicals was thus distinctly and publicly proclaimed to be the alternatives of moderate or thorough reform. It was in 1819 that Sir Francis Burdett moved his famous resolutions, which were opposed by Lord John Russell as the spokesman of the moderates. This scion of the great Whig House refused to support any "wild and visionary" schemes, or to give his vote for an inquiry "calculated to throw a slur upon the representation of the country and to fill the minds of the people with vague and indefinite alarms". Yet in the same year he moved that corrupt

---

[1] *The Life and Struggles of William Lovett; The History of Trade Unionism*, by Sidney and Beatrice Webb, p. 130; Wallas' *Life of Place*, pp. 273, 285; Bain's *James Mill*, p. 366.

boroughs be disfranchised, that the great towns and counties should be more fully represented, and that bribery—at that time unrestrained and unabashed—should be by some means made to cease. He pleaded for moderate reform, saying that to subvert the constitution would be to commit the mistake of Aladdin's servant who was deceived by the cry of "New lamps for old". "Our lamp," he declared, "is covered with dirt and rubbish, but it has a magical power." Lord John Russell, in fact, displayed the true genius of the Whigs. But he withdrew his bill on the understanding that the Government would agree to the disfranchisement of Grampound; and the suppression of that rotten borough was actually the first step taken in the direction of the reform. Next, in 1821, Mr. Lambton, better known by his subsequent title of Lord Durham, made a proposal for a bill to disfranchise rotten boroughs, to enact triennial Parliaments, and to extend the suffrage to all holders of property. Nothing came of his suggestion, but Lord John Russell moved that a hundred small boroughs should be deprived of one member each, and that forty new members be given to the large towns and sixty to the counties. His motion was supported by a considerable minority. That Lord John Russell had made himself the zealous advocate of moderate reform was rendered apparent by the fact that in 1823 and 1826 he again introduced the subject. In 1830 on no less than three occasions the question was brought before the House of Commons, and it was evident that the tide was quickly setting in the direction of reform.[1]

The attitude of the Whig party towards reform had hitherto been that of wavering indecision. The ex-

---

[1] Walpole's *Life of Lord John Russell*, vol. i.

THE SECOND PERIOD, 1789-1831.

travagances of the Radicals had gone far to make the subject one which the Whigs could not take up without risk of alienating many friends. Reform had, in fact, been rendered odious to almost all those who belonged to the upper and middle classes of society. The time had, however, come when the subject had to be grappled with and faced, and the Whig leaders were by the current of events perforce compelled to take it up. They saw that things were tending, as Earl Grey said, to "a complete separation between the higher and lower orders of society,"[1] and that to leave the reform agitation to the Radicals would be dangerous in the extreme. To enlist as many Radicals as possible upon the side of moderate reform thus became a main object of their policy, and it was one in which their efforts were attended by a large measure of success. For a brief period, at least, some famous Radicals were to be seen working shoulder to shoulder with the Whigs.

Of all Radicals, the one who worked the hardest to carry the Reform Act was Thomas Attwood. How quickly even prominent persons are forgotten is illustrated by the fact that one whom Place described as "the most influential man in England" should have already almost passed out of human memory. Yet of Thomas Attwood there now remains only the shadow of a name. Born at Halesowen in 1783, he came to Birmingham and joined a firm of bankers; and it was with that great city of the Midlands that his private and public life was in the main associated. In 1811 he was elected high bailiff, and his popularity was such that the artisans of Birmingham subscribed a sum of money to present him with a loving-cup. At first he had little inclination towards Radical

[1] *Memoirs of the Life and Times of Lord Brougham*, vol. ii., p. 342.

reform, and he looked with pitying contempt on "the poor wretches who," as he said, "clamour for Burdett and Liberty, meaning blood and anarchy". Moreover, just as he resembled one Radical, Grote, in being a banker, so too he resembled another, Cobbett, in taking up the cause of financial and currency reform. It was, indeed, his pamphlets on the currency that first made him widely known; and it was not without foundation that Disraeli wittily described him as "a provincial banker labouring under a financial monomania".[1] But though Attwood and Cobbett were agreed that the sufferings of the nation were in the main to be ascribed to the mismanagement of the national finances, they were in violent opposition over the question of the remedy. For while the former was for a system of regulated paper money and for altering the standard of value in accordance with fluctuating prices, the latter demanded a return to cash payments, accompanied with an equitable adjustment of existing obligations. Attwood acknowledged Cobbett's talents, but declared that "his ambition, his inveterate prejudices, his ignorance of the paper system, his bitter hatred of existing institutions," made him a very dangerous guide. Cobbett on his side was not so temperate in his language. He denounced Attwood as a plagiarist and accused him of desiring to keep up "an army deadweight, sinecures, places and pensions, the Stock Exchange in full swing, and the infamous borough-mongers in the height of prosperity". Thus the two would-be Radical reformers of finance had but little love for one another. Yet Attwood remained true to his convictions, and at one of the first public meetings in Birmingham, in which he played

[1] *Runnymede Letters*, No. 3.

a leading part, a petition setting forth the distressed state of the country, and praying for currency reform, was unanimously adopted. But Parliament received the petition very coldly; a fact which it is not too much to say converted Attwood into a parliamentary reformer. For, like Cobbett, he despaired of doing any good with the existing House of Commons. It was on a dark December day in 1829 that the supreme moment of his life may be said to have arrived, when he and fourteen others, met at the Royal Hotel, Birmingham, and founded the Political Union for the Protection of Public Rights. Once again, it is of great interest to note, the old principle of political association, of which we saw early examples in such societies as that for Constitutional Information, was invoked. At a great meeting held at Birmingham in January, 1830, the Political Union was established, its main object being declared to be "to obtain by every just and legal means such a reform in the Commons House of Parliament as may ensure a real and effectual representation of the lower and middle classes in that House". The first public meeting of the Union was held in the following month of May, and thus was set rolling one of the greatest political forces that England this century has seen. Vast crowds of working men, some of them descended from the very persons who had set fire to Priestley's house, used to meet on Constitution Hill and adopt resolutions in favour of reform. And just as the City of London and Westminster had been in turn the focus of democracy, so now Birmingham began to take their place. Of the Birmingham Radicals Attwood was now without dispute the chief. His, indeed, was an attractive personality. Tall and dignified in bearing, with a fine head, grave and intellectual features, an aquiline nose, grey hair and hazel eyes, he was bountifully endowed by nature with those attributes that go to make a leader of the people. It will too always redound to Attwood's credit that he used his great powers with studied moderation. "Peace, law, order, loyalty and union" he declared to be his weapons; and Grote said no more than the truth when he remarked that Attwood had "divested the physical force of the country of its terrors and of its lawlessness and has made it conducive to ends of the highest public benefit".

There were others too who worked with Attwood, who deserve a passing mention. There was Joshua Scholefield, who threatened to march to London with 100,000 men to inquire why the Reform Bill was not quickly passed, and who was Attwood's first colleague in the representation of Birmingham in Parliament; there were G. F. and P. H. Muntz; who both succeeded Attwood and Scholefield in the representation of the borough; there was Thomas Clutton Salt; there was George Edmonds, a fine orator, the friend of Cartwright, in company with whom he had suffered imprisonment for his democratic zeal, and who was afterwards the Birmingham Town Clerk; there was George Russell who was famous for a while as the publisher and seller of the political songs that were on all reformers' lips; there was "Joe" Parkes, the attorney, of whom Carlyle has left a picture; "a rather pleasant-talking, shrewd enough little fellow with bad teeth, and a knowing, flighty satirical way".[1] All these were citizens of Birmingham. Of the Radicals of Westminster and London there was no one who helped the cause as much as Francis Place, who now found the amplest scope for his resourcefulness

---

[1] Carlyle's *Reminiscences*, vol. i., p. 254; Parkes admitted that it was the Benthamites had fired his democratic zeal (Bain's *James Mill*, p. 454).

THE SECOND PERIOD, 1789-1831.   317

and practical sagacity. How he outflanked the "Rotundists" we have already seen; but his most memorable achievement remains to be described. This was the devising of the stratagem by which the Duke of Wellington was prevented from forming a Ministry in 1832—a design which, if carried out, Place considered would be fatal to any useful measure of reform. He had the acumen to perceive that a "run" upon the Bank of England, if it could be by some means brought about, would undermine the position of the Duke; so he devised a subtle plan. During the whole of one Saturday night and all the following Sunday he worked at a printer's shop in Holborn, and on Monday morning the astonished Londoners awoke to find the walls placarded with innumerable posters. They bore the words "Stop the duke—go for gold!" The effect was instantaneous, and, needless to relate, the Duke did not persevere.[1] After Place, the Radicals who most heartily co-operated in carrying the Reform Bill were Hobhouse and Burdett. To the latter the details of the bill were privately confided, and both he and Hobhouse thought that it went too far to have any chance of passing. The Radicals, as a body, had the sense to accept the bill as an instalment, valuable, indeed, for its concessions, but stopping very short of what they urgently demanded. Two Radicals only in the House of Commons had the hardihood to vote against it. Sir R. Wilson, Member for Southwark, voted

[1] Holyoake tells a curious story of Place and the Duke of Wellington. The former headed a deputation of working men to Apsley House to represent the condition of the people. The Duke listened patiently and said: "I suppose you know that I am responsible for public order. I know how to keep it. You can go." Then recalling them he said: "You seem to be men who have heads on your shoulders. Take care you keep them there" (Holyoake's *Sixty Years of an Agitator's Life*, vol. i.).

against the Government upon an amendment, though one of not supreme importance; but "Orator" Hunt, as might have been predicted from his love of egotistic ostentation, condemned the measure root and branch. He denounced it as an instrument of restriction and disfranchisement, and an attack upon the poor; he had the impudence to aver that the people, whom he claimed to represent, had gone mad about the bill. Never did any demagogue appear to greater disadvantage than did Hunt on this occasion; for in the moment of the first and one of the greatest triumphs of his party he ranged himself in the ranks of opposition.[1]

With the passing of the Reform Act in 1832, the second period of the history of the Radicals is brought to a close. Beginning with the outbreak of the French Revolution in 1789, it covered more than forty years, and might be not improperly described as one of transition between the old order and the new. Its last years were like the first; they were bright with radiant hope; but those that intervened were dark with disappointment. But though the time, for the most part, was one of retrogression and reaction, there was no sign amongst the Radicals of despondent inactivity. There was neither stagnation nor despair. The era, indeed, if we consider the philosophers, was wonderfully brilliant. It was on such days as these, dark but lighted up with rays of hope,

---

[1] *Life of Thomas Attwood*, by C. M. Wakefield, privately printed; Holyoake's *Sixty Years of an Agitator's Life;* Elihu Burritt's *Walks in the Black Country;* Cobbett's *Political Writings*, vol. vi.; Harris' *History of the Radical Party in Parliament*, p. 228; Roebuck's *History of the Whig Ministry of* 1830; *Life of Place*, by Graham Wallas; Brougham's *Memoirs of His Life and Times*, vol. iii., p. 103. It is noteworthy that Attwood had some influence over the late Professor Freeman in his early days (Stephens' *Life and Letters of Freeman*, pp. 13, 14).

THE SECOND PERIOD, 1789-1831.

that the Radicals at this time fell; but it remains to briefly sum up the salient facts, and to indicate the changes that occurred. The reformers of 1832, with some exceptions, belonged to a later generation than those of 1789; they were their lineal political descendants, but moved by new thoughts and stirred by new ideals.

In the first place it must be said that the Radicals of the time of the Reform Act differed from those who gloried in the fall of the Bastille in some essential characteristics. The general philosophy of life, the *Weltanschauung*—to borrow an expression from the Germans—of the two were not the same. For whereas the former looked at political affairs from the point of view of the abstract rights of man, the latter regarded them from that of practical utility. Both theorised and both tended to democratise the country; but the former gradually gave way before the latter. Of the older tradition, after Godwin had ceased to write on political philosophy, Shelley was the most conspicuous representative. Yet that " beautiful and ineffectual angel beating in the void his luminous wings in vain," cannot be taken seriously from the political point of view.[1] His practical influence was as nothing compared with that of Bentham and James Mill with their utilitarian materialism. This change in their outlook upon life is the cardinal fact in this period of the history of the Radicals. The altered standpoint led, moreover, to some rearrangement of their practical demands. Their ultimate aim—the control of Parliament, that is to say, by pressure from without—remained

---

[1] Southey writing in 1812 said of Shelley: "He is just what I was in 1794. . . . I tell him that all the difference between us is, that he is nineteen and I am thirty-seven" (*Life and Correspondence of Robert Southey*, vol. iii., p. 325).

the same; but whereas formerly they asserted the existence of some supposed innate and natural rights and laboured to obtain their universal recognition, they subsequently put the claim to those rights into the background and made the obtaining of better securities for good government the immediate goal of their desire. Any change, therefore, that tended to bring nearer these securities—such a change, for instance, as the Whig Reform Act of 1832—was accepted at least for what it was considered to be worth. The case of the ballot, to take a single instance, will serve to illustrate our meaning. A plan of secret voting was not deemed a thing of much value from the point of view of natural rights, but from that of securities for good government it was considered all important; and it was, therefore, placed by the utilitarian Radicals in the very forefront of their programme. So, too, by parity of reasoning, they exalted short Parliaments even above a wide extension of the suffrage.

Secondly, the course of events between 1789 and 1832 tended to accentuate and define the position of the Radicals, to make them separate and distinct, to dissociate them from the Whigs. Things had very greatly changed since the days when Wilkes had fought the battle of parliamentary privilege, when Chatham and Pitt were on the side of the reformers, and noble lords, like the Duke of Richmond, were the champions of democracy. The French Revolution and the rise of the Radicals of the type of Thomas Paine dispelled those pleasant dreams of harmony. Political life became inflamed with a spirit of bitter animosity, and the Radicals were turned into an angry, a banned and a persecuted sect. To increase the representation of the counties, and to maintain the weight, influence and position of the landed gentry, was no longer the desire of the reformer. Nay rather, the country gentleman came to be regarded by the Radicals as the bulwark of the existing Constitution, as one who battened on abuses, and was, therefore, an object of abhorrence. The Radical campaign, as carried on during the period we are now passing in review, might be summed up in a word as anti-aristocratic. The House of Lords was no longer regarded in a spirit of indifference or benevolent neutrality; and its abolition, therefore, became a prime object of reform. The aristocracy, with all its ramifications, was the deadly upas-tree which the Radicals at this time laboured to uproot, and wherever it drew nourishment, whether from the Church, the lawyers, the standing army, the colonies, or the "borough-monger" system, there the axe of the reformer was vigorously laid. The Reform Act of 1832 was the first well-directed blow.

CHAPTER III.

THE THIRD AND CONCLUDING PERIOD.

WITH the passing of the first Reform Act the Radicals entered upon a new era in their history. There was, of course, no breach of continuity with the past; there was only change of circumstance. But the conditions were much altered, so that a distinct line may be drawn between the ante-reform Radicals and those of later times. Very recent history it is, however, almost impossible to write; for as he approaches the present, difficulties more and more beset the author who attempts to relate and criticise affairs. Historical evidence—the *matériaux pour servir*—is, in the first place, less abundant; archives, memoirs, letters and the like still lie disinterred in cabinet and drawer. Freedom of speech, moreover, is restrained. It will, therefore, be impossible to peer as closely into the dusky crypts of bygone times as was done in the two preceding periods. Nevertheless the evolution of the latter-day Radical may, it is hoped, if not fully, yet at least as far as possible, be truthfully described. To place him into historical relationship with his forefathers at the time of the first Reform Act will be the purport of this chapter.

The third period, like the two former, has its men of thought and men of action; its philosophers and writers upon the one hand, its parliamentarians and agitators

THE THIRD AND CONCLUDING PERIOD.

upon the other; and just as hitherto it has been attempted to separate the two classes, and to draw distinctly the lineaments of each, so in like manner the same plan will be as far as possible adopted in the treatment of this section.

The thinkers of the party were drawn, as might have been expected, from the younger generation of the philosophical Radicals. The older men were now falling fast like leaves in autumn. Bentham himself, the great master, died in 1832; and James Mill survived him by four years only. Godwin still lingered for a while upon the stage, but he had played his part. But there was a group of young and earnest men, the chief of whom already have been named, who handed on the old tradition. There still remained Grote, Roebuck, the Austins, and others of less note, but John Stuart Mill surpassed them all as a philosophic thinker. He was unquestionably the first of the Utilitarians, as these younger philosophical Radicals were called; a party, indeed, which was much more immersed in practical politics than given to speculation. The ultimate basis of their creed had been already firmly laid by Bentham and James Mill, and in that direction there remained but little to be done. The principles of Benthamism were tacitly accepted, and John Stuart Mill alone ventured to approach them with an independent judgment. When he began to think out problems for himself, he soon perceived that there were some things in the Benthamite philosophy with which he could not possibly agree, and on some points he strongly dissented from his father. During the lifetime of the latter he usually kept his opinions to himself, but both Bentham and James Mill were obviously displeased that this "wayward intellectual deity," as Mrs. Grote called him, should have had the temerity to differ from themselves.[1] Such conduct seemed to them almost like hoisting the standard of revolt. It was not at once that the younger Mill gave a free and untrammelled expression to his views, nor did those views on all points remain unchanged. For the circumference of his mind was continually enlarging, and his final judgments on some questions differed greatly from his first. Still it is in the works of John Stuart Mill that the philosophical radicalism of later times has found its best expression, and he may be taken as its great exemplar and typical representative. It cannot, however, be too clearly understood that he refused to be considered as the exponent of the theories of a party or a sect, and that the very thought of such a thing he regarded with abhorrence. He was, he tells us, cured of "sectarian follies" by reading Condorcet's *Life of Turgot*. "The two or three pages," he says, "beginning '*il regardait toute secte comme nuisible*,' and explaining why Turgot always kept himself perfectly distinct from the Encyclopædists, sank deeply into my mind." To Turgot, indeed, John Stuart Mill was mentally near akin; his mind was like a star and dwelt apart, for there was nothing he so much valued as complete intellectual independence. It, therefore, happened that though there was no one who had been more strictly nurtured on the principles of Benthamism, yet there was no one more unwilling to be taken for a Benthamite; and he always met the allegation with an eager disavowal. Writing to Albany Fonblanque, for instance, in 1838, he denied that he had in any way identified himself with the "Philosophical Radicals" or the "Grote Conclave," as they

---

[1] J. S. Mill's *Autobiography*; Wallas' *Life of Francis Place*, p. 91.

THE THIRD AND CONCLUDING PERIOD. 325

appear to have been at that time called. "They are," said Mill, "persons whom I have nothing to do with and to whose opinions you are far more really allied than I am. . . . There may be such a conclave, but I know nothing of it, for I have never been within the door of Grote's house in Eccleston Street, and have been for the last few years completely estranged from that household." And again he passionately inquires, "What is the meaning of your insisting upon identifying me with Grote and Roebuck and the rest? Do you in your conscience think that my opinions are at all like theirs?" Mill, in fact, delighted in a position of aloofness or what might be called "glorious isolation". It was again, he tells us, a principal object of his editorship of the *London and Westminster Review* " to free philosophic radicalism from the reproach of sectarian Benthamism".[1] His political philosophy—and that alone concerns us here—was, as might have been expected from his intellectual self-reliance, very far from being identical with that of Bentham and his father; and was on some essential points independent and original. Nor is this his sole claim to special recognition; for of all thinkers of his time there was no one who more profoundly influenced the minds of active politicians; and among the Radicals, at least, he remained from first to last a strongly formative and stimulative power. Upon his teaching a whole generation may be said to have been nurtured. For a space of nearly half a century he was the great theoriser from whom in the main they drew their inspiration, and, therefore, a few words must be said about his

[1] J. S. Mill's *Autobiography;* The *Life and Labours of Albany Fonblanque*, edited by E. B. de Fonblanque, pp. 31, 32.

attitude towards the science and the practice of political affairs.[1]

John Stuart Mill resembled the Benthamites who went before him in the width and depth of his intellectual interests. To political economy, to ethics, to logic and metaphysics, his contributions were multiform and profound; but of these it would be beyond our province here to speak. It is solely as a Radical that he becomes in these pages a subject for description. In what respects and how far his political opinions differed from those of his father and of Bentham it is in the first place most pertinent to inquire.

Reserved and self-contained, somewhat formal and pedantic, John Stuart Mill concealed beneath a stern exterior a warm and feeling heart. In general society, which indeed he rarely found congenial, he did not appear to great advantage; for he was too careful of his thoughts to be a fluent conversationalist. But he was in an eminent degree compassionate and just, and, to use a happy phrase which Condorcet applied to Turgot, he resembled a volcano clothed in ice. It was indeed the altruistic element in his character that informed and coloured his political philosophy; and he might perhaps without impropriety be described as a Benthamite purified, sublimated and refined. Not that Bentham and James Mill were wanting in benevolence. The former used to say that he was selfish, but that, in his case, the vice took the form of a desire of benefiting others. But the two philosophers in the intellectual domain were cold and rigid

---

[1] Greville, an acute observer, thus described Mill: "In conversation he has not the art of managing his ideas, and is consequently hesitating and slow, and has the appearance of always working in his mind propositions or a syllogism" (*Memoirs*, vol. ii. (first series), p. 79). There is a portrait of J. S. Mill in the National Portrait Gallery by Watts.

reasoners, who exorcised from their system the sentiments and emotions. Their teaching, narrow, stunted and one-sided—a very *hortus siccus* of abstractions—was to John Stuart Mill abhorrent; yet he never shut his eyes to what he believed to be the truth; and, as Mr. Morley has well said, he united "stern science with infinite aspiration," and a "rigorous sense of what is real and practicable with bright and luminous hope".[1] That was the characteristic that formed the keynote of his life. Upon the Benthamite philosophy he brought to bear his keen and inexorable logic; and there is no one who has more plainly showed its mode of reasoning to be fundamentally defective. He exposed the fallacies of James Mill's and Bentham's methods, which, though sound in themselves, were inapplicable to political philosophy; and he refuted their main premise, that men's actions are always determined by their interests. He showed, moreover, that identity of interest between the governing body and the community at large is not in any practical sense the only thing upon which good government depends; and that this identity of interest cannot be secured by mere conditions of election. This demonstration of the inherent vices of the logical methods of the Benthamites was John Stuart Mill's great service to political philosophy; for he at the same time killed a fallacy and pointed out the right line to be followed. To the Radicals as a party his services were greater still. The unyielding harshness, the obdurate asperity, the austereness of the Benthamites had brought upon them some not unmerited reproach, but their defects were less due to their characters than to the unsoundness of their reasoning. Their

[1] John Morley's *Miscellanies*, vol. iii., p. 40.

faults were of the head and not the heart. Now it was precisely this reproach that John Stuart Mill laboured to remove. In his hands philosophical radicalism was softened and refined; its aspect was rendered more gracious and benignant; it was placed upon a higher plane; it was elevated and ennobled.

It was, however, not merely in his ratiocinative methods that John Stuart Mill differed from the Benthamites, but also in some of his matured and well-considered judgments; and on some points, indeed, he remained to the end irrevocably hostile to the whole body of Radical opinion. Upon the main thesis that the people ought to be enabled to control Parliament by pressure from without he was, of course, in absolute agreement; and there was no one more opposed to the selfishness of Governments and the oppression of numerical minorities. "To see these things," he said, "and to seek to put an end to them, by means (among other things) of giving more political power to the majority, constitutes radicalism." A better definition could probably not be made; yet he had a clear perception of the dangers of democracy. He agreed with Coleridge—whom courageously, but to the scandal of his friends, he classed with Bentham as "a great questioner of things established," and described as "the most systematic thinker" and one of the great seminal minds of his generation—that in every nationality there must be, besides the element of progression, some strong cohesive principle or the element of permanence. He admitted, that is to say, the main thesis of the great conservative philosopher, "the sage," to use Carlyle's words, who, "alone in these dark days had saved his crown of spiritual manhood, escaping the black materialisms and revolutionary deluges with 'God, Freedom, Immortality' still his".

The "black materialisms" of the Benthamites formed an intellectual ghetto, from which John Stuart Mill, thanks in part to the friendship of Maurice and of Sterling, the "Coleridgeans," had freed himself. "Few persons," he has related, "have exercised more influence over my thoughts and character than Coleridge has." This side of Mill's intellectual temper enlarged his vision in an infinite degree. He allowed, for example, the value of poetry as an educational instrument in the formation of the character—a value which the Benthamites had contemptuously denied.[1] But what concerns us more especially to consider is how he differed from the Radicals in his judgments upon political affairs; which he did on some important points. First, whereas the older class of Radicals, and many of the later, had affirmed that the suffrage was a right, he said that it was a trust; whereas they demanded universal suffrage, he regarded it with a sense of chastened fear. He had that which many Radicals had not; a keen perception of the weak side of the democratic creed. For, as he sagaciously remarked, "men, as well as women, do not need political rights in order that they may govern, but in order that they may not be misgoverned". Upon this aspect of the question he suffered no illusions. So, too, whereas the delegation theory had long been cherished by the Radicals, he rejected it with scorn. "The delegation theory of representation," he said, " seems to me false. . . . No words can exaggerate the importance in principle of leaving an unfettered discretion to the representative." Then as to the ballot—the very security for good government upon

---

[1] Mill's criticism on Wordsworth is interesting; he said he was "the poet of unpoetical natures, possessed of quiet and contemplative tastes".

which Bentham most insisted—he strenuously opposed it to the end, believing, as he did, that the performance of a trust should not be exercised in secret. But it was on female suffrage that his opinions were the strongest; and to use his own expression, he "most positively dissented" from the opinion of his father that women can be excluded from the suffrage consistently with good government. His convictions upon these points remained unalterably fixed, and he differed, therefore, from his contemporary Radicals upon some of the most important issues. Again, hoping little from short Parliaments, he looked rather to some system of proportional representation; and believing that all classes should find a spokesman in the popular legislative chamber, he favoured the return of working men to Parliament. And so it came about that in 1871 he ardently supported a candidate who avowedly came forward to maintain the cause of labour as against both Whigs and Tories.[1] Upon two points, however, he carried on the old Radical tradition, though in a somewhat qualified degree. First he believed in individualism; a creed for which his famous book *On Liberty* was an elaborate apology. Yet Mill's "sovereignty of the individual" was poles asunder from the anarchical and crude conceptions of the thinkers of the type of Thomas Paine; his love of personal freedom was temperate and sober; he knew where to limit its excess. His philosophy, indeed, was not perfectly consistent; for his views on *laissez faire* did not entirely harmonise with his ever-widening altruism; and, as the

---

[1] This Labour candidate was Odger who contested Southwark in 1871; see Webb's *History of Trade Unionism*, p. 272. Mr. Holyoake claims to have been the first Labour candidate at Tower Hamlets in 1857, and at Leicester in 1868, and to have had the support of Mill (Holyoake's *Sixty Years of an Agitator's Life*, vol. ii., p 42).

THE THIRD AND CONCLUDING PERIOD. 331

years rolled on, the dissonance increased. Speaking of his wife's and his own ultimate opinions he remarked, " but our ideal of ultimate improvement went far beyond democracy and would class us decidedly under the general designation of socialists". Upon the great question, therefore, of the proper duties of the state and of the sphere of legislation, he inclined more and more to view with favour their enlargement. In the next place he inherited a share of that optimism which in old days had been so marked a characteristic of the Radicals. The rampant enthusiasm of Priestley or of Godwin was certainly never his; but he looked forward to the future with a rational and sober-minded hope. He believed that "all the grand sources of human suffering are in a great degree, many of them almost entirely, conquerable by human care and effort," and though the progress might be slow, all obstacles might in the end be completely overcome; while he had some of that buoyancy of temperament which was entirely wanting in his father and made him take a gloomy view of the worth and interest of life.

Such very briefly was the political philosophy of John Stuart Mill, the "Saint of Rationalism," as Mr. Gladstone once felicitously styled him. That he on some points differed greatly from the Benthamites, and that to the end of his life he was on some essential questions at issue with the great body of the Radicals are indisputable facts. Yet that he was by a tacit and unanimous consent the some-time acknowledged leader of the Utilitarians is equally apparent. As he wrote to his friend Professor Nichol in 1837, "I am general referee and chamber counsel to Molesworth and others of the active Radicals".[1]

[1] See the "Unpublished Letters from J. S. Mill to Professor Nichol" in the *Fortnightly Review* for May, 1897.

Almost the whole business of philosophic thinking had in fact been left to Mill, for his followers were otherwise engaged in the actualities of life. What they tried to do, and how far their efforts were attended with success, now remains to be considered.

The Reform Act of 1832 greatly stimulated and gave a fresh impetus to Radical activity; it opened up ever-widening vistas of new worlds to conquer and subdue. Hitherto all efforts had seemed destined to be fruitless; to try to attain the popular control of Parliament was, under the old borough-monger system, to beat in vain against the bars of inexorable fate. The Reform Act admitted at least a gleam of hope; and that was much. It was a Whig measure it is true, and, therefore, was regarded by all true Radicals—as were all measures of tentative and moderate reform—as a compromise at once contemptible and weak. "Orator" Hunt, it will be remembered, opposed it altogether as a fraud upon the people, and it was, in fact, no more than a middle-class enfranchisement. In the eyes of the Radicals the new state of things was little better than the old, and they viewed the new electoral classes, " the Worshipful Company of the Ten-Pound Householders," as they were contemptuously styled, with envy and suspicion. They denounced the Act as "a damnable delusion, giving us as many tyrants as there are shopkeepers," and they stigmatised the middle-class as "the real tyrants of society". "All that is mean, and grovelling, and selfish, and rapacious, and harsh, and cold, and cruel, and luxurious, belongs to this luxurious race . . . and these are the men to whom the Whigs have entrusted the guardianship of our liberties and industry. . . . So to keep the Whigs in power, the lion must give place to the rat and the tiger to the leech."[1] That is certainly strong language, but it truly represented a large body of Radical opinion. Even the Radicals who laboured strenuously to secure the passing of the Act soon regretted its results, as Attwood did when he declared that it had produced " a House of Commons but little better than the old concern," and that he was almost sorry that he had ever had a hand in the reform when he saw " troops of sycophants and time-servers " in the legislative chamber.[2] The Act which appeared to many persons such a revolutionary measure was never heartily accepted by the Radicals; they rather viewed it, not so much as a thing of value in itself, but, as Place said, as " a commencement of the breaking up of the old rotten system "; or, as John Stuart Mill regarded it, the breaking of a spell that had kept men bound to fear of change. The ablest men among the Radicals were, therefore, naturally induced to concentrate their efforts upon influencing Parliament. To win as many seats as possible in the House of Commons, to guide it and to move it, to leaven and imbue it with their own peculiar doctrines, became the supreme object of their lives.

The results of the elections to the first reformed Parliament were certainly auspicious. Place declined all invitations to a contest, but Hobhouse and Sir Francis

---

[1] See Holyoake's *Sixty Years of an Agitator's Life*, vol. i., p. 279; and an article in the *English Historical Review* (October, 1897) on the "Unstamped Press (1815-1836)". Compare some remarks by Disraeli in a speech delivered at Aylesbury in 1855 on the Reform Act: "Everybody now considers that there was in the concoction of that bill a greater number of jobs than was ever perpetrated before . . . its nominal object was to improve the representation of the people, its great substantial object was the consolidation of Whig power (Walpole's *Life of Lord John Russell*, vol. ii., p. 296).

[2] *Life of Thomas Attwood*, p. 38.

Burdett were again returned for Westminster, while Grote headed the poll in the City of London. Joseph Hume found a seat in Middlesex, while the youthful Roebuck was returned by the Bath electors to whom Hume had introduced him. Thomas Attwood and Joshua Scholefield had the honour to be the first representatives of Birmingham, and Cobbett's ambitions were realised at Oldham. But of all the Radicals who were new to parliamentary life, the two most interesting figures were Charles Buller and Sir William Molesworth. The former, whom Disraeli in his maiden speech described as "the Daphne of Liskeard," had in his boyhood been a pupil of Carlyle; who found him "a most manageable, intelligent, cheery, and altogether welcome and intelligent phenomenon; quite a bit of sunshine in my dreary Edinburgh element".[1] He lived to perform great services to the colonies in conjunction with Lord Durham, but his brilliant talents were soon lost to the world by a too untimely death. Sir William Molesworth was a young Cornish Baronet of very great ability. Eminently handsome, with his light brown hair, florid complexion and blue expressive eyes, possessing a tall slim figure and the courtliest of manners, he looked the very ideal of the aristocrat. Yet beneath an air which was thought by some to be "foppish and conceited," he concealed a fund of sincerely democratic feeling. The circumstances of his youth were of a kind to fill him with resentment towards that section of society to which by birth and

---

[1] Carlyle's *Reminiscences*, vol. i., p. 196. Carlyle also described him as the "genialest Radical" he had ever met. Bulwer Lytton's tribute was a fine one :—

"Farewell fine humorist, finer reasoner still,
Lively as Luttrell, logical as Mill".

breeding he belonged. While a Cambridge undergraduate he challenged his tutor, by whom he thought that he had been unfairly treated, to a duel, and was in consequence expelled. His subsequent studies in Germany and Edinburgh probably further tended to unsettle his opinions; while a residence of a year or two in Italy, where he contrived to combine a life of pleasure with some systematic study, completed his conversion to advanced views in theology and politics. Coming back to England he frequented the society of Grote and James Mill, became an enthusiastic Benthamite disciple, and in consequence incurred the displeasure of his family. Nay more, his temper was embittered by the rejection of several offers of marriage on account of his undisguised avowal of Radical opinions. Becoming, if possible, more zealous than before, he came in 1834 to the rescue of his party by founding a new Radical organ, the *London Review*, which in a few years he united with the *Westminster*. Of this affair Carlyle has in his own inimitable manner drawn for us a curious and vivacious picture. "*London Review*," he says, "was at last due to the charitable faith of young Sir William Molesworth, a poorish narrow creature, but an ardent believer in Mill *Père* (James) and Mill *Fils*. 'How much will your review take to launch it, then?' asked he (all other Radical believers being so close of fist). 'Say £4000,' answered Mill. 'There, then,' writing a cheque for that amount, rejoined the other."[1] Such a manner of man was Sir William Moles-

---

[1] Carlyle's *Reminiscences*, vol. ii., p. 185. In a letter to Emerson (5th Nov., 1836) Carlyle gives a slight difference in the sum of money; "a young Radical baronet has laid out £3000 in getting the world instructed in that manner: it is very curious to see" (*Correspondence of Carlyle and Emerson*, vol. i.).

worth who in 1832 was returned as member for East Cornwall.[1]

The names that we have mentioned are few in number, but their bearers must have carried weight and influence in any legislative chamber. They were, moreover, not by any means the only Radicals who found their way into the newly constituted Parliament. How many the entire parliamentary group numbered has been differently estimated, and it is not very easy to determine. At the lowest calculation the figure has been put at forty-six, and at the highest from seventy to eighty. The discrepancy may be to some extent accounted for by the ill-defined position of the Radicals as a parliamentary party, but it is impossible to doubt that even the lowest estimate went far beyond the actual facts.[2] For there were not a few who paraded a profession of Radical opinions, but who, when it came to voting, were to be found in the same lobby with the Whigs—a cheap way of winning popular applause. Then—and this is a very curious fact which is well worth consideration in connection with the subject of Home Rule—many Irish Members were by contemporary observers classed among the Radicals, though on some questions, such as the rights of Roman Catholics, the two were fundamentally opposed. But then, as now, the Irish Nationalist and the English Radical were bound together by some tie of fellow feeling. Of this alliance even before the Reform Act there were signs that could

---

[1] *The Philosophical Radicals of 1832*, by Mrs. Grote.

[2] A writer in the *Edinburgh Review* for July, 1873, states that the Radicals in the first reformed Parliament never exceeded fifteen or twenty; but that in the Parliament of 1834 they numbered nearly fifty. See the *History of the Radical Party in Parliament*, by William Harris, pp. 234, 267.

not be mistaken. Daniel O'Connell, for example, was intimate with Bentham, and made professions of affection which were loud if not sincere. He declared himself "an humble disciple of the immortal Bentham," and in a letter to the sage written in 1829, he said, "I avowed myself on the hustings on this day to be a 'Benthamite,' and explained the leading principles of your disciples". Bentham—who playfully addressed him as "Dan, dear child"—seems to have hoped much from O'Connell, and actually expressed his firm conviction that he was "the only man perhaps in the world by whom, for many years to come, Radical reform or any approach to it can be brought upon the carpet with any the smallest chance of success". Whether his confidence in the famous Irish agitator was justified or not, hereafter will be seen; but that O'Connell for a time at least had ranged himself among the English Radicals is a fact beyond dispute.[1] When, for instance, the Radicals, who were defeated at the election of 1837, were entertained at dinner, O'Connell was conspicuous by his presence; and when Hume was defeated in Middlesex he was, by arrangement with O'Connell, elected for Kilkenny. There were some Irishmen, indeed, who, to the annoyance of their countrymen, were like Richard Lalor Sheil, "the splendid phantom," Radicals first and Nationalists only afterwards. Nevertheless it was an error to have classed the Irish with the Radicals; an error which is all the more remarkable because the latter were obviously unwilling to allow public opinion to confuse them with the former. All

[1] Bowring's *Life of Bentham*, vol. xi., pp. 9, 20. In 1830 O'Connell went so far as to move for leave to bring in a bill to establish the ballot, triennial Parliaments and universal suffrage, but only found thirteen supporters.

contact with O'Connell was usually avoided, and Grote only met him once in social intercourse at Buller's house; while Sir Francis Burdett was so much disgusted with the great agitator's insolence that he asked the managers of Brooks' Club to expel him, and on their refusal he resigned. The Radicals, in fact, felt so much repugnance to any co-operation with the Irish, that when on one occasion a scheme was formed for a Whig-Radical alliance, the negotiations failed because the Irish had been invited to take part in it.[1] Putting, therefore, the Nationalists aside, the Radicals in the first reformed Parliament did not exceed twenty at the most. At the next election, in 1835, their losses and defections were more than balanced by their gains. On the one hand, Hobhouse and Sir Francis Burdett were already showing signs of lapse—a common malady among the Radicals—towards Conservative opinions. Hobhouse had actually accepted office with the Whigs, and when in the debate on the house and window taxes he refused to vote for their repeal, he resigned his seat for Westminster, but stood for re-election. The electors, however, were not to be appeased, and they passed a resolution that "Sir F. Burdett and Sir J. C. Hobhouse, the one by opposing the strongly expressed wishes of his constituents, and the other by deserting his post of duty when his services were most needed, had forfeited the confidence of the electors of Westminster"; and they replaced Hobhouse by Colonel de Lacy Evans, who was a Radical of sterner stuff.[2] The political task-masters of Westminster were evidently men

[1] Mrs. Grote's *Personal Life of George Grote*, pp. 99, 105; Torrens' *Life of Melbourne*, vol. ii., p. 155.

[2] *The History of the Radical Party in Parliament*, by William Harris, p. 245.

who kept a careful watch upon their servants. On the other hand, there were some notable recruits to the Radical parliamentary forces. Dr. Bowring, the friend and biographer of Bentham, became the member for Kilmarnock; but the two new members for Finsbury were the men who brought to the cause the most ability and zeal. These were Thomas Wakley and Thomas Slingsby Duncombe.

Thomas Wakley, who was as much distinguished for his services as founder and editor of the *Lancet* as for his parliamentary labours, was one of the few members of the medical profession who have risen to eminence in politics. Born in 1795 he was now in the prime of life and eminently handsome. In the course of his practice as a London physician he suffered an experience which in itself was singular, and probably ultimately had some influence upon his political opinions. It so happened that the five men convicted of taking part in the so-called Thistlewood Conspiracy were hanged and afterwards decapitated; and, by some extraordinary accident which has never been explained, Wakley was suspected to be the person who carried out the last part of the dread judgment of the law. His unpopularity was such that his house was burnt down by the infuriated mob. By a curious coincidence Cobbett imagined that the conspirators had designs upon himself, and from a feeling of kinship in misfortune he sought the society of Wakley. The doctor and the journalist found a common ground of friendship, and there can be very little doubt that it was to Cobbett's influence that Wakley owed much of his political opinions.[1]

---

[1] *The Life and Times of Thomas Wakley*, by S. Squire Sprigge.

Thomas Slingsby Duncombe was a very different kind of man. He was born in Yorkshire in 1796, and as a nephew of Earl Feversham he was allied by ties of blood to an aristocratic house. His early life was passed after the manner of a nobleman of fortune. On leaving Harrow he took a commission in the Guards, became a man of fashion and a patron of the turf. In 1819 he threw up his commission and began to interest himself in politics. When in 1826 he was first returned for Hertford, there was probably no one who would have ventured to predict that this young aristocrat was destined to achieve parliamentary fame. Tall and handsome, debonair in his manners, a dandy in his dress, the very incarnation of the *jeunesse dorée*, he looked much more likely to become a lounger in the smoke-room than a favourite speaker in the House. But just as Lord George Bentinck, whom Disraeli is said to have discovered, turned his back upon the turf in order to champion the cause of the Protectionists, so did Duncombe, under the influence of Lambton, the future Earl of Durham, and moved by the perusal of the autobiographical reminiscences of Bamford, the Radical working man, begin to take more serious views of life. His maiden speech created a sensation, and it was said, whether truly or untruly it is impossible to know, that it had been written by another and committed to memory by the speaker. The "Dandy Demagogue," as he was called, thus at once bounded into fame; for his talents as a speaker were quickly placed beyond a doubt, and so long as he remained a member of the House he always raised his voice on behalf of the poor and the oppressed.[1]

[1] *The Life and Correspondence of Thomas Slingsby Duncombe*, by Thomas H. Duncombe; the *Greville Memoirs* (first series), vol. i., p. 128; vol. iii., p. 249, where Greville calls him "indefatigable for mischief, and the grand jobman of miscellaneous grievances".

That the Radicals who sat in Parliament during the first decade after the Reform Act would have achieved something might well have been expected. For, though not orators, they spoke with that force that comes only from conviction, and they were men of much more than average ability and parts. Yet they accomplished almost nothing, and their record, as they reluctantly admitted, was simply one of disappointment. True it was that the country, exhausted by the agitation for reform, was in an apathetic mood and indisposed to further change. Nevertheless, when so much is allowed, there was something about the personality of the majority of the Radicals that rendered them inapt for parliamentary life. To gain the ear and please the temper of the British House of Commons is not an easy task; and to succeed requires peculiar talents that are given to very few. Now it was in these very qualifications that the Radicals were wanting. Joseph Hume, by dint of long experience and dogged perseverance, was perhaps the one who failed the least. Grote, however, was far too doctrinaire, while Bowring was a miserable speaker and a House of Commons bore. Bald-headed, cadaverous-looking, with small eyes that twinkled beneath a pair of silver spectacles, his appearance could be scarcely called attractive, and when he rose to speak, it was usually to address a row of empty benches.[1] Cobbett died in 1835, but he lived long enough to prove that he was totally unfitted to sit in the British House of Commons. "After he came into Parliament," says Macaulay, "he was nothing. He spoke freely there when I heard him, which was often. He proved that he was quite incapable of doing anything great in debate."

[1] *Orators of the Age*, by G. H. Francis.

He displayed too want not only of tact, but also of that reverence and regard for the forms and traditions of the House which are expected from its members. He would sometimes cause a scandal by sitting upon the Treasury Bench,[1] and he went so far as to move a resolution that the King be petitioned to dismiss Sir Robert Peel for having been the author of the Act for resuming cash payments in 1819. The motion, if not received with inextinguishable laughter, found only five supporters, and it was immediately resolved that the proceedings be expunged from the minutes of the House. These are two examples of Cobbett's parliamentary manner, which, it is easy to believe, went far to discredit the Radical party as a whole. "Orator" Hunt, who died in the same year as Cobbett, displayed an even greater want of good taste, and less ability; he may be taken as an eminent illustration of Canning's famous saying that, "when firebrands touch the floor of the House they hiss and are extinguished," for at the general election of 1832 he was not returned to Parliament again. Next to Hume perhaps the most successful parliamentarian was Roebuck. Though he was insignificant in stature, and his tones were harsh and shrill, he won the attention of the House even less by his transparent honesty of purpose than by the amazing violence of his language. Even Disraeli, who did not care to waste his epigrams, taunted him with his "Saddler's Wells sarcasms" and his "melodramatic malignity".[2]

But it was rather to their want of unity and to their

---

[1] It is said that when Cobbett was asked to leave Sir Robert Peel's place, he replied, "I'll be d——d if I do". See an article in the *Nineteenth Century* for September, 1898, on "Unparliamentary Expressions," by Michael MacDonagh.

[2] *Orators of the Age*, by G. H. Francis.

THE THIRD AND CONCLUDING PERIOD. 343

mutual animosities that the failure of the Radicals was at this time mainly due. How bitterly in the ante-reform era they used to revile one another will be remembered; and now, so far from waning, the disease seemed rather to strengthen with their growth. A family party of Radicals must at this time have resembled a gladiatorial arena. Sir Francis Burdett was so disgusted that in 1837 he retired from the representation of Westminster and sought a Tory seat. The quondam demagogue became a Tory of the Tories. For some time he had been displaying symptoms of apostasy, for in 1833 he is said to have made use of the highest Tory language, and Sir Robert Peel remarked to Croker that he was " the chief Conservative in the House of Commons ". Sir Francis Burdett, in fact, though undoubtedly sincere in his democratic sympathies, was at heart a thorough aristocrat. Earl Russell has described him as " a high prerogative Tory of the days of Queen Anne," for he held that the prerogative of the Crown to choose its servants should be perfectly unfettered, and that ministers should not be allowed to sit in the House of Commons—a view which Cobbett also shared.[1] Sir John Hobhouse, who for so long had shared with Sir Francis Burdett the representation of Westminster, was to his Radical friends an almost equal disappointment.

[1] *The Correspondence and Diaries of John Wilson Croker*, vol. ii., pp. 202-3; Earl Russell's *Recollections and Suggestions*, p. 37. A good story of Lord John Russell's ready wit is related in connection with Sir F. Burdett. The Baronet, after his conversion to Toryism, made a violent speech in the House, in the course of which he said that he hated nothing so much as "the cant of patriotism," to which Lord John Russell replied that he hated something worse, " the recant of patriotism " (Tollemache's *Talks with Mr. Gladstone*). Perhaps the noble Lord had in his mind Lady Townshend's reply to one who asked her whether Whitefield had recanted; she said he had only been canting.

He took office with the Whigs, was defeated at Nottingham by a Chartist, and finally, as Lord Broughton, sought a refuge in the Elysian Fields, as Lord Beaconsfield once called the House of Lords. But to descend to lower matters, there was hardly anything upon which the Radicals agreed. Painfully conscious as they were of each other's imperfections, they poured on one another a rattling fire of recrimination and abuse. Illustrations of the fact are only too abundant. When, for instance, it was proposed to entertain Hume and Byng, the Members for Middlesex, at a dinner, the suggestion was denounced by Place and Roebuck; when a dinner was given to Wakley by the Finsbury electors, Roebuck, who was among the speakers, reproached his fellow Radicals for deserting him in Parliament, and accused Harvey, who represented Southwark, of saying things in Finsbury which he dared not repeat in Parliament; an allegation that led to a somewhat violent scene. The "damning timidity" of his professed supporters was one of Roebuck's favourite topics. To a disinterested observer this internecine strife seems to bear amusing testimony to the perennial traits of human nature and to the abiding frailties of ambition and self-love. "Hume's conduct," said Place, "has not been good during the last two sessions; no, nor that indeed of any of the reformers in the House of Commons, Roebuck's alone excepted, and his only in the last session." On the other hand Hume condemned Roebuck for being too much bent upon a policy of "thorough," and for being not enough disposed to moderation. Again, when Roebuck established his *Penny Pamphlets for the People*, Grote would not subscribe, saying that he could not identify himself with such "ultra and shocking reforms". But worse was yet to come; for over the Canadian question the two reformers quarrelled out and out, and Roebuck's friendship with the Grotes was lost for ever. So too it was with John Stuart Mill, from whom Roebuck was estranged for the most part of a life-time; but whether Mill's version of the story, that they differed over an appreciation of the merits of the poetry of Wordsworth and of Byron is the true one, or Roebuck's, that Mill's resentment was aroused by a warning that he gave him with regard to Mrs. Taylor, it is impossible to say. It is enough to note the fact that two Radicals, whose mutual sympathies and kindred views should have made the way of friendship easy, for many years scarcely spoke to one another—a truly pitiable picture for posterity to contemplate. It is little wonder that Roebuck, though he himself had, to use Kinglake's words, "appointed himself to the office of public accuser," and was, therefore, much to blame for his habit of ill-considered censure, should at last have bitterly exclaimed: "I am heartily sick of my friends. My opponents I expected would abuse me, but I have ever found that the most bitter of all my violent abusers were my intimate friends." But of the parliamentary Radicals of this time we can form the best idea from the remarks of John Stuart Mill, who, if a severe critic was a just one, and a dispassionate observer. He saw clearly their defects and diagnosed the causes of their failure. "There is," he said, "no man or men of commanding talents among the Radicals in public life, or those whose position in respect of pecuniary independence enables them to put themselves forward personally. . . . I have little hope of any of the present race of parliamentary Radicals. Some of them are full of crotchets, others fastidious and over-loaded with petty scrupulosity; none have energy except Roebuck and

Buller; Roebuck has no judgment, Buller no patient persevering industry." Nor less just was his complaint that they wanted "activity" and "enterprise"; that they left the lead of the Radicals in the House to the "old hands, to Hume and O'Connell"; that they "did very little to promote any opinions," and that they "sank into a mere *côté gauche* of the Whig party". Mill, indeed, was greatly disappointed, and when Place who was not less so, wrote to tell him that he would no longer waste his time "with men who were infirm of purpose," he told Fonblanque the contents of the letter and remarked: "I shall keep it as a memorial of the spiritless, heartless imbecility of the English Radicals". There was only too much ground for the despondency to which Mill gave utterance here; for Mrs. Grote, who made herself the chronicler of the fortunes of the Radicals, has put on record what she called "the total extinction" of the party; by which she meant that it consisted of her husband and five others. She tells a story which is eloquent in meaning. Charles Buller one night remarked to Grote, "I will tell you what you are coming to. In no very long time from this, you and I will have to 'tell' Molesworth." Macaulay had an even less exalted view of the magnitude of the democratic party; it consisted, he declared, of "Grote and his wife". To such a condition of despair had a few years spent in abusing one another reduced the parliamentary Radicals.[1]

---

[1] *Life and Letters of John Arthur Roebuck*, edited by Robert Eadon Leader, pp. 39, 77, 83, 95, 102; *Political Pamphlets for the People* (No. 9); Mrs. Grote's *Philosophical Radicals of 1832*, p. 28; Mrs. Grote's *Personal Life of George Grote*, p. 111; J. S. Mill's *Autobiography*, pp. 195-96; "Unpublished Letters from J. S. Mill to Professor Nichol," *Fortnightly Review* for May, 1897; *The Greville Memoirs* (first series), vol. iii., p. 227.

One of the most interesting aspects of the history of the Radicals since the Reform Act is their relation to the Whigs. It will not have been forgotten that the Radicals had already shown no little anxiety to dissociate themselves, and take up a separate and independent standpoint. Nay more, they openly avowed their feelings of hostility, which the Reform Act certainly did nothing to diminish. The Reform Act, which, as a Whig measure was deemed by the Radicals a timid and a miserable compromise, tended rather to increase the antipathy they felt. There are few things more remarkable than the scorn, the arrogant contempt which the Radicals ostentatiously displayed towards the very party who had done so much for the cause of the reformers. Sir William Molesworth, for example, called the Whig policy "debasing"; he said that the Whigs were "miserable wretches"; that he would rejoice to "hear their death shriek," and would "look with pleasure on their death agony". Duncombe said that they had "the voice of lions and the timidity of hares"; Place called them "a truckling set of Tories," and declared that if the parliamentary Radicals had done their duty, "the very name of Whig would have been abolished". Grote decided to retire from Parliament because he said he did not see the use of going there to sustain " Whig conservatism against the Tory conservatism ". Nor was this the feeling of the leaders only of the party ; for the London Working Men's Association reflected what the rank and file were thinking when it condemned " the hypocritical, conniving and liberty-undermining Whigs ". From the Radical point of view there seemed to be between the Whigs and Tories a distinction rather than a difference. Whiggism, as the Radicals beheld it, appeared to be a policy of dishonesty and cowardice, and as such they abhorred it. Of their prevalent feeling two illustrations must suffice. The first is that of Harriet Martineau, who was a disciple of the utilitarian school. She accused the Whigs of "blindness in regard to public opinion and the progress of the world"; of believing that they could "teach" the people all that was good for them in a coaxing and admonitory way; of "poverty and perverseness" in their notions; of "insolence" in their feelings; and she clenched the long indictment by the startling declaration that they were "a remarkably vulgar class of men".[1] The second is that of Cobden, at this time a rising politician, who was destined to become one of the founders of a new school of political opinion, which in part absorbed and in part eclipsed the old utilitarian doctrine. Speaking of the Whig ministers of 1837, he remarked that they were without principle or political honesty, and destitute of any atom of courage or independence; and he accused them of snubbing the Radicals in order that they themselves might not appear to be dangerous politicians. If this then was the kind of judgment which even the more enlightened Radicals passed upon the Whigs, it is no wonder that between the two Liberal wings there could be no workable alliance. Some proposals of co-operation were occasionally made, but they were doomed to failure in advance. Place and Roebuck, for example, disapproved of the dinner given to Hume and Byng, because it was meant to be a demonstration of good-will between Radicals and Whigs. Hume, who was one of the few Radicals who

---

[1] Harriet Martineau said that Lord John Russell and other Whigs treated Roebuck with outrageous insolence in public and private (H. Martineau's *Autobiography*, p. 346).

showed a more conciliatory spirit, was denounced for encouraging " the Whigs in every species of misdeed ". Sir William Molesworth also condemned what he was pleased to call " that accursed cry of union amongst reformers ". Once, indeed, in 1835, there was a near approach to at least a temporary union; but the plan to " brigade," as it was called, the Whigs and Radicals in Parliament, was wrecked by Hume, who wished to include the Irish members, and confided the proposal to O'Connell. How little the Radicals believed in the sincerity of the Agitator may be gathered from the fact that they suspected him of a desire to trip them up and keep the Whigs in office.[1]

Nor were the Whigs on their side much inclined to make concessions to purchase Radical support, though it was well worth their while to have it. The influence of Macaulay, for example, the most damaging critic of the Benthamite philosophy, and the greatest of all apologists for Whiggism, in itself was very great; and he told Lord John Russell that if any of the Radicals were to praise him at the expense of his colleagues, such praise would be to him more painful than their censure. Lord Grey was hardly less emphatic in declaring that nothing would induce him to be a party to anything like a concert with O'Connell and the Radicals.[2] Lord Melbourne's view was

[1] Leader's *Life and Letters of Roebuck*, pp. 83, 86; Mrs. Grote's *Philosophical Radicals of 1832; Life and Correspondence of Thomas Slingsby Duncombe*, vol. i., p. 292; *The Personal Life of George Grote*, by Mrs. Grote, pp. 99, 127; *The Life and Struggles of William Lovett*, p. 148; Miss Martineau's *Autobiography*, pp. 337, 340; Morley's *Life of Cobden*, vol. i., p. 126; vol. ii., p. 219.

[2] The Duke of Bedford writing to Lord John Russell in 1835 said: " Grey at present seems to me to have too great a horror of the Radicals " (Walpole's *Life of Lord John Russell*, vol. i., p. 219).

much the same; it was marked by that air of light disdain and easy tolerance that was characteristic of the man. They, that is to say the Utilitarians, were, he said, "all fools"; John Austin was "a damned fool," and his work on jurisprudence was "the dullest book" he ever read. Moreover he suited the action to the word, and in 1837 he refused to democratise his Cabinet by admitting two such able politicians as Lord Durham and Charles Buller. Lord Brougham, who was fond of coquetting with the Radicals, nevertheless came to the conclusion that they had been "tried and found wanting". Of all the leading Whigs perhaps the only one who showed the slightest inclination to make advances was Lord John Russell; but even his advances were not made with very willing feet. The wisest heads among the Radicals were, therefore, not long in perceiving that, so long as they remained in splendid isolation, their labours would be futile. Mrs. Grote, speaking of the year 1834, averred that there were scarcely any Radicals who were fit to enter Parliament; while John Stuart Mill spoke out with what his friends must have thought an almost brutal candour. He asserted that his party could not be anything but weak, because "the country did not contain the men". The best hope for the Radicals, he thought, lay in the acceptance of Lord Durham as their leader. The position of that nobleman was one that made him peculiarly well fitted to play the part of middleman between the Radicals and Whigs. As Lord Privy Seal in Lord Grey's Administration, he had laboured strenuously and successfully in the cause of parliamentary reform. In 1833 he differed from his colleagues, and, resigning office, was created Earl of Durham; and in the following year he found an opportunity for the display of his controversial talents by his defence of the Radicals against Brougham's vehement assaults. Now it was that Mill thought that the psychological moment had arrived: "We now see," he said, "the importance of the rallying point which Lord Durham has afforded. Any banner placed so high that what is written upon it can be read by everybody is all important towards forming a party; but Lord Durham has really acted with consummate skill and in the best possible spirit." Mill's advice was excellent indeed; but of course it was not followed. Lord Durham was a man of brilliant talents that were marred only by some infirmity of temper; but while he was too democratic in his sympathies to please the Whigs, he was not Radical enough to satisfy the democrats. Place, for instance, contemned him as "all a lord and none a man," and declared that in public life he was "defunct". As High Commissioner for Canada in 1838 he performed inestimable services to the colonies; but his official acts were disavowed and he was recalled by the Government at home. Again, as Mill believed, the time had come for the Radicals to rally round Lord Durham, who had returned home a disappointed man and full of resentment with the Whigs. Death, however, overtook him, and the Radicals were left to wander a leaderless, undisciplined band in disarray.[1]

The Radicals in the first reformed Parliament, despite their energy and talents, accomplished very little; a mere

[1] Walpole's *Life of Lord John Russell*, vol. i., p. 224; vol. ii., p. 91; *The Greville Memoirs* (first series), vol. iii., p. 138; Brougham's *Memoirs*, vol. iii., p. 401; Mrs. Grote's *Personal Life of George Grote*, p. 93; J. S. Mill's *Autobiography*, p. 215; "Unpublished Letters from J. S. Mill to Professor Nichol" in the *Fortnightly Review* for May, 1897; Mrs. Grote's *Philosophical Radicals of 1832*, p. 33.

"fortuitous concourse of atoms," they had no coherence as a party. From time to time they made spasmodic and ineffective motions for root-and-branch reform, but it was to very little purpose. The Whigs on their side, who at first, like John Russell—"Finality Jack" as he was called—affected to believe that the Reform Act was absolutely final, tried to appease the hungry Radicals by throwing them some sops of social legislation. Lord Melbourne's commissions of inquiry became a sort of by-word and a butt for the satirical sallies of the wits. Sydney Smith expressed the popular feeling with his inimitable humour; when, he said, you met a Whig whom you had not seen before, your only doubt was "not whether he was a commissioner or not, but what the department of human life might be into which he had been appointed to inquire". Praed touched lightly on the Whig dilatoriness in some bright good-natured verse:—

> To save the Church, and serve the Crown
> By letting others pull them down;
> To promise, pause, prepare, postpone,
> And end by letting things alone;
> In short to earn the people's pay
> By doing nothing every day;
> These tasks, these joys, the Fates assign
> To well-placed Whigs in Thirty-nine.[1]

But though to the Whigs these were halcyon days of tranquillity and peace, to the Radicals throughout the country the course of events was deeply disappointing. Flushed with victory and full of hope they looked on the Reform Act as merely a step, and that a short one, in the direction of the establishment of a thoroughly democratic constitution. The National Political Union had

[1] Trevelyan's *Life and Letters of Macaulay*, vol. ii., pp. 59, 61.

THE THIRD AND CONCLUDING PERIOD. 353

been formed "to obtain a full, free and effectual representation of the *middle and working classes* in the Commons House of Parliament,"[1] but in fact the working class had been left out in the cold. The hope of any further enfranchisement of the people rather receded than advanced, and the feeling of despair thus engendered gave rise to one of the most important phases of radicalism that England has experienced. This phase was Chartism.

The results of the first Reform Act may in general terms be described by saying that it threw the preponderance of political power into the hands of the middle class. One consequence was that the old party lines were partially effaced, and that the terms Whig and Tory were thought to be unfitted to suit the altered state of things. The Tories in particular, who represented the privileged *régime* of the landed aristocracy, were by the admission of the trader and manufacturer to their ranks thoroughly leavened with the new spirit of the age; they became the Conservatives of the later dispensation. Whether Croker was the first to use the word to designate the transfigured Tory party it is not very easy to decide; but it is certain that the new term was beginning to be commonly employed within a few years after the Reform Act. Sir Robert Peel, for instance, writing to Croker in 1831, referred to "those who call themselves Conservatives"; and in the following year the Duke of Wellington in a letter to the same correspondent spoke of the "Conservative party," as though the word was then in common use. Somewhat later, in 1835, Greville put on record in his diary that it was said that there was "no longer such a thing as a Tory"; Peel, he says, clearly did not intend that there should "be (as far as he is

[1] Wakefield's *Life of Thomas Attwood*, p. 139.

concerned as their leader) a Tory party, though, of course, there must be a Conservative party". Again, we find Lord John Russell in a speech delivered at Stroud in 1837 making the following declaration: "If they"—the Conservatives—"say that the distinction of Whig and Tory should no longer be kept up, I am ready in opposition to their name of Conservative to take the name of Reformer and to stand by that designation".[1] This new christening, if the expression may be allowed, of an old historic party, was eloquent in meaning; it meant the admission of the great middle class to a share in the government of the country. But that class constituted a section only of the people; and if radicalism means "the reform and control of Parliament by pressure from without," that pressure was intended to be exercised not by a privileged minority but by the people as a whole. Originally, indeed, the so-called "movement" party found little or no support among the masses of the people, to whom the cry of "King and Church" was as good as any other. When, however, they began to feel the pinch of sharp distress, they became not unwilling listeners to the tinselled declamations of such a honey-tongued demagogue as Hunt. But the more intelligent artisans, of whom Place was a superlative example, were not to be deluded by the clap-trap of brilliant generalities and an easy flow of words. Shrewd, hard-headed and clear-sighted, this superior class of workmen kept in view their own material interests rather than any political ideal; and it was, therefore, for industrial purposes mainly that they first began to band themselves together. The

---

[1] *The Diaries and Correspondence of John Wilson Croker*, vol. ii., pp. 116, 173, 198; *The Greville Memoirs* (first series), vol. iii., p. 263; Walpole's *Life of Lord John Russell*, vol. i., p. 283.

Metropolitan Trades Union of 1831 was one of the first of these associations. It, however, soon became apparent that there was little to be hoped for from an unreformed Parliament, and the Metropolitan Trades Union was turned into the National Union of the Working Classes, whose objects were intended to be in the main political. After the Reform Act had been passed, the National Union, which was thought to have done its work, was dissolved, and the Consolidated Trades Union was formed to take its place. But the working classes required a very brief experience of the reformed House of Commons to discover that from the political point of view their position had scarcely been improved. To exchange the domination of the aristocrats for that of the middle class was from their point of view like exchanging whips for scorpions. The Radicals in the House of Commons, moreover, though chosen, as Carlyle said, "to interpret and articulate the dumb deep want of the people," failed to carry out their mission ; while " the expectant millions "—to quote Carlyle again—were sitting " at a feast of the Barmecide " and bidden to fill themselves, as best they could, with the mockeries of an imaginary meal. It was on account of this conviction on the part of the still unenfranchised people that the Reform Act had failed to satisfy their aspirations, and that the Radicals in Parliament were unwilling or unable to do them any good, that in 1836 the London Working Men's Association was established. It was from this society that Chartism took its rise. While Parliament was dallying and inquiring, the working classes bestirred themselves to action.[1]

[1] *The History of Trade Unionism*, by Sidney and Beatrice Webb, pp. 130, 146 ; *Memories*, by W. J. Linton, pp. 32-35 ; *The Life and Struggles of William Lovett*, pp. 68, 73-77 ; Carlyle's *Chartism*.

To describe Chartism fully would require a volume in itself; but its place in the history of the Radicals demands a brief consideration. It may then, in the first place, be pertinently asked in what respect this radicalism of the working class—this new progressive force acting upon parallel and independent lines—differed from that which was already in existence. The answer to the question would go far to show what Chartism really was, and it may be approached from various points of view. If hostility to the aristocratic classes be taken as a test, then no Chartist could surpass the parliamentary Radicals in the violence of their language or the strength of their convictions. Take Roebuck for example. Upon what he deemed the vices of the aristocracy generally and the House of Lords in particular, he—in his salad days at least—was never weary of insisting. "A more despicable set of wretches," he said, "cannot be found than the nobles of England under the Georges. Licentious, mean, in every way thoroughly corrupt and cruel, it would be difficult to find their superiors in vice in the world's history." He averred that the majority of the hereditary Chamber naturally tended to be ignorant, grasping, imperious, suspicious, and, therefore, necessarily cruel. "They are," he said, "as cruel as they dare be, and meaner than they are they could not be. Who shall deny their cruelty while the Corn Laws and Game Laws remain? Who shall deny their meanness while the Pension List exists? Of their ignorance it is hardly necessary to speak. *That* has become a by-word and a proverb." Again, he denounced the House of Commons for their "unwise, not to say degrading, submission" to "a few ignorant, irresponsible and interested peers". In almost every institution, whether it was the army, or the colonies, or the Game Laws, Roebuck saw, or fancied that he saw, the aristocratic cloven-hoof. He, for instance, condemned the Guards in London as absolutely useless; they are, he said, "an excuse for making provision for the children of the aristocracy. They exist in order that the sons of the nobility or of rich persons may be quartered on the public purse. . . . It is evident that they are a mere excuse for aristocratic advancement." As to the colonies, he condemned them for their cost, which was far in excess of any profit they produced; but still more on account of "the malign influence" they cast upon "our liberties and domestic government, through the patronage and power which they threw into the hands of the Executive". It is also due to Roebuck that the arraignment of the Game Laws became a regular item in the political programme of the Radicals. "To the selfish purpose," he said, of "having partridges and pheasants and hares to be shot at, our squire legislators have filled the statute-book with stringent laws, which have filled the jails with prisoners. . . . These hares and pheasants and partridges are fed at the public expense." Of all landowners he was preternaturally suspicious, a fact of which an amusing illustration is recorded. When a landlord in the House of Commons moved that the tax upon dogs employed for drawing carts should be raised, Roebuck scented a sinister design, and accused the mover of acting as he did because dogs did not eat corn. Sir Robert Peel, as the Tory leader, was the object of his peculiar detestation; and in his election address to the Bath electors he spoke of that eminent statesmen in words that were an outrage alike on decency and common sense. He described him as "the evil spirit of the House of Commons"; as "malignant and envious"; he condemned "his wily machinations, his twists and turns, his utter carelessness of truth, his barefaced and brazen neglect of his former professions"; he compared his dexterity in debate to that of a horse jockey who winks at you when he means to cheat you; he likened him to Milton's Evil Spirit, whom "they found, squat like a toad, close at the ear of Eve". If, therefore, Roebuck fairly represented—and there is no reason to suppose that he did not—the feelings of the ordinary Radicals, they were as bitter towards the aristocracy as the most envenomed Chartists. Or take again the question of parliamentary reform. Grote may very well be taken to represent the opinions of the average Radical. *Ex uno disce omnes.* Of the ballot—a subject which he made peculiarly his own— he was not only the ablest and most persistent advocate in the House of Commons, where his annually recurring motions were a feature of the session; but he devised a ballot box and sent models of it up and down the country. Upon the utility of annual Parliaments he was hardly less convinced, though others expressed themselves content with a limit of three years. "One year," he said, "would be in my opinion quite sufficient and better than any longer period; two years would be tolerable, three years seriously objectionable on account of its length, and any period longer than three years not to be entertained for a moment." On the other hand he thought that the franchise should be gradually extended with the spread of education. He was singular in holding the opinion— though the idea was rather one of the nature of a devout imagination—that the House of Commons was too large, and that 300 really assiduous members were enough to carry on the business of the country. There was, therefore, only one point, that of annual Parliaments, in reference to which Grote in these days would have been considered an extremist; and the distance we have travelled since 1837 may be measured by the language of the *Times* upon his election in that year for the City of London. He had, it was said in the columns of that journal, made himself the frontispiece of a revolutionary code; he had become the representative and the peculiar organ of whatever is most chimerical in theory or most reckless in experiment, most false and revolting in hostility to our national institutions; he personified the movement system. Such was the character of the great historian of Greece as depicted in the most influential journal of his day.[1]

It would, therefore, seem at the first glance that between the Chartists and the ordinary Radicals there was very little difference. Yet it is evident that the organisation, the methods, the intellectual attitude of Chartism were distinguished by marks which were peculiarly their own. This will be made apparent if the subject is considered more in detail.

At the Crown and Anchor Tavern one day in 1837 some reformers met together at the summons of the London Working Men's Association. The meeting was a small one, and almost passed unnoticed at the time, but it was fraught with great results. A resolution was, after some debate, adopted to present a petition to Parliament demanding universal suffrage, the abolition of the property qualification, annual Parliaments, equal representation, payment of members and the ballot. The demand was

[1] *Pamphlets for the People*, edited by J. A. Roebuck; *The Life and Letters of J. A. Roebuck*, by R. E. Leader; Mrs. Grote's *Personal Life of George Grote*, p. 109; *The Minor Works of George Grote*, edited by Alexander Bain.

not a small one, and to Roebuck, as the most intrepid of the Radicals in Parliament, the task of presenting the petition was entrusted. At an adjourned meeting eight of the leading parliamentary Radicals were present, and amongst them was O'Connell, who at this time posed as a reformer, though he afterwards attacked the Chartists with all the force of his invective. The members present resolved to give Roebuck their support, and a committee was appointed to draft a bill which should embody their demands. The committee, of which Place was a very influential member, drew the outlines of a bill, which was subsequently styled the People's Charter, and gave the whole movement the name by which it speedily was known. In connection with the drafting of the bill, two points of some interest are worth a passing notice. First, the clause in favour of female suffrage in the original draft was struck out as inexpedient; and, secondly, the reform of the House of Lords was not in the first instance made one of the items of the charter. It was only at an adjourned meeting that it was decided to support Roebuck in bringing in a bill to make the House of Lords " responsible to the people ".[1]

Such, in brief, was the constitution of the Charter. The demand for universal suffrage was not, of course, a new one; but whereas many Radicals would have been content with something less, the Chartists were not willing to submit to any compromise. Equality of representation, too, was not a new demand, and the same thing may be said of annual Parliaments and the ballot. But though many Radicals would have accepted triennial Parliaments, the Chartists certainly would not. Upon

[1] *The Life and Struggles of William Lovett*, pp. 111-13, 170, 191-92.

THE THIRD AND CONCLUDING PERIOD. 361

the ballot, however, as a supreme article of faith, the Radicals of all shades were in unanimous accord. So far, then, there was nothing in the Charter which had not already been demanded with more or less insistency upon the platform and in Parliament. There were only two points which could be described in any sense as new; the abolition of the property qualification, which, though it had been demanded by the Birmingham Political Union, had hitherto been strangely overlooked; and the payment of members of Parliament. The latter was a question, indeed, which had from time to time been mooted; and the Birmingham Political Union went so far as to pass a resolution in favour of granting "wages of attendance," which were to be raised by a rate upon constituencies. But with the more deeply thinking Radicals the proposal had never found much favour. The price at which the services of a member should be appraised the Chartists did not presume to settle; for whereas in the petition the sum of £400 a year was fixed upon, in the subsequent bill all figures were omitted.[1]

We are now in a position to compare the radicalism of the Chartists with that professed by such eminent representative Radicals as Grote and Roebuck. It in the first place must be said that chartism in its origin was a strictly business-like and practical affair, and that there

[1] Wakefield's *Life of Thomas Attwood*, p. 154. Lovett devised a ballot box and a district hall or voting place. At a later period of his life (1856) he proposed to substitute for the property qualification what he called "an intellectual and moral standard". That is to say, he wished all candidates to be examined by a committee; and that after seven years' service in the House they should, if the House thought fit, be inscribed on a list of "persons competent to share in the government of the country".
—See his *Life and Struggles*, pp. 411, 369-700; and the Appendices A and B.

was in fact no striking novelty about it. Carlyle remarked that the English people regard the suffrage as "their panacea for all that goes wrong with them"; and that their sole idea of freedom is the right "to send one's twenty-thousandth part of a master of tongue-fence to National Palaver". That was exactly the thought that inspired the early Chartists. They were in no sense original; they asked only for reforms, which for the most part had already been demanded, and have since been conceded; they had no new gospel to teach or message to deliver; they were not inspired by any great ideals. In their aims and their desires from all other Radicals in fact they differed not at all. They one and all despised the aristocracy; they one and all abhorred the Whigs; they one and all contemned the House of Commons, whose members they described—to use the language of the London Working Men's Association—as "persons who cringe in the gilded circle of a court, flutter among the gaities of a ball-room to court the passing smile of royalty or whine at the ministers of the day". As to the points of the Charter there was not a Radical in Parliament who was not ready, nay eager, to support them. Thomas Attwood, for example, who in 1839 presented to the House the National Petition, was eloquent in its defence. "The first part of the petition," he said, "claims universal suffrage; it claims representation co-equal with taxation, which was the ancient law of England.... The Constitution guarantees the right of election ... and they contend that they have a constitutional right to vote by ballot. They go further and claim annual Parliaments agreeably to the Constitution. The Act of Settlement orders that Parliaments shall be triennial; and under the old practice of the Constitution they were annual. Then they go on to demand that the labour of representatives shall be rewarded. That was the ancient practice of the Constitution as exemplified by Andrew Marvel; and I could to-morrow apply to my constituents at Birmingham, the Constitution authorising the members of this House to be paid the wages of attendance by a rate on their constituents." It is worth a passing notice that chartism, as here interpreted by Attwood, was founded not so much on grounds of utility, as upon that appeal to ancient practice which in the mind of Major Cartwright amounted almost to a kind of monomania. There was in this interpretation a reversion from utilitarianism to an older type of creed. A yet more zealous advocate of chartism within the walls of Parliament was Thomas Duncombe. He obtained the commutation of the death sentences upon the Chartist leaders, and ultimately their release; he presented to Parliament the second great National Petition; he corresponded with the better class of Chartists in a genuinely sympathetic spirit. Yet though the Radicals as a whole co-operated with them, the Chartists maintained from first to last a separate position of their own, and to have been able to have kept it they must have had some peculiar idiosyncrasies.[1]

This individuality of the Chartists may be to some extent explained by several causes. First, the early Radicals, it will doubtless be remembered, relied chiefly upon political societies in order to propagate their teaching. These societies were, however, in the beginning only small and unimportant. At a later time the same principle was carried out upon an ampler scale in those political unions

[1] *Life and Struggles of William Lovett*, p. 101; Wakefield's *Life of Thomas Attwood*, p. 347.

—that of Birmingham for example—which in effect extorted the Reform Act from a most reluctant Parliament. Now in the Chartist movement the principle of association for political purposes was carried further still; a society was formed that ramified everywhere, that covered the country like a net-work. This in itself was a thing that was new, portentous and alarming. Next, the same progress may be traced in the use of public speaking. The early Radicals used it very little; they were not orators, and it was only by degrees that agitators began to see the vast potentiality of the platform. The reform campaign of 1831 was a great object lesson in its latent capabilities; the Chartists bettered the example, and spoke with a licentiousness that had been rarely known before. Lastly, the movement was one which derived its main support from the lower classes of the people; a fact which was at once its misfortune and its crime. Never before had radicalism descended to quite so deep a social stratum, unless, indeed, when Henry Hunt was in the heyday of his glory. Even the reform agitation of 1831 was the work in the main of the middle class and the Whigs. The Radicals' leaders hitherto had, generally speaking, been educated gentlemen; even fastidious in their tastes; who abhorred the common herd; who loved to preach a philosophy at a respectable distance from their hearers, but never dreamed of coming down to the market place or street, and of mingling with the masses. They had, in fact, conjured up a spirit which they dreaded and were powerless to lay. To tell the people what they ought to do was one thing; to see the people acting for themselves was quite another; it was a usurpation, an impertinence. It was then rather in their modes than in their objects and their theories that the Chartists differed from the older class of Radicals,

THE THIRD AND CONCLUDING PERIOD. 365

and from their contemporaries who had been nurtured upon the old traditions; they led a popular democratic movement in an unprecedented manner. Chartism was, in fact, with a few remarkable exceptions, thoroughly plebeian; but a sketch of the personal characteristics of its leaders will show what its nature really was more vividly than any vague abstractions.[1]

A more extraordinary group of men possessing more diversified traits or variegated talents, than the Chartists was never brought together to advocate a single cause. In the first place, a strong Hibernian strain was present in their blood. The bond of sympathy that linked together the Irish and the Radicals has already been remarked; and it is, therefore, no surprise to find that some of the most famous of the Chartists were men of Irish birth. Daniel O'Connell himself at first took up their cause; but he was probably never quite sincere, and he afterwards violently assailed it. Feargus O'Connor, the most notorious of the Chartists, was Irish in every fibre of his being. He entered public life in 1832 as the parliamentary representative of Cork; he was re-elected in 1835, but was unseated on petition. His next adventure was to contest the constituency of Oldham in opposition to a son of William Cobbett, but the result was a fiasco. Then he quarrelled with O'Connell, who, with great consideration for Anglo-Saxon feeling, "made a present of him to the English Radicals". A more fatal gift could never have been made. O'Connor was tall, strongly built and handsome, and his voice, manner and deportment

[1] The social character of the Chartists may be to some extent inferred from a statement made by Lovett about the composition of the National Convention of 1839. He says that there were fifty-three delegates, and of these three were magistrates, six were editors, two were doctors, and one a Church of England clergyman (*Life and Labours of William Lovett*, p. 201).

were such as to strike awe into the masses who hung upon his lips. Bombastic and infinitely vain, he brought ruin on the Chartists by his flame-coloured language both on the platform and in the *Northern Star*, that wildly incoherent journal of which he was the editor. His self-idolatry was sublime. "You are," said Lovett—and he said no more than the truth—"the great 'I am' of politics, the great personification of radicalism." Another Irish Chartist, and one who was in every way superior to O'Connor, was James Bronterre O'Brien. Born in 1805, the son of a wine merchant in County Longford, his extraordinary talents drew the attention of Lowell Edgeworth, the brother of the novelist, and he had him sent to school. It was to this school that Sir Walter Scott was brought to see him, and the great man is said to have been filled with wondering admiration. The youth went to Trinity College, Dublin, and was called to the bar; and coming to London, he at once plunged into the tempestuous sea of politics under the patronage of the notorious Henry Hunt. Tall and slightly stooping, with a finely intellectual cast of head and features, O'Brien soared far above his colleagues in ability. He was the only Chartist of any originality, or with any touch of genius. Not less forcible with his tongue than with his pen, his splendid talents and his learning earned him the title of the "school-master"; a fact, it must be said, that is to the credit of the Chartists, who for the most part gladly listened to his teaching. O'Connor, whom O'Brien nicknamed the "Dictator," was with his insufferable vanity an exception to the rule. Among the English leaders perhaps the two most conspicuous figures—though not the ablest or the noblest—were Richard Oastler and Joseph Rayner Stephens. The former, who had been steward to a Yorkshire squire, professed to be a Tory, and "The Altar, the Throne and the Cottage" were the words which he adopted as his motto. Yet he denounced the rich manufacturers, and the factory owners in particular, with savage fury, and under the title of "The King of the Factory Children," he became widely known as one of the most inflammatory speakers of his time. Hardly less so was Joseph Stephens, a former Wesleyan minister, who had been dismissed from his position for the part he took in politics. He proclaimed himself "a revolutionist by fire, a revolutionist by blood, to the knife, to the death," and such, indeed, he was. Of the many other Chartists, men who were justly famous in their day ; of the handsome and fluent Henry Vincent, the English "Demosthenes"; of the noble-hearted Ernest Jones; of Thomas Cooper, shoemaker, journalist, novelist and poet, it would be impossible to speak at any length without irrelevant prolixity. To consider the Chartists in their relationship to contemporary radicalism, and not to write their history, is the subject of this section of the chapter. It must, therefore, be enough to point out very briefly the reasons why a cause, by no means hopeless at the outset, was lost in dismal failure.[1]

[1] *Life and Struggles of William Lovett*, pp. 115, 158-61, 191; Holyoake's *Sixty Years of an Agitator's Life*, chap. xxii.; *History of the Chartist Movement*, by R. G. Gammage; *Dictionary of National Biography;* The *Life of Thomas Cooper*, written by himself. Cooper was a man of real literary gifts, and he was introduced by Duncombe to Disraeli in the following characteristic letter:—
"MY DEAR DISRAELI,
 I send you Mr. Cooper, a Chartist, red-hot from Stafford Jail. But don't be frightened. He won't bite you. He has written a poem and a romance; and thinks he can cut out *Coningsby* and *Sybil*. Help him if you can, and oblige yours,
"T. S. DUNCOMBE."
—(*Life of Cooper*, p. 263.)

First, the Chartists, like all other Radicals, were struck with the fatal blight of discord; they held within themselves the seeds of dissolution. It was utterly impossible for William Lovett, for example, the mild and melancholy advocate of "moral force," and O'Brien, the cultivated scholar, to work in harmony with such a firebrand as O'Connor. Nay more, from the very beginning there was a serious divergence of opinion between two sections of the party; for the two methods of "moral" and "physical" force were mutually exclusive. The gulf that yawned between the partisans of either it was impossible to bridge; and Chartism degenerated into a selfish struggle for supremacy. In parliamentary elections, for example, the Chartists could not agree upon a common policy; and when, as often happened, they had no candidate of their own, they voted sometimes for the Whigs, and sometimes for the Tories, according as caprice or spite dictated. They had no scruple in thwarting any Radical, however useful to their cause, who did not please them. When Sharman Crawfurd, the Radical member for Rochdale, proposed a scheme for obstructing all parliamentary business until the Charter was conceded, O'Connor tried his best to stop him; and when Sir John Hobhouse, that old-fashioned Radical, was a parliamentary candidate at Nottingham, O'Connor not only opposed him but actually defeated him. As time went on dissensions grew apace. The "moral force" party wished to bring within their sphere of operations such things as libraries and schools; others to tack on the temperance question; while yet again a third section desired to convert the whole movement into one of religious propagandism. Then O'Brien, who with all his fine talents was something of a dreamer, began to preach his own peculiar crotchets;

that is to say, nationalisation of the land, a symbolic currency, state industrial loans and national marts. O'Connor, who could not brook a rival, inaugurated a National Land Company, which in a short time ruined those who had staked their money in it; and Chartism was finally dismembered into a number of divergent and fragmentary segments. Such were the National Alliance, the National Association, the People's League and the National Complete Suffrage Union. When, to crown all, Ernest Jones exposed the character of O'Connor in his *History of a Democratic Movement*, Chartism was to all intents and purposes defunct. It had, in fact, wandered away from its original intention : the reform of Parliament by means of agitation within the limits of the law. The violence of its methods had alienated those who were disposed to be its friends. When Roebuck called O'Connor "a cowardly and malignant demagogue," "a rogue, a liar and a coward"; when Place said that O'Connor used "every means he could to lead and mislead the working people"; that O'Brien was "a three parts insane and savage man"; and that Stephens was "a malignant crazy man, who never seemed exhausted with bawling atrocious matter"; when even Duncombe, who had received a handsome presentation from the Charlists, was constrained to abandon them; when Attwood declared that they were "a little clique or junta of men who had little more influence over the workmen than over those of Constantinople"; when Bright accused their leaders of living on deception, it was evident that Chartism had fallen into irreparable discredit. A more disastrous record of the sacrifice of energy and talent upon the altar of self-love has never yet been told. In Chartism, indeed, the Radicals exhibited few of their virtues and almost all their vices, and it is perhaps the chapter in their history of which they have least reason to be proud.[1]

The internal dissensions, the crimes and the follies of the Chartists would in any case have wrecked them; but their end was hastened by the rise of another school of Radicals to whom, as far at least as immediate objects were concerned, they were bitterly opposed. It was, to put the matter briefly, the Anti-Corn Law agitation that proved to be the death-blow of the Chartists; for the best intellect of the Radicals was diverted into a new and widely different channel. This new movement drew its main support from the middle class and the manufacturing interests, and from the first the Chartists scented treason in it. Full of the suspicion born of ignorance, they fancied that the whole thing was a plot to thwart their efforts for parliamentary reform, and to reduce their rate of wages; they believed that a deep design was laid to increase the power of the capitalists by enabling them to obtain a larger share of wealth at the expense of the producers; they saw the cloven hoof of bourgeois tyranny in every Anti-Corn Law meeting. If only— so they argued—the points of the charter were conceded, the abolition of the Corn Laws, if desired, would quickly follow. It was therefore to no purpose that Bright and Cobden met O'Connor face to face and laboured to convince him; and there was doubtless some truth in the

---

[1] Gammage's *History of the Chartist Movement*, pp. 192-96, 253; *The Life and Letters of J. A. Roebuck*, by R. E. Leader, pp. 143, 203; Jephson's *Rise and Progress of the Platform*, vol. ii., pp. 209, 255; Wallas' *Life of Francis Place*, p. 373. There was really no sympathy between the Chartists and such a Radical as Attwood who was beyond everything a financial reformer. O'Connor used to call Attwood's financial schemes "rag-botheration".

THE THIRD AND CONCLUDING PERIOD. 371

report that some of the Tories bribed the Chartists to disturb the meetings of the Anti-Corn Law League. In their whole history there is nothing that throws a clearer light upon the real character of the Chartists than their attitude towards the League; their ignorance, their jealousy, their irreconcilable fanaticism are unmistakably exposed.[1]

The Anti-Corn Law agitation, though it was carried on by Radicals, was not an elemental part of what they believed to be their functions. It is, indeed, conceivable that, if the conditions had been other than they were, it might have been the work of Whigs or Tories. To obtain the popular control of Parliament, and not to alter tariffs was the grand aim of the Radicals; nay, rather, the very reason of their being. To cheapen the food of the people was, doubtless, a laudable desire, but there was no necessary connection between it and the democratic party. The abolition of the Corn Laws was, if the history of the Radicals be looked at from a comprehensive point of view, an event that might be described as merely incidental; it was a by-product, so to speak, of the machinery of radicalism. Yet it was one of those events that cannot be ignored; and that for several reasons. First, the successful consummation of the struggle was mainly due to the brilliant leadership, the unwearied zeal, the indefatigable labours of two of the most distinguished Radicals that England has produced: John Bright and Richard Cobden. Secondly the question of

[1] *Life and Struggles of William Lovett*, pp. 172, 173; Holyoake's *Sixty Years of an Agitator's Life*, vol. i., p. 85. Holyoake relates that Place showed him cheques given by Tories to the Chartists (Gammage's *History of the Chartist Movement*, pp. 102, 103, 254).

the Corn Laws was one of those economic questions which the Radicals by some curious idiosyncrasy have made peculiarly their own.

The attitude of the several political parties towards economic science and its practical application to affairs, is a curious subject of inquiry and one well worth consideration. Of English statesmen of the front rank perhaps the first to make political economy an object of serious and regulated study was Shelburne. He was not, indeed, a Radical himself, but he held out the hand of friendship, to Bentham, Price and Priestley, who influenced him in turn, and gave a bent and direction to his mind. For the illumination of his intellect upon the principles of trade he was indebted to several different sources. He owed something both to Adam Smith and to the well-known Dean of Gloucester, Dr. Tucker. In an interesting letter written in 1795 to Dugald Stewart there is a reference of Shelburne's to a journey which, probably in 1761, he made with Adam Smith. "I owe," he says, "to a journey I made with Mr. Smith from Edinburgh to London the difference between light and darkness through the best part of my life." So too he acknowledges his debt to Dr. Tucker. Speaking in the House of Lords in 1793 he said: "The new principles of government founded on the abolition of the old feudal system were originally propagated among us by the Dean of Gloucester, Dr. Tucker, and have since been more generally inculcated by Dr. Adam Smith in his work on *The Wealth of Nations*". But it was rather to two Frenchmen, Turgot and the Abbé Morellet, that his obligations were the greatest. Of the Abbé—who visited him at Bowood, and was for many years his constant correspondent—he said that he had "liberalised his ideas"; while for Turgot he had the greatest admiration; and when Condorcet's life of the philosopher was translated into English, Shelburne gave his powerful patronage to the preparation of the book. The disciple of masters such as these, Shelburne's view on economics were certainly more enlightened than those of most of the statesmen of his time; and he was so far advanced in his opinions that he proposed to found an independent journal to disseminate the principles of free-trade.[1] He might, therefore, rightly be called the lineal ancestor of Cobden. Next to Shelburne, the statesman who had the soundest notions of political economy was, strange to say, the Tory William Pitt; and there was nothing in his life that did him greater honour than his reverence for Adam Smith. Whenever his master—for so, the story goes, he loved to call him—came into the room, he would rise from his seat to mark his deference and respect. In his speech on the Budget in 1792 he publically expressed his admiration; he referred to him as "an author now unhappily no more, whose extensive knowledge of detail and depth of philosophical research will, I believe, furnish the best solution to every question connected with the history of commerce or with the system of political economy". Pitt, indeed, was one of the first to obtain a thorough grasp of the doctrine of free trade.

[1] Sir G. C. Lewis in his *Administrations of Great Britain from 1783 to 1830* (p. 50, note) quotes an interesting letter from Vaughan to Franklin with reference to Shelburne: "You will take pleasure in hearing that he talked of making England a free port, for which, he said, we were fitted by nature, capital, love of enterprise, maritime connections, and position between the Old and New World, and the North and South of Europe, and that those who were best circumstanced for trade could not but be gainers by having trade open". Is not this what is now called the policy of the "open door"?

Previous thinkers, to be sure, had occasional glimpses of the truth, as when Lord Halifax in one of his many pregnant sentences observed that trade was the creature of liberty. Burke too was in his remarks on trade, as he was on everything he touched, sagacious and profound; commerce, he said, flourishes most when left to itself, for interest, the great guide of commerce, is not a blind one. But Pitt was the first statesman who not only had the knowledge of sound principles but had the power and authority to apply them and put them into practice; and such was the interest he displayed in all questions of commerce and finance that he was satirised for the preference that he gave them over what some people considered to be the higher claims of science, literature and art.

> Stiff from old Turgot and his rigid school,
> He never deviates from his wholesome rule.
> Left to themselves, all find their level price,
> Potatoes, verses, turnips, Greek and rice.

The Whig leaders, however, almost all of them, for a long time looked coldly on political economy and those who laid the foundations of the science. Even the generous-minded Fox used to remark with a sneer, "Your Adam Smiths are nothing". He spoke of economic principles as "the most nonsensical," and complained that none of the definitions of the science were "intelligible," and that its reasoning was "plausible but inconclusive". Lord John Russell seems to have been of the like opinion, for he called political economy "an awful thing"; and, as though it savoured of a lack of patriotic feeling, he exclaimed: "Let us first be Englishmen and then economists". But the Radicals, to their

THE THIRD AND CONCLUDING PERIOD. 375

eternal credit be it said, never blenched before the terrors of the so-called dismal science; they dared to meet them face to face. There was Godwin, for example, who criticised the views of Malthus, and declared that reading Adam Smith gave him a feeling of contraction of the heart. The subject, indeed, was dry and unattractive; but the Radicals, who liked at the same time to enlarge the boundaries of knowledge and to further philanthropic effort, soon made it peculiarly their own. It was in 1817 that Ricardo brought out his epoch-making book; James Mill followed with his treatise in 1821; and in 1822 Place produced his pamphlet on the *Illustration and Proofs of the Principles of Population*. It is entirely characteristic of the man that he declared that he found political economy but little to his taste; and, with the self-conscious stoicism of the thorough-going Benthamite, he sententiously observed that "he who would essentially serve mankind has no choice; he must submit himself patiently to the pain he cannot avoid without abandoning his duty". Though Bentham himself gave little attention to the subject, it was unquestionably one which was studied by the philosophical Radicals in a very earnest spirit, for these indefatigable persons seem to have taken all knowledge for their province. Ricardo, James Mill, and a select band of young men engaged in mercantile pursuits used to meet at Grote's house in Threadneedle Street for study and discussion; and the Political Economy Club, the inception of which was due to Thomas Tooke, was founded under their auspices in 1821. To James Mill the task of drawing up the rules of its debates was very appropriately entrusted; and it is perhaps not too much to say that the greatest service to mankind that the early Radicals performed was to keep alive the study of a science which their modern successors are inclined to ignore because they do not like it.[1]

The traditional interest of the Radicals in the study of economic science was kept alive by John Stuart Mill, and by the founders of the Anti-Corn Law League, who, though not professed adherents of the utilitarian school, yet agreed with it in holding that economic laws existed, which no statesman worthy of the name could possibly ignore. The abolition of the Corn Laws was argued by the spokesmen of the League, as an economic question, though other considerations intervened; and it is this fact more than any other that places the Anti-Corn Law Agitators into historical relation with the utilitarian Radicals. The latter, indeed, were among the earliest supporters of the league, and Sir William Molesworth, Grote, Joseph Hume and Roebuck were members of the first Anti-Corn Law Association which was formed in London in 1836. Place too, though verging on old age, gave the movement his support, and the names of Perronet Thompson and W. J. Fox, two philosophical Radicals, will always be remembered for their inestimable labours for the cause. But though the Anti-Corn Law League, which was founded in Manchester in 1838, was strongly Radical in character, its radicalism was not the same in type as that of the utilitarian school upon the one hand or of the

---

[1] *Life of Adam Smith*, by John Rae, pp. 289, 321; Fitzmaurice's *Life of Shelburne*, vol ii., p. 234; vol. iii., p. 439; Sir G. C. Lewis's *Essays on the Administrations of Great Britain from 1783 to 1830*, p. 134 (note); *Lettres de l'Abbé Morellet à Lord Shelburne*, edited by Lord Edmond Fitzmaurice; Burke's *Plan for Economical Reform;* Lord John Russell's *Memorials of Fox;* Lord Colchester's *Diaries and Correspondence*, vol. ii., p. 71; Walpole's *Life of Lord John Russell*, vol. i., p. 366; *Personal Life of Grote*, pp. 28, 42; Bain's *James Mill*, p. 198.

Chartists on the other. The politicians of the League, in fact, were not anxious to be considered as Radicals at all, and Cobden, for example, disavowed its connection with "either Radicals or Chartists".[1] But a new class of Radicals arose by a natural process of transition after the work of the League had been accomplished. This was the so-called Manchester school of which the Anti-Corn Law League was undoubtedly the parent.

The Manchester School of politicians might be described as the dominant type of Radicals of the Victorian era; of a period, that is to say, which, roughly speaking, lasted from 1840 to the passing of the Reform Act of 1885. During all these years they held the field as *par excellence* the democratic party, and to relate their history fully would be to write the domestic history of the time. Radicals there were, indeed—Mr. Bradlaugh for example —who held extremer views and kept themselves aloof, but, comparatively speaking, their significance was small. The Manchester School, however, was the great connecting link between the Radicals of to-day and of those of the early portion of the century, and, as such, it demands a brief consideration. It remains then to inquire what were its essential characteristics, its moral traits and its intellectual attitude towards affairs.

The Manchester School, like the so-called school of the Benthamites, has been inaccurately styled; for just as Bentham had never, strictly speaking, a class of esoteric scholars who sought his oral teaching, so at Manchester there were never any political thinkers who stood to one

---

[1] Mr. Goldwin Smith in his article on the Manchester School in the *Contemporary Review* for March, 1895, says: "We were called, and were not unwilling to be called, Radicals rather than Whigs".

another in the relation of master and disciple. The term is, in fact, but an historical abridgment, and may be appropriately used to denote that there was a certain group of persons who, looking on current politics from a similar point of view, and holding like convictions about the conduct of affairs, sympathised with one another. Their general character, their mental texture, may perhaps most clearly be depicted by comparing them with the older class of Radicals whom they gradually displaced.

The philosophical Radicals applied their solvent criticism to the deepest problems that can occupy the mind of man, with the result that for the most part they became atheists or agnostics, while their successors were almost always stirred by a deep religious feeling. *Parcus deorum cultor et infrequens;* such was Bentham or James Mill. How different was Cobden, from first to last a staunch, though not a blind, adherent of the Anglican Communion! How different too was Bright! a Quaker in every fibre of his being, whose political principles were based, it may be truly said, upon a firm foundation of earnest Christian morals. It was, in fact, upon grounds of religion and morality that Bright and Cobden, at the risk of being accused of cant, tried to justify themselves. A high seriousness, indeed, was theirs. Cobden said that he believed that "a moral and even a religious spirit" might be infused into the Anti-Corn Law Agitation, which "the gross pocket question" had reduced to a somewhat sordid level. The League, too, he thought might be exalted into "a great peripatetic political university". Bright was even more emphatic; he declared that there is no permanent greatness for a nation unless it be based upon morality; he claimed that the political creed of his party was more advanced, and its political morality higher, than that of the remainder of the country; he averred that the great object of his life was "to square the policy of the country with the maxims of common sense and a plain morality".[1] Bright was essentially what has been styled a theopathic man; conversing, when in his graver moods, as though he was in the presence of the Deity, the undercurrent of his thoughts was fundamentally religious; and though there were many who denied the wisdom and the justice of his methods, there were few, indeed who questioned his honesty of purpose. It was then, first, from the religious and moral point of view that the Manchester School, at least in the persons of its leading representatives, differed most profoundly from the Radicals who went before them; for between the reverential tone of Bright and the calculated scepticism of Bentham and James Mill no greater contrast could be found. But though the new school accepted the dogmas of religion, whereas the old denied them altogether, the former was no indulgent critic of the Church Establishment, and it exceedingly disliked its privileged position. The Manchester politicians were therefore, generally speaking, Nonconformist in their sympathies. Secondly, these new Radicals were, at least in the beginning, much more economical than political reformers. The primary objects upon which the Benthamites insisted were to obtain the popular control of Parliament and absolute securities for the good government of the people; if only this aim could be accomplished—so they argued—

[1] There is a curious parallel to Bright's view of statesmanship in a letter written by Guizot to Henry Reeve in 1870. Guizot there remarks: "I moralise on politics. Good sense is the law of politics, and what I have learnt from history, above all, is that good sense is essentially moral" (*Memoirs of the Life of Henry Reeve*, vol. ii.).

then the amelioration of every social ill would quickly and inevitably follow. This belief was the Benthamite doctrine of political philosophy distilled to a quintessence. The Manchester School was, however, less concerned with securities for good government than with the immediate betterment of the condition of the people; it took its stand upon the ground of "actual economic facts". At the most—so these new Radicals believed—the popular control of Parliament was but a means, and not the best means either, towards the amelioration of the life of the English working class. To cheapen food or to raise the rate of wages were aims which the Benthamites, absorbed as they were in the work of building speculative theories, regarded as laudable but trivial, and as things with which, properly speaking, the Radical had no concern. To root up the upas-tree of aristocracy, to secure a simply democratic constitution, and not to wring piecemeal legislation from a hostile or apathetic Parliament, he believed to be his functions. It was frankly a policy of thorough. In the next place, the new school drew the majority of its members from the trading and manufacturing classes; and though, as time went on, its basis was enlarged until it embraced vast numbers of the people, it was essentially bourgeois in its type, and it is certain that at some points in its history it was decidedly unpopular. The Radicals, in short, who held the field during the middle portion of the century were, to speak in general terms, well-intentioned Nonconformists, immersed in the business of the office or the mill, who thought that the main object of the statesman should be the discovery and establishment of the conditions of profitable trade, and so indirectly to raise the standard of existence among the masses of the people. Such, in brief outline, were the distinctive marks or notes of the Manchester radicalism, of which Bright and Cobden were the most eminent representatives. There were many others, it is true—Villiers, Milner Gibson, Stansfeld, and Potter, for example—who deserve a more than passing notice; but Bright and Cobden were the master hands who directed the new policy and gave it shape and colour, and it is, therefore, to their recorded thoughts, to their expressed judgments and opinions that the inquirer will principally turn. Never surely were the principles of a party exhibited with more forcible directness, a greater amplitude, or more lucidity of diction.[1]

The attitude of the Manchester School of Radicals towards parliamentary reform is, of course, the most important question that challenges inquiry. To speak in general terms, it may be said that they desired some extension of the franchise, but as to how far it should go there was not perfect unanimity. "I have," said Cobden, " unbounded faith in the people, and would risk universal suffrage to-morrow in preference to the present franchise." He wished, in fact, thoroughly to democratise the Constitution, which he stigmatised as " a thing of monopolies and Church-craft, and sinecures, armorial hocus-pocus, primogeniture and pageantry"; while in the language which he used about Governments in general he echoed the indictment laid by Bentham. They seemed, he wrote to Bright, " as a rule to be standing conspiracies to rob and bamboozle the people ". Cobden's generous belief in the capacity of the people for self-government was probably never, and certainly not at first, shared equally by

[1] Morley's *Life of Cobden*, vol. i., pp. 126, 249; vol. ii., pp. 195, 196; *Cobden's Speeches*, edited by Professor Thorold Rogers; Goldwin Smith's article in the *Contemporary Review* for March, 1895, on the "Manchester School"; *John Bright*, by C. A. Vince, p. 231.

Bright. Somewhat Conservative in his instincts he was opposed to violent change, for, as he very truly said, it is the function of statesmanship to make the past glide quietly into the future. He would, therefore, have been satisfied with household suffrage only; and the particular reform upon which he most urgently insisted was a redistribution of seats, in order to give the larger boroughs a more equitable treatment. To some such change as this he attached a greater value than a lowering of the franchise; for he probably looked upon a democracy as not so much an excellence in itself, but as a lesser evil than the existing state of things. Both Bright and Cobden, nevertheless, insisted that any reform bill whatsoever should be drawn upon plain and simple lines. The former abhorred such things as "fancy franchises"; and Cobden declared Hare's ingenious scheme for the representation of minorities to be "incomprehensible"; he wished, he said, to see "the electoral districts as diversified as possible, and each return a single member". As to the ballot, the two men were substantially agreed that it was really less of an affair of politics than of morals; but that, as without it any extension of the suffrage would be comparatively worthless, it might be taken to be the test of genuine Liberal opinion. As to the shortening of Parliaments, they were both inclined to favour a period of three years; though, as time went on, Bright did not place so high a value upon this particular reform. To the exaction of pledges from parliamentary candidates, and to what we have called the delegation theory, Bright, as might have been expected from his strong and self-reliant character, was strenuously opposed; he avowed that he tried to shut out from his mind "any idea of controlling influence"; that there was "a higher, loftier

THE THIRD AND CONCLUDING PERIOD. 383

purer standard for a representative than even the influence of those whom he may represent"; namely, "his own intelligent conscientious convictions of duty on the question before him".[1] It was, therefore, for this very reason that such things as party programmes or party platforms were repugnant to his nature. With regard to the payment of members of Parliament, he spoke in no uncertain tones; "I am satisfied," he said, "that the results of the payment of members, in some countries at least, are highly unsatisfactory. The condition of things in the United States is deplorable." The problem of female suffrage was a difficulty which the Manchester Radicals never fairly faced; and though it was left an open question, Cobden at least on one occasion said that wives would make better voters than their husbands; while Bright went even farther. During the debate on the Reform Bill of 1867 he voted in favour of John Stuart Mill's amendment, though he did so rather out of deference to the philosopher than from a sense of absolute conviction. Such then, very briefly, were Bright's and Cobden's views upon parliamentary reform; and, therefore, those, if we strike a sort of average, of the Manchester Radicals as a body. A liberal extension of the franchise, a redistribution of seats, the adoption of the ballot, and, to add a new item, the abolition of the property qualification, formed the programme upon which they were agreed.[2]

[1] One reason why Bright advocated triennial Parliaments was that he recognised that members often pledged themselves to their constituencies, and he did not think it right that they should be bound for so long a period as seven years (*John Bright*, by C. A. Vince, p. 90).

[2] Morley's *Life of Cobden*, vol. i., pp. 128, 130; vol. ii., pp. 241, 461; *Cobden's Speeches*, edited by Professor Thorold Rogers; *John Bright*, by C. A. Vince, pp. 41, 90, 111, 125, 168, 187; Jephson's *Rise and Progress of the Platform*, vol. ii., p. 425.

In their attitude towards the question of parliamentary reform the Manchester School marked no new or striking epoch in the history of radicalism; they advanced only along the old well-beaten track. It was rather a totally different class of questions which gave the School its most distinctive note. Of these the most important was that of foreign policy. Here certainly a momentous change in Radical policy is to be noted. Formerly the old Radicals very rarely concerned themselves at all with international relations; whereas the Manchester School, mainly under the leadership of Bright, made foreign affairs a special object of attention. Nevertheless, as the apostles of non-intervention, the new School kept up the old Benthamite tradition; for perhaps there was no question whatsoever upon which Bright and Cobden felt so strongly as the duty of abstaining from interference in the affairs of other nations. Bright avowed his belief that "the whole notion of the balance of power is a mischievous delusion"; he insisted that there should be no interference "where the interests of the country are not directly and obviously assailed"; or, as he put it in memorable language, "it is not my duty to make this country the knight-errant of the human race, and to take upon herself the protection of the thousand millions of human beings who have been permitted by the Creator of all things to people this planet". In close connection with this view of foreign intervention is the no less strong opinion held by the Manchester School of Radicals upon the subject of national defence. Here again they showed themselves to be lineally descended from those early Radicals who so greatly feared the standing army. Cobden, for example, even doubted whether with large standing armies constitutional liberty could co-exist; though it was rather from reasons of economy that he and Bright condemned the growth of "bloated armaments"—a phrase of which, strange to say, Disraeli was the author. The army and navy, said Cobden, are "the great preserve of the landlord class for their younger sons"; Malta, he said, was "the great skulking hole for the navy," and the British the most warlike and aggressive people the world had ever known. Nor was Bright a whit less emphatic in his language. There was no man who in a sense was more combative than he; Roebuck called him his "pugnacious peace-loving friend"; and it was said by some wit that he must have been a prize-fighter, if he had not been a Quaker. Yet there was no one more devoted to international peace. Bentham once described war "as mischief on the largest scale," and Bright cordially agreed with him. He declared that the whole system of national defence was really "a gigantic system of out-door relief for the aristocracy of Great Britain"; that Gibraltar was held contrary to "every law of morality and honour," and that it was not the slightest use to any one "excepting to those who have pensions and occupations upon it"; he was even bold enough to say that supremacy at sea—a supremacy which Bacon well called one of England's "principal dowries"—meant arrogance and the assumption of dictatorial power, and that the sooner it became obsolete the better. Again, to colonial possessions and to what is now called the Imperialist Idea it naturally followed that the Manchester School was resolutely hostile. Cobden had the rashness to assert that the English could not govern India; he declared, in language that now sounds strange indeed, that if France took the whole of Africa it would do no harm to any one but herself; that colonies, like the army and navy, formed a paradise for the aristocracy; he even seems to have persuaded himself—such is the power of self-deception—that men were beginning to "abhor the notion of undertaking the government of colonies". Non-intervention abroad, a resolute retrenchment of the expenditure on armaments, an entire disbelief in the advantages of colonies, a haunting dread of any policy that was not essentially pacific, were the features by which the Manchester School was best known, and most strongly impressed its personality upon the national conscience. It was, in a word, to use the modern jargon, the school of "Little Englanders".[1]

The next most striking characteristic of the Manchester School of Radicals was their sturdy individualism.

> All constraint
> Except what wisdom lays on evil men is evil.

These words formed one of the watchwords of the party. Here again they kept alive the old beliefs of Priestley and Paine, James Mill and Francis Place. "I would rather," said Cobden, "live in a country where this feeling of individual freedom is jealously cherished than be without it in the enjoyment of all the principles of the French Constituent Assembly;" and with perfect consistency he held that there should be no legislative interference with the labour of adults. He had the rare courage—rare, that is to say, for a man in his position

---

[1] Morley's *Life of Cobden*, vol. ii., pp. 71, 156-58, 169, 195, 242; *Cobden's Speeches*, edited by Professor Thorold Rogers; *Bright's Speeches on Questions of Political Policy*, edited by Professor Thorold Rogers; *John Bright* by C. A. Vince, pp. 43, 62, 63. With the view of the Manchester School about colonies it is interesting to compare the thought expressed in Thucydides that it is impossible for a democracy to govern other peoples. Πολλάκις μὲν ἤδη ἔγνων τὴν δημοκρατίαν ὡς ἀδύνατόν ἐστιν ἑτέρων ἄρχειν (Thuc. 3-37).

—to avow that trade-unions were "founded upon the principle of brutal tyranny and monopoly," and that he "would rather live under a Dey of Algiers than a Trades Committee". Bright too was of the same opinion. "Most of our evils," he said, "arise from legislative interference;" and again: "if there is any principle more certain than another, it is that what a people is able to do for itself the Government should not attempt to do for it. For nothing tends so much to strengthen a people, to make them powerful, great and good, as the constant exercise of all their faculties on public objects, and the carrying out of public works and objects by voluntary contributions among themselves." Once more, in a speech he made in 1873 he described the history of England when looked at from the point of view of domestic legislation as "mainly a history of the conquests of freedom". That true liberalism, in fact, meant a policy of what is conveniently spoken of as a *laissez faire* he heartily believed. Like Cobden, therefore, he assailed with some virulence, and though not always quite wisely, all appeals for legislative interference with the labour of adults; he looked askance at trade-unions, and at the presence of working men's representatives in Parliament; he even attacked the temperance party for trying to place unjustifiable restrictions upon the licensed victuallers.[1]

A few other traits of the Manchester School remain to be considered. Their attitude towards the House of Lords was one of suspicion and dislike; not so much because of its legislative functions, as because it was the

[1] Morley's *Life of Cobden*, vol. i., pp. 299-301; *Cobden's Speeches*, edited by Professor Thorold Rogers; *Bright's Speeches on Questions of Public Policy*, edited by Professor Thorold Rogers; *John Bright*, by C. A. Vince, pp. 39, 233-34.

most prominent representative of those two plague-spots, as they believed them to be, of aristocracy and landlordism. "The governing feudal class," said Cobden, "exists only by the violation of sound principles of political economy, and therefore the very institution is hostile to the interests of the masses;"—an observation that embodied the general feeling of the School towards the Upper House.[1] Bright also, although he generally showed the Peers the mercy of his silence, could, when they annoyed him by their action, in his occasional comments be terribly severe; as when he said that whereas it was formerly believed that the path to the Temple of Honour lay through the Temple of Virtue, "the law-making peer goes into the Temple of Honour through the sepulchre of a dead ancestor". Yet he was disposed to moderation, and he looked forward not so much to the abolition of the House as to the curtailment of its functions. It was landlordism, indeed, much more than the hereditary principle that he peculiarly abhorred, and it was the continued ascendency of the landed interest in the House of Commons, notwithstanding the great Reform Act, that caused him to insist upon an extension of the franchise. "This House," he once indignantly exclaimed, "is a club of landowners legislating for landowners." Antipathy to the landed gentry, a class of men whom he depicted as incorrigibly selfish, and as delighting to keep their tenants ignorant, servile and dependent, was quite as much as sympathy for the workers in the towns an element of force in the Anti-Corn Law agitation. Bright's hatred of

---

[1] Cobden allowed his prejudice against what he called government in the interests of the great families to warp even some of his most statesmanlike views. See a letter from Cobden to Captain Cowper Coles (1864) on turret-ships, published in the *Times* of 6th December, 1898.

the Game Laws was based upon the same ideas; so too was his contemptuous dislike—a dislike which Cobden fully shared—for the ancient universities. In this respect they showed themselves true sons of their Radical forefathers. Bentham led the way with his indictment of Oxford as the home of mendacity and fraud; Cobbett followed with his denunciations of what he described as dens of dunces; and then came Attwood, who had the temerity to say that Oxford and Cambridge were "the ruin of England," and that it took a man twenty years to unlearn all the nonsense that he learnt there. Cobden and Bright uttered the same sentiments, only in rather different language. The former used to lament the ignorance of modern affairs which undergraduates displayed, and of Oxford he remarked that the education given there was "the largest investment for the smallest return of all the academics of the world". Bright, who had the real literary gift of felicity of language, described Oxford in an epigram; it was, he said, "the home of dead languages and undying prejudices". So little appreciation had he of the place whose "progressive emulation" Dr. Johnson so much admired.[1]

A few words must be given to a consideration of the Manchester School of Radicals in their historical relations to the past and to the present. It is, in the first place, worth a passing notice that the centre of radicalism had shifted once again. Formerly laid in the City of London, it had moved to Westminster, thence to Birmingham, and now it had travelled north to Manchester. It is curious

---

[1] Morley's *Life of Cobden*, vol. ii., p. 396; *Cobden's Speeches*, edited by Professor Thorold Rogers; *John Bright*, by C. A. Vince, pp. 30, 31, 41, 185; Wakefield's *Life of Thomas Attwood* (letter to his wife in 1837).

to observe how completely the political character of the City of London had been changed. It was, in fact, utterly distrusted by the Radicals, as was admitted by John Bright. "Well," he once said, "I never knew the City to be right. Men who are deep in great monetary transactions, and who are steeped to the lips sometimes in perilous speculations, are not able to take broad and dispassionate views of political questions of this nature." Cobden too denounced what he called the "mummeries" of the Corporation. But in many respects the new School carried on the old traditions; as, for example, in their insistence upon parliamentary reform as a means to increase the power of control of the people over the Government; in their non-intervention doctrine; in their hatred of the aristocracy and the landlords; in their anti-imperialism; in their demands for retrenchment and for economy; in their courageous individualism; in their contempt for academic learning. They retained even some of the old-fashioned cheery optimism. Cobden at all events used to pride himself upon what he called his "Bonapartian feeling"; or, as he put it, "Dame Fortune, like other fair ones, loves a brisk and confident wooer". There was much in Bentham's creed, there were some things even in Paine's, with which Bright and Cobden would have cordially agreed. Yet the radicalism of the Manchester School was of a new and different type. Much less doctrinaire and prone to speculation upon the principles of government, it sought a surer foothold upon economic facts. Desiring to bring material comfort to the masses of the people, its immediate aims were in some ways rather social than political. While the Benthamites insisted upon what would have amounted to a constitutional revolution, the Manchester School looked rather to the practically possible. Content to move slowly and advance step by step, they did not lose sight of the ultimate ends in view, but accepted legislation by instalments. As practical reformers, therefore, the Manchester Radicals accomplished infinitely more for the betterment of the people than the philosophical extremists. But if the School had its virtues, it also had its vices; it had the defects of its qualities in a very marked degree. For its view of life was bounded by a narrowly circumscribed horizon; thoroughly bourgeois in its character, it was prone to look upon the nation as a great industrial workshop; to reduce the functions of statesmanship to that of securing the conditions of profitable trade, and to regard the growth of wealth and its diffusion amongst all classes of society as the supreme end of national life. It was because war was the greatest obstacle to commerce that the Manchester Radicals were such zealous advocates of peace.[1] The leaders of the party, and doubtless many of the rank and file, were men of high principles, deep piety and genuine benevolence. But the party as a whole was not inspired by great ideals or elevating sentiments. Not Pericles, who called on the Athenians to beautify their city, but Benjamin Franklin, with his sublimated common sense, his practical sagacity and mechanical acumen, was of the

---

[1] It would almost appear as if Cobden thought that war was justifiable if it brought with it as a result profitable trade. He admired Chatham, who, he said, "went abroad in the spirit of a commercial traveller more than any minister we ever had," and lamented that it was no longer possible to make commerce "flourish by war" (Speech at Rochdale, 1864). Yet Chatham had so little knowledge of economics that he swore that he "never would allow the colonies even to manufacture a hob-nail for themselves" (Campbell's *Lives of the Chancellors*, vol. viii., p. 263).

type of manhood it admired. Unable to appreciate the noble sentiment of Burke, that to love our country we must make it lovely first, it found pleasure in the sight of the factory chimney and its smoke; while no sound fell so wooingly on the ears of these "Philistine" Radicals, as perhaps they may be called, as the crash of the hammer or the humming of the loom. Distrusting culture and disdainful of the study of the humanities, they went far to make politics a mere affair of the cashbox and the ledger; for, as Cobden himself reluctantly admitted, "the gross pocket question" became one of all-absorbing interest. In a well-known passage of one of his most celebrated poems, Lord Tennyson thus described one of the characters he created:—

> This broad-brimmed hawker of holy things,
> Whose ear is stuffed with his cotton, and rings
> Even in dreams to the chink of his pence.

The reading public instinctively applied the lines to Bright, but they were wrong, for no personal attribution was intended. Yet the satire was meant to refer to a type of politician which at that time was common, and in some members of the Manchester School was not difficult to recognise.[1] Carlyle once described Cobden as an inspired bagman who preached a calico millennium, and the saying was not less apposite than witty. The popular judgment, as is usual, was harsh and undiscriminating; but resting, as it did, upon a real though imperfect perception of the facts, it was not altogether wrong. "The cocknosed Rochdale Radical," to quote Carlyle again, was not the enemy

---

[1] *John Bright* by C. A. Vince, p. 238. See an interesting correspondence on this subject in *Literature* for the 13th and 27th of August, 1898.

THE THIRD AND CONCLUDING PERIOD. 393

of his country that his opponents sometimes thought him; and to speak of Bright and Cobden, as people sometimes did, as the members for the United States, conveyed an imputation that was certainly unjust. "Little Englandism," if a wrong, is at least an intelligible creed, and one which men of sense may hold, and it is not unpatriotic. Yet, after making all allowances, the Manchester School will be rightly remembered by posterity as being of all the various types of Radicals the one of the dullest imaginative power, of the narrowest mental vision, and the least animated by high conceptions of the future of the Anglo-Saxon race. The *imperi porrecta majestas* was a notion that transcended the intelligence of this once powerful group of politicians. These were grave defects, which brought their retribution with them.

When Bright passed away full of years and full of honours in 1889, the Manchester type of radicalism was already on the wane. Neo-radicalism, if we may be permitted so to call the radicalism of to-day, was already beginning to appear. It will be well, therefore, to pause for a moment and consider what the Manchester Radicals accomplished.

A moment's reflection will make one important fact apparent; that if radicalism be properly defined as the endeavour to reform and control Parliament by pressure from without, and to make its members habitually subservient to its constituents, then the activity of the Manchester School was in many of its manifestations beside the mark. To abolish the Corn Laws; to pioneer Free Trade; to plead the cause of religious equality; to preach the anti-imperialist crusade; were things, which, whatever may be thought of them, formed no essential part of Radical policy at all. But in two ways, direct and indirect, the Manchester School did much to democratise the Constitution. Directly, they laboured successfully and strenuously for the extension of the suffrage, for redistribution of seats and for the ballot; but indirectly they performed even more important services than these. They popularised the use of political associations and public meetings; they exalted the platform to a height that it had never reached before, for Bright was the greatest English orator of his time. This popularisation of the use of public speaking was perhaps their greatest service to the democratic cause; for it is only within the last fifty years or so that the platform has become the common organ for conducting political campaigns—a fact that it is difficult to realise. Yet it is true that Mr. Gladstone was "the first English minister who was accustomed on a large scale to bring his policy in great meetings directly before the people," and that "he completely discarded the old tradition that a leading minister or ex-minister should confine himself almost exclusively to parliamentary utterances, and should only on rare occasions address the public outside".[1] That he did so was in a great measure due to the examples of Cobden and Bright. Next the Manchester School of Radicals took a very active part in obtaining the removal of those vexatious restrictions on the press, the newspaper stamp duties, the "taxes on knowledge," as one, who was by no means a Radical, Bulwer Lytton, very happily described them. The change that has come over the conditions of the press since their abolition can only be adequately recognised by comparing the journals of that time and of this. In the days of Barnes and Delane it was wittily remarked that if the apostles had

---

[1] Lecky, Preface to the Second Edition of *Democracy and Liberty.*

THE THIRD AND CONCLUDING PERIOD. 395

been living then, they would have had no chance against the *Times*. Cobbett called it the " bell-wether of the well-dressed rabble," and it was, in fact, the only journal that profoundly influenced opinion.[1] The Manchester Radicals, in short, familiarised the people with the habits and the instruments upon which self-government must ultimately rest. To have done this was the great merit of the Manchester School, and in the general history of radicalism it is a fact of great importance.

We are now in a position to be able to take a comprehensive survey of the history of the Radicals; to see what they aimed at; how far they have succeeded; in what they have failed and why; and what changes they have undergone in character.

The old Whigs, steeped to the lips in the traditions of the great aristocratic houses, with their cultured tastes and courtly manners, instinctively abhorred the persons' of the Radicals. *Malignum spernere volgus;* these words or something like them might have formed a fitting motto for these Liberals of the old school. They barely condescended to admit even Burke to the charmed circle of their councils. Shelburne was an exception, it is true, for he brought Radicals to Bowood, but in so doing he risked his reputation. Even as late as 1834, when someone in the House of Commons suggested that in the future Radicals should be admitted to the Cabinet, the proposal was received with derision upon the ministerial benches. The Court too threw the great weight of its influence against the democratic side, for William the Fourth, it is well known, expressed his anxiety to exclude

---

[1] On the former condition of the press, see an article in the *English Historical Review* for October, 1897, on "The Unstamped Press, 1815-1836".

them from all places of authority and trust. But little by little some of the ablest Radicals, Hobhouse, Buller, and Sir William Molesworth, for example, made themselves indispensable allies and were admitted into office; and when Cobden in 1859 refused the Presidency of the Board of Trade, the event was generally thought to mark an epoch in English parliamentary life. The language used by Palmerston, one of the most Conservative of the Whigs, and who, as Premier, made the offer, is worth a passing notice; he said that he wished his Cabinet "to contain representatives of all sections of the Liberal party". These are words that seem to indicate that the old Whig exclusiveness was slowly giving way before the onset of the democratic tide. There is a story that when Guizot heard of the offer made to Cobden, he remarked that it was the end of "*la grande politique*" in England; and if he really said so, he displayed an acute perception of the tendency of political affairs. For there was an end to the Government monopoly of the aristocratic houses. When Bright, therefore, who was actually the first Nonconformist to become a Cabinet Minister, took office, the event did not cause the least surprise, though it was distasteful to many of the Whigs. Lord Westbury, for example, expressed their prevalent feeling in a letter to Henry Reeve in 1868 in the characteristic exclamation: " Why, fancy Granville, Clarendon and the rest, pigging heads and tails with John Bright in the same truckle-bed ". Yet even in this very year we find Bradlaugh clamouring in the old style of the *Westminster* Reviewers for the abolition of the government of the Whigs. "Whiggism," he said, almost echoing the very language of James Mill, " is hypocritical; while professing to be Liberal, it never initiates a good measure or hinders a bad one." Since

THE THIRD AND CONCLUDING PERIOD. 397

then a change has occurred, the magnitude of which it is difficult to realise; the old party lines have been partially obliterated; a section of the Whigs have left the Liberals altogether; even the ancient party names have been rendered to some extent inapplicable to the existing state of things, now that the Liberals have adopted the policy of Home Rule. But it may in general terms be said that the democratisation of affairs has enabled the Radicals to capture and absorb the Liberal party. At first an insignificant, a despised, an almost persecuted sect, then grudgingly admitted as allies, they would seem to have ended by almost identifying themselves with one of the great historical parties of the country. The triumph seems a great one, but it has been purchased at a price, and is, perhaps, not as complete as appears upon the surface.[1]

Take, for instance, the question of parliamentary reform, for the carriage of which the Radicals have taken so much credit to themselves. Yet, if the history of the subject be impartially examined, their claim to have been the great party of reform cannot be allowed without considerable deductions. That the reform and popular control of Parliament has been for all practical purposes accomplished of course must be admitted; but to say that this result is wholly due to the efforts of the Radicals would be to misinterpret history. They did not even originate the movement; they were not the first to step into the field, for Chatham certainly was beforehand with them here. He had strong opinions on the subject and well-defined

---

[1] Mrs. Grote's *Personal Life of George Grote*, p. 96; Brougham's *Memoirs*, vol. iii., p. 403; *Memoirs of the Life of Henry Reeve*, vol. ii., p. 148.

ideas, which he left as a legacy to his political successors. Many Whigs and even Tories at this time looked upon the reform of Parliament with no unfavourable eye, and if the French Revolution had not caused a senseless panic, Pitt would almost certainly have carried out the plans that Chatham had designed. Of parliamentary reform, therefore, the Radicals had from the beginning no monopoly. Nor is this all. The reforms which have been since then accomplished, have been won only by the active co-operation of the Whigs, and sometimes of the Tories. Alone the Radicals would have been powerless to effect them, though it is true that by their importunate insistency and unweariable zeal they kept reform before the country through good report and ill. To this extent and to this only, their claim to be the authors of parliamentary reform can be allowed; and it is a notable fact that most of the particular reforms upon which they placed the greatest value appear to be farther off from being realised than ever. Such, for instance, are short Parliaments, whether annual or triennial; the bondage of representatives by signed and written pledges; the mending or ending of that hereditary Chamber where so many Radicals have found an euthanasia; universal suffrage, and the payment of members. The country gives no sign that it desires a single one of these reforms. Even the more practicable measures of "one man, one vote," and "one vote, one value," awaken no enthusiasm among the masses of the people. From the strict and narrow point of view of parliamentary reform, therefore, the purpose of the Radicals has failed; it still in its main points awaits fulfilment. Indeed, as hereafter will be shown, it is not too much to say that but for the Radical extravagancies such reform as has been accomplished would have come much earlier than it did.

The great triumphs of the Radicals were in fact gained very early in their history, when Wilkes and Horne Tooke were in the heyday of their glory. To protect the people against the encroachments of their natural representatives; to check the arrogant assumptions of parliamentary privilege; to guard the rights of the electors; to unveil the mysteries of Parliament by establishing the right to the reporting of debates;[1] these were the objects for which the early Radicals contended. Their victory was immediate and great; the citadel of unwarranted pretensions, like the walls of Jericho, fell at the first sound of the attack. Again, if the development of such liberalising institutions as the platform and political societies be considered, the popular party cannot take the whole credit to themselves. True it is that the early Radicals may justly claim here also to have been the pioneers, and to have made possible the later achievements of the orator and the electioneering agent. They sowed the seeds from which posterity has reaped the crops. Nay, more; when all things are considered, when the balance of account is fairly struck, it will perhaps be found that it is in these respects that the labours of the Radicals have been most fruitful in results. For it is to the rights of free association, and of public speech, and to a knowledge and intelligent criticism of parliamentary proceedings that the advance of democracy is in the long run mainly due. Yet even this great result

---

[1] It is noteworthy that Mr. Gladstone thought at one time that the Division Lists of the House of Commons ought not to be published, and that it should be left to each member to tell, if he pleased, his constituents how he voted (Robbin's *The Early Public Life of W. E. Gladstone*, p. 204). He seems to have had no high opinion of parliamentary reporting: "The speeches in Parliament are ill reported even now" (Tollemache's *Talks with Mr. Gladstone*, p. 55).

has flowed from the co-ordinated labours of many different classes of which the Radicals were only one. It is remarkable, indeed, how little they influenced the course of English history, for they were often men of brilliant parts, of indomitable courage, of great and disinterested zeal. They had robustness of faith; they suffered for what they conceived to be righteousness' sake; they sought knowledge as the pearl of great price; they loved truth and pursued it; they earnestly desired to be, as Place claimed that he desired to be, useful to mankind; they learned the luxury of doing good; they glowed, as it were, with a moral incandescence. Their lives, consecrated as they were to noble purposes, were a constant rebuke to that immoral thoughtlessness of the generality of men, which Turgot said filled his mind with *sæva indignatio*. Of few men can it be so confidently said, as it may be said of Bentham and of Cartright, for example, that happy in the consciousness of pure and lofty motives, they moved with inward glory crowned. Yet their history is largely one of abandoned policies and discredited philosophies. It is almost painful to reflect that so many fine qualities should have been wasted upon labours so barren of results. What were the causes of this unfruitfulness it will be of some interest to inquire.

In the first place, during a long period of their history the Radicals condemned themselves to labour under some systems of political philosophy that were fundamentally unsound; they were, moreover, a race of doctrinaires, the the slaves of theory and immersed in speculation. Lord Melbourne said of the doctrinaire Radicals that they were fools but honest men; and he was in a measure right. The English are a people, who, as Arthur Young, that observant traveller, remarked, are much absorbed in politics; yet, patient of anomalies, they are the least given to theorising of any nation in the world. England, in fact, does not afford congenial soil for philosophic politicians. Yet the history of the Radicals presents us with two conspicuous examples of this fatal eccentricity, which was the *vitium originis* of their nature. The first was the metaphysical philosophy of the abstract rights of man. The idea of abstract rights did not, indeed, arise immediately from the Wilkes agitation; yet it derived from that event some of its force and actuality. The contest between the House of Commons and the Middlesex electors appeared —so the Radical philosophers imagined—to demonstrate the truth of their convictions; and to show that the right of every man to have a share in choosing and controlling his parliamentary representatives was indefeasible and personal. But the theory drew its main support from Burke's "cannibal philosophers"—the French revolutionary thinkers; and the philosophy of abstract rights was not altogether wrongly described by the Anti-Jacobin poet, as "Condorcet filtered through the dregs of Paine". Allured by glittering generalities, and neglecting what Bacon called the *vera illa et media axiomata* for the *maxime generalia*, these metaphysicians wandered far astray. It was upon the "metapoliticians," to use a happy phrase of Stein's, that Burke poured out the vials of his passionate indignation. He made it, as it were, almost the mission of his life to forewarn his countrymen, to quote from Wordsworth's graphic sketch,—

Against all systems built on abstract rights.[1]

---

[1] It is curious that Oliver Goldsmith should have described Burke as being "too fond of the right to pursue the expedient". This is just what Burke was not. See Wordsworth's Prelude for his description of Burke.

Of these visionary structures, falsely bright with imaginative gilding, he plainly saw the danger, and he likened them to the

> great Serbonian bog
> 'Twixt Damietta and Mount Cassius old
> Where armies whole have sunk.

He condemned that view of human actions that strips them of all outward relations and leaves them cold and shivering "in all the nakedness and solitude of metaphysical abstraction"; he abhorred that "mechanic philosophy" which destroyed our sentiments of love, veneration, admiration and attachment. "Nothing," he said, "can be conceived more hard than the heart of a thorough-bred metaphysician. It comes nearer to the cold malignity of a wicked spirit than to the frailty and passion of a man. It is like that of the principle of evil himself, incorporeal, pure, unmixed, dephlegmated, defecated evil. The geometricians and the chymists bring the one from the dry bones of their diagrams, and the other from the foot of their furnaces, dispositions that make them worse than indifferent about those feelings and habitudes, which are the supports of the moral world. . . . These philosophers consider men in their experiments no more than they do mice in an air-pump, or in a recipient of mephitic gas." These words may be taken to illustrate the saying that Burke's most splendid flights of eloquence were produced in fits of rage; and, doubtless, when we think of Price's gentle spirit—and it was against Price that his declamation was directed—the invective seems a little overstrained. Yet Burke's passionate indictment was based on reason, nay more, on common sense. For the philosophy of abstract rights, besides being faulty reasoning, was full of peril, as events subsequently proved. The

THE THIRD AND CONCLUDING PERIOD. 403

Jacobins used to say that they would rather turn France into a graveyard than not regenerate it in the way that they desired, and they were persons, who, like Mirabeau, meant every word they said. They were maddened, so to speak, by drinking too deeply of their philosophic draughts. From the French horrors the English people were preserved by their distaste for theorisation and their saving fund of common sense.[1]

The metaphysical view of politics flourished for a while, but, never striking root, it quickly withered. The race of doctrinaires was, however, not extinct; it reappeared in a new and aggravated form; in the persons, that is to say, of the Benthamites or utilitarian Radicals. Burke by this time was in his grave, but it may be confidently said that if he had lived he would with equal vigour have denounced the newer fashions of philosophy. Benthamism was certainly, as a theory of government, superior to that of the abstract rights of man; it was a more scientific system. But as thorough-going doctrinaires the Benthamites have rarely if ever been surpassed. No thinkers ever dogmatised so rigorously upon the principles of government, and none ever took such a maimed, distorted view of human nature. They looked out upon a sun-lit world, so to speak, through dark and narrow

---

[1] See Burke's *Reflections on the French Revolution*, and his *Letter to a Noble Lord*. The same judgment on abstract rights was expressed by Burke in a variety of ways, *e.g.*, "The circumstances are what render every civil and political scheme beneficial or noxious to mankind"; "nothing universal can be rationally affirmed on any moral or any political subject". Halifax long before Burke enunciated a curiously similar proposition: "Circumstances must come in, and are to be made a part of which we are to judge; positive decisions are always dangerous, more especially in politics". See Halifax's *Rough Draft*.

windows. The notion of the abstract rights of man had at least this much in its favour; that it glittered and allured; that it stirred the feelings and awakened the enthusiasm of multitudes of people. But there was no soul-animating fire in the doctrine of utility, which, so far from being popular, was the appanage of a few distinguished thinkers. Their morbid system of analysis simply petrified the feelings. The "futilitarians," as the Benthamites were nicknamed, had scarcely any perception of the truth that life is green but theory is grey, as Goethe poetically put it; and they, therefore, never obtained a hold of any large section of the people. Nearly seventy years have passed since Bentham moved and lived, and the echoes of his voice have not yet completely died away; and though he has been compared to Samson, who perished in the wreck of the building he destroyed, the influence that he wielded is not even now entirely spent. Yet Benthamism has slowly but certainly declined; and though its failure astonished its professors, the rest of the world felt no surprise at all. To most people, on the contrary, the decline and fall of Benthamism seemed a perfectly natural event. For these philosophic politicians might be compared to Swift's wise men in Laputa, who could only be aroused to the realities of life by blows upon their faces; or to Thales, who, as Plato relates, fell into a well while intently gazing at the stars; they were blind, in short, to the limits of the practical and possible. Sir Robert Peel was once twitted by Disraeli for expounding his parliamentary bills as though he was tracing back the genesis of the steam-engine to the tea-kettle. But though he dwelt upon his measures with the fulness of the deeply contemplating statesman, he accomplished more in one session than the whole Radical party in a dozen. He played, it has been said, upon the House of Commons like an old fiddle; but that assembly was an instrument upon which the Radicals could scarcely sound a single note.

In the second place, the Radicals by the violence of their language, by their extravagant demands, by their impatience of delay, and by their unfettered licence of invective, did immeasurable harm to the cause they strove to serve. It would be hard to overrate the extent of these self-inflicted injuries; indeed, it is no exaggeration to affirm that of all parties the Radicals have—though unconsciously of course—most impeded the advent of reform. The publication, for example, of Paine's *Rights of Man*, coming at the moment that it did, was the greatest imaginable blow to the progress of democracy in England; it shattered the hopes of the reformers for quite a generation; it diverted Pitt—whom Addington described as the most sanguine man he had ever known—from a course of liberal legislation into one of undisguised reaction. The effects of jacobinical radicalism were felt for many years; for, as Mr. Gladstone well said in the House of Commons in 1864, "it went far to establish the doctrine that the masses of every community were in permanent antagonism with the laws under which they lived, and were disposed to regard those laws, and the persons by whom the laws were made and administered as their natural enemies". This state of feeling survived even the Reform Act, which, moderate though it was, was exceedingly deplored by many reasonable people.[1] A doctrine more unhappy or

---

[1] It is curious to note that in a debate at the Oxford Union upon the Reform Bill Mr. Gladstone moved an amendment censuring the Government for having introduced a measure "which threatens not only to

one more unfavourable to the progress of democracy than that which Mr. Gladstone here described it would be difficult to conceive; but that it should actually have existed for a considerable time is one of those facts for which the Radicals must in the main be held responsible.

Thirdly, the Radicals have never appreciated as they should have done the altruism of the English aristocracy. If there be any truth in the saying that civilisation is the work of aristocrats, the history of England would prove it more fully than that of any other country. It may be doubted whether any aristocracy or landed gentry in the world has ever laboured so diligently or with such disinterested zeal. Before democracy was possible, they ruled the country and made her history glorious; it was their sons who won her victories and extended the confines of her empire. A fine story is related of Lord Granville, to whom as minister in 1762 the preliminary articles of the Treaty of Paris were submitted. He was an eminent example of the old type of academic statesmen, of whom it is to be feared that Mr. Gladstone was the last. Their age like that of chivalry is gone. But however that may be, Lord Granville belonged to that aristocratic class which the Radicals detested, but whose self-sacrificing labours posterity should gratefully remember. He was at the time when the Treaty was submitted to him very ill; but he preferred the fulfilment of his duty to the prolongation of his life, and with a singular propriety he applied to himself these noble lines from Homer :—

---

change the form of our government, but ultimately to break up the very foundations of social order in the country . . . " (Robbins' *The Early Public Life of W. E. Gladstone*, p. 99).

THE THIRD AND CONCLUDING PERIOD. 407

> Could all our care elude the gloomy grave,
> Which claims no less the fearful than the brave,
> For lust of fame I should not vainly dare
> In fighting fields, nor urge thy soul to war.
> But since, alas! ignoble age must come,
> Disease and death's inexorable doom;
> The life which others pay, let us bestow,
> And give to fame, what we to nature owe.[1]

It was in such a spirit as this that the nobility of England—a nobility which Burke called the Corinthian capital of polished society—have sacrificed for their country's sake their leisure and their ease; a fact to which the Radicals have too often closed their eyes. Even Bright, with all his sincerity, was reluctant to admit it. "Palaces, baronial castles, great halls," he said, "do not make the nation. The nation in every country dwells in the cottage." It would be more accurate to say that the nation dwells in both. The Radicals, however, have lost by their injustice as much as they have gained; for they have made their bitterest enemies out of those whom they would have found the most powerful of allies. It is, moreover, in this connection worth remarking that the efforts of the Radicals, long continued and unflagging, to undermine the ascendency of the landed interest in English politics have been almost entirely futile. That the ascendency of the land-

---

[1] *Iliad*, xii. 324 (Pope's translation); M. Arnold's *Lectures on translating Homer*. Cp. Kidd's *Social Evolution*, pp. 173, 180. The English noblemen, even when most ineffective in office, often showed a great deal of unselfish self-sacrifice. Such was the Duke of Grafton with his "lounging opinions," as Shelburne called them. See the introduction to the *Autobiography of the Duke of Grafton*, edited by Sir William Anson; and *The American Revolution*, by Sir George Trevelyan, p. 55.

owners was the key-stone of the Constitution was one of those cardinal articles of faith which no one, Whig or Tory, at one time ever questioned. Of the fact there is abundant illustration. Both Chatham and Pitt, for instance, made the increase of the representation of the counties an essential portion of their proposals of reform; Shelburne said that "he never heard a reflecting man doubt the county representation being the great restorative principle of the Constitution," and he spoke no more than the truth. Burke insisted on the principle with characteristic vehemence; property, he said, could never be safe unless "it be out of all proportion predominant in the representation," and that too "in great masses of accumulation". Dr. Johnson justified the House of Lords by the assertion that it was right that influence should be in proportion to property; while Coleridge took the philosophic view that the state derives its principle of permanence, by which it is enabled to subsist, from the owners of the land. Nor was this old tradition shaken by the passing of the Reform Act; on the contrary it so steadily persisted that it was made a fundamental ground for demanding the abolition of the Corn Laws. This landed interest dogma, if it may be permitted thus briefly to describe it, has in fact continually endured. We find Croker, for example, writing to Lord Brougham in 1843 about "the existence of a landed gentry which has made England what she has been and is; without which no representative government can last"; and telling Lord Lonsdale in 1846 that "the only permanent government possible in this country must be founded on the landed interests". Nor was this view of the importance of the representation of the soil an insular peculiarity of the English, for French thinkers held it just as firmly. The Abbé Morellet, for example, an avowed Anglomaniac, writing to Lord Shelburne in 1791, affirmed that the French Constitution was defective, inasmuch as it was not based on landed property, which in his opinion was the only base upon which any good and durable Constitution of a great country could be founded. Long afterwards, Guizot in a letter to Croker expressed the same opinion; "the landed interest," he said, "is the very foundation of society, the source of its grandeur, as it is of its security, its morality and power ".[1]

Now to this great body of opinion the doctrine of the Radicals was in flagrant contradiction; to Chatham's theory of the representation of the soil, for example, their counter principle of the representation not of property but of persons, not of things but of men, was fundamentally opposed. These were two conflicting dogmas which it was impossible to reconcile. The personal feeling of antipathy of the Radicals to the landlords, however, was only gradually developed; and it only reached its zenith during the twenty years that preceded the Reform Act. Then it was that Cobbett amid a chorus of approval from his party described the English country gentlemen "as the most base of all the creatures that God has ever suffered to disgrace the human shape". Since then hatred of the landed interest has always been with the Radicals a more or less animating force; it inspired, no impartial critic can deny, much bitter feeling into the agitation for the

---

[1] Fitzmaurice's *Life of Shelburne*, vol. ii., p. 223; Burke's *Reflections on the French Revolution;* Coleridge's *Constitution of the Church and State;* Boswell's *Life of Johnson; The Croker Papers*, vol. iii., pp. 13, 71, 196-97; *Lettres de l'Abbé Morellet à Lord Shelburne*, edited by Lord Edmond Fitzmaurice (Letter, 6th February, 1791).

repeal of the Corn Laws and the Game Laws.[1] Yet notwithstanding the assaults that have been made upon them, the landed gentry still remain a strongly influential, a controlling and a modifying force. Their importance in English institutions, whether social or political, has often been observed by foreign writers. M. Taine, for example, in his *Notes on England* called the landed gentry "the natural representatives" of the people; and a later French writer, who is deservedly esteemed for his insight and power of accurate observation, has made some excellent remarks upon the subject. He has shown that, putting aside all comparison of the French Senate and the English House of Lords, the landed and agricultural interests are much better represented in the House of Commons than in the Chamber of Deputies. What the agricultural interest may be considered to comprise it is not easy to determine with exactness, for the term is rather vague. But M. Demolins has made some statistical comparisons, which at any rate possess considerable value in reference to the matter now in hand. He has, to sum up his calculations, brought out the fact that, whereas in the present House of Commons there are one hundred and thirty-two representatives of what may be called in general terms the agricultural interest, in the Chamber of Deputies there are only seventy-two. And this, though France is much more an agricultural country than the British Islands. The inference is obvious; that the

---

[1] Cobbett's *Rural Rides.* Some of the Radical arguments against the Game Laws were exceedingly absurd. Cartright, for instance, said that they prevented the oppressed householders from bearing arms and performing the duties of their allegiance (*The Appeal, Civil and Military,* second edition, 1799).

landed gentry still remain in English politics a considerable force.[1]

In the next place, the Radicals have failed to see that one of the great facts of human nature is its love of settled habit ; and that men's conduct is in the long run oftenest determined by their innate dislike of change. To this common feeling, to which some writers have given the name of misoneism, the British are by no means strangers. As Carlyle said, John Bull is a born Conservative ; for he has a reasoned veneration for the traditional and the old ; he has what Burke called " the ancient permanent sense " ; seeking to find the "latent wisdom" in long-established custom, he attempts the cure of evils with " pious awe and trembling solicitude ". To innovation he generally, at first at least, displays " a sullen resistance " that it is hard to overcome. Moreover, even when the Radicals have perceived this existence of what may be called almost a psychological law of human nature, they have failed to estimate its power. John Bright once said that the House of Commons hated change with an animosity that nothing could assuage ; yet this very natural feeling awakened in his mind only contempt and indignation. Whether the British people are too Conservative or not it would be idle to inquire ; but there is one thing that is certain ; the fact, that is to say, that the Radicals by flouting and defying this side of human nature have done their cause immeasurable harm. Even Rousseau, with all his revolutionary fervour, had the wisdom to perceive that it is the excellence of old institutions that preserves them. Yet how many English Radicals have begun with

---

[1] *A quoi tient la Supériorité des Anglo-Saxons*, par Edmond Demolins ; *France*, by J. E. C. Bodley, vol. ii., p. 148.

the assumption that whatever is, is bad! How often have they obstructed the acceptance of reforms—even reforms the most urgently required—by their disdain for the feelings, the prejudices, and the conscientious scruples of great masses of the people! The spirit of compromise, caring little for the exactitude of logic and not impatient of anomaly, is a peculiarly English characteristic; and whenever the Radicals defy it and denounce it, as if it almost were a crime, they go far to put themselves beyond the hope of making themselves practically useful to the state.

Lastly the Radicals have persistently confused the results of reform and of democracy with those of civilisation and of the progress of national prosperity. Blinded by self-love, prone to see in the betterment of society the fruit of their individual efforts only, they have failed impartially to analyse events. Of the task of tracing out the true relations of causes and effects—a task at no time easy even for the least interested critics—they have proved themselves incapable. John Stuart Mill, perhaps alone, had the acumen to perceive, and the candour to admit, that among the beneficial changes for which the Radicals had assumed the credit there were many which in reality were quite as much the work of other people. If a retrospect be made of the amelioration that has taken place in the conditions, both moral and material, of the English people during the Victorian era, and if the causes of the change be impartially examined, it will be found that the progress has been due to the simultaneous and co-operating efforts of persons of all shades of opinion both religious and political. In the good work, so fruitful of beneficent results, no sect or party, not even the Radicals, can claim an exclusive or predominating share. Speaking of the House of Commons as it was from 1832 to 1868, that once sturdy Radical John Arthur Roebuck observed that a history of its work would present a picture "unparalleled in the legislative history of mankind" for "wise reforms wisely executed, for courage attended by wisdom, by truth and by honour". That is no exaggerated praise; but even Roebuck would hardly have denied that during the whole of that period the great majority of the House was composed not of Radicals but of Tories and of Whigs. It is, indeed, not too much to say that the democrats, intent as they were on carrying out thorough constitutional changes, treated much useful legislation with comparative neglect. There is scarcely a single improvement in English social institutions for which the better minds among both Whigs and Tories did not plead with eloquence and power. Many of the reforms that were demanded in the *Westminster Review*—public economy, Catholic emancipation, free trade and law reform are instances in point—had already been put forward in the great quarterly organ of the Whigs. But there is an even stronger case than this. Southey, after he had thrown aside the follies of his youth, was regarded as a Tory of an almost reactionary type; and the *Quarterly Review*, to which he was one of the most constant of contributors, was for many years the greatest organ of Conservative opinion. "It was," said a country squire, "the best book in the world next to God's Bible." Yet Southey in its pages urged many ameliorative measures which, most of them, have since been carried out with the happiest results. National education, the diffusion of good and cheap literature, colonisation, the establishment of savings-banks, the reform of the criminal law, factory legislation, commutation of tithes, were among the things he advocated, to mention but a few. He even pleaded for reforms —the abolition of flogging in the army and navy, the amendment of the poor and game laws, and agricultural allotments, for example—for which the Radicals have claimed and received almost the whole of the credit. Nevertheless, by constantly ascribing to a single set of causes the results which were really due to many, they have greatly narrowed their sphere of practical utility.[1]

A space of nearly one hundred and thirty years separates the Radicals of to-day from their ancestors of 1769. During all that time there has been a continuous evolutionary process, which we have tried very briefly to trace and to describe; and it will be of some interest to inquire what changes radicalism has undergone in the course of its development. How, in short, does the present-day Radical differ from those who have gone before him?

It must in the first place be remarked that, if the popular control of Parliament be the ultimate object of the Radicals, their great work has already been substantially performed. Their final cause, their *raison d'être* has gone; they have reached the promised land of fulfilment and fruition. The doctrine of the control of Parliament by the people was, moreover, strictly speaking, at no time in the exclusive possession of the Radicals. Burke, for instance, said that the House of Commons could not control the Government unless it was itself controlled by

---

[1] J. S. Mill's *Dissertations*, vol. ii., p. 62; *Life and Letters of Roebuck*, p. 327; *The Edinburgh Review* for January, 1874. Bentham relates that he was disturbed at his residence in Queen's Square Place by the cries of the soldiers being flogged in the barracks close by. It was this personal experience of Bentham's that caused the abolition of flogging to be made an important part of the Radical programme.

its electors.¹ The difference between the Radicals and Whigs was rather one of means than of ends, but it was a difference that cut deep. The former sought for the means of control in what may be called the "delegate" theory of parliamentary representation, a theory which they tried to carry out in practice by the plan of taking pledges from parliamentary candidates. The question of the relationship of members to their constituents is at the present time perplexed and undetermined; for though the control of Parliament by the people is an indisputable fact, yet it is maintained by means of quite another kind from those which the early Radicals proposed. The result is somewhat paradoxical, for while the system of pledges has been contemptuously rejected, yet the theory that a member is a delegate tacitly prevails in English politics. That members of the House of Commons have tended, and do tend, to lose their independence it is impossible to doubt. A distinguished French publicist, M. Boutmy, for instance, has remarked the fact; and he thinks that in consequence a deterioration of the tone of politicians is likely to occur. Mr. E. L. Godkin, an American writer, whose judgments are entitled to respect, has expressed much the same opinion; "the delegate theory," he says, "has been gaining ground in England, and in America has almost completely succeeded in asserting its sway, so that we have seen many cases recently in which members of Congress have openly declared their dissent from the measure for which they voted in obedience to their constituents".² Yet with a curious inconsistency

[1] Burke's *Thoughts on the Causes of the Present Discontents*.
[2] *Le Développement de la Constitution et de la Société politique en Angleterre*, par E. Boutmy, pp. 354-55; Godkin's *Unforeseen Tendencies of Democracy*, p. 134.

the Radicals, no less than the Liberals and Conservatives, indignantly refuse to bind themselves with pledges, and even repudiate the notion that they are delegates in any sense whatever. That notion, however, may be clearly traced to them; for they were the first to plan the system of exacting written pledges and of giving "instructions" to parliamentary representatives. The Radical members of Parliament, and Radical candidates have, notwithstanding these attempts, been as eager to parade their independence as the most thorough-paced Conservatives. In the constituency of Westminster, for example, where Place introduced the modern electioneering methods, both Sir John Hobhouse and Sir Francis Burdett declared "that none but fools demanded pledges, and none but fools gave them". When the Reform Act was passed, it was believed by its opponents that the "delegate" theory would prevail to an extent that would revolutionise the House of Commons. In a letter, for instance, written in 1837, Croker reminded Sir Robert Peel that they had "all foreseen that the Reform Act must tend to a system of delegation and dependence". So too A. H. Hallam in a letter to Tennyson describing his impressions of the opening of the first reformed Parliament, made use of remarkable language to express the same idea: "Yesterday I saw," he said "(perhaps) the last King of England go down to open the first assembly of delegates from a sovereign people".[1] The prediction that the "delegate" theory would eventually leaven English politics has been in a sense abundantly fulfilled, but in quite a different way than was supposed. The delegation is indirect and

[1] *The Correspondence and Diaries of J. W. Croker*, vol. ii., p. 320; *The Life of Lord Tennyson*, vol. i., p. 92.

unavowed, but it is there. No self-respecting candidate consents to bind himself with pledges or to lower himself to the position of a mere agent or attorney, but he has but little independence, his protests notwithstanding. The control of Parliament works in ways, that, though all powerful, are subtle and unseen. The methods of election, the universal use of the platform, the sleepless vigilance of the press, the fierce light that is thrown upon the conduct of every public man, all exert an influence which it is impossible to resist. Yet since the Reform Act, no less than before, parliamentary representatives and candidates have delighted in assuming an air of independence; and the ultra-Liberals, perhaps, in a manner the most spirited of all. Lord Brougham—a Whig of Radical propensities—claimed this independence in the very plainest terms; " the people's power," he said, " being transferred to the representative body for a limited time, the people are bound not to exercise their influence so as to control the conduct of their representatives, as a body, on the measures that come before them ". And again, he pointed out that " the most serious risk to which the representative principle is exposed in a democracy arises from the people, and their disposition to take back a portion of the power which they have entrusted to their deputies, by controlling them in its exercise on questions of a peculiarly interesting nature ". That is excellently said, but it surely conveys what in these days is a counsel of perfection. Or take again the case of the late Professor Freeman, who, when he stood as a parliamentary candidate, thus boldy stated his position: " I hold also," he said, " that no member of Parliament should pledge himself to vote this way or that on matters of detail. If I ever sit in the House of Commons, I will sit there as a representative and not as a delegate."[1] The opinions of two such representative Radicals as John Bright and John Stuart Mill have been previously referred to, and what they said upon the question need not be repeated here. It will suffice to remark that no one more clearly than they has recognised the fact that the electors, if they chose, could put their representatives into fetters, or has more earnestly exhorted them to refrain from making an unwise and illiberal misuse of the powers that they possessed. The attitude of the Radicals towards the question would appear to be strangely inconsistent. They have desired the end, but they have often kicked against submission to the means. The early Radicals, indeed, did not shrink from insisting on pledges and the like for the attainment of the purpose; but these self-denying ordinances could not be easily endured. The new Radicals, no less strongly than the old, demand the complete control of Parliament by the people; and one—Mr. Labouchere—has had the courage to affirm that the choice of a leader is of no importance to his party, because it is the duty of its chiefs not to lead but to follow. But the Radicals of to-day are even less willing to surrender their own individual independence than was formerly the case. The fact is that the popular control of Parliament has been

[1] Jephson's *Rise and Progress of the Platform*, vol. ii., p. 566; *The Life and Letters of E. A. Freeman*, by W. R. W. Stephens, vol. i., p. 209; *Electoral Address at Wallingford* (1859). It is of some interest to note Professor Freeman's views upon the history of representation. Writing to the Rev. R. E. Bartlett on 2nd August, 1854, he says: "You should also try to work out the difference between a representative of the whole body of citizens, and only chosen for convenience' sake by the citizens of a certain locality, and a delegate, the mere mouth-piece of local wishes. The former is our present idea, but I conceive the latter was the original one" (vol. i., p. 173).

eventually accomplished through the gradual progress of democracy, and not by the means the early Radicals desired. It is, indeed, not too much to say that, if the "delegate" theory, as the Radicals defined it, had prevailed, the prestige of Parliament would grievously have suffered. What was the origin of political representation is one of those obscure problems which it is very difficult to solve, but it seems probable that its sources were the two ideas of agency and vicarious liability. The two were generally blended, but not everywhere in quite the same proportions. In countries where the Roman law was dominant, the idea of agency prevailed; but where, as in England, that law had little sway, the idea of agency gave way before that of vicarious liability. Now, as an agent is not permitted to exceed the instructions of his principal, it follows that in countries where parliamentary representatives are merely looked upon as agents, their Parliaments tend to lose their self-dependence and to languish—a tendency which can historically be proved to have occurred. Now it is precisely this idea of agency that the Radicals have attempted to import into our constitutional principles; but it was too alien to strike root. That the "Mother of Parliaments" would have suffered loss of power and dignity, if the attempt had been successful, it is impossible to doubt.[1]

[1] I am indebted for this view of the origin of political representation to a very illuminating article on the subject in the *Contemporary Review* for December, 1898, by Mr. Edward Jenks. It is worth noting that under the old pocket-borough system the nominee representatives were under great obligations to their patrons, so that they, many of them, had probably less liberty of action than the Radicals supposed. See Boutmy's *Le Développement de la Constitution et de la Société Politique en Angleterre*, p. 291.

In close connection with the vexed question of the control of Parliament lies the attitude of the Radicals towards the House of Commons. Very striking in this respect is the contrast between the old order and the new; for the early Radicals abhorred—and the term is not too strong—the Lower Chamber as the grand obstacle to reform, to liberty, and the enfranchisement of the people. They made no secret of their feeling of contempt, and they expressed it in very vigorous language. Sir Francis Burdett used to talk of the House in slighting terms as "the room over the way," and of Members as "a band of notorious oligarchs"; he disliked, he said, attending Parliament because he hated "bad company and late hours". Bentham, to be sure, at one time wished to find a seat, though he was wont to speak sarcastically of the "Honourable House". His disciple Place was more outspoken; he called it "rascally" and an "atrocious assembly," and he stubbornly refused to come forward as a candidate. Even Bright sometimes spoke of it with disdain; he said that it cared very little for the great internal interests of the country, and that it was reckless, not to say profligate, in the expenditure of public money. He said that if the Clerk of the House were to stand at Temple Bar with orders to tap upon the shoulder every well dressed and apparently cleanly washed man who passed through until he had numbered 658, and if the Crown were to summon them to Parliament, it was his honest conviction that a better House of Commons would be formed than that which actually existed. No Radical in these days would indulge in language such as this. There are some persons—*laudatores temporis acti*— who profess to lament a falling off in the quality of Parliament; but the Radical of to-day must necessarily admire a legislative chamber that is the express image of the sovereign people. To do otherwise would be to stultify himself. In this respect, at least, the new Radicals differ greatly from the old.[1]

Much greater changes than this, however, have occurred; and in some ways, indeed, the new Radicals have moved to an opposite extreme. The first great change may be noted in the sphere of foreign politics. The old Radical idea might be summarised by saying that the less Great Britain interfered with the affairs of other countries the better it would be. James Mill, for example, expressed the doctrine very well when he observed that "the desire, so often expressed, that we should interfere to establish good government all over the world, is most alarming, and, if assented to in any degree, would lead to the worst of consequences. . . . The business of a nation," he went on to remark, "is with its own affairs." It would not be quite accurate to say that what may be called the non-interference theory was universally accepted by every class of Radicals; for the London Working Men's Association conceived and carried out a system of international addresses. These, however, were specially composed in the interests of the so-called solidarity of labour. Again a small group of Republicans, some of them the disciples of Mazzini, were constant in their efforts to promulgate their principles abroad. Mr. Bradlaugh, at any rate, was once deputed by a republican congress at Birmingham to convey a message of congratulation to the Republicans of Spain. But these attempts at foreign interference were

---

[1] Cobbett's *Political Writings*, vol. v.; *A History of the Last Hundred Days of English Freedom*, Letter 4; Wallas' *Life of Place*, p. 100; *John Bright*, by C. A. Vince, pp. 96, 118.

exceptions to the rule; for, generally speaking, the old doctrine was steadily maintained. It was so strenuously insisted on by the school of Bright and Cobden that it became its most distinctive badge. The new Radicals, however, take a very different view; they have, with few exceptions, discarded an outworn and unfashionable creed. Their clamour for active interference in Armenia and in Crete is witness to the fact. That the White Man has a burden, which it is his duty to take up, as Mr. Rudyard Kipling has expressed it, they seem to have been convinced at last.[1]

The second great change is to be found in the sphere of home affairs, and arises from that much-vexed philosophic question of the duties of Government and of the field of legislation. How strongly individualist was the old Radical character has been already shown, and to illustrate the fact anew would be merely idle repetition. But there is one piece of testimony that is so forcible and striking that it may, without irrelevance, be mentioned here: the fact, that is to say, that the modern anarchists place the early Radical writers, Paine and Godwin, for example, among their prototypes and the founders of their creed. There is connected with this subject a very curious incident which is worth a passing notice. Burke, when a young and unknown man, wrote a *reductio ad absurdum* of the principles of anarchy in his ironical *Vindication of Natural Society*. Godwin said that it proved in good earnest the very things which under the guise of satire it laboured to refute; and, therefore, by a singular freak of

---

[1] Bain's *James Mill*, p. 366; *The Life and Struggles of William Lovett*, pp. 90, 98; *Memories*, by W. J. Linton; *Life of Charles Bradlaugh*, by Mrs. Bradlaugh-Bonner, vol. i., p. 353.

destiny the name of Burke has been placed along with that of Paine amongst the anarchical philosophers. No better illustration of the rampant individualism of the early Radicals could be found than the remarkable fact that their best remembered writers are still quoted by those thinkers of to-day who seek to find a reasoned basis for the principles of anarchy. The idea of *laissez faire* was at first vague and indeterminate, and it had long to wait before it took a strictly philosophic shape. When John Stuart Mill brought out his famous book *On Liberty*, the plan of which, like a second Gibbon, he conceived while ascending the steps of the Capitol in Rome; when he affirmed that "the only purpose for which power can be rightfully exercised over any member of a civilised community against his will is to prevent harm to others," he gave a scientific form to a doctrine which the older Radicals had held, but to which they came for reasons they were scarcely able to explain. There is perhaps no principle which the Radicals have so consistently sustained or one which has so profoundly influenced their policy and conduct as that which John Stuart Mill so brilliantly worked out in that extraordinary book. But all this has changed in recent years. Bright was the last of the great Radicals who manfully through good and ill report upheld the ancient faith—the principle that it is the right of every man to be allowed to conduct his own affairs with as little interference as is possible by the state. His teaching has already in the ears of the new Radicals an antiquated sound.[1]

---

[1] *English Thought in the Eighteenth Century*, by Leslie Stephen, vol. ii., p. 224; Nettlau's *Bibliographie de l'Anarchie;* Boutmy's *Le Développement de la Constitution et de la Société politique en Angleterre*, p. 348.

But it is rather in their traits, their character, their temperament and disposition that the new Radicals contrast so strongly with the old. The latter had, at least, some well-defined ideas, some clearly thought out principles, which informed and permeated their views of life. They knew exactly what they wanted, and, knowing it, they pursued it with unconquerable zeal. With all their deficiencies and mental limitations, there was much about many of the old Radicals which we cannot but admire. True it is that led astray by the false lights of abstractions and assumptions they lost themselves in a labyrinth of inextricable mazes; true it is that they were unable to discern "the falsehood of extremes," and that their minds were but rarely illumined by any imaginative glow. But they were no light half-believers of their casual creeds; the principles they held, they grasped with hooks of steel. They were men who signified somewhat, as Cromwell would have said. If they held unpopular opinions they had the courage to avow them; for to be a Radical was formerly no light or trivial matter. It is only in recent years that the old ferocity in politics has completely died away. In the time of the Tudors or the Stuarts, if a man took a strong line in politics, he ran some risk of a state trial, the Tower and the scaffold; as Macaulay said, it was at one period as dangerous to be a Whig as to be a highwayman. The ferocity was lessened by degrees, but while it lasted the Radicals were the persons who suffered from it most.[1] A man of good birth and position in

[1] The old antipathy to the Radicals is illustrated in an amusing way by a story told by Carlyle; he says that he once met with a stage-coach driver who used to address scornfully persons whom he disliked as "you Radical" (*Carlyle's Reminiscences*, vol. i., p. 246). Another illustration is afforded from Mr. Gladstone's school life. He wrote in the *Eton Miscellany*

society who ventured to display any democratic sympathies was disowned by his friends, and became socially *déclassé*. To persevere, he had to be cast in an heroic mould. There was, for example, no circle of society, however distinguished, to which the presence of Grote would not have added lustre ; yet for years this highly cultured man—who lamented that he lived in "an age of steam and cant"—was debarred by his political opinions from the social intercourse for which he was so admirably fitted.[1] Active radicalism might bring, and often did bring, imprisonment and ruin. Wilkes, for instance, was outlawed and imprisoned ; yet even he, "an unworthy representative of good principles," as Mr. Gladstone called him, has a claim upon our sympathy. The picture too of Bentham devoting his vast talents and a long life of unremitting and unrewarded toil to the amelioration of mankind is surely one of the most touching and heroic which history has to show. The sight of that venerable figure in the old Hermitage at Queen's Square Place, whether among his books and papers or pacing round his garden, is one upon which the imagination loves to dwell. There was an artless simplicity about some of the old school of Radicals which was refreshing because it was so obviously sincere. Cartwright was "in his simplicity sublime " ; while Bentham is said to have been boyish to the end. In his constitution youth and age

---

that he had admitted among his staff of writers "one who would rather keep company with a hyæna than with a Radical " (Robbins' *Early Public Life of Mr. Gladstone*, p. 68).

[1] After the Grotes had begun to enter society Sydney Smith is said to have remarked to Mrs. Grote : "Now that you have been seduced, my dear, I may tell you that your virtue was sometimes uncommonly disagreeable " (*Edinburgh Review* for July, 1873).

were by some magic touch so nicely intermingled that he was in some respects never really young and never really old. A robust cheeriness, a rosy optismism—now, alas! too rare—at one time used to colour the lives of the reformers. For they were men who were full of expectations; the promised land lay still before them; they had their victories yet to win. But the new Radicals are enjoying the fulfilment of much of their desire. It may, indeed, perhaps be said that the old Radicals thought too well of human nature and too nobly of mankind, for they showed that, while they were painfully alive to present evils and were anxious to remove them, they could still retain their faith in human progress and a lively sense of hope. With quietness and confidence they looked forward to the time when their principles would be universally accepted, and would dominate the world. "Twenty years after I am dead," said Bentham, "I shall be a despot." This is the kind of faith that removes mountains, and the radicalism that produced it must have had a wonderful vitality for which we at present look in vain. Who of the latter-day Radicals would venture to make a similar prediction of himself? Such firmness of conviction, such disinterested zeal, such limitless philanthropy, and such optimism are at present far to seek. If the premises of the old Radicals were false, their reasoning, at least, was luminous, and their arguments were logical. They were intellectually sincere; their creed was easy to define; it might be almost compressed into a syllogism. But upon what principle the new radicalism is now based, or what unity underlies the various items of its programme it is difficult to see; and to put into a few words what it consists of, would be a task beyond the wit of man. Whether the present-day Radicals are agreed upon any principles may well be doubted. Dr. Johnson used to say that to treat your adversary with respect was to give him an advantage that he did not deserve; but this tactical mistake is one into which the Radicals have never been liable to fall. Nay rather, to bicker and to quarrel and to vituperate one another they have been always much too prone, as there has been unfortunately only too much occasion to observe. But this fissiparous tendency—this movement from homogeneity to heterogeneity, as an evolutionist would call it—was never before so unmistakably apparent. The new Radicals are not agreed whether they wish for Home Rule all round, or Home Rule for Ireland only; it is, indeed, by no means certain whether it has been abandoned altogether or only for a time. They are not agreed whether they wish to end the House of Lords or only to amend it; whether they wish to strengthen it or weaken it; whether they desire two legislative chambers or only one. The Abbé Siéyès defended the single chamber system by propounding a dilemma; if, he said, the Upper House agrees with the Lower, it is superfluous; if it disagrees, it ought to be abolished. For such a compact argument we should ask the modern Radicals in vain. They insist on the principle of "one man one vote," but of that of "one vote, one value," which a fair system of redistribution would involve, they will not hear a word. So too, with regard to the new Imperialist idea; for while some clamour for foreign intervention, a remnant still keep the ancient faith; but whether the former are prepared to find the necessary means by increased armaments is not so very certain. This is not statesmanship, but what Junius would have called "the ominous oscillation of a pendulum". Never before have the Radicals presented so disorganised, so undisciplined a body.

Carlyle once said that there was a "paralytic" type of radicalism, and it surely must be that which we are confronted with to-day Even as long ago as 1887, John Bright, then verging on the confines of old age, and bidding farewell to public life, spoke in melancholy tones of the condition of the party to which he had given such lustre and distinction. "The moral sense," he said, "of the Liberal party seems to have become depraved, and all that we boasted of in its former character has for the time forsaken it."[1] What would he have said if he had been living at this hour? Happy he to have been spared the sight of a veritable *débâcle* of the party of which he was so proud.

But though the new Radicals are distinguished by their points of disagreement, it must in fairness be allowed that they are sometimes of the same opinion, and that when then do agree their unanimity is wonderful. They at least clamour with one voice for legislative interference; they join hands in casting from them that idea of *laissez faire* which they once so heartily professed. Their work, as the old Radicals conceived it, was to tear off the bonds of privilege and prejudice, to liberate the oppressed and to strike off the fetters which clogged the energies and industry of the individual man. They sought to obtain the greatest happiness for humanity by a sturdy individualism, and they believed that the surest way to reach the goal in view was to secure to every man his independence. Their work, in a word, was one of disenthralment. So believing, they set themselves the mission—like Knights of the Holy Ghost, to use Heine's strange similitude—of redressing human wrong. But all

---

[1] *John Bright*, by C. A. Vince., p. 202.

that is now changed; for if there is one thing that is especially distinctive of modern radicalism, it is its constant cry for legislation; it is suffering from a fit of what Mirabeau called "la plus funeste maladie des gouvernements modernes," namely, "la fureur de gouverner". The bureaucratic temper appears to be a form of disposition to which democracy is liable to excess. Under the plea of protecting persons against themselves and the consequences of their follies and their faults, legislation is demanded that is too often of a coercive and irritating kind. The Radical policy is branded everywhere with that odious word compulsion. The education question will serve to illustrate the fact. Priestley used to protest against the establishment of a stereotyped form of education by the state; Bentham and Place valued highly—no one more so—the education of the people, but they did not propose to go to Parliament for the enactment of a scheme; they set to work themselves to establish Lancasterian and chrestomathic schools. Roebuck again, though he certainly believed that it was the duty of the state to educate the people, insisted that in matters of religion allowances should be made for differences of opinion. "So believing," he said, "I shall certainly support every plan for the education of the people by the state which does not interfere with the religious feelings and opinions of the parents and guardians of the children to be educated." It is precisely this kind of interference—which would compel parents to send their children to schools where denominational teaching is forbidden—against which the supporters of the voluntary schools so earnestly protest. In the same spirit this disciple of Bentham attacked the extreme temperance and Sabbatarian parties; he called them "canting hypocrites" and "two muddy streams," which after running some distance side by side, "had at last united their waters, and now they formed one foaming muddy river, which it was very difficult to stem, and very disagreeable to see and smell". That seems strong language to employ; but he believed that the extreme temperance and Sabbatarian advocates intended to deprive the working class of those enjoyments which the rich would be permitted to retain. The modern Radicals, on the other hand, would compel a large minority to go without the use of intoxicating liquors, if the majority in any district should require it; and they would deprive a publican of his means of livelihood without some reasonable compensation. They ask Parliament to extend the long arm of interference in other ways besides; to prohibit a man from working more than eight hours a day; and to prevent him making terms, however beneficial, with his employer for getting compensation for injuries received in the course of his employment. For "contracting out," as it is called, is what the new radicalism peculiarly abhors. It is of course true that the Conservative party have always been more prone than their opponents to impose regulations on industries by law—as the earlier Factory Acts have testified. But in these days they are the defenders of liberty against the Radical attacks; and though they have passed the Compensation for Accidents Act of 1896, they have done it in a much more liberal form than the Opposition would have liked. Again, the Radicals propose—though this is not surprising, nor is it altogether new—that every Member of Parliament should be compelled, however reluctantly, to receive the wages of attendance from the state. These would be some of the characteristics of the Radical Utopia. It is conceivable, indeed, that a social order involving loss of personal freedom might, things being what they are, be the best for human nature; but a policy that seeks to frame society in this way is not liberalism, and he deceives himself who imagines that it is. It is a bastard form of liberalism that trenches upon liberty.[1]

A moment's reflection will discover the last but not the least important difference between the old radicalism and the new. The former was, in the main, concerned with the ultimate principles of government, and it was around those principles that discussion chiefly centred. It is now difficult to realise the excitement that was once aroused by the brilliant sparring, for example, of James Mill on the one hand and Macaulay and Mackintosh on the other. The bulk of mankind, as Burke very truly said, are, while they are well and happy, not excessively curious about theories of politics and of government, and, he added, a propensity to resort to theories of this kind is a sure sign of an ill-conducted state. It may, therefore, be taken as a proof of the improved condition of the people that any such discussion as that on the identity of interest in the governors and governed would, except, perhaps, in academic circles, be now deemed entirely futile. Men in these days prefer to put idle logomachies aside, and to consider particular measures on the more limited but more useful grounds of practical expediency. Theorising upon the forms of government used to be in an especial manner the distinguishing characteristic of the Radicals, and the intellectual trait that divided them most sharply from the Whigs. For whereas the latter thought that abstract

---

[1] Leader's *Life and Letters of John Arthur Roebuck*, pp. 185, 295.

constitutional systems were, comparatively speaking, of very little moment, the former believed that their importance was supreme. Of Pope's celebrated lines :—

> For forms of government let fools contest:
> That which is best administered is best,

Bentham said that it was " one of the most foolish couplets that was ever written—if written with knowledge ".[1] His remark is strikingly typical of the Radical point of view, and it stands almost at the very antipodes of thought in its distance from the sentiment expressed by Dr. Johnson in the lines that he added to Goldsmith's *Traveller* :—

> How small of all that human hearts endure,
> That part which kings or laws can cause or cure.

The massive sagacity of the Doctor is plainly manifested here; for he belonged to that numerous class of thinkers who believe that the form of government is by no means as important as the character of the men who make and administer the laws. Most schemes of political improvement, he said, are " very laughable things "; and he added that he would not give half a guinea to live under one form of government rather than another. That perhaps may be thought to be an extravagant Tory view; but Burke, who was the very incarnation of Whiggism, was of much the same opinion. When he declaimed against the folly of overrating " the wisdom and the power of human legislation," he, in effect, condemned that exaggerated language about the potentialities of government

---

[1] Bowring's *Life of Bentham, Works,* vol. x., p. 532.

which was beginning to be heard.[1] The new Radicals, though still fond of theorising, must be constrained by force of circumstances to allow that Burke and Johnson were substantially correct. For during the present century the world has enlarged its experience. It has, in fact, discovered that monarchs and aristocracies have often acted, and do constantly act, in the interests of the governed; that identity of interest in the governors and the governed is not necessarily a security for good government at all; that the governed do not always know their true interest, nor pursue it when they know it.[2] The reasoning of the old Radicals was one-sided and misleading, and both their premises and deductions were far too absolute in character. True it is that in their days the condition of the mass of the population was often very bad; that there was scarcity, poverty, ignorance and leaden-eyed despair; and

---

[1] Boswell's *Johnson*; *Burke's Speech on the Taxation of America*.

[2] It is curious to consider the different opinions of political writers on this question. Compare the following. Rousseau said: " Of themselves, the people always desire what is good, but do not always discern it. The general will is always right, but the judgment which guides it is not always enlightened" (*Social Contract*, chapter vi.). Macchiavelli said: " I will venture to assert against all that the people is more constant, more judicious, more prudent than any prince. And it is not without reason that the voice of the people is compared to the voice of a god" (Villari's *Macchiavelli*, vol. iii., p. 319). In his *Rough Draft of a New Model at Sea*, Lord Halifax said: "I will not deny but that 'Interest will not lie' is a right maxim, whenever it is sure to be understood. . . . A nation is a great while before they can see, and generally they must feel first before their sight is quite cleared. This maketh it so long before they can see their interest, that for the most part it is too late for them to pursue it; if men must be supposed always to follow their true interest, it must be meant of a new manufactory of mankind by God Almighty; there must be some new clay, the old stuff never yet made any such infallible creature."

that the governing class did not always consider the best interests of the people. But the world now possesses an experience of democracy and representative government which it was formerly impossible to have; and it is no extravagance to say that out of England the representative system has proved itself to be but very moderately successful. For extravagance and corruption some modern democracies have been as bad as any oligarchy or monarch ever was. Even in England the character of the Radicals in this respect has greatly changed since the days of Joseph Hume. It is true that now and then one of them is found to raise a warning voice; but the Radicals quite as much as the Conservatives make incessant demands upon the Treasury. They are always wanting money for this scheme or for that. The democratic form of government, in fact, demands more courage, integrity and intelligence than Bentham ever dreamed of. Rousseau, fanatic though he was, showed greater wisdom here. If there was, he said, a nation of gods, it would be governed democratically; but so perfect a government would be unsuitable to men.[1] Burke once said that "a perfect democracy is the most shameless thing in the world"; and the Radicals themselves have, with a curious inconsistency, used language that implied the truth of his remark. In the same breath that they have claimed the right of self-government for the people, they have denied their fitness to receive it. When Burke spoke of the

---

[1] Rousseau, *Social Contract*, chap. iv. Compare his statement in the same chapter: "Taking the term in its strict sense, there never has existed, and never will exist, any true democracy. It is contrary to the natural order that the majority should govern and that the minority should be governed."

populace as "the swinish multitude," the democrats were furiously enraged; yet no one has spoken more harshly of the people than they. Place, for instance, said that he was not too ignorant to see that "the common people must ever be imbecile when not encouraged and supported by others who have money and influence". Roebuck too declared that "the masses" show "profound ignorance, and necessarily inveterate prejudice," and he reluctantly admitted that the danger of placing power in the hands of the ignorant could only be avoided by 'careful and slow proceedings". In like manner, John Stuart Mill justified what appeared to be a cooling of his democratic ardour by saying that he dreaded "the ignorance and especially the selfishness and brutality" of the people, so long as their education remained so wretchedly imperfect.[1] Nor is this all. It is worthy of remark that both James and John Stuart Mill spent the greater portion of their lives in administering, under the East India Company, a form of government that was in flagrant contradiction to the theories they professed. Nor did any one defend the rule of what was in effect a vivifying despotism more strenuously than they. A more remarkable example of the habit of preaching one thing and practising another it would be difficult to find. John Stuart Mill had, however, sometimes a dim perception that a democratic form of government was not quite the *summum bonum* that most Radicals fancied that it was; for he once told Professor Nichol that he would like to see Ireland governed like India; "I

---

[1] The Radicals have often resembled the fastidious Gelo, the tyrant of Syracuse, who found the people very unpleasant to live with: δημοῦ ξυνοίκημα ἀχαριτώτατον (Herodotus, bk. vii., ch. clvi.).

myself," he said, "have always been for a good stout despotism ".[1]

Whether democracy is the best form of government it would be now-a-days a barren question to dispute. For whether we welcome it or not; whether we say with Mazzini that it is the self-government of the people under the leadership of the best and wisest; whether we call it an aristocracy of orators sometimes interrupted by a monarchy of one;[2] whether we agree with Bismarck that it resembles the government of a household by the nursery; or with Talleyrand that it is an aristocracy of blackguards; it is present for evil or for good. The doctrine of the government by the majority may be obnoxious to criticism. Lord Houghton said that it meant that everybody wished to govern others but to be exempt from government himself; Disraeli—who has somewhere styled the representative system "a fatal drollery"—said that self-government was in terms a contradiction, because power must be necessarily exercised by a minority of numbers; even Paine, who had a sense of humour, once observed that as the fools outnumber the wise, the minority should govern. But however that may be, the Radicals have ground for exultation. If the consummation of democracy —and democracy implies the control of Parliament by the people—has been the grand object to which their predecessors devoted their labours and their lives, then we are driven to the conclusion that their work has been ac-

---

[1] Wallas' *Life of Place*, p. 117; Leader's *Life and Letters of John Arthur Roebuck*; J. S. Mill's *Autobiography*; Unpublished Letters from J. S. Mill to Professor Nichol, in the *Fortnightly Review* for May, 1897.

[2] Cp. *The Government of Athens under Pericles*: λόγῳ μὲν δημοκρατία, ἔργῳ δὲ ὑπὸ τοῦ πρώτου ἀνδρὸς ἀρχή (Thuc. 2-65).

complished, and that the radicalism of the old traditional type is a spent and waning force. If this be the case, the distractions and divisions of the Liberal party of to-day can be naturally explained. For the old-world Radical lags superfluous on the stage. What the future Radical will be it is not easy to predict, but that he will be a very different person it seems impossible to doubt.

INDEX.

Address to the Addressers, Paine's, 112.
Anarchists, their claim to Burke, Godwin and Paine, 122, 422.
American war, the, 45, 89.
Ancients, their views of human progress, 2.
Anglo-mania in France, 13, 14.
Anti-Corn Law agitation, 370, 371, 376.
Ashburton, Lord, offends Bentham, 182.
Aristotle quoted, 106 *note*.
Aristocracy, Radical hostility to, 406, 407.
Attwood, Thomas, 313-316, 362, 369.
Austin, Charles, 214.
Austin, John, 215, 350.

BACON, Lord, on the study of political philosophy by the young, 106 *note*.
Ballot, the, 96, 188, 330.
Bamford, Samuel, on demagogues, 275; on Cobbett, 306; his personality, 307.
Barbauld, Mrs., 110; her criticism of Godwin's *Political Justice*, 120 *note*.
Barracks, Blackstone on, 98; Paine on, 116.
Bastille, the anniversary of the fall of, 102; the true condition of, 103 *note*; H. Tooke treasures a fragment of, 103.
Beccaria, Bentham's indebtedness to, 180.
Beckford, the Lord Mayor, 51, 56, 93.
Beddoes, Dr., his Pneumatic Institution at Bath, 169.
Bentham on Horne Tooke, 51; his indebtedness to Priestley, 80, 179; his denunciation of Fox, 165; his love of chemistry, 170; on the spread of scientific knowledge, 172; his personality, 172-176, 425; on Oxford, 173; on the dressing of the hair, 173; his dislike of Wilkes, 174, 178; attends Blackstone's lectures, 174; his resemblance to Franklin, 176; his radicalism, 177, 186, 191, 228, 233, 234; his intellectual development, 178-183; his indebtedness to Helvetius, 179; his *Fragment on Government*, 181; befriended by Shelburne, 181; on the English government, 186, 187; his optimism, 190, 237, 426; his Panopticon,

190; on simplicity in government, 190; on the sphere of government, 190; his influence in Spain, 192; his mode of composition, 222; his method of inquiry, 226; his literary judgments, 226, 227; on Sir S. Romilly, 246; on Brougham, 247, 248; on Sir F. Burdett, 264; on "Orator" Hunt, 278; on Cobbett, 291, 305; on war, 385; on flogging in the army, 414 *note.*

Benthamites, the, 185, 195, 196, 225, 232, 324.

Birmingham, riots at, 140; the Political Union, 315.

Black, Mr., of the *Morning Chronicle,* 286.

Black Dwarf, the, 283.

Blackstone, on barracks, 98; his lectures, 174, 181.

Blaquière, a Benthamite apostle, 193.

Blue-stocking clubs, 14.

Bolingbroke on the representation of the land, 20.

Borrow, George, on Bentham's influence in Spain, 192 *note.*

Boutmy, M., quoted, 415.

Bowring, Sir John, 219, 341.

Bradlaugh, Mr., on the Whigs, 396; a republican, 421.

Bright, John, on the Chartists, 369; his personality, 378, 395; on the House of Commons, 411, 420; on Liberal demoralisation, 428.

Brougham, Lord, on Priestley, 80; his relations to Bentham, 195; on the Radicals, 350; on parliamentary representation, 417.

Bull, Alderman, 57.

Buller, Charles, 334, 346, 350.

Burdett, Sir Francis, 254, 255, 264, 265, 266; his committal to the Tower, 258-260; fined and imprisoned, 291; his Toryism, 303, 343; on the House of Commons, 420.

Burdettites, the, 265.

Burke, on Whiggism, 11 *note;* on the representation of the land, 20, 408; on the House of Lords, 17, 95; on reform, 23; his Liberal sentiments, 23; his abhorrence of radicalism, 23, 401, 402; disliked by Bentham, 24 *note;* first uses the word franchise, 24 *note;* on the party system, 25; on Wilkes, 42; on parliamentary reporting, 61; on "high bred republicans," 64; on Price's sermon, 83; his election speeches, 84; on the Constitutional Society, 86; the origin of his *Reflections on the French Revolution,* 82, 110; on Godwin's *Political Justice,* 120; on the French Revolution, 133; on Lafayette, 134; on Condorcet, 134; his conversation with Arthur Young on Gibbon, 134 *note;* on the Dissenters, 139; on Thelwall, 153; on the scientific method in politics, 171, 401, 402, 403 *note;* on self-interest, 198; claimed by the Anarchists, 422; on the sphere of legislation, 432.

Burns influenced by the French Revolution, 104.

INDEX. 441

Buxton, Sir Fowell, on the Radicals, 245; on Sir F. Burdett, 255.
Byng, Mr., his story of the Whigs, 157.
Byron, Lord, on Wilkes, 30; his lines on Hobhouse, 261; his lines on Cobbett and Paine's bones, 288 *note*.

CAMDEN, his discharge of Wilkes, 35; he offends Bentham, 182.
Campbell, Lord, on the trials of Hardy and others, 157 *note*.
Canning, his youthful radicalism, 103; on parliamentary representation, 268.
Carlisle, Richard, 282.
Carlyle on Paine, 109 *note;* on the Benthamites, 230; on the Radicals, 230, 355; on Cobbett, 304; on Coleridge, 328; on Buller, 334; on Sir W. Molesworth, 335; on the English political panacea, 362; on Cobden and Bright, 392, 393; on English Conservatism, 411; his anecdote of Radicals, 424 *note*.
Cartwright, John, on Burke, 24 *note;* his personality, 67-73; writes the first work on reform, 69; on parliamentary representation, 69, 269; on the House of Lords, 96; on the payment of members, 97; on the standing army, 71, 73 *note*, 99; his connection with the Society of the Friends of the People, 161; a dinner given to, 257.
Cavendish, Sir H., his parliamentary reports, 59.
Chartism, 356-370.
Chatham, Lord, his unique position, 6, 8, 22, 26; as a reformer, 19, 20, 22, 155; on the party system, 25; his reverence for the King, 25; his elevation to the peerage, 27; on Lord Mayor Beckford, 51; admired by Cobden, 391 *note*.
Chesterfield, Lord, on the standing army, 98.
Christie, Thomas, 170.
Churchill, the satirical poet, 32.
City, the, of London, instructs its representatives, 29, 30 *note*, 57; a centre of radicalism, 55-57, 391; its addresses to the Crown, 50-51; its treatment of the Roman Catholics, 90; its subsequent conservatism, 251, 390.
Civilisation, results of, confused with those of democracy, 412.
Cobbett, William, brings Paine's bones to England, 117, 288 *note;* on the Whigs, 245; on Sir F. Burdett, 266, 267; on "Orator" Hunt, 277; his personality, 287-306; on Paine, 288; on Wilkes, 288; on Price, 288; his persecution of Priestley, 288; on the landed interest, 409; on the colonies, 303; his relations to Attwood, 314; his friendship with Wakley, 339; his failure in Parliament, 341.
Cobden, Richard, his description of Grote, 210; on the Whigs, 348; his personality, 378-395; his admiration for Chatham, 391 *note*.

Coleridge, on opposites and contraries, 10 *note;* on the principles of progress and permanence, 10 *note;* on the representation of the land, 21; on Horne Tooke, 48; on metaphysical systems, 67; on Priestley as the founder of the Unitarians, 77 *note;* his youthful radicalism, 104; on Godwin, 120; on the irreligion of the Radicals, 131; on hair powder, 137; on Holcroft, 151 *note;* on Thelwall, 153, 154 *note;* John Stuart Mill on, 328; Carlyle on, 328.

Colonies, Benthamite view of, 288; Manchester School's view of, 385; Cobbett's view of, 303; Chatham on, 391 *note.*

Combination Laws, 308, 309.

Commons, House of, its relations to the Crown, 17, 18; its former unpopularity, 18; its corruption, 18; its treatment of Wilkes, 43; Radicals' contempt for, 253; how regarded, 388, 411, 413, 420.

Common Sense, Paine's, 109.

Compensation for Accidents Act, the, 430.

Compromise, Cartwright on, 72; Mazzini on, 72; Jebb on, 74; Paine on, 116.

Comte on permanence and progress, 10 *note;* his law of the three stages, 167.

Condorcet, his optimism, 4 *note;* Godwin compared with, 123, 126, 127 *note;* Burke on, 134.

DAY, Thomas, 66.

Debates, reporting of, 58-63, 258, 301, 399.

Declaration of Rights, Bentham on, 184.

Delegates, members of Parliament regarded as, 23, 34, 43, 93, 268-270, 329, 382, 415-419.

Democracy, modern experience of, 433; Rousseau on, 433 *note*, 434 *note;* Burke on, 434; Place on, 435; J. S. Mill on, 435; Mazzini on, 436; Bismarck on, 436; Talleyrand on, 436; Lord Houghton on, 436.

Demolins, M., on the representation of the land in France, 411.

Diderot congratulates Wilkes, 40.

Disraeli on Thomas Attwood, 314; on the Reform Act of 1832, 333 *note;* on representative government, 436.

Dissenters, the, unpopularity of, 139; Burke on, 139.

Diversions of Purley, the, 48.

De Tocqueville on taxation in England, 129.

De Quincey on opposites and contraries, 10 *note;* on Paine, 116.

Dumont, his relations to Bentham, 188, 192, 197.

Duncombe, T. S., 340, 347, 363, 367 *note*, 369.

Durham, Lord, 169 *note*, 245, 312, 350, 351.

INDEX. 443

EAST INDIA COMPANY, the, James and J. S. Mill in, 435.
Edinburgh Review, the, 217, 218.
Eldon, Lord, on parliamentary representation, 268, 298.
Erskine, his radicalism, 103; his defence of Paine, 143; of Hardy and others, 155; on the Society of the Friends of the People, 159.
Essay on Woman, the, 86.
Examiner, the, 284, 285.

FÉNELON, his influence on Bentham, 179.
Female suffrage, 188, 201, 330, 360, 383.
Flower, Benjamin, advocates the ballot, 96 *note*.
Fonblanque, Albany, 286, 324.
Foreign policy, Benthamite view of, 239, 421; Cobbett's view of, 303; the Manchester School's view of, 384, 385.
Fox, C. J., 28, 85, 90, 103, 142, 146 *note*, 162, 163, 164, 165, 166.
Fox, W. J., 376.
Foy, General, on Bentham, 176.
Franchise, first use of the word in politics, 24.
Franklin, Benjamin, on the representation of the land, 21; on Wilkes, 40; on payment of members, 97; his resemblance to Bentham, 176.
Freeman, Professor, on parliamentary representation, 417, 418 *note*.
French and English, intercourse of, 12-14.
French Revolution, the, 79, 83, 101-107, 110, 132-134, 162, 183, 184.
Frost, John, 144.

GAGGING BILLS, the, 142.
Game Laws, the, 149, 356, 357, 410 *note*.
George III., 5, 6, 18, 25, 26, 31, 34 *note*, 42, 61, 141.
Gerrald, trial of, 145.
Gibbon on Whigs and Tories, 9; on the country gentlemen, 21; on Wilkes, 30; on the French Revolution, 110, 134; on parliamentary reform, 158; on the anti-slavery agitation, 158; on the scientific method, 171; on Oxford, 173.
Gladstone, Mr., on Wilkes, 46 *note*; on parliamentary reporting, 63, 399 *note*; on J. S. Mill, 331; on the effects of the French Revolution, 405; on the Reform Act of 1832, 405 *note*; his use of the platform, 394.
Gloucester, city of, exacts pledges from its representatives, 30.
Glynn, Serjeant, 56, 57.
Godkin, Mr., quoted, on parliamentary representation, 415.
Godwin, William, on H. Tooke, 48, 104; his personality, 118-126; his relations with Thelwall, 154; his relations with Place, 205 *note*; on Burke's *Vindication of Natural Society*, 422.
Goethe on mathematics, 171.

Goldsmith, Oliver, Bentham's criticism of his *Deserted Village*, 226; his lines on Burke, 401 *note;* his *Traveller* quoted, 432; government, sphere of, views of, 79, 82, 114, 121, 122, 191, 240, 387, 432.

Grafton, Duke of, 407 *note*.

Granville, Lord, story of his quoting Homer, 406.

Greville, H., on the Tories, 353; on J. S. Mill, 326 *note;* on Duncombe, 340 *note*.

Grey, Earl, on reform, 158, 313; on the Radicals, 246, 349.

Grote on James Mill, 197, 229; his personality, 205 *note*, 209, 210; his social ostracism, 243, 425; on Attwood, 316; quarrels with Roebuck, 345; on the Whigs, 347; and the Political Economy Club, 375; his radicalism, 358; the *Times* on, 359.

Grote, Mrs., on James Mill, 196, 229; on the Radicals, 347.

"Grote Conclave," the, 324.

Guizot, M., on morality in politics, 379 *note;* on the representation of the land, 409; on Cobden's invitation to office, 396.

HAIR-POWDER, use of, 104, 136, 137.

Halifax, Lord, on Whigs and Tories, 9; on payment of members, 97; on free trade, 375; on abstractions in politics, 403 *note;* on democracy, 433 *note*.

Hallam, A. H., on the reformed Parliament, 416.

Hanover, the House of, 17.

Hardy, Thomas, 147.

Harrington, a republican, 63; on the ballot, 96.

Hazlitt on Southey, 107; on Godwin, 119, 120; on Bentham, 192.

Helvetius, his influence on Bentham, 179.

Herodotus quoted, 435 *note*.

Hobhouse, John C., 236, 261, 262, 270, 338, 344, 368.

Hogarth, his caricature of Wilkes, 30, 40 *note*.

Holcroft, T., 149, 150.

Hollis, T., 65.

Homer quoted, 407.

Home Rule, Irish, Benthamite view of, 239; J. S. Mill on, 436.

Horsley, Bishop, his view of government, 11.

Hume, David, on the House of Commons, 7 *note;* on self-interest in governors, 7 *note;* on the divine right of kings, 9; on the unpopularity of the Scotch, 26; his definition of Whigs and Tories, 16 *note;* on the standing army, 71; on the ballot, 96; on the principle of utility, 180; James Mill's indebtedness to, 198.

Hume, Joseph, 210-212, 253; on colonies, 239; Cobbett on, 296; on the landed interest, 300.

INDEX. 445

Hunt, John and Leigh, 31, 284, 285.
Hunt, "Orator," on the Whigs, 245; on Sir F. Burdett, 265, 276-280; opposes the Reform Bill, 318.
Huskisson, his youthful radicalism, 104.
Hutcheson on the greatest happiness of the greatest number, 180.

INDIVIDUALISM, different views of, 79, 82, 114, 116, 240, 241, 302, 330, 386, 387, 423, 428-430.
Instructions to members of parliaments, different views of, 29, 30, 38, 56, 57, 70, 75, 77, 93, 382, 416-418.
Imperialism, 385.

JACOBITES, 6, 7 *note*, 9.
Jacobinical Radicals, 107.
Jebb on parliamentary reporting, 58 *note*; his personality and political opinions, 74, 75, 85, 99.
Jenks, Mr., on the origin of representation, 419.
Johnson, Dr., on petitions, 15; on kingship, 16; on the House of Commons, 18; on Wilkes, 31, 41; on Churchill, 32; on H. Tooke, 48; his parliamentary reports, 59,; on Mrs. Macaulay, 65; on the Whigs, 89; on representation, 93; on general elections, 94; on the House of Lords, 95 *note*; Bentham on, 226; on forms of government, 432.
Jones, Ernest, 367, 369.
Jones, Sir William, 86.
Jones, John Gale, 259.
Junius on the Wilkes agitation, 41, 42, 44.

LABOUCHERE, Mr., on party leaders, 418.
Labour representatives, 330.
Land, the representation of, 20, 87, 88, 145, 298-300, 408-410.
Lamb, Lady Caroline, 124, 256.
Landor, W. S., his radicalism, 104.
Lafayette, Burke on, 134.
Lauderdale, Earl, his radicalism, 103.
Lecky, Mr., quoted, 17, 394.
Lewis, Sir G. C., on opposites and contraries, 10 *note*.
Legislatorial attorney, the, 271.
Liberty in small states, 78, 82.
Locke on government, 224.
Lords, House of, 17, 95, 96.
London, the, and the *London and Westminster Reviews*, 325, 335.

Loughborough, Lord, on parliamentary reporting, 59; disliked by Bentham, 182; on the press, 282.
Lovett, William, 307, 308, 310, 361 note.
Lunar, the, Society, 140.
Luttrell, Colonel, 40, 41.
Lyndhurst, Lord, his youthful radicalism, 103.

MACAULAY, Lord, on the Benthamites, 230; on Cobbett, 341; on the Radicals, 346, 349.
Macaulay, Mrs. Catherine, 64, 65, 110.
Macchiavelli quoted, 433 note.
Mackintosh, Sir James, 110, 164, 229.
Malthus, Cobbett's denunciation of, 305.
Manchester School, the, 377-395.
Mansfield, Lord, his relations to Bentham, 174, 178, 182.
Martineau, Miss H., on the Whigs, 348.
Marvell, Andrew, 97, 363.
Mazzini on the two schools of historians, 4 note; on compromise, 72; on democracy, 436.
Middlesex elections, 41 et seq.
Mill, James, 48, 193-202, 275, 421; his acerbity of temper, 229; on colonies, 238.
Melbourne, Lord, on the utilitarians, 350.
Mill, John Stuart, on the principles of permanence and progress, 10 note; his use of the term "personal" representation, 69 note; his education, 213; his connection with the *Westminster Review*, 220, 221; on the Benthamites, 225, 233; his political opinions, 323-331; on Wordsworth, 329 note; his quarrel with Roebuck, 345; his criticism of the Radicals, 345, 346; on Lord Durham, 351; on progress and democracy, 412.
Mirabeau on bureaucracy, 429.
Molesworth, Sir William, 334, 335-347, 349.
Montesquieu on the English Constitution, 13, 236; as a scientist, 169.
More, Hannah, 136.
Morellet, the Abbé, 13, 76 note, 98, 181, 372, 409.

NASH, the Lord Mayor, 57.
National Union of the Working Classes, 355.
Norfolk, the Duke of, 164.
North Briton, the, 32, 34, 43.

OASTLER, Richard, 367.
Obstruction in Parliament, early instance, 61.

INDEX. 447

O'Brien, J. B., 366, 368, 369.
O'Connell, Daniel, 337, 338, 349, 359, 365.
O'Connor, Feargus, 365, 366, 368, 369.
Oliver, Richard, 56, 57, 62.
Onslow, Colonel, on the reporting of debates, 60.
Onslow, the ex-Speaker, on the reporting of debates, 60.
Optimism a, characteristic of the Radicals, 4, 331, 390, 426.
Owen, Robert, 240, 310.

P's, the three of liberty, 16.
Paine, Thomas, 108-118; and Burke's *Reflections on the French Revolution*, 110; his *Rights of Man*, 110; claimed by the anarchists, 122; his radicalism, 128, 129; his unpopularity, 135; his letters to the Attorney-General, 143; as a scientist, 169; on government by minorities, 436.
Palmerston, Lord, offers office to Cobden, 396.
Pamphlet, the age of the, 92.
Pantisocrats, the, 105.
Parkes, "Joe," 316.
Parliament, the unreported, 59.
Parr, Dr., 41, 145.
Party system, the, 9-11, 25.
Payment of members, 97, 361.
Pearson, Mr., his pessimism, 5 *note*.
Peel, Sir R., on Sir F. Burdett, 343; on the Conservatives, 353; Roebuck's abuse of, 356, 357; Disraeli on, 404.
Persius, Bentham's favourite quotation from, 177.
Peterloo Riot, the, 279.
Petitions, 15, 16, 85, 274.
Philosophical Radicals, the, 168, 172, 221-223.
Pitt, his youthful preference for the House of Commons, 27 *note;* his proposals for reform, 87, 88, 155; Coleridge on, 134; on Godwin's *Political Justice*, 135; on Paine's *Rights of Man*, 157; on the Society of the Friends of the People, 161; on Fox, 162; his dread of the Radicals, 162 *note;* on Adam Smith, 373; his views on trade, 374.
Place, Francis; on Cartwright, 72 *note;* and the London Corresponding Society, 148; his political opinions, 203-207, 241, 376; his individualism, 241; on the Whigs, 245, 347; on the City Corporation, 252; as an electioneering organiser, 253; his influence on Joseph Hume, 211, 253; his contempt for the House of Commons, 253, 420; on Sir F. Burdett, 260, 268; on parliamentary pledges, 269, 270; on the Reformed Parliament, 333; and the repeal of the Combination Laws

Plato, James Mill's indebtedness to, 198.
Pledges, parliamentary, 30, 53, 269, 270.
Poe, on Godwin's mode of composition, 127 *note*.
Political economy, different views of, 296, 372-375.
Political Justice, Godwin's, 119, 120, 125, 127.
Political societies, 46, 47, 52, 85, 86.
Political Register, Cobbett's, 289, 290.
Poole, Thomas, his description of Paine, 109 *note*; his social ostracism, 135.
Pope's *Essay on Man* quoted, 432.
Porson, his witticism on Gilbert Wakefield, 163 *note*.
Potatoes, Cobbett's denunciation of, 302, 304.
Praed, his verses quoted, 352.
Press, the, 14, 43, 58, 282.
Price, Richard, 81-84, 102, 105 *note*.
Priestley, Joseph, 76-80, 103, 140, 141.
Printers, the case of the, 61.
Privilege, parliamentary, 37, 43, 44, 60, 61.
Progress, the idea of, 2-5.
Progress and permanence, the principles of, 10 *note*.
Public meetings, first, 46, 47 *note*.

Quarterly Review, 217, 413.

RADICALS, origin of, 5, 17; their unpopularity, 135-138, 141, 424 *note*; influence of the French Revolution on, 101-107; opprobrium of the name, 243; dissensions of, 344; their study of political economy, 375; their absorption of the Liberal party, 397; their disinterested zeal, 400, 424, 426; their proneness to speculative theories, 401-404; old and new, 414-437; their religious opinions, 130, 131, 378.
Radicalism, a creed of youth, 106, 319 *note*.
Reeves, John, 163.
Reform Act, the, 332, 333, 355.
Renan, on the Indo-European and Semitic conceptions of a golden age, 4 *note*.
Republicans, a group of, 63.
Ricardo, David, 207, 208, 296, 375.
Richmond, Duke of, 87, 95, 154.
Rickman, Thomas, 170.
Rights, natural, Burke on, 23.
Rights of Man, Paine's, 110.
Rockingham, Lord, 28, 84.

INDEX. 449

Roebuck, J. A., 215, 229, 356, 357, 413, 429.
Roman Catholics, intolerant treatment of, 90.
Romilly, Sir S., on the Constitutional Society, 86; on Godwin's *Political Justice*, 120; his attitude to the Radicals, 246, 247; on parliamentary seats, 251.
Rotundists, the, 310.
Rousseau, on Wilkes, 37 *note;* offers to legislate, 65; his view of English liberty, 70 *note;* on liberty in small states, 78 *note;* his work on musical notation, 169; on democracy, 433 *note*, 434 *note*.
Russell, Lord John, 311, 312, 343, 354.

SANDWICH, Lord, 36.
Saville, Sir George, 84.
Sawbridge, Alderman, 55.
Scientific knowledge, spread of, 169.
Scientific method in politics and morals, 171.
Scott, Sir Walter, attends state trials at Edinburgh, 146; on Joseph Hume, 212; Bentham on, 227; and the Burdettites, 265; on the press, 282; Cobbett on, 292.
Scotch, the, their unpopularity in England, 26, 27.
Scotland, state trials in, 144-146.
Shakespeare quoted, 106 *note*.
Shelburne, Lord, on Whigs and Tories, 75, 99, 382, 383; on the representation of the land, 20; his friendship for Priestley, 76; his friendship for Price, 81; on short Parliaments, 94; his friendship for Bentham, 181; on political economy, 372, 373.
Shelley, 126, 279 *note*, 306, 319 *note*.
Sheridan, R., 144, 162, 163.
Short Parliaments, 19, 75, 94, 99, 382, 383.
Sidney, Algernon, 63.
Smith, Adam, on Price, 81; Cobbett on, 296; Shelburne on, 372.
Smith, Goldwin, cited, 377 *note*.
Smith, Sydney, sayings of, quoted, 222, 229, 352, 425.
Smollett, 32.
Socialism, 241, 310, 331.
Society, the, of the Supporters of the Bill of Rights, 47, 52, 53, 61; Society, the, for Constitutional Information, 74, 86; Society, the, for Commemorating the Revolution of 1688, 83, 102; Society, the Constitutional, 86, 111, 112 *note;* Society, the London Corresponding, 147, 148, 204; Society, the, of the Friends of the People, 159, 160, 165; Society, the Hampden, 273; Society, the Union, 274.

Spain, influence of Bentham in, 192.
Spence, Thomas, 309.
Spurs, use of in the House of Commons by county members, 21.
Standing army, suspicion of, 71, 98, 301.
Stanhope, Earl, 69 *note*, 103, 105 *note*, 169.
Stephen, Mr. Leslie, cited, 123.
Stephens, Joseph, 367, 369.
Swift, on Whigs and Tories, 9 ; on short Parliaments, 19, 94 *note ;* on the standing army, 98.

TAINE, M., on Jacobinism as the creed of youth, 106; on the English landed gentry, 410.
Taxation in England, 129.
Tennyson, Lord, cited, 392.
Thelwall, J., 136, 149, 151-153, 154.
Thompson, Perronet, 376.
Thrale, Mrs., on Wilkes, 31 *note.*
Thucydides quoted, 386 *note,* 436 *note.*
Thurlow, Lord, 152, 157 *note.*
Tierney, Mr., saying of, quoted, 245.
Times, the, 301, 395.
Tooke, Horne, 47, 48, 49, 50, 51, 52, 54, 107, 119; his wit, 155 *note.*
Tooke, Thomas, 375.
Trials, state, 144-146, 154-156.
Tucker, Dean, 78, 239, 372.
Turgot, J. S. Mill compared with, 324 ; Shelburne's indebtedness to, 372.

UNITARIANS, Priestley, the founder of, 77.
Universities, the Radical distrust of the, 297, 389.
Utilitarian Society, the, 213.

VINCENT, H., 367.
Voltaire, on the eighteenth century, 12 ; as a scientist, 169.

WAKEFIELD, Gilbert, 163.
Wakley, Thomas, 339.
Walker, Thomas, 143.
Walpole, Horace, on Wilkes, 30, 40; on Churchill, 32; on the *North Briton,* 33 ; on the City of London, 55 ; on a group of republicans, 63 ; on Mrs. Macaulay, 64 ; on Radical philosophers, 138 ; on Priestley, 141 ; on Price, 102, 105 *note;* on the Amazonian allies, 110.
Watson, Bishop, on the Radicals, 131.

Watt, James, 170.
Wellington, the Duke of, 317, 353.
Westbury, Lord, on John Bright's admission to office, 396.
Wesley, John, 136.
Westminster, the constituency of, 85, 252-255.
Westminster Review, the, 217-221.
Whigs and Tories, 9-11, 16 *note*, 354; their theory of trusteeship, 11; their disruption, 157; their dilatoriness, 352; their exclusiveness, 395, 396; their relations to the Radicals, 218, 244, 245, 347-350.
Whitefield, prays for Wilkes, 40.
Wilberforce, W., on English luxury, 129; on the Radicals, 131; on parliamentary representation, 268.
Wilkes, John, 28, 30, 31-40; his radicalism, 44-46, 54, 55, 62, 78 *note*.
Winterbotham, Mr., trial of, 143.
Wollstonecraft, Mary, 110 *note*, 125, 127 *note*.
Wolseley, Sir Charles, 271, 281.
Woodfall as a parliamentary reporter, 60.
Wooler, T. J., 283, 289.
Working men, Radical, 354, 355.
Wordsworth, his youthful radicalism, 104, 136; on Godwin's *Political Justice*, 120; his relations to Thelwall, 136, 153; J. S. Mill's criticism on, 329 *note*; on Burke, 401.
Wyvill, Christopher, 85, 88, 96.

YOUNG, Arthur, on taxation in England, 129; on the Radicals, 131; his conversation with Burke, 134 *note*.
Youth, radicalism, the creed of, 106, 319 *note*.

MESSRS. LONGMANS, GREEN, & CO.'S
CLASSIFIED CATALOGUE
OF
WORKS IN GENERAL LITERATURE.

History, Politics, Polity, Political Memoirs, &c.

Abbott.—A HISTORY OF GREECE. By EVELYN ABBOTT, M.A., LL.D.
Part I.—From the Earliest Times to the Ionian Revolt. Crown 8vo., 10s. 6d.
Part II.—500-445 B.C. Cr. 8vo., 10s. 6d.

Acland and Ransome.—A HANDBOOK IN OUTLINE OF THE POLITICAL HISTORY OF ENGLAND TO 1896. Chronologically Arranged. By A. H. DYKE ACLAND, M.P., and CYRIL RANSOME, M.A. Crown 8vo., 6s.

ANNUAL REGISTER (THE). A Review of Public Events at Home and Abroad, for the year 1897. 8vo., 13s.
Volumes of the ANNUAL REGISTER for the years 1863-1896 can still be had. 18s. each.

Amos.—PRIMER OF THE ENGLISH CONSTITUTION AND GOVERNMENT. By SHELDON AMOS, M.A. Cr. 8vo., 6s.

Arnold.— INTRODUCTORY LECTURES ON MODERN HISTORY. By THOMAS ARNOLD, D.D., formerly Head Master of Rugby School. 8vo., 7s. 6d.

Baden-Powell.—THE INDIAN VILLAGE COMMUNITY. Examined with Reference to the Physical, Ethnographic, and Historical Conditions of the Provinces; chiefly on the Basis of the Revenue-Settlement Records and District Manuals. By B. H. BADEN-POWELL, M.A., C.I.E. With Map. 8vo., 16s.

Bagwell.—IRELAND UNDER THE TUDORS. By RICHARD BAGWELL, LL.D. (3 vols). Vols. I. and II. From the first Invasion of the Northmen to the year 1578. 8vo., 32s. Vol. III. 1578-1603. 8vo., 18s.

Ball.—HISTORICAL REVIEW OF THE LEGISLATIVE SYSTEMS OPERATIVE IN IRELAND, from the Invasion of Henry the Second to the Union (1172-1800). By the Rt. Hon. J. T. BALL. 8vo., 6s.

Besant.—THE HISTORY OF LONDON. By Sir WALTER BESANT. With 74 Illustrations. Crown 8vo., 1s. 9d. Or bound as a School Prize Book, 2s. 6d.

Brassey (LORD).—PAPERS AND ADDRESSES.
NAVAL AND MARITIME, 1872-1893. 2 vols. Crown 8vo., 10s.
MERCANTILE MARINE AND NAVIGATION, from 1871-1894. Cr. 8vo., 5s.
IMPERIAL FEDERATION AND COLONISATION FROM 1880-1894. Crown 8vo., 5s.
POLITICAL AND MISCELLANEOUS, 1861-1894. Crown 8vo., 5s.

Bright.—A HISTORY OF ENGLAND. By the Rev. J. FRANCK BRIGHT, D.D.
Period I. MEDIÆVAL MONARCHY: A.D. 449-1485. Crown 8vo., 4s. 6d.
Period II. PERSONAL MONARCHY: 1485-1688. Crown 8vo., 5s.
Period III. CONSTITUTIONAL MONARCHY: 1689-1837. Cr. 8vo., 7s. 6d.
Period IV. THE GROWTH OF DEMOCRACY: 1837-1880. Crown 8vo., 6s.

Buckle.—HISTORY OF CIVILISATION IN ENGLAND. By HENRY THOMAS BUCKLE. 3 vols. Crown 8vo., 24s.

Burke.—A HISTORY OF SPAIN, from the Earliest Times to the Death of Ferdinand the Catholic. By ULICK RALPH BURKE, M.A. 2 vols. 8vo., 32s.

Chesney.—INDIAN POLITY: a View of the System of Administration in India. By General Sir GEORGE CHESNEY, K.C.B. With Map showing all the Administrative Divisions of British India. 8vo., 21s.

Corbett.—DRAKE AND THE TUDOR NAVY, with a History of the Rise of England as a Maritime Power. By JULIAN S. CORBETT. With Portrait, Illustrations and Maps. 2 vols. 8vo., 36s.

Creighton.—A HISTORY OF THE PAPACY FROM THE GREAT SCHISM TO THE SACK OF ROME (1378-1527). By M. CREIGHTON, D.D., Lord Bishop of London. 6 vols. Cr. 8vo., 6s. each.

Cuningham.—A SCHEME FOR IMPERIAL FEDERATION: a Senate for the Empire. By GRANVILLE C. CUNINGHAM of Montreal, Canada. Cr. 8vo., 3s 6d.

History, Politics, Polity, Political Memoirs, &c.—*contd*

Curzon.—PERSIA AND THE PERSIAN QUESTION. By the Right HON. GEORGE N. CURZON, M.P. With 9 Maps, 96 Illustrations, Appendices, and an Index. 2 vols. 8vo., 42*s*.

De Tocqueville.—DEMOCRACY IN AMERICA. By ALEXIS DE TOCQUEVILLE. 2 vols. Crown 8vo., 16*s*.

Dickinson.—THE DEVELOPMENT OF PARLIAMENT DURING THE NINETEENTH CENTURY. By G. LOWES DICKINSON, M.A. 8vo., 7*s*. 6*d*.

Froude (JAMES A.).
THE HISTORY OF ENGLAND, from the Fall of Wolsey to the Defeat of the Spanish Armada. 12 vols. Crown 8vo., 3*s*. 6*d*. each.

THE DIVORCE OF CATHERINE OF ARAGON. Crown 8vo., 3*s*. 6*d*.

THE SPANISH STORY OF THE ARMADA, and other Essays. Cr. 8vo., 3*s*. 6*d*.

THE ENGLISH IN IRELAND IN THE EIGHTEENTH CENTURY. 3 vols. Crown 8vo., 10*s*. 6*d*.

ENGLISH SEAMEN IN THE SIXTEENTH CENTURY. Crown 8vo., 6*s*.

THE COUNCIL OF TRENT. Cr. 8vo., 3*s*. 6*d*.

SHORT STUDIES ON GREAT SUBJECTS. 4 vols. Cr. 8vo., 3*s*. 6*d*. each.

CÆSAR: a Sketch. Cr. 8vo., 3*s*. 6*d*.

Gardiner (SAMUEL RAWSON, D.C.L., LL.D.).
HISTORY OF ENGLAND, from the Accession of James I. to the Outbreak of the Civil War, 1603-1642. 10 vols. Crown 8vo., 6*s*. each.

A HISTORY OF THE GREAT CIVIL WAR, 1642-1649. 4 vols. Cr. 8vo., 6*s*. each.

A HISTORY OF THE COMMONWEALTH AND THE PROTECTORATE, 1649-1660. Vol. I., 1649-1651. With 14 Maps. 8vo., 21*s*. Vol. II., 1651-1654. With 7 Maps. 8vo., 21*s*.

WHAT GUNPOWDER PLOT WAS. With 8 Illustrations and Plates. Crown 8vo., 5*s*.

Gardiner (SAMUEL RAWSON, D.C.L., LL.D.)—*continued*.
CROMWELL'S PLACE IN HISTORY. Founded on Six Lectures delivered the University of Oxford. 8vo., 3*s*. 6*d*.

THE STUDENT'S HISTORY OF ENGLAND. With 378 Illustrations. Cr. 8vo. *Also in Three Volumes*, price 4*s*. each.
Vol. I. B.C. 55-A.D. 1509. 173 Illustrations.
Vol. II. 1509-1689. 96 Illustrations.
Vol. III. 1689-1885. 109 Illustrations.

Greville.—A JOURNAL OF THE REIGN OF KING GEORGE IV., KING WILLIAM IV., AND QUEEN VICTORIA. By CHARLES C. F. GREVILLE, formerly Clerk of the Council. 8 vols. Cr. 8vo., 3*s*. 6*d*. each.

HARVARD HISTORICAL STUDIES.
THE SUPPRESSION OF THE AFRICAN SLAVE TRADE TO THE UNITED STATES OF AMERICA, 1638-1870. W. E. B. DU BOIS, Ph.D. 8vo.
THE CONTEST OVER THE RATIFICATION OF THE FEDERAL CONSTITUTION IN MASSACHUSETTS. By S. B. HARDING, A.M. 8vo., 6*s*.
A CRITICAL STUDY OF NULLIFICATION IN SOUTH CAROLINA. By D. F. HOUSTON, A.M. 8vo., 6*s*.
NOMINATIONS FOR ELECTIVE OFFICE IN THE UNITED STATES. By FREDERICK W. DALLINGER, A.M. 7*s*. 6*d*.
A BIBLIOGRAPHY OF BRITISH MUNICIPAL HISTORY, including Gilds and Parliamentary Representation. By CHARLES GROSS, Ph.D. 8vo.
THE LIBERTY AND FREE SOIL PARTIES IN THE NORTH-WEST. By THEODORE CLARKE SMITH, 8vo., 7*s*. 6*d*.

Historic Towns.—Edited by E. A. FREEMAN, D.C.L., and Rev. WILLIAM HUNT, M.A. With Maps and Plans. Crown 8vo., 3*s*. 6*d*. each.

Bristol. By Rev. W. Hunt.	London. By Rev. W. J. Loftie.
Carlisle. By Mandell Creighton, D.D.	Oxford. By Rev. W. Boase.
Cinque Ports. By Montagu Burrows.	Winchester. By G. W. Kitchin, D.D.
Colchester. By Rev. E. L. Cutts.	York. By Rev. James Raine.
Exeter. By E. A. Freeman.	New York. By Theodore Roosevelt.
	Boston (U.S.). By Henry Cabot Lodge.

History, Politics, Polity, Political Memoirs, &c.—*continued.*

...yce (P. W., LL.D.).

A SHORT HISTORY OF IRELAND, from the Earliest Times to 1608. Crown 8vo., 10s. 6d.

A CHILD'S HISTORY OF IRELAND, from the Earliest Times to the Death of O'Connell. With Map and 160 Illustrations. Crown 8vo., 3s. 6d.

...aye and Malleson.—HISTORY OF THE INDIAN MUTINY, 1857-1858. By Sir JOHN W. KAYE and Colonel G. B. MALLESON. With Analytical Index and Maps and Plans. 6 vols. Crown 8vo., 3s. 6d. each.

...ang (ANDREW).

PICKLE THE SPY, or, The Incognito of Prince Charles. With 6 Portraits. 8vo., 18s.

ST. ANDREWS. With 8 Plates and 24 Illustrations in the Text by T. HODGE. 8vo., 15s. net.

...ecky (WILLIAM EDWARD HARTPOLE).

HISTORY OF ENGLAND IN THE EIGHTEENTH CENTURY.

Library Edition. 8 vols. 8vo.

Vols. I. and II., 1700-1760, 36s. Vols. III. and IV., 1760-1784, 36s. Vols. V. and VI., 1784-1793, 36s. Vols. VII. and VIII., 1793-1800, 36s.

Cabinet Edition. ENGLAND. 7 vols. Cr. 8vo., 6s. each. IRELAND. 5 vols. Crown 8vo., 6s. each.

HISTORY OF EUROPEAN MORALS FROM AUGUSTUS TO CHARLEMAGNE. 2 vols. Crown 8vo., 16s.

HISTORY OF THE RISE AND INFLUENCE OF THE SPIRIT OF RATIONALISM IN EUROPE. 2 vols. Crown 8vo., 16s.

DEMOCRACY AND LIBERTY. 2 vols. 8vo., 36s.

Macaulay (LORD).

THE LIFE AND WORKS OF LORD MACAULAY. '*Edinburgh*' *Edition.* 10 vols. 8vo., 6s. each.

Vols. I.-IV. HISTORY OF ENGLAND.

Vols. V.-VII. ESSAYS; BIOGRAPHIES; INDIAN PENAL CODE; CONTRIBUTIONS TO KNIGHT'S 'QUARTERLY MAGAZINE'.

Vol. VIII. SPEECHES; LAYS OF ANCIENT ROME; MISCELLANEOUS POEMS.

Vols. IX. and X. THE LIFE AND LETTERS OF LORD MACAULAY. By the Right Hon. Sir G. O. TREVELYAN, Bart.

This Edition is a cheaper reprint of the Library Edition of LORD MACAULAY'S *Life and Works.*

COMPLETE WORKS.

'*Albany*' *Edition.* With 12 Portraits. 12 vols. Crown 8vo., 3s. 6d. each.
Cabinet Edition. 16 vols. Post 8vo., £4 16s.
'*Edinburgh*' *Edition.* 8 vols. 8vo., 6s. each.
Library Edition. 8 vols. 8vo., £5 5s.

HISTORY OF ENGLAND FROM THE ACCESSION OF JAMES THE SECOND.
Popular Edition. 2 vols. Cr. 8vo., 5s.
Student's Edit. 2 vols. Cr. 8vo., 12s.
People's Edition. 4 vols. Cr. 8vo., 16s.
Cabinet Edition. 8 vols. Post 8vo., 48s.
'*Edinburgh*' *Edition.* 4 vols. 8vo., 6s. each.
'*Albany*' *Edition.* 6 vols. Crown 8vo., 3s. 6d. each.
Library Edition. 5 vols. 8vo., £4.

CRITICAL AND HISTORICAL ESSAYS, WITH LAYS OF ANCIENT ROME, in 1 volume.
Popular Edition. Crown 8vo., 2s. 6d.
Authorised Edition. Crown 8vo., 2s. 6d., or 3s. 6d., gilt edges.
'*Silver Library*' *Edition.* Crown 8vo., 3s. 6d.

CRITICAL AND HISTORICAL ESSAYS.
Student's Edition. 1 vol. Cr. 8vo., 6s.
People's Edition. 2 vols. Cr. 8vo., 8s.
'*Trevelyan*' *Edit.* 2 vols. Cr. 8vo., 9s.
Cabinet Edition. 4 vols. Post 8vo., 24s.
'*Edinburgh*' *Edition.* 4 vols. 8vo., 6s. each.
Library Edition. 3 vols. 8vo., 36s.

History, Politics, Polity, Political Memoirs, &c.—*conti*

Macaulay (LORD).—*continued.*

ESSAYS which may be had separately, price 6*d.* each sewed, 1*s.* each cloth.

Addison and Walpole.	Ranke and Gladstone.
Croker's Boswell's Johnson.	Milton and Machiavelli.
Hallam's Constitutional History.	Lord Byron. Lord Clive.
Warren Hastings.	Lord Byron,and The
The Earl of Chatham (Two Essays).	Comic Dramatists of the Restoration.
Frederick the Great.	

MISCELLANEOUS WRITINGS.

People's Edition. 1 vol. Cr. 8vo., 4*s.* 6*d.*
Library Edition. 2 vols. 8vo., 21*s.*
Popular Edition. Cr. 8vo., 2*s.* 6*d.*
Cabinet Edition. Including Indian Penal Code, Lays of Ancient Rome, and Miscellaneous Poems. 4 vols. Post 8vo., 24*s.*

SELECTIONS FROM THE WRITINGS OF LORD MACAULAY. Edited, with Occasional Notes, by the Right Hon. Sir G. O. Trevelyan, Bart. Cr. 8vo., 6*s.*

MacColl. — THE SULTAN AND THE POWERS. By the Rev. MALCOLM MAC-COLL, M.A., Canon of Ripon. 8vo., 10*s.* 6*d.*

Mackinnon. — THE UNION OF ENGLAND AND SCOTLAND: a Study of International History. By JAMES MACKINNON, Ph.D., Examiner in History to the University of Edinburgh. 8vo., 16*s.*

May.—THE CONSTITUTIONAL HISTORY OF ENGLAND since the Accession of George III. 1760-1870. By Sir THOMAS ERSKINE MAY, K.C.B. (Lord Farnborough). 3 vols. Crown 8vo., 18*s.*

Merivale (THE LATE DEAN).
HISTORY OF THE ROMANS UNDER THE EMPIRE. 8 vols. Cr. 8vo., 3*s.* 6*d.* each.
THE FALL OF THE ROMAN REPUBLIC: a Short History of the Last Century of the Commonwealth. 12mo., 7*s.* 6*d.*
GENERAL HISTORY OF ROME, from the Foundation of the City to the Fall of Augustulus, B.C. 753-A.D. 476. With 5 Maps. Crown 8vo., 7*s.* 6*d.*

Montague.—THE ELEMENTS OF LISH CONSTITUTIONAL HISTOR' F. C. MONTAGUE, M.A. Cr. 8vo.,

Richman.—APPENZELL: Pure cracy and Pastoral Life in Rhoden. A Swiss Study. By] B. RICHMAN, Consul-General United States to Switzerland. Maps. Crown 8vo., 5*s.*

Seebohm (FREDERIC).
THE ENGLISH VILLAGE COMM Examined in its Relations Manorial and Tribal System With 13 Maps and Plates. 8v
THE TRIBAL SYSTEM IN WALES Part of an Inquiry into the St and Methods of Tribal Society. 3 Maps. 8vo., 12*s.*

Sharpe.—LONDON AND THE KIN a History derived mainly fro Archives at Guildhall in the cus the Corporation of the City of L By REGINALD R. SHARPE, D.C.: cords Clerk in the Office of the Clerk of the City of London. 8vo., 10*s.* 6*d.* each.

Smith.—CARTHAGE AND THE C/ GINIANS. By R. BOSWORTH : M.A., With Maps, Plans, &c 8vo., 3*s.* 6*d.*

Stephens.—A HISTORY OF THE F REVOLUTION. By H. MORSE STE 8vo. Vols. I. and II., 18*s.* each.

Stubbs.—HISTORY OF THE UNIV OF DUBLIN, from its Foundation End of the Eighteenth Century. W. STUBBS. 8vo., 12*s.* 6*d.*

Sutherland.—THE HISTO AUSTRALIA AND NEW ZEALAN 1606-1890. By ALEXANDER S LAND, M.A., and GEORGE S LAND, M.A. Crown 8vo., 2*s.* 6

Taylor.—A STUDENT'S MANU THE HISTORY OF INDIA. By (MEADOWS TAYLOR, C.S.I., &c 8vo., 7*s.* 6*d.*

Todd.—PARLIAMENTARY GOVER IN THE BRITISH COLONIES. By AI TODD, LL.D. 8vo., 30*s.* net.

LONGMANS & CO.'S STANDARD AND GENERAL WORKS.   5

History, Politics, Polity, Political Memoirs, &c.—*continued*.

Wakeman and Hassall.—ESSAYS INTRODUCTORY TO THE STUDY OF ENGLISH CONSTITUTIONAL HISTORY. By Resident Members of the University of Oxford. Edited by HENRY OFFLEY WAKEMAN, M.A., and ARTHUR HASSALL, M.A. Crown 8vo., 6*s*.

Walpole.—HISTORY OF ENGLAND FROM THE CONCLUSION OF THE GREAT WAR IN 1815 TO 1858. By SPENCER WALPOLE. 6 vols. Crown 8vo., 6*s*. each.

Wood-Martin.—PAGAN IRELAND: an Archæological Sketch. A Handbook of Irish Pre-Christian Antiquities. By W. G. WOOD-MARTIN, M.R.I.A. With 512 Illustrations. Crown 8vo., 15*s*.

Wylie.—HISTORY OF ENGLAND UNDER HENRY IV. By JAMES HAMILTON WYLIE, M.A., one of H.M. Inspectors of Schools. 4 vols. Crown 8vo. VoL I., 1399-1404, 10*s*. 6*d*. Vol. II. 15*s*. Vol. III. 15*s*. Vol. IV. 21*s*.

Biography, Personal Memoirs, &c.

Armstrong.—THE LIFE AND LETTERS OF EDMUND J. ARMSTRONG. Edited by G. F. SAVAGE ARMSTRONG. Fcp. 8vo., 7*s*. 6*d*.

Bacon.—THE LETTERS AND LIFE OF FRANCIS BACON, INCLUDING ALL HIS OCCASIONAL WORKS. Edited by JAMES SPEDDING. 7 vols. 8vo., £4 4*s*.

Bagehot. — BIOGRAPHICAL STUDIES. By WALTER BAGEHOT. Cr. 8vo., 3*s*. 6*d*.

Blackwell.—PIONEER WORK IN OPENING THE MEDICAL PROFESSION TO WOMEN: Autobiographical Sketches. By Dr. ELIZABETH BLACKWELL. Cr. 8vo., 6*s*.

Buss.—FRANCES MARY BUSS AND HER WORK FOR EDUCATION. By ANNIE E. RIDLEY. With 5 Portraits and 4 Illustrations. Crown 8vo., 7*s*. 6*d*.

Carlyle.—THOMAS CARLYLE: a History of his Life. By JAMES ANTHONY FROUDE. 1795-1835. 2 vols. Crown 8vo., 7*s*. 1834-1881. 2 vols. Crown 8vo., 7*s*.

Digby.—THE LIFE OF SIR KENELM DIGBY, *by one of his Descendants*, the Author of 'The Life of a Conspirator,' 'A Life of Archbishop Laud,' etc. With 7 Illustrations. 8vo., 16*s*.

Duncan.—ADMIRAL DUNCAN. By the EARL OF CAMPERDOWN. With 3 Portraits. 8vo., 16*s*.

Erasmus.—LIFE AND LETTERS OF ERASMUS. By JAMES ANTHONY FROUDE. Crown 8vo., 6*s*.

FALKLANDS. By the Author of 'The Life of Sir Kenelm Digby,' 'The Life of a Prig,' etc. With Portraits and other Illustrations. 8vo., 10*s*. 6*d*.

Faraday. — FARADAY AS A DISCOVERER. By JOHN TYNDALL. Cr. 8vo., 3*s*. 6*d*.

FOREIGN COURTS AND FOREIGN HOMES. By A. M. F. Crown 8vo., 7*s*. 6*d*.

Fox.—THE EARLY HISTORY OF CHARLES JAMES FOX. By the Right Hon. Sir G. O. TREVELYAN, Bart.
Library Edition. 8vo., 18*s*.
Cabinet Edition. Crown 8vo., 6*s*.

Halifax.—THE LIFE AND LETTERS OF SIR GEORGE SAVILE, BARONET, FIRST MARQUIS OF HALIFAX. With a New Edition of his Works, now for the first time collected and revised. By H. C. FOXCROFT. With 2 Portraits. 2 vols. 8vo., 36*s*.

Hamilton.—LIFE OF SIR WILLIAM HAMILTON. By R. P. GRAVES. 8vo. 3 vols. 15*s*. each. ADDENDUM. 8vo., 6*d*.

Havelock.—MEMOIRS OF SIR HENRY HAVELOCK, K.C.B. By JOHN CLARK MARSHMAN. Crown 8vo., 3*s*. 6*d*.

Haweis.—MY MUSICAL LIFE. By the Rev. H. R. HAWEIS. With Portrait of Richard Wagner and 3 Illustrations. Crown 8vo., 7*s*. 6*d*.

Holroyd.—THE GIRLHOOD OF MARIA JOSEPHA HOLROYD (Lady Stanley of Alderly). Recorded in Letters of a Hundred Years Ago, from 1776-1796. Edited by J. H. ADEANE. With 6 Portraits. 8vo., 18*s*.

Jackson.—STONEWALL JACKSON AND THE AMERICAN CIVIL WAR. By Lieut.-Col. G. F. R. HENDERSON, York and Lancaster Regiment. With 2 Portraits and 33 Maps and Plans. 2 vols. 8vo., 42*s*.

Biography, Personal Memoirs, &c.—continued.

Lejeune.—MEMOIRS OF BARON LE-JEUNE, Aide-de-Camp to Marshals Berthier, Davout, and Oudinot. Translated. 2 vols. 8vo., 24s.

Luther.—LIFE OF LUTHER. By JULIUS KÖSTLIN. With Illustrations from Authentic Sources. Translated from the German. Crown 8vo., 3s. 6d.

Macaulay.—THE LIFE AND LETTERS OF LORD MACAULAY. By the Right Hon. Sir G. O. TREVELYAN, Bart., M.P.
Popular Edit. 1 vol. Cr. 8vo., 2s. 6d.
Student's Edition. 1 vol. Cr. 8vo., 6s.
Cabinet Edition. 2 vols. Post 8vo., 12s.
Library Edition. 2 vols. 8vo., 36s.
'Edinburgh Edition.' 2 vols. 8vo., 6s. each.

Marbot.—THE MEMOIRS OF THE BARON DE MARBOT. Translated from the French. 2 vols. Crown 8vo., 7s.

Max Müller.—AULD LANG SYNE. By the Right Hon. Professor F. MAX MÜLLER. With Portrait. 8vo., 10s. 6d.

Meade. — GENERAL SIR RICHARD MEADE AND THE FEUDATORY STATES OF CENTRAL AND SOUTHERN INDIA : a Record of Forty-three Years' Service as Soldier, Political Officer and Administrator. By THOMAS HENRY THORNTON, C.S.I., D.C.L. With Portrait, Map and 16 Illustrations. 8vo., 10s. 6d. net.

Nansen.—FRIDTJOF NANSEN, 1861-1893. By W. C. BRÖGGER and NORDAHL ROLFSEN. Translated by WILLIAM ARCHER. With 8 Plates, 48 Illustrations in the Text, and 3 Maps. 8vo., 12s. 6d.

Newdegate.— THE CHEVERELS OF CHEVEREL MANOR. By Lady NEWDIGATE-NEWDEGATE, Author of 'Gossip from a Muniment Room'. With 6 Illustrations from Family Portraits. 8vo., 10s. 6d.

Place.—THE LIFE OF FRANCIS PLACE. By GRAHAM WALLAS. 8vo., 12s.

Rawlinson.—A MEMOIR OF MAJOR-GENERAL SIR HENRY CRESWICKE RAWLINSON, Bart., K.C.B. By GEO. RAWLINSON, M.A., F.R.G.S., Canon of Canterbury. With an Introduction by Field-Marshal LORD ROBERTS of Kandahar, V.C. With Map, 3 Portraits and an Illustration. 8vo., 16s.

Reeve.—MEMOIRS OF THE LIFE AND CORRESPONDENCE OF HENRY REEVE, C. B., D.C.L., late Editor of the 'Edinburgh Review' and Registrar of the Privy Council. By J. KNOX LAUGHTON, M.A. 2 vols. 8vo.

Romanes.—THE LIFE AND LETTERS OF GEORGE JOHN ROMANES, M.A., LL.D., F.R.S. Written and Edited by his Wife. With Portrait and 2 Illustrations. Cr. 8vo., 6s.

Seebohm.—THE OXFORD REFORMERS —JOHN COLET, ERASMUS AND THOMAS MORE : a History of their Fellow-Work. By FREDERIC SEEBOHM. 8vo., 14s.

Shakespeare.—OUTLINES OF THE LIFE OF SHAKESPEARE. By J. O. HALLIWELL-PHILLIPPS. With Illustrations and Facsimiles. 2 vols. Royal 8vo., £1 1s.

Shakespeare's TRUE LIFE. By JAS. WALTER. With 500 Illustrations by GERALD E. MOIRA. Imp. 8vo., 21s.

Verney.—MEMOIRS OF THE VERNEY FAMILY.
Vols. I. and II. DURING THE CIVIL WAR. By FRANCES PARTHENOPE VERNEY. With 38 Portraits, Woodcuts and Facsimile. Royal 8vo., 42s.
Vol. III. DURING THE COMMONWEALTH. 1650-1660 By MARGARET M. VERNEY. With 10 Portraits, &c. Royal 8vo., 21s.

Wellington.—LIFE OF THE DUKE OF WELLINGTON. By the Rev. G. R. GLEIG, M.A. Crown 8vo., 3s. 6d.

Wills.—W. G. WILLS, DRAMATIST AND PAINTER. By FREEMAN WILLS. With Photogravure Portrait 8vo., 10s. 6d.

Travel and Adventure, the Colonies, &c.

Arnold.—SEAS AND LANDS. By Sir EDWIN ARNOLD. With 71 Illustrations. Cr. 8vo., 3s. 6d.

Baker (Sir S. W.).
EIGHT YEARS IN CEYLON. With 6 Illustrations. Crown 8vo., 3s. 6d.
THE RIFLE AND THE HOUND IN CEYLON. With 6 Illustrations. Cr. 8vo.,

Ball.—THE ALPINE GUIDE. By the late JOHN BALL, F.R.S., &c., President of the Alpine Club. A New Edition, Reconstructed and Revised on behalf of the Alpine Club, by W. A. B. COOLIDGE.
Vol. I. THE WESTERN ALPS. The Alpine Region, South of the Rhone Valley, from the Col de Tenda to the Simplon Pass. With 9 New and

Travel and Adventure, the Colonies, &c.—*continued.*

Bent.—THE RUINED CITIES OF MASHONALAND: being a Record of Excavation and Exploration in 1891. By J. THEODORE BENT. With 117 Illustrations. Crown 8vo., 3s. 6d.

Brassey.—VOYAGES AND TRAVELS OF LORD BRASSEY, K.C.B., D.C.L., 1862-1894. Arranged and Edited by Captain S. EARDLEY-WILMOT. 2 vols. Cr. 8vo., 10s.

Brassey (The late LADY).

A VOYAGE IN THE 'SUNBEAM'; OUR HOME ON THE OCEAN FOR ELEVEN MONTHS.
Cabinet Edition. With Map and 66 Illustrations. Crown 8vo., 7s. 6d.
Silver Library Edition. With 66 Illustrations. Crown 8vo., 3s. 6d.
Popular Edition. With 60 Illustrations. 4to., 6d. sewed, 1s. cloth.
School Edition. With 37 Illustrations. Fcp., 2s. cloth, or 3s. white parchment.

SUNSHINE AND STORM IN THE EAST.
Cabinet Edition. With 2 Maps and 114 Illustrations. Crown 8vo., 7s. 6d.
Popular Edition. With 103 Illustrations. 4to., 6d. sewed, 1s. cloth.

IN THE TRADES, THE TROPICS, AND THE 'ROARING FORTIES'.
Cabinet Edition. With Map and 220 Illustrations. Crown 8vo., 7s. 6d.
Popular Edition. With 183 Illustrations. 4to., 6d. sewed, 1s. cloth.

THREE VOYAGES IN THE 'SUNBEAM'. Popular Edition. With 346 Illustrations. 4to., 2s. 6d.

Browning.—A GIRL'S WANDERINGS IN HUNGARY. By H. ELLEN BROWNING. With Map and 20 Illustrations. Crown 8vo., 3s. 6d.

Churchill.—THE STORY OF THE MALAKAND FIELD FORCE. By Lieut. WINSTON L. SPENCER CHURCHILL. With Maps and Plans. Cr. 8vo., 7s. 6d.

Crawford. — SOUTH AMERICAN SKETCHES. By ROBERT CRAWFORD,

Froude (JAMES A.).
OCEANA: or England and her Colonies. With 9 Illustrations. Crown 8vo., 3s. 6d.
THE ENGLISH IN THE WEST INDIES: or the Bow of Ulysses. With 9 Illustrations. Cr. 8vo., 2s. bds., 2s. 6d. cl.

Howitt.—VISITS TO REMARKABLE PLACES, Old Halls, Battle-Fields, Scenes illustrative of Striking Passages in English History and Poetry. By WILLIAM HOWITT. With 80 Illustrations. Crown 8vo., 3s. 6d.

Knight (E. F.).
THE CRUISE OF THE 'ALERTE': the Narrative of a Search for Treasure on the Desert Island of Trinidad. With 2 Maps and 23 Illustrations. Crown 8vo., 3s. 6d.
WHERE THREE EMPIRES MEET: a Narrative of Recent Travel in Kashmir, Western Tibet, Baltistan, Ladak, Gilgit, and the adjoining Countries. With a Map and 54 Illustrations. Cr. 8vo., 3s. 6d.
THE 'FALCON' ON THE BALTIC: a Voyage from London to Copenhagen in a Three-Tonner. With 10 Full-page Illustrations. Cr. 8vo., 3s. 6d.

Lees and Clutterbuck.—B. C. 1887: A RAMBLE IN BRITISH COLUMBIA. By J. A. LEES and W. J. CLUTTERBUCK. With Map and 75 Illustrations. Cr. 8vo., 3s. 6d.

Max Müller.—LETTERS FROM CONSTANTINOPLE. By Mrs. MAX MÜLLER. With 12 Views of Constantinople and the neighbourhood. Crown 8vo., 6s.

Nansen (FRIDTJOF).
THE FIRST CROSSING OF GREENLAND. With numerous Illustrations and a Map. Crown 8vo., 3s. 6d.
ESKIMO LIFE. With 31 Illustrations. 8vo., 16s.

Oliver.—CRAGS AND CRATERS: Rambles in the Island of Réunion. By WILLIAM DUDLEY OLIVER, M.A. With 27 Illustrations and a Map. Cr.

Travel and Adventure, the Colonies, &c.—*continued*.

Smith.—CLIMBING IN THE BRITISH ISLES. By W. P. HASKETT SMITH. With Illustrations by ELLIS CARR, and Numerous Plans.

Part I. ENGLAND. 16mo., 3s. 6d.

Part II. WALES AND IRELAND. 16mo., 3s. 6d.

Stephen.—THE PLAYGROUND OF EUROPE. By LESLIE STEPHEN. New Edition, with Additions and 4 Illustrations. Crown 8vo., 6s. net.

THREE IN NORWAY. By Two of Them. With a Map and 59 Illustrations. Cr. 8vo., 2s. boards, 2s. 6d. cloth

Tyndall.—THE GLACIERS OF THE ALPS: being a Narrative of Excursions and Ascents. An Account of the Origin and Phenomena of Glaciers, and an Exposition of the Physical Principles to which they are related. By JOHN TYNDALL F.R.S. With 61 Illustrations. Crown 8vo., 6s. 6d. net.

Vivian.—SERVIA: the Poor Man's Paradise. By HERBERT VIVIAN, M.. 8vo., 15s.

Sport and Pastime.

THE BADMINTON LIBRARY.

Edited by HIS GRACE THE DUKE OF BEAUFORT, K.G., and

A. E. T. WATSON.

Complete in 28 Volumes. Crown 8vo., Price 10s. 6d. each Volume, Cloth.

*** *The Volumes are also issued half-bound in Leather, with gilt top. The price c. be had from all Booksellers.*

ARCHERY. By C. J. LONGMAN and Col. H. WALROND. With Contributions by Miss LEGH, Viscount DILLON, &c. With 2 Maps, 23 Plates, and 172 Illustrations in the Text. Crown 8vo., 10s. 6d.

ATHLETICS. By MONTAGUE SHEARMAN. With 6 Plates and 52 Illustrations in the Text. Crown 8vo., 10s. 6d.

BIG GAME SHOOTING. By CLIVE PHILLIPPS-WOLLEY.

Vol. I. AFRICA AND AMERICA. With Contributions by Sir SAMUEL W. BAKER, W. C. OSWELL, F. C. SELOUS, &c. With 20 Plates and 57 Illustrations in the Text. Crown 8vo., 10s. 6d.

Vol. II. EUROPE, ASIA, AND THE ARCTIC REGIONS. With Contributions by Lieut.-Colonel R. HEBER PERCY, Major ALGERNON C. HEBER PERCY, &c. With 17 Plates and 56 Illustrations in the Text. Crown 8vo., 10s. 6d.

BILLIARDS. By Major W. BROADFOOT, R.E. With Contributions by A.] BOYD, SYDENHAM DIXON, W. J FORD, &c. With 11 Plates, 19 Illustrations in the Text, and numerous Diagrams. Crown 8vo., 10s. 6d.

COURSING AND FALCONRY.] HARDING COX and the Hon. GERAI LASCELLES. With 20 Plates and 56 Illustrations in the Text. Crov 8vo., 10s. 6d.

CRICKET. By A. G. STEEL, and t Hon. R. H. LYTTELTON. With Co tributions by ANDREW LANG, W. (GRACE, F. GALE, &c. With 12 Plat and 53 Illustrations in the Text. Crov 8vo., 10s. 6d.

CYCLING. By the EARL OF ALB MARLE, and G. LACY HILLIER. Wi 19 Plates and 44 Illustrations in t Text. Crown 8vo., 10s. 6d.

Sport and Pastime —*continued.*

THE BADMINTON LIBRARY—*continued.*

'ANCING. By Mrs. LILLY GROVE, F.R.G.S. With Contributions by Miss MIDDLETON, The Honourable Mrs. ARMYTAGE, &c. With Musical Examples, and 38 Full-page Plates and 93 Illustrations in the Text. Crown 8vo., 10s. 6d.

RIVING. By His Grace the DUKE OF BEAUFORT, K.G. With Contributions by other Authorities. With 12 Plates and 54 Illustrations in the Text. Crown 8vo., 10s. 6d.

ENCING, BOXING, AND WRESTLING. By WALTER H. POLLOCK, F. C. GROVE, C. PREVOST, E. B. MITCHELL, and WALTER ARMSTRONG. With 18 Plates and 24 Illustrations in the Text. Crown 8vo., 10s. 6d.

ISHING. By H. CHOLMONDELEY-PENNELL.

Vol. I. SALMON AND TROUT. With Contributions by H. R. FRANCIS, Major JOHN P. TRAHERNE, &c. With 9 Plates and numerous Illustrations of Tackle, &c. Crown 8vo., 10s. 6d.

Vol. II. PIKE AND OTHER COARSE FISH. With Contributions by the MARQUIS OF EXETER, WILLIAM SENIOR, G. CHRISTOPHER DAVIES, &c. With 7 Plates and numerous Illustrations of Tackle, &c. Crown 8vo., 10s. 6d.

OLF. By HORACE G. HUTCHINSON. With Contributions by the Rt. Hon. A. J. BALFOUR, M.P., Sir WALTER SIMPSON, Bart., ANDREW LANG, &c. With 32 Plates and 57 Illustrations in the Text. Cr. 8vo., 10s. 6d.

HUNTING. By His Grace the DUKE OF BEAUFORT K.G., and MOWBRAY MORRIS. With Contributions by the EARL OF SUFFOLK AND BERKSHIRE, Rev. E. W. L. DAVIES, G. H. LONGMAN, &c. With 5 Plates and 54 Illustrations in the Text. Crown 8vo., 10s. 6d.

MOUNTAINEERING. By C. T. DENT. With Contributions by Sir W. M. CONWAY, D. W. FRESHFIELD, C. E. MATHEWS, &c. With 13 Plates and 95 Illustrations in the Text. Crown 8vo., 10s. 6d.

POETRY OF SPORT (THE).—Selected by HEDLEY PEEK. With a Chapter on Classical Allusions to Sport by ANDREW LANG, and a Special Preface to the Badminton Library by A. E. T. WATSON. With 32 Plates and 74 Illustrations in the Text. Crown 8vo., 10s. 6d.

RACING AND STEEPLE-CHASING. By the EARL OF SUFFOLK AND BERKSHIRE, W. G. CRAVEN, the HON. F. LAWLEY, ARTHUR COVENTRY, and ALFRED E. T. WATSON. With Frontispiece and 56 Illustrations in the Text. Crown 8vo., 10s. 6d.

RIDING AND POLO. By Captain ROBERT WEIR, the DUKE OF BEAUFORT, the EARL OF SUFFOLK AND BERKSHIRE, the EARL OF ONSLOW, &c. With 18 Plates and 41 Illustrations in the Text. Crown 8vo., 10s. 6d.

ROWING. By R. P. P. ROWE and C. M. PITMAN. With Contributions by C. P. SEROCOLD, F. C. BEGG, and S. LE B. SMITH. PUNTING. By P. W. SQUIRE. With 20 Plates and 55 Illustrations in the Text; also 4 Maps of the Oxford and Cambridge Boat-race and Metropolitan Championship Course, Henley Course, Oxford Course, and Cambridge Course. Crown 8vo., 10s. 6d.

SEA FISHING. By JOHN BICKERDYKE, Sir H. W. GORE-BOOTH, ALFRED C. HARMSWORTH, and W. SENIOR. With 22 Full-page Plates and 175 Illustrations in the Text. Crown 8vo., 10s. 6d.

Sport and Pastime—*continued*.
THE BADMINTON LIBRARY—*continued*.

SHOOTING.

Vol. I. FIELD AND COVERT. By LORD WALSINGHAM and Sir RALPH PAYNE-GALLWEY, Bart. With Contributions by the Hon. GERALD LASCELLES and A. J. STUART-WORTLEY. With 11 Plates and 94 Illustrations in the Text. Crown 8vo., 10s. 6d.

Vol. II. MOOR AND MARSH. By LORD WALSINGHAM and Sir RALPH PAYNE-GALLWEY, Bart. With Contributions by LORD LOVAT and LORD CHARLES LENNOX KERR. With 8 Plates and 57 Illustrations in the Text. Crown 8vo., 10s. 6d.

SKATING, CURLING, TOBOGGANING. By J. M. HEATHCOTE, C. G. TEBBUTT, T. MAXWELL WITHAM, Rev. JOHN KERR, ORMOND HAKE, HENRY A. BUCK, &c. With 12 Plates and 272 Illustrations in the Text. Cr. 8vo., 10s. 6d.

SWIMMING. By ARCHIBALD SINCLAIR and WILLIAM HENRY, Hon. Secs. of the Life-Saving Society. With 13 Plates and 106 Illustrations in the Text. Cr. 8vo., 10s. 6d.

TENNIS, LAWN TENNIS, RACQUETS, AND FIVES. By J. M. and C. G. HEATHCOTE, E. O. PLEYDELL-BOUVERIE, and A. C. AINGER. With Contributions by the Hon. A. LYTTELTON, W. C. MARSHALL, Miss L. DOD, &c. With 12 Plates and 67 Illustrations in the Text. Crown 8vo., 10s. 6d.

YACHTING.

Vol. I. CRUISING, CONSTRUCTION OF YACHTS, YACHT RACING RULES, FITTING-OUT, &c. By Sir EDWARD SULLIVAN, Bart., THE EARL OF PEMBROKE, LORD BRASSEY, K.C.B., C. E. SETH-SMITH, C.B., G. L. WATSON, R. T. PRITCHETT, E. F. KNIGHT, &c. With 21 Plates and 93 Illustrations in the Text, and from Photographs. Crown 8vo., 10s. 6d.

Vol. II. YACHT CLUBS, YACHTING IN AMERICA AND THE COLONIES, YACHT RACING, &c. By R. T. PRITCHETT, THE MARQUIS OF DUFFERIN AND AVA, K.P., THE EARL OF ONSLOW, JAMES MCFERRAN, &c. With 35 Plates and 160 Illustrations in the Text. Crown 8vo., 10s. 6d.

FUR, FEATHER AND FIN SERIES.
Edited by A. E. T. WATSON.

Crown 8vo., price 5s. each Volume.

* *The Volumes are also issued half-bound in Leather, with gilt top. The price can be had from all Booksellers.*

THE PARTRIDGE. *Natural History*, by the Rev. H. A. MACPHERSON; *Shooting*, by A. J. STUART-WORTLEY; *Cookery*, by GEORGE SAINTSBURY. With 11 Illustrations and various Diagrams in the Text. Crown 8vo., 5s.

THE GROUSE. *Natural History*, by the Rev. H. A. MACPHERSON; *Shooting*, by A. J. STUART-WORTLEY; *Cookery*, by GEORGE SAINTSBURY. With 13 Illustrations and various Diagrams in the Text. Crown 8vo., 5s.

THE PHEASANT. *Natural History*, by the Rev. H. A. MACPHERSON; *Shooting*, by A. J. STUART-WORTLEY; *Cookery*, by ALEXANDER INNES SHAND. With 10 Illustrations and various Diagrams. Crown 8vo., 5s.

THE HARE. *Natural History*, by the Rev. H. A. MACPHERSON; *Shooting*, by the Hon. GERALD LASCELLES; *Coursing*, by CHARLES RICHARDSON; *Hunting*, by J. S. GIBBONS and G. H. LONGMAN; *Cookery*, by Col. KENNEY HERBERT. With 9 Illustrations. Cr. 8vo., 5s.

Sport and Pastime—*continued*.

FUR, FEATHER AND FIN SERIES—*continued*.

RED DEER. *Natural History*, by the Rev. H. A. MACPHERSON; *Deer Stalking*, by CAMERON OF LOCHIEL. *Stag Hunting*, by Viscount EBRINGTON; *Cookery*, by ALEXANDER INNES SHAND. With 10 Illustrations. Crown 8vo., 5s.

THE RABBIT. By J. E. HARTING, &c. With Illustrations. [*In preparation.*

WILDFOWL. By the Hon. JOHN SCOTT MONTAGU. With Illustrations. [*In preparation.*

THE SALMON. By the Hon. A. E. GATHORNE-HARDY. With Chapters on the Law of Salmon-Fishing by CLAUD DOUGLAS PENNANT; Cookery, by ALEXANDER INNES SHAND. With 8 Illustrations. Crown 8vo., 5s.

THE TROUT. By the MARQUESS OF GRANBY. With Chapters on Breeding by Colonel F. H. CUSTANCE; Cookery, by ALEXANDER INNES SHAND. With 12 Illustrations. Crown 8vo., 5s.

André.—COLONEL BOGEY'S SKETCH-BOOK. Comprising an Eccentric Collection of Scribbles and Scratches found in disused Lockers and swept up in the Pavilion, together with sundry After-Dinner Sayings of the Colonel. By R. ANDRÉ, West Herts Golf Club. Oblong 4to., 2s. 6d.

BADMINTON MAGAZINE (THE) OF SPORTS AND PASTIMES. Edited by ALFRED E. T. WATSON ('Rapier'). With numerous Illustrations. Price 1s. Monthly. Vols. I.-VI., 6s. each.

DEAD SHOT (THE): or, Sportsman's Complete Guide. Being a Treatise on the Use of the Gun, with Rudimentary and Finishing Lessons on the Art of Shooting Game of all kinds. Also Game-driving, Wildfowl and Pigeon-shooting, Dog-breaking, etc. By MARKSMAN. With numerous Illustrations. Crown 8vo., 10s. 6d.

Ellis.—CHESS SPARKS; or, Short and Bright Games of Chess. Collected and Arranged by J. H. ELLIS, M.A. 8vo., 4s. 6d.

Folkard.—THE WILD-FOWLER: A Treatise on Fowling, Ancient and Modern; descriptive also of Decoys and Flight-ponds, Wild-fowl Shooting, Gunning-punts, Shooting-yachts, &c. Also Fowling in the Fens and in Foreign Countries, Rock-fowling, &c., &c., by H. C. FOLKARD. With 13 Engravings on Steel, and several Woodcuts. 8vo.,

Ford.—THE THEORY AND PRACTICE OF ARCHERY. BY HORACE FORD. New Edition, thoroughly Revised and Re-written by W. BUTT, M.A. With a Preface by C. J. LONGMAN, M.A. 8vo., 14s.

Francis.—A BOOK ON ANGLING: or, Treatise on the Art of Fishing in every Branch; including full Illustrated List of Salmon Flies. By FRANCIS FRANCIS. With Portrait and Coloured Plates. Crown 8vo., 15s.

Gibson.—TOBOGGANING ON CROOKED RUNS. By the Hon. HARRY GIBSON. With Contributions by F. DE B. STRICKLAND and 'LADY-TOBOGGANER'. With 40 Illustrations. Crown 8vo., 6s.

Graham.—COUNTRY PASTIMES FOR BOYS. By P. ANDERSON GRAHAM. With 252 Illustrations from Drawings and Photographs. Crown 8vo., 3s. 6d.

Lang.—ANGLING SKETCHES. By A. LANG. With 20 Illustrations. Crown 8vo., 3s. 6d.

Lillie.—CROQUET: its History, Rules, and Secrets. By ARTHUR LILLIE, Champion Grand National Croquet Club, 1872; Winner of the 'All-Comers' Championship,' Maidstone, 1896. With 4 Full-page Illustrations by LUCIEN DAVIS, 15 Illustrations in the Text, and 27 Diagrams. Crown 8vo., 6s.

Longman.—CHESS OPENINGS. By FREDERICK W. LONGMAN. Fcp. 8vo., 2s. 6d.

Madden.—THE DIARY OF MASTER WILLIAM SILENCE: A Study of Shakespeare and of Elizabethan Sport. By the Right Hon. D. H. MADDEN, Vice-Chancellor of the University of Dublin.

Sport and Pastime—*continued.*

Maskelyne.—SHARPS AND FLATS: a Complete Revelation of the Secrets of Cheating at Games of Chance and Skill. By JOHN NEVIL MASKELYNE, of the Egyptian Hall. With 62 Illustrations. Crown 8vo., 6s.

Park.—THE GAME OF GOLF. By WILLIAM PARK, Junr., Champion Golfer, 1887-89. With 17 Plates and 26 Illustrations in the Text. Crown 8vo., 7s. 6d.

Payne-Gallwey (Sir RALPH, Bart.).
LETTERS TO YOUNG SHOOTERS (First Series). On the Choice and Use of a Gun. With 41 Illustrations. Cr. 8vo., 7s. 6d.

LETTERS TO YOUNG SHOOTERS (Second Series). On the Production, Preservation, and Killing of Game. With Directions in Shooting Wood-Pigeons and Breaking-in Retrievers. With Portrait and 103 Illustrations. Crown 8vo., 12s. 6d.

LETTERS TO YOUNG SHOOTERS (Third Series). Comprising a Short Natural History of the Wildfowl that are Rare or Common to the British Islands, with Complete Directions in Shooting Wildfowl on the Coast and Inland. With 200 Illustrations. Cr. 8vo., 18s.

Pole.—THE THEORY OF THE MODERN SCIENTIFIC GAME OF WHIST. By WILLIAM POLE. Fcp. 8vo., 2s. 6d.

Proctor.—HOW TO PLAY WHIST: WITH THE LAWS AND ETIQUETTE OF WHIST. By RICHARD A. PROCTOR. Crown 8vo., 3s. 6d.

Ribblesdale.—THE QUEEN'S HOUNDS AND STAG-HUNTING RECOLLECTIONS. By LORD RIBBLESDALE, Master of the Buckhounds, 1892-95. With Introductory Chapter on the Hereditary Mastership by E. BURROWS. With 24 Plates and 35 Illustrations in the Text, including reproductions from Oil Paintings in the possession of Her Majesty the Queen at Windsor Castle and Cumberland Lodge, Original Drawings by G. D. GILES, and from Prints and Photographs. 8vo., 25s.

Ronalds.—THE FLY-FISHER'S ENTOMOLOGY. By ALFRED RONALDS. With 20 Coloured Plates. 8vo., 14s.

Thompson and Cannan. HAND-IN-HAND FIGURE SKATING. By NORCLIFFE G. THOMPSON and F. LAURA CANNAN, Members of the Skating Club. With an Introduction by Captain J. H. THOMSON, R.A. With Illustrations. 16mo., 6s.

Wilcocks. THE SEA FISHERMAN: Comprising the Chief Methods of Hook and Line Fishing in the British and other Seas, and Remarks on Nets, Boats, and Boating. By J. C. WILCOCKS. Illustrated. Crown 8vo., 6s.

Veterinary Medicine, &c.

Steel (JOHN HENRY).
A TREATISE ON THE DISEASES OF THE DOG. With 88 Illustrations. 8vo., 10s. 6d.
A TREATISE ON THE DISEASES OF THE OX. With 119 Illustrations. 8vo., 15s.
A TREATISE ON THE DISEASES OF THE SHEEP. With 100 Illustrations. 8vo., 12s.
OUTLINES OF EQUINE ANATOMY: a Manual for the use of Veterinary Students in the Dissecting Room. Crown 8vo., 7s. 6d.

Fitzwygram.—HORSES AND STABLES. By Major-General Sir F. FITZWYGRAM, Bart. With 56 pages of Illustrations. 8vo., 2s. 6d. net.

Schreiner. — THE ANGORA GOAT (published under the auspices of the South African Angora Goat Breeders' Association), and a Paper on the Ostrich (reprinted from the *Zoologist* for March, 1897). By S. C. CRONWRIGHT SCHRIENER. With 26 Illustrations. 8vo., 10s. 6d.

'**Stonehenge.**'—THE DOG IN HEALTH AND DISEASE. By 'STONEHENGE'. With 78 Wood Engravings. 8vo., 7s. 6d.

Youatt (WILLIAM).
THE HORSE. Revised and enlarged. By W. WATSON, M.R.C.V.S. With 52 Wood Engravings. 8vo., 7s. 6d.
THE DOG. Revised and enlarged. With 33 Wood Engravings. 8vo., 6s.

Mental, Moral, and Political Philosophy.
LOGIC, RHETORIC, PSYCHOLOGY, &c.

Abbott.—THE ELEMENTS OF LOGIC. By T. K. ABBOTT, B.D. 12mo., 3*s*.

Aristotle.
THE ETHICS: Greek Text, Illustrated with Essay and Notes. By Sir ALEXANDER GRANT, Bart. 2 vols. 8vo., 32*s*.
AN INTRODUCTION TO ARISTOTLE'S ETHICS. Books I.-IV. (Book X. c. vi.-ix. in an Appendix.) With a continuous Analysis and Notes. By the Rev. EDWARD MOORE, D.D. Cr. 8vo., 10*s*. 6*d*.

Bacon (FRANCIS).
COMPLETE WORKS. Edited by R. L. ELLIS, JAMES SPEDDING, and D. D. HEATH. 7 vols. 8vo., £3 13*s*. 6*d*.
LETTERS AND LIFE, including all his occasional Works. Edited by JAMES SPEDDING. 7 vols. 8vo., £4 4*s*.
THE ESSAYS: with Annotations. By RICHARD WHATELY, D.D. 8vo., 10*s*. 6*d*.
THE ESSAYS: Edited, with Notes. By F. STORR and C. H. GIBSON. Cr. 8vo., 3*s*. 6*d*.
THE ESSAYS. With Introduction, Notes, and Index. By E. A. ABBOTT, D.D. 2 vols. Fcp. 8vo., 6*s*. The Text and Index only, without Introduction and Notes, in One Volume. Fcp. 8vo., 2*s*. 6*d*.

Bain (ALEXANDER).
MENTAL SCIENCE. Crown 8vo., 6*s*. 6*d*.
MORAL SCIENCE. Crown 8vo., 4*s*. 6*d*.
The two works as above can be had in one volume, price 10*s*. 6*d*.
SENSES AND THE INTELLECT. 8vo., 15*s*.
EMOTIONS AND THE WILL. 8vo., 15*s*.
LOGIC, DEDUCTIVE AND INDUCTIVE. Part I., 4*s*. Part II., 6*s*. 6*d*.
PRACTICAL ESSAYS. Crown 8vo., 2*s*.

Bray.—THE PHILOSOPHY OF NECESSITY; or Law in Mind as in Matter. By CHARLES BRAY. Crown 8vo., 5*s*.

Crozier (JOHN BEATTIE).
HISTORY OF INTELLECTUAL DEVELOPMENT: on the Lines of Modern Evolution.
Vol. I. Greek and Hindoo Thought; Græco-Roman Paganism; Judaism; and Christianity down to the Closing of the Schools of Athens by Justinian, 529 A.D. 8vo., 14*s*.

Crozier (JOHN BEATTIE)—*continued.*
CIVILISATION AND PROGRESS; being the Outlines of a New System of Political, Religious and Social Philosophy. 8vo., 14*s*.

Davidson.—THE LOGIC OF DEFINITION, Explained and Applied. By WILLIAM L. DAVIDSON, M.A. Crown 8vo., 6*s*.

Green (THOMAS HILL). The Works of. Edited by R. L. NETTLESHIP.
Vols. I. and II. Philosophical Works 8vo., 16*s*. each.
Vol. III. Miscellanies. With Index to the three Volumes, and Memoir. 8vo., 21*s*.
LECTURES ON THE PRINCIPLES OF POLITICAL OBLIGATION. 8vo., 5*s*.

Hodgson (SHADWORTH H.).
TIME AND SPACE: a Metaphysical Essay. 8vo., 16*s*.
THE THEORY OF PRACTICE: an Ethical Inquiry. 2 vols. 8vo., 24*s*.
THE PHILOSOPHY OF REFLECTION. 2 vols. 8vo., 21*s*.
THE METAPHYSIC OF EXPERIENCE. 4 vols. I. General Analysis of Experience. II. Positive Science. III. Analysis of Conscious Action. IV. The Real Universe. 4 vols. 8vo., 36*s*. net.

Hume.—THE PHILOSOPHICAL WORKS OF DAVID HUME. Edited by T. H. GREEN and T. H. GROSE. 4 vols. 8vo., 56*s*. Or separately, Essays. 2 vols. 28*s*. Treatise of Human Nature. 2 vols. 28*s*.

James.—THE WILL TO BELIEVE, and other Essays in Popular Philosophy. By WILLIAM JAMES, M.D., LL.D., &c. Crown 8vo., 7*s*. 6*d*.

Justinian.—THE INSTITUTES OF JUSTINIAN: Latin Text, chiefly that of Huschke, with English Introduction, Translation, Notes, and Summary. By THOMAS C. SANDARS, M.A. 8vo., 18*s*.

Kant (IMMANUEL).
CRITIQUE OF PRACTICAL REASON, AND OTHER WORKS ON THE THEORY OF ETHICS. Translated by T. K. ABBOTT, B.D. With Memoir. 8vo., 12*s*. 6*d*.
FUNDAMENTAL PRINCIPLES OF THE METAPHYSIC OF ETHICS. Translated by T. K. ABBOTT, B.D. Crown 8vo., 3*s*.

14　*LONGMANS & CO.'S STANDARD AND GENERAL WORKS.*

Mental, Moral and Political Philosophy—*continued.*

Kant (IMMANUEL)—*continued.*
INTRODUCTION TO LOGIC, AND HIS ESSAY ON THE MISTAKEN SUBTILTY OF THE FOUR FIGURES. Translated by T. K. ABBOTT. 8vo., 6s.

Killick.—HANDBOOK TO MILL'S SYSTEM OF LOGIC. By Rev. A. H. KILLICK, M.A. Crown 8vo., 3s. 6d.

Ladd (GEORGE TRUMBULL).
OUTLINES OF DESCRIPTIVE PSYCHOLOGY: a Text-Book of Mental Science for Colleges and Normal Schools. 8vo., 12s.

PHILOSOPHY OF KNOWLEDGE: an Inquiry into the Nature, Limits and Validity of Human Cognitive Faculty. 8vo., 18s.

PHILOSOPHY OF MIND: an Essay on the Metaphysics of Psychology. 8vo., 16s.

ELEMENTS OF PHYSIOLOGICAL PSYCHOLOGY. 8vo., 21s.

OUTLINES OF PHYSIOLOGICAL PSYCHOLOGY. A Text-Book of Mental Science for Academies and Colleges. 8vo., 12s.

PRIMER OF PSYCHOLOGY. Crown 8vo., 5s. 6d.

Lutoslawski.—THE ORIGIN AND GROWTH OF PLATO'S LOGIC. By W. LUTOSLAWSKI. 8vo., 21s.

Max Müller (F.).
THE SCIENCE OF THOUGHT. 8vo., 21s.
THREE INTRODUCTORY LECTURES ON THE SCIENCE OF THOUGHT. 8vo., 2s. 6d. net.

Mill.—ANALYSIS OF THE PHENOMENA OF THE HUMAN MIND. By JAMES MILL. 2 vols. 8vo., 28s.

Mill (JOHN STUART).
A SYSTEM OF LOGIC. Cr. 8vo., 3s. 6d.
ON LIBERTY. Cr. 8vo., 1s. 4d.
CONSIDERATIONS ON REPRESENTATIVE GOVERNMENT. Crown 8vo., 2s.
UTILITARIANISM. 8vo., 2s. 6d.

Mill (JOHN STUART)—*continued.*
EXAMINATION OF SIR WI HAMILTON'S PHILOSOPHY. 8vc
NATURE, THE UTILITY OF REL AND THEISM. Three Essays. 8

Romanes.—MIND AND MOTION MONISM. By GEORGE JOHN ROM LL.D., F.R.S. Crown 8vo., 4

Stock (ST. GEORGE).
DEDUCTIVE LOGIC. Fcp. 8vo.,
LECTURES IN THE LYCEUM; or, totle's Ethics for English Re Edited by ST. GEORGE S Crown 8vo., 7s. 6d.

Sully (JAMES).
THE HUMAN MIND; a Text-bc Psychology. 2 vols. 8vo., 21s.
OUTLINES OF PSYCHOLOGY. 8vo., 9s.
THE TEACHER'S HANDBOOK OF CHOLOGY. Crown 8vo., 6s. 6d.
STUDIES OF CHILDHOOD. 8vo. 1
CHILDREN'S WAYS: being Sele from the Author's ' Studies of hood,' with some additional N With 25 Figures in the Text. 8vo., 4s. 6d.

Sutherland. — THE ORIGIN GROWTH OF THE MORAL INST By ALEXANDER SUTHERLAND, 2 vols. 8vo., 28s.

Swinburne.—PICTURE LOGIC: Attempt to Popularise the Scien Reasoning. By ALFRED JAMES BURNE, M.A. With 23 Woo Crown 8vo., 5s.

Weber.—HISTORY OF PHILOS By ALFRED WEBER, Professor University of Strasburg, Translat FRANK THILLY, Ph.D. 8vo., 16

Whately (ARCHBISHOP).
BACON'S ESSAYS. With Annota 8vo., 10s. 6d.
ELEMENTS OF LOGIC. Cr. 8vo.,
ELEMENTS OF RHETORIC. Cr. 4s. 6d.
LESSONS ON REASONING. Fcp. 1s. 6d.

Mental, Moral and Political Philosophy—*continued*.

ller (Dr EDWARD, Professor in the University of Berlin).

THE STOICS, EPICUREANS, AND SCEPTICS. Translated by the Rev. O. J. REICHEL, M.A. Crown 8vo., 15s.

OUTLINES OF THE HISTORY OF GREEK PHILOSOPHY. Translated by SARAH F. ALLEYNE and EVELYN ABBOTT. Crown 8vo., 10s. 6d.

Zeller (Dr EDWARD)—*continued*.

PLATO AND THE OLDER ACADEMY. Translated by SARAH F. ALLEYNE and ALFRED GOODWIN, B.A. Crown 8vo., 18s.

SOCRATES AND THE SOCRATIC SCHOOLS. Translated by the Rev. O. J. REICHEL, M A Crown 8vo., 10s. 6d.

ARISTOTLE AND THE EARLIER PERIPATETICS. Translated by B. F. C. COSTELLOE, M.A., and J. H. MUIRHEAD, M.A. 2 vols. Cr. 8vo., 24s.

MANUALS OF CATHOLIC PHILOSOPHY.
(Stonyhurst Series.)

MANUAL OF POLITICAL ECONOMY. By C. S. DEVAS, M.A. Cr. 8vo., 6s. 6d.

ST PRINCIPLES OF KNOWLEDGE. By OHN RICKABY, S.J. Crown 8vo., 5s.

NERAL METAPHYSICS. By JOHN RICKABY, S.J. Crown 8vo., 5s.

GIC. By RICHARD F. CLARKE, S J. Crown 8vo., 5s.

MORAL PHILOSOPHY (ETHICS AND NATURAL LAW). By JOSEPH RICKABY, S.J. Crown 8vo., 5s.

NATURAL THEOLOGY. By BERNARD BOEDDER, S.J. Crown 8vo., 6s. 6d.

PSYCHOLOGY. By MICHAEL MAHER, S.J. Crown 8vo., 6s. 6d.

History and Science of Language, &c.

vidson.—LEADING AND IMPORTANT ENGLISH WORDS: Explained and Exemplified. By WILLIAM L. DAVIDSON, M.A. Fcp. 8vo., 3s. 6d.

rrar.—LANGUAGE AND LANGUAGES. By F. W. FARRAR, D.D., F.R.S., Cr. vo., 6s.

aham.—ENGLISH SYNONYMS, Classed and Explained: with Practical Exercises. By G. F. GRAHAM. Fcap vo., 6s.

ax Müller (F.).

THE SCIENCE OF LANGUAGE, Founded on Lectures delivered at the Royal Institution in 1861 and 1863. 2 vols. Crown 8vo., 10s.

BIOGRAPHIES OF WORDS, AND THE HOME OF THE ARYAS. Crown 8vo., 5s.

Max Müller (F.)—*continued*.

THREE LECTURES ON THE SCIENCE OF LANGUAGE, AND ITS PLACE IN GENERAL EDUCATION, delivered at Oxford, 1889. Crown 8vo., 3s. net.

Roget. — THESAURUS OF ENGLISH WORDS AND PHRASES. Classified and Arranged so as to Facilitate the Expression of Ideas and assist in Literary Composition. By PETER MARK ROGET, M.D., F.R.S. Recomposed throughout, enlarged and improved, partly from the Author's Notes, and with a full Index, by the Author's Son, JOHN LEWIS ROGET. Crown 8vo., 10s. 6d.

Whately.—ENGLISH SYNONYMS. By E. JANE WHATELY. Fcap. 8vo., 3s.

Political Economy and Economics.

Ashley.—ENGLISH ECONOMIC HISTORY AND THEORY. By W. J. ASHLEY. Cr. 8vo., Part I., 5s. Part II., 10s. 6d.

Bagehot.—ECONOMIC STUDIES. By WALTER BAGEHOT. Cr. 8vo., 3s. 6d.

Brassey.—PAPERS AND ADDRESSES ON WORK AND WAGES. By Lord BRASSEY. Crown 8vo., 5s.

Channing.—THE TRUTH ABOUT AGRICULTURAL DEPRESSION: An Economic Study of the Evidence of the Royal Commission. By FRANCIS ALLSTON CHANNING, M.P., one of the Commission. Crown 8vo., 6s.

Devas.—A MANUAL OF POLITICAL ECONOMY. By C. S. DEVAS, M.A. Crown 8vo., 6s. 6d.

Dowell.—A HISTORY OF TAXATION AND TAXES IN ENGLAND, from the Earliest Times to the Year 1885. By STEPHEN DOWELL (4 vols. 8vo.). Vols. I. and II. The History of Taxation, 21s. Vols. III. and IV. The History of Taxes, 21s.

Jordan.—THE STANDARD OF VALUE. By WILLIAM LEIGHTON JORDAN. Crown 8vo., 6s.

Macleod (HENRY DUNNING).
BIMETALISM. 8vo., 5s. net.
THE ELEMENTS OF BANKING. Crown 8vo., 3s. 6d.
THE THEORY AND PRACTICE OF BANKING. Vol. I. 8vo., 12s. Vol. II. 14s.

Macleod (HENRY DUNNING)—*cont.*
THE THEORY OF CREDIT. 8vo. Vol. I. 10s. net. Vol. II., Part I., 10s. net. Vol. II. Part II., 10s. net.
INDIAN CURRENCY. 8vo., 2s. 6d. net.

Mill.—POLITICAL ECONOMY. By JOHN STUART MILL.
Popular Edition. Crown 8vo., 3s 6d.
Library Edition. 2 vols. 8vo., 30s.

Mulhall.—INDUSTRIES AND WEALTH OF NATIONS. By MICHAEL G. MULHALL, F.S.S. With 32 Full-page Diagrams. Crown 8vo., 8s. 6d.

Soderini.—SOCIALISM AND CATHOLICISM. From the Italian of Count EDWARD SODERINI. By RICHARD JENERY-SHEE. With a Preface by Cardinal VAUGHAN. Crown 8vo., 6s.

Symes.—POLITICAL ECONOMY: a Short Text-book of Political Economy. With a Supplementary Chapter on Socialism. By J. E. SYMES, M.A. Crown 8vo., 2s. 6d.

Toynbee.—LECTURES ON THE INDUSTRIAL REVOLUTION OF THE 18th CENTURY IN ENGLAND. By ARNOLD TOYNBEE. With a Memoir of the Author by BENJAMIN JOWETT, D.D. 8vo., 10s. 6d.

Webb (SIDNEY and BEATRICE).
THE HISTORY OF TRADE UNIONISM. With Map and full Bibliography of the Subject. 8vo., 18s.
INDUSTRIAL DEMOCRACY: a Study in Trade Unionism. 2 vols. 8vo., 25s. net.
PROBLEMS OF MODERN INDUSTRY. 8vo., 7s. 6d.

STUDIES IN ECONOMICS AND POLITICAL SCIENCE.

Issued under the auspices of the London School of Economics and Political Science.

THE HISTORY OF LOCAL RATES IN ENGLAND: Five Lectures. By EDWIN CANNAN, M.A. Crown 8vo., 2s. 6d.

GERMAN SOCIAL DEMOCRACY. By BERTRAND RUSSELL, B.A. With an Appendix on Social Democracy and the Woman Question in Germany by ALYS RUSSELL, B.A. Cr. 8vo., 3s. 6d.

SELECT DOCUMENTS ILLUSTRATING THE HISTORY OF TRADE UNIONISM.
1. The Tailoring Trade. Edited by W. F. GALTON. With a Preface by SIDNEY WEBB, LL.B. Crown 8vo., 5s.

LOCAL VARIATIONS OF RATES AND WAGES. By F. W. LAURENCE, B.A., Fellow of Trinity College, Cambridge.
[*In the press.*

DEPLOIGE'S REFERENDUM EN SUISSE. Translated with Introduction and Notes, by C. P. TREVELYAN, M.A.
[*In preparation.*

SELECT DOCUMENTS ILLUSTRATING THE STATE REGULATION OF WAGES. Edited, with Introduction and Notes, by W. A. S. HEWINS, M.A.
[*In preparation.*

HUNGARIAN GILD RECORDS. Edited by Dr. JULIUS MANDELLO, of Budapest.
[*In preparation.*

THE RELATIONS BETWEEN ENGLAND AND THE HANSEATIC LEAGUE. By Miss E. A. MACARTHUR. [*In preparation.*

THE ECONOMIC POLICY OF COLBERT. By A. J. SARGENT, B.A. [*In preparation.*

Evolution, Anthropology, &c.

Clodd (EDWARD).

THE STORY OF CREATION : a Plain Account of Evolution. With 77 Illustrations. Crown 8vo., 3s. 6d.

A PRIMER OF EVOLUTION: being a Popular Abridged Edition of 'The Story of Creation'. With Illustrations. Fcp. 8vo., 1s. 6d.

Lang.—CUSTOM AND MYTH: Studies of Early Usage and Belief. By ANDREW LANG. With 15 Illustrations. Crown 8vo., 3s. 6d.

Lubbock.—THE ORIGIN OF CIVILISATION and the Primitive Condition of Man. By Sir J. LUBBOCK, Bart., M.P. With 5 Plates and 20 Illustrations in the Text. 8vo., 18s.

Romanes (GEORGE JOHN).

DARWIN, AND AFTER DARWIN: an Exposition of the Darwinian Theory, and a Discussion on Post-Darwinian Questions.
Part I THE DARWINIAN THEORY. With Portrait of Darwin and 125 Illustrations. Crown 8vo., 10s. 6d.
Part II. POST-DARWINIAN QUESTIONS: Heredity and Utility. With Portrait of the Author and 5 Illustrations. Cr. 8vo., 10s. 6d.
Part III. POST-DARWINIAN QUESTIONS: Isolation and Physiological Selection. Crown 8vo., 5s.

AN EXAMINATION OF WEISMANNISM. Crown 8vo., 6s.

ESSAYS. Edited by C. LLOYD MORGAN, Principal of University College, Bristol. Crown 8vo., 6s.

Classical Literature, Translations, &c.

Abbott.—HELLENICA. A Collection of Essays on Greek Poetry, Philosophy, History, and Religion. Edited by EVELYN ABBOTT, M.A., LL.D. Crown 8vo., 7s. 6d.

Æschylus.—EUMENIDES OF ÆSCHYLUS. With Metrical English Translation. By J. F. DAVIES. 8vo., 7s.

Aristophanes.—THE ACHARNIANS OF ARISTOPHANES, translated into English Verse. By R. Y. TYRRELL. Cr. 8vo., 1s.

Aristotle.—YOUTH AND OLD AGE, LIFE AND DEATH, AND RESPIRATION. Translated, with Introduction and Notes, by W. OGLE, M.A., M.D., F.R.C.P. 8vo., 7s. 6d.

Becker (W. A.). Translated by the Rev. F. Metcalfe, B.D.

GALLUS: or, Roman Scenes in the Time of Augustus. With 26 Illustrations. Post 8vo., 3s. 6d.

CHARICLES: or, Illustrations of the Private Life of the Ancient Greeks. With 26 Illustrations. Post 8vo., 3s. 6d.

Butler.— THE AUTHORESS OF THE ODYSSEY, WHERE AND WHEN SHE WROTE, WHO SHE WAS, THE USE SHE MADE OF THE ILIAD AND HOW THE POEM GREW UNDER HER HANDS. By SAMUEL BUTLER, Author of 'Erewhon,' &c. With 14 Illustrations and 4 Maps. 8vo., 10s. 6d.

Cicero.—CICERO'S CORRESPONDENCE. By R. Y. TYRRELL. Vols. I., II., III. 8vo., each 12s. Vol. IV., 15s. Vol. V., 14s.

Homer. — THE ILIAD OF HOMER. Freely rendered into English Prose for the use of those that cannot read the original. By SAMUEL BUTLER, Author of 'Erewhon,' 'Life and Habit,' etc. Crown 8vo., 7s. 6d.

Horace.—THE WORKS OF HORACE, rendered into English Prose. With Life, Introduction, and Notes. By WILLIAM COUTTS, M.A. Crown 8vo., 5s. net.

Lang.—HOMER AND THE EPIC. By ANDREW LANG. Crown 8vo., 9s. net.

Lucan.—THE PHARSALIA OF LUCAN. Translated into Blank Verse. By Sir EDWARD RIDLEY. 8vo., 14s.

Mackail.—SELECT EPIGRAMS FROM THE GREEK ANTHOLOGY. By J. W. MACKAIL. Edited with a Revised Text, Introduction, Translation, and Notes 8vo., 16s.

Rich.—A DICTIONARY OF ROMAN AND GREEK ANTIQUITIES. By A. RICH, B.A. With 2000 Woodcuts. Crown 8vo., 7s. 6d.

Classical Literature, Translations, &c.—*continued.*

Sophocles.—Translated into English Verse. By ROBERT WHITELAW, M.A., Assistant Master in Rugby School. Cr. 8vo., 8s. 6d.

Tacitus.—THE HISTORY OF P. CORNELIUS TACITUS. Translated into English, with an Introduction and Notes, Critical and Explanatory, by ALBERT WILLIAM QUILL, M.A., T.C.D. 2 Vols. Vol. I., 8vo., 7s. 6d., Vol. II., 8vo., 12s. 6d.

Tyrrell.—TRANSLATIONS INTO GREEK AND LATIN VERSE. Edited by R. Y. TYRRELL. 8vo., 6s.

Virgil.—THE ÆNEID OF VIRGIL. Translated into English Verse by JOHN CONINGTON. Crown 8vo., 6s.

THE POEMS OF VIRGIL. Translated into English Prose by JOHN CONINGTON. Crown 8vo., 6s.

THE ÆNEID OF VIRGIL, freely translated into English Blank Verse. By W. J. THORNHILL. Crown 8vo., 7s. 6d.

THE ÆNEID OF VIRGIL. Translated into English Verse by JAMES RHOADES.
Books I.-VI. Crown 8vo., 5s.
Books VII.-XII. Crown 8vo., 5s.

Poetry and the Drama.

Allingham (WILLIAM).

IRISH SONGS AND POEMS. With Frontispiece of the Waterfall of Asaroe. Fcp. 8vo., 6s.

LAURENCE BLOOMFIELD. With Portrait of the Author. Fcp. 8vo., 3s. 6d.

FLOWER PIECES; DAY AND NIGHT SONGS; BALLADS. With 2 Designs by D. G. ROSSETTI. Fcp. 8vo., 6s.; large paper edition, 12s.

LIFE AND PHANTASY: with Frontispiece by Sir J. E. MILLAIS, Bart., and Design by ARTHUR HUGHES. Fcp. 8vo., 6s.; large paper edition, 12s.

THOUGHT AND WORD, AND ASHBY MANOR: a Play. Fcp. 8vo., 6s.; large paper edition, 12s.

BLACKBERRIES. Imperial 16mo., 6s.

Sets of the above 6 vols. may be had in uniform half-parchment binding, price 30s.

Armstrong (G. F. SAVAGE).

POEMS: Lyrical and Dramatic. Fcp. 8vo., 6s.

KING SAUL. (The Tragedy of Israel, Part I.) Fcp. 8vo., 5s.

KING DAVID. (The Tragedy of Israel, Part II.) Fcp. 8vo., 6s.

Armstrong (G. F. SAVAGE)—*continued.*

KING SOLOMON. (The Tragedy of Israel, Part III.) Fcp. 8vo., 6s.

UGONE: a Tragedy. Fcp. 8vo., 6s.

A GARLAND FROM GREECE: Poems. Fcp. 8vo., 7s. 6d.

STORIES OF WICKLOW: Poems. Fcp. 8vo., 7s. 6d.

MEPHISTOPHELES IN BROADCLOTH: a Satire. Fcp. 8vo., 4s.

ONE IN THE INFINITE: a Poem. Cr. 8vo., 7s. 6d.

Armstrong.—THE POETICAL WORKS OF EDMUND J. ARMSTRONG. Fcp. 8vo., 5s.

Arnold.—THE LIGHT OF THE WORLD: or, the Great Consummation. By Sir EDWIN ARNOLD. With 14 Illustrations after HOLMAN HUNT. Crown 8vo., 6s.

Beesly (A. H.).

BALLADS, AND OTHER VERSE. Fcp. 8vo., 5s.

DANTON, AND OTHER VERSE. Fcp. 8vo., 4s. 6d.

Bell (Mrs. HUGH).

CHAMBER COMEDIES: a Collection of Plays and Monologues for the Drawing Room. Crown 8vo., 6s.

FAIRY TALE PLAYS, AND HOW TO ACT THEM. With 91 Diagrams and 52 Illustrations. Crown 8vo., 6s.

Poetry and the Drama—*continued.*

Cochrane (ALFRED).
THE KESTREL'S NEST, and other Verses. Fcp. 8vo., 3s. 6d.
LEVIORE PLECTRO: Occasional Verses. Fcp. 8vo., 3s. 6d.

Douglas.—POEMS OF A COUNTRY GENTLEMAN. By Sir GEORGE DOUGLAS, Bart. Crown 8vo., 3s. 6d.

Goethe.
FAUST, Part I., the German Text, with Introduction and Notes. By ALBERT M. SELSS, Ph.D., M.A. Cr. 8vo., 5s.
THE FIRST PART OF THE TRAGEDY OF GOETHE'S FAUST IN ENGLISH. By THOS. E. WEBB, LL.D. New and Cheaper Edition, with the Death of Faust, from the Second Part. Crown 8vo., 6s.

Gurney (Rev. ALFRED, M.A.).
DAY-DREAMS: Poems. Cr. 8vo, 3s. 6d.
LOVE'S FRUITION, and other Poems. Fcp. 8vo., 2s. 6d.

Hampton.—FOR REMEMBRANCE. A Record of Life's Beginnings. Three Poetical Quotations for Every Day in the Year for Birth, Baptism, Death. Illustrative of our Life, Temporal, Spiritual, Eternal. Interleaved for Names. Compiled by the Lady LAURA HAMPTON. Fcp. 8vo., 3s. 6d.

Ingelow (JEAN).
POETICAL WORKS. 2 vols. Fcp. 8vo., 12s. Complete in One Volume. Crown 8vo., 7s. 6d.
LYRICAL AND OTHER POEMS. Selected from the Writings of JEAN INGELOW. Fcp. 8vo., 2s. 6d.; cloth plain, 3s. cloth gilt.

Lang (ANDREW).
GRASS OF PARNASSUS. Fcp. 8vo., 2s. 6d. net.
THE BLUE POETRY BOOK. Edited by ANDREW LANG. With 100 Illustrations. Crown 8vo., 6s.

Layard.—SONGS IN MANY MOODS. By NINA F. LAYARD. AND THE WANDERING ALBATROSS, &c. By ANNIE CORDER. In one volume. Crown 8vo., 5s.

Lecky.—POEMS. By W. E. H. LECKY. Fcp. 8vo., 5s.

Lytton (THE EARL OF) (OWEN MEREDITH).
THE WANDERER. Cr. 8vo., 10s. 6d.
LUCILE. Crown 8vo., 10s. 6d.
SELECTED POEMS. Cr. 8vo., 10s. 6d.

Macaulay.—LAYS OF ANCIENT ROME, WITH IVRY, AND THE ARMADA. By Lord MACAULAY.
Illustrated by G. SCHARF. Fcp. 4to., 10s. 6d.
———— Bijou Edition. 18mo., 2s. 6d., gilt top.
———— Popular Edition. Fcp. 4to., 6d. sewed, 1s. cloth.
Illustrated by J. R. WEGUELIN. Crown 8vo., 3s. 6d.
Annotated Edition. Fcp. 8vo., 1s. sewed, 1s. 6d. cloth.

MacDonald (GEORGE, LL.D.).
A BOOK OF STRIFE, IN THE FORM OF THE DIARY OF AN OLD SOUL: Poems. 18mo., 6s.
RAMPOLLI: GROWTHS FROM A LONG-PLANTED ROOT; being Translations, new and old (mainly in verse), chiefly from the German; along with 'A Year's Diary of an Old Soul'. Crown 8vo., 6s.

Moffat.—CRICKETY CRICKET: Rhymes and Parodies. By DOUGLAS MOFFAT. With Frontispiece by Sir FRANK LOCKWOOD, Q.C., M.P., and 53 Illustrations by the Author. Crown 8vo., 2s. 6d.

Morris (WILLIAM).
POETICAL WORKS—LIBRARY EDITION. Complete in Ten Volumes. Crown 8vo., price 6s. each :—
THE EARTHLY PARADISE. 4 vols. 6s. each.
THE LIFE AND DEATH OF JASON. 6s.
THE DEFENCE OF GUENEVERE, and other Poems. 6s.
THE STORY OF SIGURD THE VOLSUNG, and the Fall of the Niblungs. 6s.
LOVE IS ENOUGH; or, The Freeing of Pharamond: a Morality; and POEMS BY THE WAY. 6s.

Poetry and the Drama—*continued*.

Morris (WILLIAM)—*continued*.
THE ODYSSEY OF HOMER. Done into English Verse. 6s.
THE ÆNEIDS OF VIRGIL. Done into English Verse. 6s.

Certain of the Poetical Works may also be had in the following Editions:—
THE EARTHLY PARADISE.
Popular Edition. 5 vols. 12mo., 25s.; or 5s. each, sold separately.
The same in Ten Parts, 25s.; or 2s. 6d. each, sold separately.
Cheap Edition, in 1 vol. Cr. 8vo., 7s. 6d.
LOVE IS ENOUGH; or, The Freeing of Pharamond: a Morality. Square crown 8vo., 7s. 6d.
POEMS BY THE WAY. Square crown 8vo., 6s.
*** For Mr. William Morris's Prose Works, see pp. 22 and 31.

Nesbit.—LAYS AND LEGENDS. By E. NESBIT (Mrs. HUBERT BLAND). First Series. Crown 8vo., 3s. 6d. Second Series, with Portrait. Crown 8vo., 5s.

Riley (JAMES WHITCOMB).
OLD FASHIONED ROSES: Poems. 12mo., 5s.
A CHILD-WORLD: POEMS. Fcp. 8vo. 5s.
RUBÁIYÁT OF DOC SIFERS. With 43 Illustrations by C. M RELYEA. Crown 8vo., 6s.
THE GOLDEN YEAR. From the Verse and Prose of JAMES WHITCOMB RILEY. Compiled by CLARA E. LAUGHLIN. Fcp. 8vo.

Romanes.—A SELECTION FROM POEMS OF GEORGE JOHN ROMANES, M.A., LL.D., F.R.S. With an duction by T. HERBERT WA President of Magdalen College, O Crown 8vo., 4s. 6d.

Russell.—SONNETS ON THE SOI an Anthology compiled by the MATTHEW RUSSELL, S.J. Crown 3s. 6d.

Shakespeare.—BOWDLER'S F. SHAKESPEARE. With 36 Woo 1 vol. 8vo., 14s. Or in 6 vols. 8vo., 21s.
THE SHAKESPEARE BIRTHDAY I By MARY F. DUNBAR. 32mo.,

Tupper.—POEMS. By JOHN I TUPPER. Selected and Edite WILLIAM MICHAEL ROSSETTI. (8vo., 5s.

Wordsworth.—SELECTED P. By ANDREW LANG. With I gravure Frontispiece of Rydal M With 16 Illustrations and num Initial Letters By ALFRED PAR A.R.A. Crown 8vo., gilt edges, ;

Wordsworth and Coleridg DESCRIPTION OF THE WORDSW AND COLERIDGE MANUSCRIPTS II POSSESSION OF Mr. T. NORTON I MAN. Edited, with Notes, by W. WHITE. With 3 Facsimile Repr tions. 4to., 10s. 6d.

Fiction, Humour, &c.

Allingham.—CROOKED PATHS. By FRANCIS ALLINGHAM. Cr. 8vo., 6s
Anstey.—VOCES POPULI. Reprinted from 'Punch'. By F. ANSTEY. First Series. With 20 Illustrations by J. BERNARD PARTRIDGE. Cr. 8vo., 3s. 6d.
Beaconsfield (THE EARL OF).
NOVELS AND TALES.
Complete in 11 vols. Cr. 8vo., 1s. 6d. each.

Vivian Grey.	Sybil.
TheYoungDuke,&c.	Henrietta Temple.
Alroy, Ixion, &c.	Venetia.
Contarini Fleming, &c.	Coningsby.
	Lothair.
Tancred.	Endymion.

NOVELS AND TALES. The Hughenden Edition. With 2 Portraits and 11 Vignettes. 11 vols. Cr. 8vo., 42s.

Deland (MARGARET).
PHILIP AND HIS WIFE. Cr. 8vo.,:
THE WISDOM OF FOOLS: Stories. 8vo., 5s.
OLD CHESTER TALES. Crown 8

Diderot.—RAMEAU'S NEPHEW Translation from Diderot's Autogr Text. By SYLVIA MARGARET I Crown 8vo., 3s. 6d.

Dougall.—BEGGARS ALL. B DOUGALL. Crown 8vo., 3s. 6d.

Fiction, Humour, &c.—continued.

Doyle (A. Conan).
MICAH CLARKE: a Tale of Monmouth's Rebellion. With 10 Illustrations. Cr. 8vo., 3s. 6d.
THE CAPTAIN OF THE POLESTAR, and other Tales. Cr. 8vo., 3s. 6d.
THE REFUGEES: a Tale of the Huguenots. With 25 Illustrations. Crown 8vo., 3s. 6d.
THE STARK-MUNRO LETTERS. Cr. 8vo., 3s. 6d.

Farrar (F. W., Dean of Canterbury).
DARKNESS AND DAWN: or, Scenes in the Days of Nero. An Historic Tale. Cr. 8vo., 7s. 6d.
GATHERING CLOUDS: a Tale of the Days of St. Chrysostom. Crown 8vo., 7s. 6d.

Fowler (Edith H.).
THE YOUNG PRETENDERS. A Story of Child Life. With 12 Illustrations by PHILIP BURNE-JONES. Cr. 8vo., 6s.
THE PROFESSOR'S CHILDREN. With 24 Illustrations by ETHEL KATE BURGESS. Crown 8vo., 6s.

Froude.—THE TWO CHIEFS OF DUNBOY: an Irish Romance of the Last Century. By JAMES A. FROUDE. Cr. 8vo., 3s. 6d.

Gilkes.—KALLISTRATUS: An Autobiography. A Story of the Hannibal and the Second Punic War. By A. H. GILKES, M.A., Master of Dulwich College. With 3 Illustrations by MAURICE GREIFFENHAGEN. Crown 8vo., 6s.

Graham.—THE RED SCAUR: a Story of the North Country. By P. ANDERSON GRAHAM. Crown 8vo., 6s.

Gurdon.—MEMORIES AND FANCIES: Suffolk Tales and other Stories; Fairy Legends; Poems; Miscellaneous Articles. By the late LADY CAMILLA GURDON, Author of 'Suffolk Folk-Lore'. Crown 8vo., 5s.

Haggard (H. Rider).
HEART OF THE WORLD. With 15 Illustrations, Crown 8vo., 3s. 6d.
JOAN HASTE. With 20 Illustrations. Cr. 8vo., 3s. 6d.
THE PEOPLE OF THE MIST. With 16 Illustrations. Crown 8vo., 3s. 6d.
MONTEZUMA'S DAUGHTER. With 24 Illustrations. Crown 8vo., 3s. 6d.
SHE. With 32 Illustrations. Cr. 8vo. 3s. 6d.

Haggard (H. Rider)—continued.
ALLAN QUATERMAIN. With 31 Illustrations. Crown 8vo., 3s. 6d.
MAIWA'S REVENGE. Crown 8vo., 1s. 6d.
COLONEL QUARITCH, V.C. Cr. 8vo., 3s. 6d.
CLEOPATRA. With 29 Illustrations Crown 8vo., 3s. 6d.
BEATRICE. Cr. 8vo., 3s. 6d.
ERIC BRIGHTEYES. With 51 Illustrations. Cr. 8vo., 3s. 6d.
NADA THE LILY. With 23 Illustrations. Cr. 8vo., 3s. 6d.
ALLAN'S WIFE. With 34 Illustrations. Crown 8vo., 3s. 6d.
THE WITCH'S HEAD. With 16 Illustrations. Crown 8vo., 3s. 6d.
MR. MEESON'S WILL. With 16 Illustrations. Crown 8vo., 3s. 6d.
DAWN. With 16 Illustrations. Crown 8vo. 3s. 6d.

Haggard and Lang.—THE WORLD'S DESIRE. By H. RIDER HAGGARD and ANDREW LANG. With 27 Illustrations. Crown 8vo., 3s. 6d.

Harte.—IN THE CARQUINEZ WOODS, and other Stories. By BRET HARTE. Cr. 8vo., 3s. 6d.

Hope.—THE HEART OF PRINCESS OSRA. By ANTHONY HOPE. With 9 Illustrations by JOHN WILLIAMSON. Crown 8vo., 6s.

Hornung.—THE UNBIDDEN GUEST. By E. W. HORNUNG. Cr. 8vo., 3s. 6d.

Jerome.—SKETCHES IN LAVENDER: Blue and Green. By JEROME K. JEROME, Author of 'Three Men in a Boat,' &c. Crown 8vo., 6s.

Joyce.—OLD CELTIC ROMANCES: Twelve of the most beautiful of the Ancient Irish Romantic Tales. Translated from the Gaelic. Cr. 8vo., 3s. 6d.

Lang.—A MONK OF FIFE: a Story of the Days of Joan of Arc. By ANDREW LANG. With 13 Illustrations by SELWYN IMAGE. Crown 8vo., 3s. 6d.

Levett-Yeats (S.).
THE CHEVALIER D'AURIAC. Crown 8vo., 6s.
A GALAHAD OF THE CREEKS, and other Stories. Crown 8vo., 6s.
THE HEART OF DENISE, and other Stories. Crown 8vo., 6s.

Fiction, Humour, &c.—*continued*.

Lyall (EDNA).
THE AUTOBIOGRAPHY OF A SLANDER. Fcp. 8vo., 1s. sewed.
Presentation Edition. With 20 Illustrations by LANCELOT SPEED. Cr. 8vo., 2s. 6d. net.
THE AUTOBIOGRAPHY OF A TRUTH. Fcp. 8vo., 1s. sewed; 1s. 6d. cloth.
DOREEN: The Story of a Singer. Cr. 8vo., 6s.
WAYFARING MEN. Crown 8vo., 6s.
HOPE THE HERMIT: a Romance of Borrowdale. Crown 8vo., 6s.

Melville (G. J. WHYTE).
The Gladiators. | Holmby House.
The Interpreter. | Kate Coventry.
Good for Nothing. | Digby Grand.
The Queen's Maries. | General Bounce.
Cr. 8vo., 1s. 6d. each.

Merriman.—FLOTSAM: a Story of the Indian Mutiny. By HENRY SETON MERRIMAN. With Frontispiece and Vignette by H. G. MASSEY, A.R.E. Crown 8vo., 3s. 6d.

Morris (WILLIAM).
THE SUNDERING FLOOD. Crown 8vo., 7s. 6d.
THE WATER OF THE WONDROUS ISLES. Crown 8vo., 7s. 6d.
THE WELL AT THE WORLD'S END. 2 vols., 8vo., 28s.
THE STORY OF THE GLITTERING PLAIN, which has been also called The Land of the Living Men, or The Acre of the Undying. Square post 8vo., 5s. net.
THE ROOTS OF THE MOUNTAINS, Written in Prose and Verse. Square crown 8vo., 8s.
A TALE OF THE HOUSE OF THE WOLFINGS. Written in Prose and Verse. Square crown 8vo., 6s.
A DREAM OF JOHN BALL, AND A KING'S LESSON. 12mo., 1s. 6d.
NEWS FROM NOWHERE; or, An Epoch of Rest. Post 8vo., 1s. 6d.
*** For Mr. William Morris's Poetical Works, see p. 19.

Newman (CARDINAL).
LOSS AND GAIN: The Story of a Convert. Crown 8vo. Cabinet Edition, 6s.; Popular Edition, 3s. 6d.
CALLISTA: A Tale of the Third Century. Crown 8vo. Cabinet Edition, 6s.; Popular Edition, 3s. 6d.

Oliphant.—OLD MR. TRE[Mrs. OLIPHANT. Crown 8[

Phillipps-Wolley.—SNA[of the Lone Mountain. B LIPPS-WOLLEY. With 13 I Crown 8vo., 3s. 6d.

Quintana.—THE CID C, an Historical Romance. ANTONIO DE TRUEBA Y LA (Translated from the Spanish J. GILL, M.A., T.C.D. Cro

Rhoscomyl (OWEN).
THE JEWEL OF YNYS GA[a hitherto unprinted Cha History of the Sea Rover Illustrations by LANCEI Crown 8vo., 3s. 6d.
BATTLEMENT AND TOWER: With Frontispiece by WOODVILLE. Crown 8v[
FOR THE WHITE ROSE OF Story of the Jacobite Ris Crown 8vo., 6s.

Sewell (ELIZABETH M.).
A Glimpse of the World. | Am
Laneton Parsonage. | Cle[
Margaret Percival. | Ger
Katharine Ashton. | Ho
The Earl's Daughter. | Aft[
The Experience of Life. | Urs
Cr. 8vo., 1s. 6d. each, cloth p] each, cloth extra, gilt edg[

Stevenson (ROBERT LOUIS
THE STRANGE CASE OF [AND MR. HYDE. Fcp sewed, 1s. 6d. cloth.
THE STRANGE CASE OF [AND MR. HYDE; with O Crown 8vo., 3s. 6d.
MORE NEW ARABIAN N[DYNAMITER. By ROB STEVENSON and FANN] GRIFT STEVENSON. C 3s. 6d.
THE WRONG BOX. By Ro STEVENSON and LLOYD Crown 8vo., 3s. 6d.

Suttner.—LAY DOWN Y (*Die Waffen Nieder*): Th graphy of Martha Tilling. VON SUTTNER. Transla HOLMES. Crown 8vo., 1s.

Taylor. — EARLY ITALI STORIES. Edited and Retc TAYLOR. With 12 Illustra J. FORD.

LONGMANS & CO.'S STANDARD AND GENERAL WORKS. 23

Fiction, Humour, &c.—*continued.*

Hope (ANTHONY).
E WARDEN. Cr. 8vo., 1s. 6d.
RCHESTER TOWERS. Cr. 8vo., 1s. 6d.
ford (L. B.).
DDY MARGET. Crown 8vo., 6s.
\ KILDARE: a Matrimonial Problem.
Crown 8vo., 6s.
. SMITH : a Part of his Life. Crown
!vo., 2s. 6d.
E BABY'S GRANDMOTHER. Crown
!vo., 2s. 6d
USINS. Crown 8vo., 2s. 6d.
OUBLESOME DAUGHTERS. Crown
!vo., 2s. 6d.
ULINE. Crown 8vo., 2s. 6d.
CK NETHERBY. Crown 8vo., 2s. 6d.
E HISTORY OF A WEEK. Crown
!vo. 2s. 6d.
ITIFF-NECKED GENERATION. Crown
!vo. 2s. 6d.
N, and other Stories. Cr. 8vo., 2s. 6d.
E MISCHIEF OF MONICA. Crown
!vo., 2s. 6d.
E ONE GOOD GUEST. Cr. 8vo. 2s. 6d.
LOUGHED,' and other Stories. Crown
!vo., 2s. 6d.
E MATCHMAKER. Cr. 8vo., 2s. 6d.

Watson.—RACING AND CHASING : a Volume of Sporting Stories and Sketches. By ALFRED E. T. WATSON, Editor of the ' Badminton Magazine'. With 52 Illustrations. Crown 8vo., 7s. 6d.

Weyman (STANLEY).
THE HOUSE OF THE WOLF. Cr. 8vo., 3s. 6d.
A GENTLEMAN OF FRANCE. Cr. 8vo., 6s.
THE RED COCKADE. Cr. 8vo., 6s.
SHREWSBURY. With 24 Illustrations. Crown 8vo., 6s.

Whishaw (FRED.).
A BOYAR OF THE TERRIBLE: a Romance of the Court of Ivan the Cruel, First Tzar of Russia. With 12 Illustrations by H. G. MASSEY, A.R.E. Cr. 8vo., 6s.
A TSAR'S GRATITUDE. Cr. 8vo., 6s.

Woods.—WEEPING FERRY, and other Stories. By MARGARET L. WOODS, Author of 'A Village Tragedy'. Crown 8vo., 6s.

Popular Science (Natural History, &c.).

ler.—OUR HOUSEHOLD INSECTS. Account of the Insect-Pests found Dwelling-Houses. By EDWARD A. TLER, B.A., B.Sc. (Lond.). With ; Illustrations. Crown 8vo., 3s. 6d.

neaux (W.).
E OUTDOOR WORLD; or, The Young Collector's Handbook. With 18 Plates, 16 of which are coloured, nd 549 Illustrations in the Text. Crown 8vo., 7s. 6d.
TTERFLIES AND MOTHS (British). With 12 coloured Plates and 241 Illustrations in the Text. Crown 8vo., 's. 6d.
FE IN PONDS AND STREAMS. With ! coloured Plates and 331 Illustrations in the Text. Cr. 8vo., 7s. 6d.

twig (Dr. GEORGE).
E SEA AND ITS LIVING WONDERS. With 12 Plates and 303 Woodcuts. !vo., 7s. net.
E TROPICAL WORLD. With 8 Plates and 172 Woodcuts. 8vo., 7s. net.
E POLAR WORLD. With 3 Maps, 8 Plates and 85 Woodcuts. 8vo., 7s. net.

Hartwig (Dr. GEORGE)—*continued.*
THE SUBTERRANEAN WORLD. With 3 Maps and 80 Woodcuts. 8vo., 7s. net.
THE AERIAL WORLD. With Map, 8 Plates and 60 Woodcuts. 8vo., 7s. net.
HEROES OF THE POLAR WORLD. 19 Illustrations. Crown 8vo., 2s.
WONDERS OF THE TROPICAL FORESTS. 40 Illustrations. Crown 8vo., 2s.
WORKERS UNDER THE GROUND. 29 Illustrations. Crown 8vo., 2s.
MARVELS OVER OUR HEADS. 29 Illustrations. Crown 8vo., 2s.
SEA MONSTERS AND SEA BIRDS. 75 Illustrations. Crown 8vo., 2s. 6d.
DENIZENS OF THE DEEP. 117 Illustrations. Crown 8vo., 2s. 6d.
VOLCANOES AND EARTHQUAKES. 30 Illustrations. Crown 8vo., 2s. 6d.
WILD ANIMALS OF THE TROPICS. 66 Illustrations. Crown 8vo., 3s. 6d.

Helmholtz.—POPULAR LECTURES ON SCIENTIFIC SUBJECTS. By HERMANN VON HELMHOLTZ. With 68 Woodcuts. 2 vols. Crown 8vo., 3s. 6d. each.

Popular Science (Natural History, &c.).

Hudson (W. H.).
BRITISH BIRDS. With a Chapter on Structure and Classification by FRANK E. BEDDARD, F.R.S. With 16 Plates (8 of which are Coloured), and over 100 Illustrations in the Text. Crown 8vo., 7s. 6d.

BIRDS IN LONDON. With 17 Plates and 15 Illustrations in the Text. 8vo., 12s.

Proctor (RICHARD A.).
LIGHT SCIENCE FOR LEISURE HOURS. Familiar Essays on Scientific Subjects. 3 vols. Crown 8vo., 5s. each vol. Cheap edition, Crown 8vo., 3s. 6d.

ROUGH WAYS MADE SMOOTH. Familiar Essays on Scientific Subjects. Crown 8vo., 3s. 6d.

PLEASANT WAYS IN SCIENCE. Crown 8vo., 3s. 6d.

NATURE STUDIES. By R. A. PROCTOR, GRANT ALLEN, A. WILSON, T. FOSTER and E. CLODD. Crown 8vo., 3s. 6d.

LEISURE READINGS. By R. A. PROCTOR, E. CLODD, A. WILSON, T. FOSTER, and A. C. RANYARD. Cr. 8vo., 3s. 6d.

⁎ For Mr. Proctor's other books see Messrs. Longmans & Co.'s Catalogue of Scientific Works.

Stanley.—A FAMILIAR HISTORY OF BIRDS. By E. STANLEY, D.D., formerly Bishop of Norwich. With 160 Illustrations. Crown 8vo., 3s. 6d.

Wood (Rev. J. G.).
HOMES WITHOUT HANDS: a Description of the Habitation of Animals, classed according to the Principle of Construction. With 140 Illustrations. 8vo., 7s. net.

Wood (Rev. J. G.)—continued.
INSECTS AT HOME. a Popular Account of British Insects, their Structure, Habits and Transformations. With 700 Illustrations. 8vo., 7s. net.

INSECTS ABROAD: a Popular Account of Foreign Insects, their Structure, Habits and Transformations. With 600 Illustrations. 8vo., 7s. net.

BIBLE ANIMALS: a Description of every Living Creature mentioned in the Scriptures. With 112 Illustrations. 8vo., 7s. net.

PETLAND REVISITED. With 33 Illustrations. Cr. 8vo., 3s. 6d.

OUT OF DOORS; a Selection of Original Articles on Practical Natural History. With 11 Illustrations. Cr. 8vo., 3s. 6d.

STRANGE DWELLINGS: a Description of the Habitations of Animals, abridged from 'Homes without Hands'. With 60 Illustrations. Cr. 8vo., 3s. 6d.

BIRD LIFE OF THE BIBLE. 32 Illustrations. Crown 8vo., 3s. 6d.

WONDERFUL NESTS. 30 Illustrations. Crown 8vo., 3s. 6d.

HOMES UNDER THE GROUND. 28 Illustrations. Crown 8vo., 3s. 6d.

WILD ANIMALS OF THE BIBLE. 29 Illustrations. Crown 8vo., 3s. 6d.

DOMESTIC ANIMALS OF THE BIBLE. 23 Illustrations. Crown 8vo., 3s. 6d.

THE BRANCH BUILDERS. 28 Illustrations. Crown 8vo., 2s. 6d.

SOCIAL HABITATIONS AND PARASITIC NESTS. 18 Illustrations. Crown 8vo., 2s.

Works of Reference.

Longmans' GAZETTEER OF THE WORLD. Edited by GEORGE G. CHISHOLM, M.A., B.Sc. Imp. 8vo., £2 2s. cloth, £2 12s. 6d. half-morocco.

Maunder (Samuel).
BIOGRAPHICAL TREASURY. With Supplement brought down to 1889. By Rev. JAMES WOOD. Fcp. 8vo.. 6s.

Maunder (Samuel)—continued.
TREASURY OF GEOGRAPHY, Physical, Historical, Descriptive, and Political. With 7 Maps and 16 Plates. Fcp. 8vo., 6s.

THE TREASURY OF BIBLE KNOWLEDGE. By the Rev. J. AYRE, M.A. With 5 Maps, 15 Plates, and 300 Woodcuts. Fcp. 8vo., 6s.

LONGMANS & CO.'S STANDARD AND GENERAL WORKS. 25

Works of Reference—*continued.*

Maunder (Samuel)—*continued.*

TREASURY OF KNOWLEDGE AND LIBRARY OF REFERENCE. Fcp. 8vo., 6*s.*

HISTORICAL TREASURY: Fcp. 8vo., 6*s.*

SCIENTIFIC AND LITERARY TREASURY. Fcp. 8vo., 6*s.*

THE TREASURY OF BOTANY. Edited by J. LINDLEY, F.R.S., and T. MOORE, F.L.S. With 274 Woodcuts and 20 Steel Plates. 2 vols. Fcp. 8vo., 12*s.*

Roget.—THESAURUS OF ENGLISH WORDS AND PHRASES. Classified and Arranged so as to Facilitate the Expression of Ideas and assist in Literary Composition. By PETER MARK ROGET, M.D., F.R.S. Recomposed throughout, enlarged and improved, partly from the Author's Notes and with a full Index, by the Author's Son, JOHN LEWIS ROGET. Crown 8vo., 10*s.* 6*d.*

Willich.—POPULAR TABLES for giving information for ascertaining the value of Lifehold, Leasehold, and Church Property, the Public Funds, &c. By CHARLES M. WILLICH. Edited by H. BENCE JONES. Crown 8vo., 10*s.* 6*d.*

Children's Books.

Buckland.—TWO LITTLE RUNAWAYS. Adapted from the French of LOUIS DESNOYERS. By JAMES BUCKLAND. With 110 Illustrations by CECIL ALDIN.

Crake (Rev. A. D.).

EDWY THE FAIR; or, the First Chronicle of Æscendune. Crown 8vo., 2*s.* 6*d.*

ALFGAR THE DANE: or, the Second Chronicle of Æscendune. Cr. 8vo., 2*s.* 6*d.*

THE RIVAL HEIRS: being the Third and Last Chronicle of Æscendune. Crown 8vo., 2*s.* 6*d.*

THE HOUSE OF WALDERNE. A Tale of the Cloister and the Forest in the Days of the Barons' Wars. Crown 8vo., 2*s.* 6*d.*

BRIAN FITZ-COUNT. A Story of Wallingford Castle and Dorchester Abbey. Crown 8vo., 2*s.* 6*d.*

Lang (ANDREW)—EDITED BY.

THE BLUE FAIRY BOOK. With 138 Illustrations. Crown 8vo., 6*s.*

THE RED FAIRY BOOK. With 100 Illustrations. Crown 8vo., 6*s.*

THE GREEN FAIRY BOOK. With 99 Illustrations. Crown 8vo., 6*s.*

THE YELLOW FAIRY BOOK. With 104 Illustrations. Crown 8vo., 6*s.*

THE PINK FAIRY BOOK. With 67 Illustrations. Crown 8vo., 6*s.*

THE BLUE POETRY BOOK. With 100 Illustrations. Crown 8vo., 6*s.*

THE BLUE POETRY BOOK. School

Lang (ANDREW)—*continued.*

THE TRUE STORY BOOK. With 66 Illustrations. Crown 8vo., 6*s.*

THE RED TRUE STORY BOOK. With 100 Illustrations. Crown 8vo., 6*s.*

THE ANIMAL STORY BOOK. With 67 Illustrations. Crown 8vo., 6*s.*

THE ARABIAN NIGHTS ENTERTAINMENTS. With Illustrations. Crown 8vo., 6*s.*

Meade (L. T.).

DADDY'S BOY. With Illustrations. Crown 8vo., 3*s.* 6*d.*

DEB AND THE DUCHESS. With Illustrations. Crown 8vo., 3*s.* 6*d.*

THE BERESFORD PRIZE. With Illustrations. Crown 8vo., 3*s.* 6*d.*

THE HOUSE OF SURPRISES. With Illustrations. Crown 8vo., 3*s.* 6*d.*

Praeger. (S. ROSAMOND).

THE ADVENTURES OF THE THREE BOLD BABES: Hector, Honoria and Alisander. A Story in Pictures. With 24 Coloured Plates and 24 Outline Pictures. Oblong 4to., 3*s.* 6*d.*

THE FURTHER DOINGS OF THE THREE BOLD BABES. With 25 Coloured Plates and 24 Outline Pictures. Oblong 4to., 3*s.* 6*d.*

Stevenson.—A CHILD'S GARDEN OF VERSES. By ROBERT LOUIS STEVENSON. fcp. 8vo., 5*s.*

Sullivan.—HERE THEY ARE! More

Children's Books—continued.

Upton (FLORENCE K., and BERTHA).
THE ADVENTURES OF TWO DUTCH DOLLS AND A 'GOLLIWOGG'. With 31 Coloured Plates and numerous Illustrations in the Text. Oblong 4to., 6s.

THE GOLLIWOGG'S BICYCLE CLUB. With 31 Coloured Plates and numerous Illustrations in the Text. Oblong 4to., 6s.

Upton (FLORENCE K., and BERTHA *continued*.
THE VEGE-MEN'S REVENGE. With Coloured Plates and numerous Illustrations in the Text. Oblong 4to.,
THE GOLLIWOGG AT THE SEA-SII With Coloured Plates and Illust tions in the Text. Oblong 4to., 6.

Wordsworth.—THE SNOW GARDI and other Fairy Tales for Children. ELIZABETH WORDSWORTH. With Illustrations by TREVOR HADD(Crown 8vo., 3s. 6d.

Longmans' Series of Books for Girls.
Price 2s. 6d. each.

ATELIER (THE) DU LYS: or an Art Student in the Reign of Terror.
BY THE SAME AUTHOR.
Mademoiselle Mori: a Tale of Modern Rome.
In the O!den Time: a Tale of the Peasant War in Germany.
The Younger Sister.
That Child.
Under a Cloud.
Hester's Venture.
The Fiddler of Lugau.
A Child of the Revolution.

ATHERSTONE PRIORY. By L. N. COMYN.

THE STORY OF A SPRING MORNING, &c. By Mrs. MOLESWORTH. Illustrated.

THE PALACE IN THE GARDEN. By Mrs. MOLESWORTH. Illustrated.

NEIGHBOURS. By Mrs. MOLESWORTH.

THE THIRD MISS ST. QUENTIN. By Mrs. MOLESWORTH.

VERY YOUNG; and QUITE ANOTH STORY. Two Stories. By JEAN IN(LOW.

CAN THIS BE LOVE? By LOUISA PA!

KEITH DERAMORE. By the Author 'Miss Molly'.

SIDNEY. By MARGARET DELAND.

AN ARRANGED MARRIAGE. By DO! THEA GERARD.

LAST WORDS TO GIRLS ON LIFE SCHOOL AND AFTER SCHOOL. MARIA GREY.

STRAY THOUGHTS FOR GIRLS. LUCY H. M. SOULSBY, Head Mistr of Oxford High School. 16mo., 1s. net.

The Silver Library.
CROWN 8VO. 3s. 6d. EACH VOLUME.

Arnold's (Sir Edwin) Seas and Lands. With 71 Illustrations. 3s. 6d.

Bagehot's (W.) Biographical Studies. 3s. 6d.

Bagehot's (W.) Economic Studies. 3s. 6d.

Bagehot's (W.) Literary Studies. With Portrait. 3 vols. 3s. 6d. each.

Baker's (Sir S. W.) Eight Years in Ceylon. With 6 Illustrations. 3s. 6d.

Baker's (Sir S. W.) Rifle and Hound in Ceylon. With 6 Illustrations. 3s. 6d.

Baring-Gould's (Rev. S.) Curious Myths of the Middle Ages. 3s. 6d.

Baring-Gould's (Rev. S.) Origin and Development of Religious Belief. 2 vols. 3s. 6d. each.

Becker's (W. A.) Gallus: or, Ron Scenes in the Time of Augustus. W 26 Illustrations. 3s. 6d.

Becker's (W. A.) Charicles: or, Illus tions of the Private Life of the Anci Greeks. With 26 Illustrations. 3s.

Bent's (J. T.) The Ruined Cities of I shonaland. With 117 Illustratio 3s. 6d.

Brassey's (Lady) A Voyage in the 'S! beam'. With 66 Illustrations. 3s.

Clodd's (E.) Story of Creation: a Pl Account of Evolution. With 77 Ill trations. 3s. 6d.

LONGMANS & CO.'S STANDARD AND GENERAL WORKS. 27

The Silver Library—*continued*.

ybeare (Rev. W. J.) and Howson's 'ery Rev. J. S.) Life and Epistles of :. Paul. With 46 Illustrations. 3s. 6d.
gall's(L.)Beggars All; a Novel. 3s.6d.
le's (A. Conan) Micah Clarke: a Tale of Monmouth's Rebellion. With 10 lustrations. 3s. 6d.
le's (A. Conan) The Captain of the)lestar, and other Tales. 3s. 6d.
le's (A. Conan) The Refugees: A ale of the Huguenots. With 25 lustrations, 3s. 6d.
le's (A. Conan) The Stark Munro itters. 3s. 6d.
ide's (J. A.) The History of England,)m the Fall of Wolsey to the Defeat the Spanish Armada. 12 vols. . 6d. each.
ide's (J. A.) The English in Ireland, vols. 10s. 6d.
ide's (J. A.) The Divorce of Catherine Aragon. 3s. 6d.
ide's (J. A.) The Spanish Story of e Armada, and other Essays. 3s. 6d.
ide's (J. A.) Short Studies on Great ibjects. 4 vols. 3s. 6d. each.
ide's (J. A.) The Council of Trent. 6d.
ide's (J. A.) Thomas Carlyle: a istory of his Life.
95-1835. 2 vols. 7s.
34-1881. 2 vols. 7s.
ide's (J. A.) Cæsar: a Sketch. 3s. 6d.
de's (J. A.) Oceana; or, England d her Colonies. With 9 Illustra- ins. 3s. 6d.
ide's (J. A.) The Two Chiefs of Duny: an Irish Romance of the Last :ntury. 3s. 6d.
f's (Rev. G. R.) Life of the Duke of ellington. With Portrait. 3s. 6d.
'ille's (C. C. F.) Journal of the ligns of King George IV., King illiam IV., and Queen Victoria. /ols, 3s. 6d. each.
gard's (H. R.) She: A History of iventure. 32 Illustrations. 3s. 6d.
gard's (H. R.) Allan Quatermain. ith 20 Illustrations. 3s. 6d.
gard's (H. R.) Colonel Quaritch, C.: a Tale of Country Life. 3s. 6d.
gard's (H. R.) Cleopatra. With 29 ustrations. 3s. 6d.
gard's (H. R.) Eric Brighteyes. ith 51 Illustrations. 3s. 6d.
gard's (H. R.) Beatrice. 2s. 6d.

Haggard's (H. R.) Heart of the World. With 15 Illustrations. 3s. 6d.
Haggard's (H. R.) Montezuma's Daughter. With 25 Illustrations. 3s. 6d.
Haggard's (H. R.) The Witch's Head. With 16 Illustrations. 3s. 6d.
Haggard's (H. R.) Mr. Meeson's Will. With 16 Illustrations. 3s. 6d.
Haggard's (H. R.) Nada the Lily. With 23 Illustrations. 3s. 6d.
Haggard's (H. R.) Dawn. With 16 Illustrations. 3s. 6d.
Haggard's (H. R.) The People of the Mist. With 16 Illustrations. 3s. 6d.
Haggard's (H. R.) Joan Haste. With 20 Illustrations. 3s. 6d.
Haggard (H. R.) and Lang's (A.) The World's Desire. With 27 Illus. 3s. 6d.
Harte's (Bret) In the Carquinez Woods, and other Stories. 3s. 6d.
Helmholtz's (Hermann von) Popular Lectures on Scientific Subjects. With 68 Illustrations. 2 vols. 3s. 6d. each.
Hornung's (E. W.) The Unbidden Guest. 3s. 6d.
Howitt's (W.) Visits to Remarkable Places. With 80 Illustrations. 3s. 6d.
Jefferies' (R.) The Story of My Heart: My Autobiography. With Portrait. 3s. 6d.
Jefferies' (R.) Field and Hedgerow. With Portrait. 3s. 6d.
Jefferies' (R.) Red Deer. 17 Illus. 3s. 6d.
Jefferies' (R.) Wood Magic: a Fable. 3s. 6d.
Jefferies' (R.) The Toilers of the Field. With Portrait from the Bust in Salisbury Cathedral. 3s. 6d.
Kaye (Sir J.) and Malleson's (Colonel) History of the Indian Mutiny of 1857-8. 6 vols. 3s. 6d. each.
Knight's (E. F.) The Cruise of the 'Alerte': the Narrative of a Search for Treasure on the Desert Island of Trinidad. With 2 Maps and 23 Illustrations. 3s. 6d.
Knight's (E. F.) Where Three Empires Meet: a Narrative of Recent Travel in Kashmir, Western Tibet, Baltistan, Gilgit. With a Map and 54 Illustrations. 3s. 6d.
Knight's (E. F.) The 'Falcon' on the Baltic. With Map and 11 Illustrations. 3s. 6d.
Kœstlin's (J.) Life of Luther. With 62 Illustrations, &c. 3s. 6d.
Lang's (A.) Angling Sketches. 20 Illustrations. 3s. 6d.

The Silver Library—continued.

Lang's (A.) Custom and Myth: Studies of Early Usage and Belief. 3s. 6d.

Lang's (Andrew) Cock Lane and Common-Sense. With a New Preface. 3s. 6d.

Lees (J. A.) and Clutterbuck's (W.J.)B.C. 1887, A Ramble in British Columbia. With Maps and 75 Illustrations. 3s. 6d.

Macaulay's (Lord) Essays and Lays of Ancient Rome. With Portrait and Illustration. 3s. 6d.

Macleod's (H. D.) Elements of Banking. 3s. 6d.

Marbot's (Baron de) Memoirs. Translated. 2 vols. 7s.

Marshman's (J. C.) Memoirs of Sir Henry Havelock. 3s. 6d.

Merivale's (Dean) History of the Romans under the Empire. 8 vols. 3s. 6d. ea.

Merriman's (H. S.) Flotsam: a Story of the Indian Mutiny. 3s. 6d.

Mill's (J. S.) Political Economy. 3s. 6d.

Mill's (J. S.) System of Logic. 3s. 6d.

Milner's (Geo.) Country Pleasures: the Chronicle of a Year chiefly in a garden. 3s. 6d.

Nansen's (F.) The First Crossing of Greenland. With Illustrations and a Map. 3s. 6d.

Phillipps-Wolley's (C.) Snap: a Legend of the Lone Mountain. With 13 Illustrations. 3s. 6d.

Proctor's (R. A.) The Moon. 3s. 6d.

Proctor's (R. A.) The Orbs Around Us. 3s. 6d.

Proctor's (R. A.) The Expanse of Heaven. 3s. 6d.

Proctor's (R. A.) Other Worlds than Ours. 3s. 6d.

Proctor's (R. A.) Our Place among Infinities: a Series of Essays contrasting our Little Abode in Space and Time with the Infinities around us. Crown 8vo., 3s. 6d.

Proctor's (R. A.) Other Suns than Ours. 3s. 6d.

Proctor's (R. A.) Rough Ways made Smooth. 3s. 6d.

Proctor's (R. A.) Pleasant Ways in Science. 3s. 6d.

Proctor's (R. A.) Myths and Marvels of Astronomy. 3s. 6d.

Proctor's (R. A.) Light Science for Leisure Hours. First Series. 3s. 6d.

Proctor's (R. A.) Nature Studies. 3s. 6d.

Proctor's (R. A.) Leisure Readings. By R. A. PROCTOR, EDWARD CLODD, ANDREW WILSON, THOMAS FOSTER and A. C. RANYARD. With Illustrations. 3s. 6d.

Rossetti's (Maria F.) A Shadow of Dante. 3s. 6d.

Smith's (R. Bosworth) Carthage and the Carthaginians. With Maps, Plans &c. 3s. 6d.

Stanley's (Bishop) Familiar History of Birds. With 160 Illustrations. 3s. 6d.

Stevenson's (R. L.) The Strange Case of Dr. Jekyll and Mr. Hyde; with other Fables. 3s. 6d.

Stevenson (R. L.) and Osbourne's (L.) The Wrong Box. 3s. 6d.

Stevenson (Robt. Louis) and Stevenson (Fanny van de Grift) More New Arabian Nights.—The Dynamiter. 3s. 6d.

Weyman's (Stanley J.) The House of the Wolf: a Romance. 3s. 6d.

Wood's (Rev. J. G.) Petland Revisited. With 33 Illustrations. 3s. 6d.

Wood's (Rev. J. G.) Strange Dwellings. With 60 Illustrations. 3s. 6d.

Wood's (Rev. J. G.) Out of Doors. With 11 Illustrations. 3s. 6d.

Cookery, Domestic Management, &c.

Acton.—MODERN COOKERY. By ELIZA ACTON. With 150 Woodcuts. Fcp. 8vo., 4s. 6d.

Bull (THOMAS, M.D.).
HINTS TO MOTHERS ON THE MANAGEMENT OF THEIR HEALTH DURING THE PERIOD OF PREGNANCY. Fcp. 8vo., 1s. 6d.
THE MATERNAL MANAGEMENT OF CHILDREN IN HEALTH AND DISEASE. Fcp. 8vo., 1s. 6d.

De Salis (Mrs.).
CAKES AND CONFECTIONS À LA MODE. Fcp. 8vo., 1s. 6d.

DOGS: a Manual for Amateurs. Fcp. 8vo., 1s. 6d.

DRESSED GAME AND POULTRY À LA MODE. Fcp. 8vo., 1s. 6d.

DRESSED VEGETABLES À LA MODE. Fcp. 8vo., 1s. 6d.

Cookery, Domestic Management, &c.—*continued.*

De Salis (Mrs.)—*continued.*
DRINKS À LA MODE. Fcp. 8vo., 1s. 6d.
ENTRÉES À LA MODE. Fcp. 8vo., 1s. 6d.
FLORAL DECORATIONS. Fcp. 8vo., 1s. 6d.
GARDENING À LA MODE. Fcp. 8vo.
 Part I. Vegetables. 1s. 6d.
 Part II. Fruits. 1s. 6d.
NATIONAL VIANDS À LA MODE. Fcp. 8vo., 1s. 6d.
NEW-LAID EGGS. Fcp. 8vo., 1s. 6d.
OYSTERS À LA MODE. Fcp. 8vo., 1s. 6d.
PUDDINGS AND PASTRY À LA MODE. Fcp. 8vo., 1s. 6d.
SAVOURIES À LA MODE. Fcp. 8vo., 1s. 6d.
SOUPS AND DRESSED FISH À LA MODE. Fcp. 8vo., 1s. 6d.
SWEETS AND SUPPER DISHES À LA MODE. Fcp. 8vo., 1s. 6d.

De Salis (Mrs.)—*continued.*
TEMPTING DISHES FOR SMALL INCOMES. Fcp. 8vo., 1s. 6d.
WRINKLES AND NOTIONS FOR EVERY HOUSEHOLD. Cr. 8vo., 1s. 6d.

Lear.—MAIGRE COOKERY. By H. L. SIDNEY LEAR. 16mo., 2s.

Poole.—COOKERY FOR THE DIABETIC. By W. H. and Mrs. POOLE. With Preface by Dr. PAVY. Fcp. 8vo., 2s. 6d.

Walker (JANE H.).
 A BOOK FOR EVERY WOMAN.
 Part I. The Management of Children in Health and out of Health. Cr. 8vo., 2s. 6d.
 Part II. Woman in Health and out of Health. Crown 8vo, 2s. 6d.
 A HANDBOOK FOR MOTHERS: being Simple Hints to Women on the Management of their Health during Pregnancy and Confinement, together with Plain Directions as to the Care of Infants. Cr. 8vo., 2s. 6d.

Miscellaneous and Critical Works.

Allingham.—VARIETIES IN PROSE. By WILLIAM ALLINGHAM. 3 vols. Cr. 8vo, 18s. (Vols. 1 and 2, Rambles, by PATRICIUS WALKER. Vol. 3, Irish Sketches, etc.)

Armstrong.—ESSAYS AND SKETCHES. By EDMUND J. ARMSTRONG. Fcp. 8vo., 5s.

Bagehot.—LITERARY STUDIES. By WALTER BAGEHOT. With Portrait. 3 vols. Crown 8vo., 3s. 6d. each.

Baring-Gould.—CURIOUS MYTHS OF THE MIDDLE AGES. By Rev. S. BARING-GOULD. Crown 8vo., 3s. 6d.

Boyd (A. K. H.) ('A.K.H.B.').
 And see MISCELLANEOUS THEOLOGICAL WORKS, p. 32.
 AUTUMN HOLIDAYS OF A COUNTRY PARSON. Crown 8vo., 3s. 6d.
 COMMONPLACE PHILOSOPHER. Crown 8vo., 3s. 6d.
 CRITICAL ESSAYS OF A COUNTRY PARSON. Crown 8vo., 3s. 6d.
 EAST COAST DAYS AND MEMORIES. Crown 8vo., 3s. 6d.
 LANDSCAPES, CHURCHES AND MORALITIES. Crown 8vo., 3s. 6d.
 LEISURE HOURS IN TOWN. Crown 8vo., 3s. 6d.
 LESSONS OF MIDDLE AGE. Cr. 8vo., 3s. 6d.
 OUR LITTLE LIFE. Two Series. Cr.

Miscellaneous and Critical Works—*continued.*

Butler (SAMUEL).
EREWHON. Cr. 8vo., 5*s*.
THE FAIR HAVEN. A Work in Defence of the Miraculous Element in our Lord's Ministry. Cr. 8vo., 7*s*. 6*d*.
LIFE AND HABIT. An Essay after a Completer View of Evolution. Cr. 8vo., 7*s*. 6*d*.
EVOLUTION, OLD AND NEW. Cr. 8vo., 10*s*. 6*d*.
ALPS AND SANCTUARIES OF PIEDMONT AND CANTON TICINO. Illustrated. Pott 4to., 10*s*. 6*d*.
LUCK, OR CUNNING, AS THE MAIN MEANS OF ORGANIC MODIFICATION? Cr. 8vo., 7*s*. 6*d*.
EX VOTO. An Account of the Sacro Monte or New Jerusalem at Varallo-Sesia. Crown 8vo., 10*s*. 6*d*.

CHARITIES REGISTER, THE ANNUAL, AND DIGEST. Volume for 1898 : being a Classified Register of Charities in or available in the Metropolis. With an Introduction by C. S. LOCH, Secretary to the Council of the Charity Organisation Society, London. 8vo., 4*s*.

Clough.—A STUDY OF MARY WOLLSTONECRAFT, AND THE RIGHTS OF WOMEN. By EMMA RAUSCHENBUSCH-CLOUGH, Ph.D. 8vo., 7*s*. 6*d*.

Dreyfus.—LECTURES ON FRENCH LITERATURE. Delivered in Melbourne by IRMA DREYFUS. With Portrait of the Author. Large crown 8vo., 12*s*. 6*d*.

Evans.—THE ANCIENT STONE IMPLEMENTS, WEAPONS, AND ORNAMENTS OF GREAT BRITAIN. By Sir JOHN EVANS, K.C.B., D.C.L., LL.D., F.R.S., etc. With 537 Illustrations. Medium 8vo., 28*s*.

Gwilt.—AN ENCYCLOPÆDIA OF ARCHITECTURE. By JOSEPH GWILT, F.S.A.

Hime. — STRAY MILITARY PAPERS. By Lieut.-Colonel H. W. L. HIME (late Royal Artillery). 8vo., 7*s*. 6*d*.
CONTENTS.—Infantry Fire Formations—On Marking at Rifle Matches—The Progress of Field Artillery—The Reconnoitering Duties of Cavalry.

Indian Ideals (No. 1).
NÂRADA SÛTRA: an Inquiry into Love (Bhakti-Jijnâsâ). Translated from the Sanskrit, with an Independent Commentary, by E. T. STURDY. Crown 8vo., 2*s*. 6*d*. net.

Jefferies (RICHARD).
FIELD AND HEDGEROW. With Portrait. Crown 8vo., 3*s*. 6*d*.
THE STORY OF MY HEART: my Autobiography. With Portrait and New Preface by C. J. LONGMAN. Crown 8vo., 3*s*. 6*d*.
RED DEER. With 17 Illustrations by J. CHARLTON and H. TUNALY. Crown 8vo., 3*s*. 6*d*.
THE TOILERS OF THE FIELD. With Portrait from the Bust in Salisbury Cathedral. Crown 8vo., 3*s*. 6*d*.
WOOD MAGIC: a Fable. With Frontispiece and Vignette by E. V. B. Cr. 8vo., 3*s*. 6*d*.

Johnson.—THE PATENTEE'S MANUAL: a Treatise on the Law and Practice of Letters Patent. By J. & J. H. JOHNSON, Patent Agents, &c. 8vo., 10*s*. 6*d*.

Joyce.—THE ORIGIN AND HISTORY OF IRISH NAMES OF PLACES. By P. W. JOYCE, LL.D. Seventh Edition. 2 vols. Crown 8vo., 5*s*. each.

Lang (ANDREW).
MODERN MYTHOLOGY. 8vo., 9*s*.
LETTERS TO DEAD AUTHORS. Fcp. 8vo., 2*s*. 6*d*. net.
BOOKS AND BOOKMEN. With 2 Coloured Plates and 17 Illustrations. Fcp. 8vo., 2*s*. 6*d*. net.
OLD FRIENDS. Fcp. 8vo., 2*s*. 6*d*. net.
LETTERS ON LITERATURE. Fcp. 8vo.,

LONGMANS & CO.'S STANDARD AND GENERAL WORKS. 31

Miscellaneous and Critical Works—*continued.*

Max Müller (F.).
INDIA: WHAT CAN IT TEACH US? Cr. 8vo., 3s. 6d.
CHIPS FROM A GERMAN WORKSHOP.
Vol. I. Recent Essays and Addresses. Cr. 8vo., 5s.
Vol. II. Biographical Essays. Cr. 8vo., 5s.
Vol. III. Essays on Language and Literature. Cr. 8vo., 5s.
Vol. IV. Essays on Mythology and Folk Lore. Crown 8vo., 5s.
CONTRIBUTIONS TO THE SCIENCE OF MYTHOLOGY. 2 vols. 8vo., 32s.

Milner.—COUNTRY PLEASURES: the Chronicle of a Year chiefly in a Garden. By GEORGE MILNER. Cr. 8vo., 3s. 6d.

Morris (WILLIAM).
SIGNS OF CHANGE. Post 8vo., 4s. 6d.
HOPES AND FEARS FOR ART. Cr. 8vo., 4s. 6d.
AN ADDRESS DELIVERED AT THE DISTRIBUTION OF PRIZES TO STUDENTS OF THE BIRMINGHAM MUNICIPAL SCHOOL OF ART, 21ST FEBRUARY, 1894. 8vo., 2s. 6d. net.

Orchard.—THE ASTRONOMY OF 'MILTON'S PARADISE LOST'. By T. N. ORCHARD. 13 Illustrations. 8vo., 6s. net.

Poore(GEORGE VIVIAN, M.D., F.R.C.P.).
ESSAYS ON RURAL HYGIENE. With 13 Illustrations. Crown 8vo., 6s. 6d.
THE DWELLING HOUSE. With 36 Illustrations. Crown 8vo., 3s. 6d.

Proctor.—STRENGTH: How to get Strong and keep Strong, with Chapters on Rowing and Swimming, Fat, Age, and the Waist. By R. A. PROCTOR. With 9 Illustrations. Cr. 8vo, 2s.

PROGRESS IN WOMEN'S EDUCATION IN THE BRITISH EMPIRE. Being the Report of the Education Section, Victorian Era Exhibition, 1897. Edited by the COUNTESS OF WARWICK. With 10 Illustrations. Crown 8vo., 6s.

Richmond.—BOYHOOD : a Plea for Continuity in Education. By ENNIS RICHMOND. Crown 8vo., 2s. 6d.

Rossetti.—A SHADOW OF DANTE : being an Essay towards studying Himself, his World, and his Pilgrimage. By MARIA FRANCESCA ROSSETTI. Crown 8vo., 3s. 6d.

Solovyoff.—A MODERN PRIESTESS OF ISIS (MADAME BLAVATSKY). Abridged and Translated on Behalf of the Society for Psychical Research from the Russian of VSEVOLOD SERGYEEVICH SOLOVYOFF. By WALTER LEAF, Litt. D. Cr. 8vo., 6s.

Soulsby (LUCY H. M.).
STRAY THOUGHTS ON READING. Small 8vo., 2s. 6d. net.
STRAY THOUGHTS FOR GIRLS. 16mo., 1s. 6d. net.
STRAY THOUGHTS FOR MOTHERS AND TEACHERS. Fcp. 8vo., 2s. 6d. net.
STRAY THOUGHTS FOR INVALIDS. 16mo., 2s. net.

Stevens.—ON THE STOWAGE OF SHIPS AND THEIR CARGOES. With Information regarding Freights, Charter-Parties, &c. By ROBERT WHITE STEVENS. 8vo., 21s.

Turner and Sutherland.—THE DEVELOPMENT OF AUSTRALIAN LITERATURE. By HENRY GYLES TURNER and ALEXANDER SUTHERLAND. With 5 Portraits and an Illust. Cr. 8vo., 5s.

White.—AN EXAMINATION OF THE CHARGE OF APOSTASY AGAINST WORDSWORTH. By WILLIAM HALE WHITE. Crown 8vo., 3s. 6d.

Miscellaneous Theological Works.

*** *For Church of England and Roman Catholic Works see* MESSRS. LONGMANS & CO.'s *Special Catalogues.*

Balfour.—THE FOUNDATIONS OF BELIEF: being Notes Introductory to the Study of Theology. By the Right Hon. ARTHUR J. BALFOUR, M.P. 8vo., 12s. 6d.

Bird (ROBERT).
A CHILD'S RELIGION. Crown 8vo., 2s.

Bird (ROBERT)—*continued.*
JESUS, THE CARPENTER OF NAZARETH. Twelfth Edition. Crown 8vo, 5s.
To be had also in Two Parts, price 2s. 6d. each.
Part. I.—GALILEE AND THE LAKE OF GENNESARET.

Miscellaneous Theological Works—*continued.*

Boyd (A. K. H.) ('A.K.H.B.').
OCCASIONAL AND IMMEMORIAL DAYS: Discourses. Crown 8vo., 7s. 6d.
COUNSEL AND COMFORT FROM A CITY PULPIT. Crown 8vo., 3s. 6d.
SUNDAY AFTERNOONS IN THE PARISH CHURCH OF A SCOTTISH UNIVERSITY CITY. Crown 8vo., 3s. 6d.
CHANGED ASPECTS OF UNCHANGED TRUTHS. Crown 8vo., 3s. 6d.
GRAVER THOUGHTS OF A COUNTRY PARSON. Three Series. Crown 8vo., 3s. 6d. each.
PRESENT DAY THOUGHTS. Crown 8vo., 3s. 6d.
SEASIDE MUSINGS. Cr. 8vo., 3s. 6d.
'TO MEET THE DAY' through the Christian Year; being a Text of Scripture, with an Original Meditation and a Short Selection in Verse for Every Day. Crown 8vo., 4s. 6d.

Gibson.—THE ABBÉ DE LAMENNAIS AND THE LIBERAL CATHOLIC MOVEMENT IN FRANCE. By the HON. W. GIBSON. With Portrait. 8vo., 12s. 6d.

Kalisch (M. M., Ph.D.).
BIBLE STUDIES. Part I. Prophecies of Balaam. 8vo., 10s. 6d. Part II. The Book of Jonah. 8vo., 10s. 6d.
COMMENTARY ON THE OLD TESTAMENT: with a new Translation. Vol. I. Genesis. 8vo., 18s. Or adapted for the General Reader. 12s. Vol. II. Exodus. 15s. Or adapted for the General Reader. 12s. Vol. III. Leviticus, Part I. 15s. Or adapted for the General Reader. 8s. Vol. IV. Leviticus, Part II. 15s. Or adapted for the General Reader. 8s.

Lang.—THE MAKING OF RELIGION. By ANDREW LANG. 8vo., 12s.

Macdonald (GEORGE).
UNSPOKEN SERMONS. Three Series. Crown 8vo., 3s. 6d. each.
THE MIRACLES OF OUR LORD. Crown 8vo., 3s. 6d.

Martineau (JAMES)—*continued.*
ENDEAVOURS AFTER THE CHRISTIAN LIFE. Discourses. Cr. 8vo., 7s. 6d.
THE SEAT OF AUTHORITY IN RELIGION. 8vo., 14s.
ESSAYS, REVIEWS, AND ADDRESSES. 4 Vols. Crown 8vo., 7s. 6d. each. I. Personal; Political. II. Ecclesiastical; Historical. III. Theological; Philosophical. IV. Academical; Religious.
HOME PRAYERS, with Two Services for Public Worship. Crown 8vo. 3s. 6d.

Max Müller (F.).
THE ORIGIN AND GROWTH OF RELIGION, as illustrated by the Religions of India. The Hibbert Lectures, delivered at the Chapter House, Westminster Abbey, in 1878. Crown 8vo., 5s.
INTRODUCTION TO THE SCIENCE OF RELIGION: Four Lectures delivered at the Royal Institution. Cr. 8vo.,3s. 6d.
NATURAL RELIGION. The Gifford Lectures, delivered before the University of Glasgow in 1888. Cr. 8vo., 5s.
PHYSICAL RELIGION. The Gifford Lectures, delivered before the University of Glasgow in 1890. Cr. 8vo., 5s.
ANTHROPOLOGICAL RELIGION. The Gifford Lectures, delivered before the University of Glasgow in 1891. Cr. 8vo., 5s.
THEOSOPHY; or, PSYCHOLOGICAL RELIGION. The Gifford Lectures, delivered before the University of Glasgow in 1892. Cr. 8vo., 5s.
THREE LECTURES ON THE VEDÁNTA PHILOSOPHY, delivered at the Royal Institution in March, 1894. 8vo., 5s.

Romanes.—THOUGHTS ON RELIGION. By GEORGE J. ROMANES, LL.D., F.R.S. Crown 8vo., 4s. 6d.

Vivekananda.—YOGA PHILOSOPHY: Lectures delivered in New York, Winter

www.ingramcontent.com/pod-product-compliance
Lightning Source LLC
Chambersburg PA
CBHW020832020526
44114CB00040B/565